Theodore Dreiser and American Culture

Drawing by William J. Glackens, "That Fairyland of Theatres and gaudy Palaces which is Broadway," included in Dreiser's magazine article, "Whence the Song," ***Harper's Weekly,*** **8 December 1900.**

Theodore Dreiser and American Culture

New Readings

Edited by
Yoshinobu Hakutani

Newark: University of Delaware Press
London: Associated University Presses

Associated University Presses
440 Forsgate Drive
Cranbury, NJ 08512

Associated University Presses
16 Barter Street
London WC1A 2AH, England

Associated University Presses
P.O. Box 338, Port Credit
Mississauga, Ontario
Canada L5G 4L8

The paper used in this publication meets the requirements of the American National Standard of Permanence of Paper for Printed Library Materials Z39.48-1984.

Library of Congress Cataloging-in-Publication Data

Theodore Dreiser and American culture : new readings / edited by Yoshinobu Hakutani.
p. cm.
Includes bibliographical references (p.) and index.
ISBN 0-87413-714-4 (alk. paper)
1. Dreiser, Theodore, 1871–1945—Criticism and interpretation. 2. National characteristics, American, in literature. 3. Culture in literature. I. Hakutani, Yoshinobu, date
PS3507.R55 Z8475 2000
813′.52—dc21 99-088356

PRINTED IN THE UNITED STATES OF AMERICA

For the International Dreiser Society

Contents

Acknowledgments 9
List of Abbreviations 11
Introduction 13

Part I: Essays in Criticism and History

Sister Carrie: Novel and Romance 23
YOSHINOBU HAKUTANI

Dreiser, *Sister Carrie*, and Mrs. Doubleday: Gender and Social Change at the Turn of the Century 39
MARSHA S. MOYER

Alcohol and Drinking in *Sister Carrie* 56
JAMES L. W. WEST III

"But a Single Point in a Long Tragedy": *Sister Carrie*'s Equivocal Style 65
KIYOHIKO MURAYAMA

Jolly Mrs. Yerkes Is Home from Abroad: Dreiser and the Celebrity Culture 79
PHILIP GERBER

Men Strike, Women Sew: Gendered Labor Worlds in Dreiser's Social Protest Art 104
LAURA HAPKE

Working Out to Work Through: Dreiser in Muldoon's Body Shop of Shame 115
KATHY FREDERICKSON

This Sex Which Is One: Language and the Masculine Self in *Jennie Gerhardt* 138
STEPHEN C. BRENNAN

Part II: Essays of Intertextuality and Interauthoriality

Obscuring the Home: Textual Editing and Dreiser's *Jennie Gerhardt* 161
ANNEMARIE KONING WHALEY

From Travel Guide to Autobiography: Recovering the Original of *A Traveler at Forty* 177
RENATE VON BARDELEBEN

Interlocking, Intermeshing Fantasies: Dreiser and *Dearest Wilding* 187
MIRIAM GOGOL

Dreiser and American Literary Paganism: A Reading of the Trilogy of Desire 203
SHAWN ST. JEAN

Expansive and Unnameable Desire in American Fiction: From "Naturalism" to Postmodernism 214
LAWRENCE E. HUSSMAN

Dreiser, Fitzgerald, and the Question of Influence
THOMAS P. RIGGIO 234

Wright, Dreiser, and Spatial Narrative 248
YOSHINOBU HAKUTANI

Urban Frontiers, Neighborhoods, and Traps: The City in Dreiser's *Sister Carrie*, Farrell's *Studs Lonigan*, and Wright's *Native Son* 274
ROBERT BUTLER

Bibliography 291

List of Contributors 306

Index 311

Acknowledgments

This collection has become a reality, thanks to the many Dreiser meetings held in the past decade, beginning with the Brockport, N.Y., Conference in October 1990, directed by Philip Gerber, and continuing in conjunction with the annual American Literature Association Conference, alternately held in San Diego and Baltimore. The earlier, shorter versions of several of the essays included in the collection were originally presented in those conferences. For preparation of the book, I would like to thank, in particular, Thomas P. Riggio, James L. W. West III, and Michiko Hakutani for their help and encouragement. I am also grateful to Professor Donald C. Mell, Chair, Board of Editors, and the anonymous readers for the University of Delaware Press for their useful, incisive comments and suggestions.

Over the years my studies in American literature have generously been supported by a number of academic leaves and grants-in-aid provided by the Kent State University Research Council.

List of Abbreviations

The following abbreviations parenthetically refer to Dreiser's books.

AAT—An American Tragedy
BAM—A Book about Myself
B—The Bulwark
D—Dawn
F—The Financier
G—The "Genius"
AHH—A Hoosier Holiday
JG—Jennie Gerhardt
SC—Sister Carrie
S—The Stoic
T—The Titan
ATF—A Traveler at Forty

Introduction

IN RECENT YEARS, JOURNAL ARTICLES AND CONFERENCE PAPERS ON Dreiser have increasingly used psychoanalytical, feminist, new historicist, and comparative literary methodologies. The present collection of essays has brought together for the first time the work of critics who approach Dreiser from these perspectives. Building on the pioneering work of the Pennsylvania Dreiser Edition, the book also examines old, neglected, or unpublished texts, and explores questions of intertextuality and interauthoriality that recent reading has brought to light.

For this project I have gathered a group of Dreiser scholars intent upon providing new approaches to Dreiser. Most of the contributors are not only well-known critics of Dreiser but also established scholars in other areas of American studies. This book, then, is of interest not only to Dreiserians but to students and writers in related fields of inquiry such as American cultural history, women's studies, and textual criticism. Since some of the contributors are not American, the book provides a cross-cultural perspective that will attract students of American studies abroad as well.

A central concern of this volume is the intertextual and literary relationships between Dreiser and key American writers in modern times such as Stephen Crane, Frank Norris, F. Scott Fitzgerald, James T. Farrell, and Richard Wright. Although Dreiser's impact on American literary realism has been acknowledged, only a few scholars have challenged the naturalistic cliches that have long dominated Dreiser criticism. Amy Kaplan's *The Social Construction of American Realism* (1988) and, earlier, Ellen Moers's *Two Dreisers* (1969) and my *Young Dreiser* (1980) and *Selected Magazine Articles of Theodore Dreiser* (1985–87) all have attempted to widen our appreciation of both Dreiser's literary, cultural roots and his authorial, interauthorial impacts. There have been, however, no in-depth comparative studies investigating the important relations between Dreiser and other writers, many of whom were not "realists" or "naturalists" in the narrow sense of the term, and the nexus between Dreiser's vision of American culture and other traditions. This book attempts to stimulate the reader's interest in cultural studies.

Both the lack of methodological sophistication on the part of critics and the blindness to Dreiser's literary influence can be traced to the vagaries of literary history since the Second World War. When modernist criticism flourished in mid-century, Dreiser's work was undervalued. In recent years, the novelist's legacy has regained its proper place in literary history. Today we are aware that Dreiser exerted a powerful influence on authors, even in the decades after his death. For example, Allen Tate, an eminent New Critic who apotheosized modernism, called Dreiser, Faulkner, and Hemingway the three most important American novelists of the twentieth century; and we remember that Robert Penn Warren, himself a famous New Critic, celebrated Dreiser in *Homage to Theodore Dreiser*. These examples suggest that as the new century begins and the centennial of *Sister Carrie* approaches, the importance of Dreiser, in his own time and in ours, can hardly be overstated. Earlier American writers like Willa Cather, Sinclair Lewis, Sherwood Anderson, and F. Scott Fitzgerald acknowledged their debt to Dreiser, as did a score of younger writers, including James T. Farrell, Richard Wright, Nelson Algren, Jack Conroy, Louis Auchincloss, Norman Mailer, Saul Bellow, and James Dickey. Wright, perhaps the most influential African American novelist, and a major American writer, wrote in his famous autobiography *Black Boy* (1945):

> I read Dreiser's *Jennie Gerhardt* and *Sister Carrie* and they revived in me a vivid sense of my mother's suffering; I was overwhelmed. I grew silent, wondering about the life around me. It would have been impossible for me to have told anyone what I derived from these novels, for it was nothing less than a sense of life itself. All my life had shaped me for the realism, the naturalism of the modern novel, and I could not read enough of them.

Wright went on to say it was "these books—written by men like Dreiser, Masters, Mencken, Anderson, and Lewis—" that enabled him to envision "imaginative constructions of heroic or tragic deeds" in American life.

Although creative and scholarly writers have paid tribute to Dreiser, few have taken into account the achievements the textual scholars and editors have made since the 1980s. It is time for criticism to redefine the importance of Dreiser's vision to American culture on the basis of the continuously expanding Dreiser canon. The immediate goal of the project is twofold. On the one hand, the essays selected for the book provide new critical and historical interpretations based on the sources and texts established in the Dreiser Edition. On the other, the essays in Part II explore the intertextual and interauthorial discourse underlying Dreiser's work.

In one way or another, many of the essays concern or reflect upon *Sister Carrie*. In Part I, my "*Sister Carrie*: Novel and Romance" attempts to read the two versions in the ambivalence between romance and novel, a dualism that runs through American fiction. Marsha S. Moyer, in "Dreiser, *Sister Carrie*, and Mrs. Doubleday: Gender and Social Change at the Turn of the Century," observes that the novel stirred the interests of those who stood for "artistic and individual freedom," a modernism which high modernist writers failed to appreciate. Moyer questions the validity of separating a literary text like *Sister Carrie* from its historical context, a motto New Critics conflated with modernist criticism. In "Alcohol and Drinking in *Sister Carrie*," James L. W. West III speculates Dreiser's motives for cutting out several passages about alcohol in the 1900 edition. This kind of textual scholarship, so far from "a cold, logical, dispassionate consideration of dry textual evidence," suggests what poststructural, deconstructive critics have long suspected: as a product of American culture, *Sister Carrie* is an unstable, unsettled but volatile text that ironically offers various readings and representations.

Kiyohiko Murayama's " 'But a Single Point in a Long Tragedy': *Sister Carrie*'s Equivocal Style" uses and shows the limitations of new historicist theory. Murayama questions Walter Benn Michaels's observation that Dreiser endorses capitalism as a system that provides humanity with happiness. Taking the side of Fredric Jameson's view that Dreiser is the greatest novelist representing American culture, Murayama considers what Jameson calls "a fundamental and exilarating heterogeneity" the novelistic structure that buttresses *Sister Carrie*. Murayama also characterizes Dreiser's narrative method in this novel as a use of Bakhtinian dialogism rather than of Hegelian dialectics: the overall narrative voice reflects the insoluble contradiction of human life rather than of synthesis and resolution.

In "Jolly Mrs. Yerkes Is Home from Abroad: Dreiser and the Celebrity Culture," Philip Gerber as a historical, biographical critic has traced the very processes of Dreiser's composition of *The Financier*. Based on the thousands of manuscript notes Dreiser compiled in preparation of his third novel-to-be, Gerber has examined, among other things, Dreiser's portrait of Emilie Grigsby, the real-life mistress of Charles T. Yerkes, who was revealed after the financier's death to be the daughter of the madame of an upper-class brothel in Louisville, Kentucky. Most importantly, the essay captures the celebrity culture underlying that novel, a metonymic representation of American life.

Laura Hapke's "Men Strike, Women Sew: Gendered Labor Worlds in Dreiser's Social Protest Art," also taking a historical approach, examines the male and female proletarian worlds around the turn of the nineteenth century that indicate male dominance over working women. Dreiser's early work, especially *Sister Carrie* and *Jennie Gerhardt*, as Hapke shows, makes the historical reading evocative and provocative in reading the text as well as rendering history: much of Dreiser's magazine and biographical writing is so closely interrelated with his fiction. Dreiser's close representations of the social, economic, and cultural phenomena make Hapke note: "If to a certain extent he transcends such fiction, he also shares the prejudices that permeate it."

Kathy Frederickson's "Working Out to Work Through: Dreiser in Muldoon's Body Shop of Shame" and Stephen C. Brennan's "This Sex Which Is One: Language and the Masculine Self in *Jennie Gerhardt*" both use psychoanalytic theories. Frederickson psychoanalyzes Dreiser's sense of shame as exhibited in the sketch "Culhane, the Solid Man," collected in *Twelve Men*. Based on Dreiser's experience with William Muldoon, a Jewish wrestler, who helped Dreiser recover from his psychic depression, the story sheds light on Dreiser's concept of the masculine body. Even though Dreiser wrote about his friendship with Muldoon in *A Hoosier Holiday*, "Thereafter my life changed and I was much better. . . . I am not theorizing; I am stating facts," Frederickson, applying Freudian psychoanalysis, observes: "Muldoon would consider shame the 'feminine' character trait 'par excellence,' particularly for 'sissies and mamma's boys and pet heirs.' " In keeping with Luce Irigaray's theory of phallocracy, Brennan characterizes Lester Kane and other men as individuals who regard language as a system of representing masculine "unity," authority, and unified ideology. While Lester has inherited his father's language, Jennie has acquired a transcendentalist worldview. As Brennan notes, her language, transcending a system of rigid signifiers, functions as a semiotic system of free signifiers, in which the body, nature, is the primal signifier for life's mystery. In terms of Irigaray's psychoanalysis, Brennan observes that Jennie, finding herself in the "*nonsuture of her lips*" and knowing the happiness "*of never being simply one*," enters into the world of "a ceaseless exchange of herself with the other."

Part II begins with Annemarie Koning Whaley's "Obscuring the Home: Textual Editing and Dreiser's *Jennie Gerhardt*" and Renate von Bardeleben's "From Travel Guide to Autobiography: Recovering the Original of *A Traveler at Forty*," both of which conclusively show, by analyzing sources and variant texts uncovered by the Pennsylvania Dreiser Edition, that Dreiser's books had been compromised and subverted by their original editors and publishers. Comparing the two editions of *Jennie Gerhardt*, Whaley demonstrates that the Harpers version (1911) suffers from the cuts and that, should the cuts not have been made, the novel would have depicted a closer familial tie in the

Gerhardt family. Dreiser, Whaley notes, intended to describe the Gerhardt family as close and "somewhat idyllic" against the backdrop of a fragmented society, from which Dreiser himself had suffered. And the Pennsylvania edition (1992) makes his portrait of Jennie even more altruistic and "wholly 'sacrificial.'" von Bardeleben, on the other hand, shows with well-annotated evidence that much of the authorial intention for *A Traveler at Forty* was sacrificed in the interests of the publishers. She also suggests that Dreiser fell victim to his own desire to finance his travels to Europe and pursue women "of his heart."

Based on the recently published love memoir of Yvette Eastman, wife of the American editor and writer Max Forrester Eastman, Miriam Gogol's "Interlocking, Intermeshing Fantasies: Dreiser and *Dearest Wilding*" explores Yvette's adolescent relationship with the older Dreiser. "There is no question," Gogol sees, "that Eastman was in search of the 'giant father' to compensate for the loss of her own father at an early age." Gogol's discovery of the twenty-seven letters Dreiser also wrote to Suzanne, Yvette's younger sister, from 1929 to 1930, has led to Gogol's observation that the old Dreiser's pursuit of adolescent women like Yvette and Suzanne is symptomatic of "verging on pedophilia." Gogol, then, analyzes both Yvette's and Dreiser's motives in terms of "relational psychoanalysis": each seeks a partner for his or her own identity, Yvette in search of a father figure and Dreiser a young woman. In Dreiser's case, the search for a woman is "compulsively repeated. That's why even Dreiser described himself as driven in his search for 'not one but three or four, even five women at once.'"

While Shawn St. Jean's "Dreiser and American Literary Paganism: A Reading of the Trilogy of Desire" relates Dreiser's concept of manhood and power to a classic tradition, Lawrence E. Hussman's "Expansive and Unnameable Desire in American Fiction: From 'Naturalism' to Postmodernism" examines the concept of male desire as represented in modern American fiction. St. Jean attempts to deconstruct the traditional concepts of romanticism, naturalism, and realism, and proposes to read Dreiser's characterization of Frank Cowperwood in the light of Greek mythology. "His novels," St. Jean remarks, "represent life alternately as he saw it, read about it, deplored it, wished it could be. He imported to American life the moral and theological perspective of a past civilization, abandoning those of his own milieu." To Hussman, American literary naturalists' "anguished search for substance and salvation" in the absence of God persists in postmodern American fiction. This body of fiction concerns the constant, cyclic generation of male desire that marks humanity in post-religious American culture. *The "Genius"*, a typical example of this fiction, Hussman observes, finds its descendant in Woody Allen's alter ego affirmation, "Women are God":

the search for sexual fulfillment, always accompanied by disillusionment, nevertheless serves modern and postmodern American culture as a sign of resilience, perseverance, and cyclicity.

The last three essays in Part II discuss the literary and cultural nexus between Dreiser and those who followed the way he had paved for them. Thomas P. Riggio's "Dreiser, Fitzgerald, and the Question of Influence" is concerned with the relationship in which the two popular novelists regarded each other not only as an inspiration but as a rival. Their stylistic differences notwithstanding, as Riggio points out, their affinity rests on "a prose whose tonalities are inseparable from their understanding of the world": *An American Tragedy* and *The Great Gatsby*, two of the masterpieces that portray modern American life, are cast in the mode of pathos rather than of tragedy. My "Wright, Dreiser, and Spatial Narrative" not only shows that Dreiser was Wright's mentor and "father" but suggests that, since many of the postmodern African American writers were influenced by Wright, they can be regarded as Dreiser's "grandchildren." Robert Butler's "Urban Frontiers, Neighborhoods, and Traps: The City in Dreiser's *Sister Carrie*, Farrell's *Studs Lonigan*, and Wright's *Native Son*" focus on the three great novels of Chicago. Both *Studs Lonigan* and *Native Son* use the image of the window, through which American urban life is depicted, a realistic modernist technique Dreiser uses in *Sister Carrie*. While Dreiser develops the image romantically and Farrell revises it realistically, Wright radically inverts it in *Native Son* to assail the blatantly racist society against which Bigger Thomas must battle. "Unlike Max who is ultimately described as a 'blind man,'" Butler sees, "Bigger has a lucid awareness that the only windows which can provide him with hope are the windows of his soul."

Theodore Dreiser and American Culture

Part I
Essays in Criticism and History

Sister Carrie: Novel and Romance

YOSHINOBU HAKUTANI

NOW THAT BOTH VERSIONS OF *SISTER CARRIE* HAVE LONG BEEN STUDIED, one can realize that the 1900 edition is less naturalistic than supposedly thought.[1] In establishing the 1981 version, the editors restored about thirty-six thousand words which had been cut from the 1900 edition of the novel. What is most revealing about their work is not that they dealt with the problems of corruption and censorship that had plagued the composition of the novel in 1899–1900. Nor is it that the editors noted numerous stylistic changes between the two versions, the alterations which have to do with Dreiser's choice of words. But the Pennsylvania edition has revealed once and for all that Dreiser, by making substantial block cuts, intended to tell a far less grim story of Hurstwood and, in turn, to romanticize Carrie's rise to stardom. That *Sister Carrie* (1900) contains more elements of romance than naturalistic criticism has accorded a Dreiserian novel is not unique in American fiction. This type of narrative seems to have derived from the two traditions: the romance and the novel. The romantic narrative is characterized by authorial implicitness, ambiguity, and sentimentality, while the realistic narrative is written with authorial explicitness, structural clarity, and social detail.

Sister Carrie (1900) has a curious critical history. It has become legend that the book, though accepted and printed by Doubleday and Company, was withheld from market because Frank Doubleday, and his wife in particular, detested Dreiser's theme and treatment.[2] To some readers in 1900, Carrie is an "immoral" girl society fails to punish; nor does she regret her relations with the two older men. While Hurstwood, Carrie's lover, commits suicide in the gutter, Carrie rises to stardom on Broadway. Another reason for the controversy the novel stirred in 1900 was the deterministic worldview it seems to express. "Scholars," Lars Åhnebrink wrote in 1950, "generally agree that naturalism in the United States came of age in the writings of Theodore Dreiser, whose first novel, *Sister Carrie* (1900), is a fairly typical work of the movement."[3] But this reading of *Sister Carrie* has been challenged. Some critics, while recognizing the influences of social environment on Dreiser's characters, also recognize as strongly the human aspirations generated from within.[4]

The difficulty in interpreting Dreiser's narrative has partly risen from the definition of the term "naturalism." A character, according to the doctrine, is a product of the forces over which he or she has no control. The two most important sources of influence are heredity and environment. Some of our earlier critics, however, have used the term a bit loosely in applying it to American fiction, and to Dreiser in particular. In fact, we do not find as much naturalism in American literature as some have supposed. In Zola's novels, for example, one can easily find that Zola's characterization conforms to the theory. Gervaise in *L'Assommoir* is made a victim of her genetic heredity and social environment. Despite her goodness, she takes to drink not only because her husband is alcoholic but because alcoholism runs in her family. In American naturalism, on the other hand, one's heredity is not as important an issue as it is in Zola's fiction. It is in the national character that people in America cherish individualism and self-reliance, and a novelist like Dreiser has ingrained his characters with this spirit. As Carrie Meeber leaves home for Chicago, she is endowed with the spirit of independence. Save for the parting kisses she receives from her parents and her temporarily living with the Hansons in the beginning, her relations to her family are seldom mentioned in the story.

While American literature has produced some excellent naturalistic novels, many of the novels called "naturalistic" are naturalistic in a rather limited sense. Given a unique culture and history, the naturalistic philosophy has proved uncongenial, in the main, to the American temperament. How strongly naturalism influenced an American novelist depends on the novel. Clyde Griffiths in *An American Tragedy*, as Dreiser observes, suffers from a weak mind and easily succumbs to economic, social, and sexual temptations. Although Clyde is portrayed more deterministically than Carrie, he is also motivated by human aspirations as strongly as she is. "Clyde," as Irving Howe characterized him, "is pitiable, his life and fate are pitiable; yet at the end we feel a somber exaltation, for we know that *An American Tragedy* does not seek to persuade us that human existence need be without value or beauty."[5] The difference between a Zolaesque novel and an American novel like Dreiser's is that the American novel, despite the overwhelming forces of circumstance, expresses the strong will of an individual. The American novelist, in general, tries to uphold the stature of the individual and endow the character with autonomy and responsibility.

This spirit of individualism appears in various forms of aspiration. It can be one's pursuit of happiness, one's realization of a dream, or one's quest for freedom and independence. Even though life ends in tragedy for Clyde, his effort to realize his dream of success elicits sympathy and understanding. If Henry Fleming in *The Red Badge of Courage* becomes a hero at the end, Crane has transcended the limitations imposed by Zolaesque naturalism. Bigger Thomas in Richard Wright's *Native Son* is made a victim of racism and condemned to die as a murderer, but this defeat is ironically a triumph for the man who has rejected society's rules and values and established his own. If romantics like Emerson and Whitman exalted the individual to the level of divinity, American naturalists, by challenging the strictures of society, reaffirmed human aspirations.

For Dreiser to make a realistic novel less naturalistic was to reduce the social and economic forces which would otherwise be beyond a character's control. One of the most remarkable changes in the two versions of *Sister Carrie* was the ending of the book. The original version ends with this grim, deterministic passage:

> It seemed as if he thought awhile for now he arose and turned the gas out, standing calmly in the blackness, hidden from view. After a few moments in which he reviewed nothing, but merely hesitated, he turned the gas on again, but applying no match. Even then he stood there, hidden wholly in that kindness which is night, while the uprising fumes filled the room. When the odor reached his nostrils he quit his attitude and fumbled for the bed.
>
> "What's the use," he said wearily, as he stretched himself to rest. (*SC* 1981: 499)

In Zolaesque naturalism, characters like Gervaise and Nana are simpleminded and often susceptible to the forces outside them. A character like the Hurstwood of the original manuscript is easily destroyed by social and economic forces. But Dreiser's intent was not to portray Hurstwood as did Zola but to suggest that Hurstwood falls victim to forces within him. For Dreiser, such a portrait gives Hurstwood's story more poignancy and pathos than does Zola's treatment of Gervaise in *L'Assommoir*. The effect in general was to reduce the forces of society and to increase the stature of the individual. Dreiser thus takes pains to show that Hurstwood's deterioration toward the end of the book is caused by forces within him: Hurstwood is made a victim of his psychic predisposition.

The change in Dreiser's treatment of Hurstwood at the end of the book has a corollary in the structural changes made in the rest of the book. In Chapter XI, for example, several paragraphs in which Dreiser posits his naturalistic philosophy are eliminated. The deleted opening paragraph reads:

> In considering Carrie's mental state, the culmination of reasoning which held her at anchorage in so strange a harbor, we must fail of a just appreciation if

> we do not give due weight to those subtle influences, not human, which environ and appeal to the young imagination when it drifts. Trite though it may seem, it is well to remember that in life, after all, we are most wholly controlled by desire. The things that appeal to desire are not always visible objects. Let us not confuse this with selfishness. . . . Selfishness is the twin-screw motive power of the human steamer. It drives unchangingly, unpoetically on. Its one danger is that of miscalculation. Personalties such as Carrie's would come under the former category. The art by which her rather confused consciousness of right and duty might be overcome is not easily perceived. (*SC* 1981: 97)

In the second paragraph, which is also cut, Dreiser sums up his argument: "In the progress of all such minds environment is a subtle, persuasive control. It works hand in hand with desire. For instance, by certain conditions which her intellect was scarcely able to control, she was pushed into a situation where for the first time she could see a strikingly different way of living from her own" (*SC* 1981: 97). By deleting these passages, Dreiser entitled the chapter "The Persuasion of Fashion: Feeling Guards o'er Its Own," and resumed his portrait of Carrie as a feeling and autonomous individual. Indeed, Dreiser was intent upon creating feminine subjectivity for his heroine.

What makes Dreiser less realistic in his portrayal of characters than he appears to be is his expression of compassion.[6] If Flaubert is considered a realist, Dreiser has more affinity with a romantic naturalist like Frank Norris than with a realist. Flaubert believed in the environmental influences on character and demonstrated the tragedy of Emma Bovary by the bourgeois society of which she was a necessary part. "Great Art," Flaubert wrote to George Sand, "is scientific and impersonal. By an effort of the mind you must put yourself into your characters, not draw them to you. That, at least, is the method."[7] If Flaubert strove to be impersonal in treatment, Dreiser took a pride in being personally involved with his characters. As a result, Dreiser paid far more attention to the emotions of the individual than to the events of society.

As Dreiser was drawn to Carrie's personal sentiments, he tried to stave off whatever influences society might have exerted upon Carrie. The technique he used in such a story was to render her portrait, in part, in symbolic or mythic terms, as shown from the beginning of the story. In Chapter I, entitled "The Magnet Attractive: A Waif amid Forces," Carrie is rendered: "A half-equipped little knight she was, venturing to reconnoitre the mysterious city and dreaming wild dreams of some vague, far-off supremacy, which should make it prey and subject—the proper penitent, grovelling at a woman's slipper."[8] A corollary tendency of this method is that as Dreiser stresses the mythic qualities in his portrayal, he minimizes the impact of realistic details upon the character. Dreiser's strategy is hardly unique. Novelists of myth and romance, like Scott and Fielding, as Richard Chase pointed out, "ignore the whole reality of time and place and the whole illuminating cultural context, which more than other literary forms the novel reflects."[9]

Dreiser's reference to the specific details indicating the time, place, and context of Carrie's travel to Chicago is excised in the second paragraph of the first chapter:

> Since infancy her ears had been full of its fame. Once the family had thought of moving there. If she secured good employment they might come now. Anyhow it was vast. There were lights and sounds and a roar of things. People were rich. There were vast depots. This onrushing train was merely speeding to get there. (*SC* 1981: 3)

In place of this passage, Dreiser resumes his tale of the small town girl's pilgrimage to a big city: "When a girl leaves her home at eighteen, she does one of two things. Either she falls into saving hands and becomes better, or she rapidly assumes the cosmopolitan standard of virtue and becomes worse" (*SC* 1900: 2). Whether such a passage is retained to evoke a myth of success or to ignore the details that would otherwise make Carrie's story too realistic, the significance of this shift has more to do with the structure of the novel than the style of writing.

That Dreiser at the outset of the story has his eye more intensively on the innocent feelings of his heroine than he does on her immediate surroundings sets a distinct pattern of development for the rest of the story. Whenever the plot veers too closely to social and realistic material, there emerges a conscious effort to return to portrayal of individual sentiments. In fact, Carrie in the original manuscript is not so innocent and naive as she appears to be in the novel. Deleted from the 1900 edition are the passages which specifically mentioned the sexual exploitation rampant in Chicago. In her struggle to land a job she runs into a prospective employer, "a most sensual-faced individual" (*SC* 1981: 27), whose interview implies that she would be hired if she became his mistress. As her affair with Drouet fades away, she begins to think seriously about obtaining another job with a fake crayon-portrait establishment called the "Great American Art Company," whose manager "was nevertheless anxious to get near him some girl of good looks and weak principles on whom he might practice his art of seduction" (*SC* 1981: 257). Although she does not have to take the job because Hurstwood appears on the scene as her next savior, she still thinks that "the day had gone by and five dollars was five dollars. Insignificant as the sum seemed compared with what had been her allowance and state of living, she thought in her fear that it might be necessary to take it" (*SC* 1981: 259). On their flight to New York, she is not a coy mistress as presented in the novel. As Hurstwood inflates his hopes of establishing a new life for them in a new city, she herself quickly responds and joins him in their quest.

The most obvious difference between the novel and the manuscript is the fewer actual or social details in the novel.[10] The 1900 edition does contain some dense detail that makes the novel realistic; it has been hailed as an example of social realism in American literature. This characteristic of the novel is further intensified in the original manuscript. The actual names of places and persons included in the manuscript are cut out in the 1900 edition: for example, "the Fair," the World's Fair at Chicago in 1893; "Schlesinger and Mayer's," presumably a well-known dress shop on Michigan Avenue in the 1890s; "Armour," the businessman and philanthropist Philip D. Armour,[11] and "Marshall Field," the famous department store tycoon.[12] Drouet drives Carrie to a section of the city where many millionaires lived. "Say Carrie," Drouet calls her attention, "see that house on ahead there?" Dreiser then adds:

> He pointed to a rather awkward brick and stone affair, not at all beautiful in its decorative effect, which was set down in a rather extensive green lawn—a very fair example of the mixed and uncertain architecture characteristic of the city at that time.
>
> Carrie nodded.
>
> "That's Pullman's," he said.[13]
>
> The two gazed at the great sleeping-car magnate's residence with undisguised interest.
>
> "Say, but he's got the money. Twenty million dollars. Think of that!" (*SC* 1981: 100)

The first published version is also free of sexual or erotic allusions. The 1900 edition contains some sexual references, but compared to the manuscript version, it is less informal, realistic, and contemporary. Drouet's attitude toward Carrie is described less idealistically than that of Hurstwood, but still Dreiser's description of Drouet's sentiments is free of sexual connotations. Earlier in the story Dreiser once catches a glimpse of Drouet in a blissful mood: "He was as much affected by this show of finery and gayety as she. He pressed her arm warmly. Once she looked up, her even teeth glistening through her smiling lips, her eyes alight. As they were moving out he whispered down to her, 'You look lovely!' " (*SC* 1900: 88). In the manuscript, however, the same passage includes in its midst this sentence: "He felt a keen wave of desire" (*SC* 1981: 77). As Drouet's relationship with Carrie becomes more intimate,

Dreiser's description of the mistress includes more sexual representations and signifiers:

> With Drouet's experience and opinion for a guide she had learned to select colors and shades which had value in relation to her complexion. Her dresses draped her becomingly, for she wore excellent corsets and laced herself with care. Her hair had grown out even more luxuriantly than before. . . . She had always been of cleanly instincts and now that opportunity afforded, she kept her body sweet. . . . She had some color in her cheeks, a large soft eye, a plump, dainty chin and a round, full neck. Altogether, and at all times, she was pleasing to look upon. (*SC* 1981: 146)

Moreover, the dialogue in the original manuscript often sounds more colloquial than does that in the novel. The manuscript includes some profane utterances, such as Lord, God, and Christ, but Dreiser eliminated them in the 1900 edition. Hurstwood says "George," his own name, instead of "Jesus." Similarly, Mrs. Hurstwood calls her daughter "Jessica" rather than "Jess." On one occasion he bursts into rage when Mrs. Hurstwood writes him "I want you to send the money I asked for at once. I need it to carry out my plans. You can stay away if you want to. It doesn't matter in the least. But I must have some money. So don't delay, but send it by the boy." In response, as originally written, Hurstwood says, "Damn her. . . . Damn her. . . . I'll make her change her tone if I've got to wring her neck" (*SC* 1981: 235–36). In the novel, Hurstwood says softly: "Damn her! . . . I'll make it hot for her if she causes me trouble. I'll make her change her tone if I have to use force to do it!" (*SC* 1900: 257).

The original version of *Sister Carrie* also is full of the economic references which find no place in the novel. Dreiser originally indicated, for example, that the four-dollar weekly rent Carrie pays her sister and her husband would pay for their monthly rent, "seventeen dollars." With the savings, Hanson could make an investment in the "two lots which were valued at two hundred dollars each, far out on the West Side" (*SC* 1981: 13). Economic references made later in the story, when Hurstwood is out of work and winter arrives in New York, also provides as crucial detail and verisimilitude to make *Sister Carrie* a truly realistic novel. Hurstwood, now drifting into the lobby of a hotel, overhears a conversation by "two big mining millionaires from the West" (*SC* 1981: 357), one of whom talks about meeting his wife in France and the other is excited about going on a vacation in Florida with his wife. When Hurstwood sits and reads a newspaper by the radiator in his room, he learns, as Dreiser writes,

> Great attention was given to the details of the storm by the newspapers, which played up the distress of the poor in large type. Italians, doing all the

small–bushel business in coal throughout the city, raised the price. A vast excitement about cold, hunger, starvation and the like was really worked up by the papers until nearly everyone felt some of the terrors of winter, although they were not suffering at all. (*SC* 1981: 360)

Such economic references aside, the original manuscript of the novel contains numerous signifiers for the social status of an individual or a group of people. By contrast, Dreiser in the novel is less conscious of social class; his characterization is more personal and individualistic. Interestingly, Dreiser said of Henry James: "I would reject most of James as too narrowly and thinly class-conscious."[14] It is not surprising that Dreiser omitted some allusions to class-consciousness which would have detracted from expressing personal feelings.

When Carrie in Chicago plays on an amateur stage the role of Laura, a girl rescued off the streets and raised by a New York society woman, the role, Dreiser writes, "affected Carrie deeply. It reminded her somehow of her own state. She caught the infection of sorrow, sympathized with it wholly and consequently mastered it easily." When a suitor from the upper class finds out Laura's background, Dreiser comments with a touch of satire: "Society would not brook a marriage with so low a creature." One of the men who tries to write the lines for the play, referring to Laura's story, remarks: "The best blood of New York is insulted by the girl's presence" (*SC* 1981: 162–63). Later in New York, Hurstwood, working as a scab during the railroad strike, becomes a victim of jeers and catcalls, many of which are excised from the 1900 edition. Stemming from a violent class warfare, such representations dramatize various scenes of the workers against the capitalists, the police against the mob, the middle class against the upper as well as lower classes. In the 1900 edition, these social and political signifiers are either toned down or eliminated entirely.

Another way of considering *Sister Carrie* less realistic than usually perceived is to recognize a paucity of moralism in the book. Dreiser is generally regarded as a writer least interested in moral issues. "Dreiser's world," Louis Auchincloss has noted, "seems closer to us than that of Henry James or Edith Wharton because he was not interested in the moral fashions of his time."[15] Isabel Archer and Carrie Meeber, both American women and fictional contemporaries, are presented in stark contrast. James's heroine is endowed not only with intelligence but with altruism. Dreiser's is not aware of her own mind, nor does she think precisely about her condition or analyze her problem. In short, Isabel is a thinker, Carrie a dreamer. To portray Carrie as does Drieser, he finds it necessary to reduce the analytical or philosophical commentary that would get in the way of the development of the story. Such passages would have appealed less to her heart than they would to her mind.

The introduction of a young, innocent girl as a "half-equipped little knight" (*SC* 1900: 3) helps the reader to understand what Dreiser has in mind. Dreiser's conception of his heroine is clearly sentimental and idealistic. The romance, then, begins on one summer afternoon in 1889, when Carrie, from a small town in Wisconsin, goes to Chicago aboard a train. In the rest of her journey, the battle of life, the clashes of her dreams against the sordid reality, is repeated. The image of her sister's dreary flat and of herself walking in miserable weather from one sweatshop to another for employment chills Carrie's spirit, and it becomes inevitable that this "little soldier of fortune took her good turn in an easy way" by accepting the twenty dollars Drouet insists is a loan. When Drouet wants to buy Carrie a new jacket, the saleswoman helps her on with it, and "by accident" (*SC* 1900: 67–79), it fits her perfectly. As these events suggest, her course of action is largely determined by chance and unconscious direction, the elements which contribute to a melodrama.

Carrie's rise, furthermore, parallels a neat pattern formulated by her instincts always craving for better things. Apparently, the incidental forces controlling life command that, whatever achievement one makes, he or she be always dissatisfied. Discontent, the inevitable result of longing, is nevertheless a symptom of romantic sensibility. This representation of desire is true of Carrie. To her the boys trying to attract her attention at the factory appear glaringly inferior to Drouet. When he introduces her to Hurstwood, she instinctively feels that Hurstwood belongs to a higher class of men. She is more strongly attracted to Hurstwood than to Drouet because Hurstwood is more intelligent than Drouet and because Hurstwood, as Dreiser says, "paid that peculiar deference to women which every member of the sex appreciates" (*SC* 1900: 106).

As Carrie's desire for happiness suggests, Dreiser's account of human action is markedly different from that of a typical naturalist like Zola. Dreiser is moved more deeply by abstractions, mysteries, and accidents in life than by people and their daily activities. Early in the book he observes the ambivalent position in which humankind is placed:

> Among the forces which sweep and play throughout the universe, untutored man is but a wisp in the wind. Our civilisation is still in a middle stage, scarcely beast, in that it is no longer wholly guided by instinct; scarcely human, in that it is not yet wholly guided by reason. . . . As a beast, the forces of life aligned him with them; as a man, he has not yet wholly learned to align himself with the forces. In this intermediate stage he wavers—neither drawn in harmony with nature by his instincts nor yet wisely putting himself in harmony by his own free-will. (*SC* 1900: 83)

Dreiser thus makes his realism a means of restoring to the novel some of the dramatic mysteries and colorful events that used to be incorporated into a romance. He has a penchant for mythic or analogic expressions as he calls Carrie "a knight" or man "a wisp in the wind." And Dreiser is known to use clothes and furniture as symbolic images.[16] His idea of the novel is closer to that of Frank Norris than to that of William Dean Howells. In *The Octopus*, Norris portrays a dead girl being reincarnated in the wheat: "In the wheat he waited for her. He saw her coming. She was simply dressed. No fanciful wreath of tube-roses was about her head now, no strange garment of red and gold enveloped her now. It was no longer as ephemeral illusion of the night, evanescent, mystic, but a simple country girl coming to meet her lover." In dramatizing the mysterious forces of nature represented by the wheat, Norris concludes his story: "In that little, isolated group of human insects, misery, death, and anguish spun like a wheel of fire. *But the* WHEAT *remained*. Untouched, unassailable, undefiled, that mighty world-force, that nourisher of nations, wrapped in Nirvanic calm, indifferent to the human swarm, gigantic, resistless, moved onward in its appointed grooves."[17]

Whereas naturalists like Norris and Hardy are emotionally involved with the mysterious forces of the universe, realists like James and Howells are morally concerned with the events and manners of society that appear to control human behavior. In accounting for the downfall of a young couple in *A Modern Instance*, Atherton, Howells's mouthpiece, says:

> The Hubbards were full of natural goodness, I dare say, when they didn't happen to cross each other's wishes. No, it's the implanted goodness that saves,—the seed of righteousness treasured from generation to generation, and carefully watched and tended by disciplined fathers and mothers in the hearts where they have dropped it. The flower of this implanted goodness is what we call civilization.[18]

This is sound morality but a bad state of mind for a novelist like Dreiser. His purpose of writing was not so much to delve into the realm of social criticism as to dramatize the psychology of human behavior. In contemplating Hurstwood's action, Dreiser is more impressed by accidental and mysterious phenomena than he is by the moral sanctions society imposes upon the individual. Hurstwood's story, in fact, contains as many elements of romance as Carrie's, for the very abstractness and profundity of romance allows it to formulate human truths of the heart rather than moral truths of society. For Hurstwood, the difference between this young, pretty, innocent girl and his petty, vain, nagging wife becomes equally obvious. Mrs. Hurstwood is a sophisticated woman; she is well informed in social mores and well polished in her manners. When he becomes acquainted with Carrie, Hurstwood is enjoying the zenith of his career. His position is respected in his circle, and economically he belongs to the class just below that of the luxuriously rich. At the age of forty, his flight from such a position is doomed from the beginning. But, swayed by his blind infatuation with the girl, he commits a blunder. And, when Hurstwood accompanies Carrie and Drouet to a show, he carelessly tells his friends the classic lie that his wife is unable to come with him because of illness. Hurstwood's action is always motivated by adventure, not by the kind of planning an ordinary businessman would contemplate.

Predictably, Hurstwood's adventure is accompanied by chance and accident. To elope with Carrie, Hurstwood is tempted to steal money from the safe at Fitzgerald and Moy's, his employer. The embezzlement eventually is to undo his fortune, but he does not steal the money on purpose. This incident creates irony on his fate. "After he had all the money in the hand bag," Dreiser describes,

> a revulsion of feeling seized him. He would not do it—no! Think of what a scandal it would make. . . . He took out the two boxes and put all the money back. In his excitement he forgot what he was doing, and put the sums in the wrong boxes. . . .
>
> While the money was in his hand the lock clicked. It had sprung! Did he do it? He grabbed at the knob and pulled vigorously. It had closed. (*SC* 1900: 288–89)

There is no way for Hurstwood to explain the incident to his employer and he has stolen the money in spite of himself. His moral victory is ironically invalidated by sheer chance and he has become a victim of cruel fate.[19] But, in the Pennsylvania edition, Dreiser writes: "He took them out and straightened the matter, but now the terror had gone. Why be afraid? Could he not get away? What would be the use of remaining? He would never get such a chance again. He emptied the good money into the satchel. There was something fascinating about the soft green stack—the loose silver and gold. He felt sure now that he could not leave that. No, no. He would do it" (*SC* 1981: 270–71). In this predicament Hurstwood acts a calculating, willful criminal, whereas in the novel fate and chance seem to bail out Hurstwood, a romantic lover.

In a romantic novel, such scenes as depicted in the 1900 edition are more successful in convincing the reader of the dilemma a character faces. Having come to know Hurstwood and Carrie in the circumstances of their extraordinary lives, the reader is able to feel for them as their romance unfolds. Indeed they envision an existence apart from the victims they have become. As the fortune of Hurstwood, dubbed "Wheeler," falls that of Carrie rises. In describing this crucial turn of events, Dreiser is freely creating realistic signifiers such as "wheel of fortune," "wheeler-dealer," "carrier," and "carryall." As a myth of success, however, the story must shift its focus from Hurstwood to Carrie. Dreiser, then, dramatically portrays her successes on the stage, showing her rapidly rising reputation on the road throughout the country. Far from his final scene in the manuscript version, where he turns the gas on to end his misery, the final scene of the novel, by stark contrast, signifies a hopeful outlook on life Carrie comes to cherish.

The rearrangement of such a grim scene as Hurstwood's suicide suggests that one's striving for the ideal, despite one's occasional misfortune, is the keynote of *Sister Carrie*. And this call for the ideal is the essential motivation of each character in the novel. Even if Dreiser accepts the world as it is and things as they are, he could still assert in the end: "Not evil, but longing for that which is better, more often directs the steps of erring. Not evil, but goodness more often allures the feeling mind unused to reason" (*SC* 1900: 556). Most significantly, the 1900 edition of the novel ends with this often quoted passage in which Dreiser tells his heroine:

> Oh, Carrie, Carrie! Oh, blind strivings of the human heart! Onward, onward, it saith, and where beauty leads, there it follows. Whether it be the tinkle of a lone sheep bell o'er some quiet landscape, or the glimmer of beauty in sylvan places, or the show of soul in some passing eye, the heart knows and makes answer, following. It is when the feet weary and hope seems vain that the heartaches and the longings arise. Know, then, that for you is neither surfeit nor content. In your rocking-chair, by your window dreaming, shall you long, alone. In your rocking-chair, by your window, shall you dream such happiness as you may never feel. (*SC* 1900: 557)

Dreiser finally sees Carrie in her famous rocking chair as she broods over the mystery of life, just as he did in his own life, without understanding anything more clearly than the day she first left home for Chicago. This is *not* so hopeless a situation a young girl like Carrie must face in life as it appears.[20] Because Carrie at the end of the story is not completely happy, she ponders a possible relationship with Ames, an intellectual, who recommends that she read Balzac's novels. But banishing Ames from her further thoughts suggests her realization that happiness is always elusive and that as her standards become higher, she will be less satisfied in life. This awareness, which buttresses Dreiser's concept of romance, also tells Carrie's thought and action.

Not only does the ending of the story differ between the novel and the manuscript, but Carrie's lovers are drawn with a number of discrepancies. In the novel Drouet assumes the role of a congenial fellow Carrie is eager to trust, but Drouet's character as Dreiser originally conceived is less compassionate. Drouet, as presented in the manuscript, is a confirmed philanderer and an occasional hypocrite:

> He had but one idol—the perfect woman. He found her enshrined in many a pretty petticoat. On his trade pilgrimages he was like to forget Carrie entirely. She came into his mind when all later divinities were out, or when he was on his way back to Chicago. Then her beauty and the cosy quarters in which she was installed loomed up before him with considerable fascination, and he was delighted to get back. He would enter Carrie's presence with all the spirit of a lover—away from her would forsake her memory with the ease of the unattached masher, which, after all, he was. (*SC* 1981: 105–6)

When Carrie becomes suspicious of Drouet's intention to marry her, Drouet tries to calm her fears by concocting a real estate deal and promising to marry when it goes through. "He dragged in the reference to the fictitious real estate deal," Dreiser adds, "as a sop to Carrie's matrimonial desires. He wanted her to feel contented with her state, the while he winged his merry, thoughtless round" (*SC* 1981: 135).

Hurstwood in the manuscript version is even more lustful and hypocritical than Drouet. Though Hurstwood pretends to be genuinely in love with Carrie, he is as heartless a philanderer as is Drouet. Since he is more intelligent and polished in his manners than his rival Drouet, he is a ruthless and calculating individual as conceived by Dreiser. In the 1900 edition, Hurstwood is drawn on a popular businessman who likes to socialize but he is also a gentleman:

> He loved to go out and have a good time once in a while—to go to the races, the theatres, the sporting entertainments at some of the clubs. He kept a horse and neat trap, had his wife and two children, who were well established in a neat house on the North Side near Lincoln Park, and was altogether a very acceptable individual of our great American upper class—the first grade below the luxuriously rich. (*SC* 1900: 50)

But the Pennsylvania edition reveals that Dreiser deleted a lengthy phrase stating that Hurstwood loved to go to "those more unmentionable resorts of vice—the gilded chambers of shame with which Chicago was then so liberally cursed" (*SC* 1981: 44).

Furthermore, Hurstwood's demeanor on his flight to New York by way of Montreal, as described in the manuscript, is expedient; Hurstwood is quite explicit about his plans, an action which seldom evokes the feelings of a romance. In the 1900 edition, such detail is excised in keeping with a delightful mood in which Hurstwood is presented. In the following passage Dreiser is a transcendentalist in spirit:

> Meanwhile, he accepted his present situation with Carrie, getting what joy out of it he could.
>
> Out came the sun by noon, and poured a golden flood through their open windows. Sparrows were twittering. There were laughter and song in the air. Hurstwood could not keep his eyes from Carrie. She seemed the one ray of sunshine in all his trouble. Oh, if she would only love him wholly—only throw her arms around him in the blissful spirit in which he had seen her in the little park in Chicago—how happy he would be! (*SC* 1900: 316)

Another deleted passage referring to their stopover in Montreal reveals how Hurstwood's mind, as told in the manuscript, is preoccupied with their mundane, domestic shopping list even while Hurstwood is in a romantic mood. Such incongruity in Dreiser's characterization is quite plausible in realistic fiction, but it would be awkward at best in a romance.

What makes a realistic novel naturalistic as well as romantic is the expression of the sentiments generated by the individual whose search for happiness is idealistic rather than materialistic, humanistic rather than social and economic. The two versions of *Sister Carrie* suggest that during the composition of the book Dreiser himself was ambivalent in presenting this story to the public. Although it is not true that the 1900 version is a pure romance while the 1981 edition is a realistic and naturalistic novel, it is interesting to recognize how clearly this dualism in an American narrative emerges in the story of Sister Carrie.

Notes

1. See *Sister Carrie*, the Pennsylvania edition. Later page references to this edition are indicated in parentheses as *SC* 1981.

2. Perhaps the influence of the publisher's wife has been exaggerated; Doubleday himself could have been sufficiently influenced by a personal dislike for Dreiser's subject matter. For a publishing history of the novel, see Jack Salzman, "The Publication of *Sister Carrie*: Fact and Fiction." Salzman observes: "Not only have we misunderstood the order of events and various commitments involved in the publication of *Sister Carrie*, but we may have also exaggerated the role played by Frank Norris, while perhaps unjustifiably condemning Mrs. Doubleday" (127).

3. See Lars Åhnebrink, *The Beginnings of Naturalism in American Fiction*, v.

4. Redefining *Sister Carrie* (1900) with Frank Norris's *McTeague* and Stephen Crane's *The Red Badge of Courage* from this modified point of view, Donald Pizer noted: "The naturalist often describes his character, as though they

are conditioned and controlled by environment, heredity, instinct, or chance. But he also suggests a compensating humanistic value in his characters or their fates which affirm the significance of the individual and of his life." See Pizer, "Nineteenth-Century American Naturalism: An Essay in Definition," 3. Also see William J. Handy, "A Re-examination of Dreiser's *Sister Carrie*," 380–89; Yoshinobu Hakutani, "Dreiser and French Realism"; and "*Sister Carrie* and the Problem of Literary Naturalism."

5. See Irving Howe, "Afterword," in *An American Tragedy*, 1925, (New York: New American Library, 1964), 827.

6. Randall Stewart observes: "Dreiser is the most compassionate of writers. . . . Dreiser, when confronted by human troubles, is overwhelmed by pity and perplexity. He doesn't know what to do about life." See Stewart, "Dreiser and the Naturalistic Heresy," 112.

7. See George J. Becker, ed. *Documents of Modern Literary Realism*, 95.

8. *Sister Carrie* (New York: Doubleday, Page & Company, 1900), 3. Further textual references to this edition are indicated in parentheses as *SC* 1900.

9. Richard Chase, *The American Novel and Its Tradition*, 245.

10. In discussing the danger of realism in fiction, James Fenimore Cooper argued that fiction succeeds better "by delineations of principles, and of character, in their classes, than by a too fastidious attention to originals." See Chase, 56. In the manuscript version of *Sister Carrie*, Dreiser, influenced by his wife Jug, was apparently concerned with the historical accuracy of his descriptions. Jug wrote in the manuscript such questions as "When did the word 'drummer' come into use?" "Was Waukesha a Chicago resort in 1884?" "When did the 'flat' come into use?" "Was Chicago's population 500,000 in 1884? When and where were the first department stores established?" See Alfred Kazin, "Introduction: Theodore Dreiser and *Sister Carrie* Restored," in *Sister Carrie* (New York: Penguin, 1981), xiii.

11. A year before Dreiser wrote *Sister Carrie* he also had written a magazine article, "Life Stories of Successful Men—No. 10: Philip D. Armour."

12. Dreiser also wrote a magazine article on Marshall Field. See "Life Stories of Successful Men—No. 12."

13. At the time of writing the original version of *Sister Carrie*, Dreiser wrote a long detailed article about G. M. Pullman, the designer of the Pullman car and the town near Chicago where the famous sleeping-car was manufactured. See "The Town of Pullman."

14. See F. O. Matthiessen, *Theodore Dreiser*, 56.

15. See Louis Auchincloss, "Introduction," in *Sister Carrie* (Columbus: Charles E. Merrill, 1969), xi.

16. F. O. Matthiessen is the earliest critic to notice Dreiser's use of clothes symbolism: "Dreiser's few basic and recurrent symbolic images serve to underscore this view. The symbol he makes most of—as we have already seen—is that of clothes, which Veblen was singling out at the same time, in *The Theory of the Leisure Class*, as giving a peculiarly representative expression of 'pecuniary culture.' Clothes in Dreiser are the chief means of display, of lifting a character above where he was, and by that fact above somewhere else. They lure—but really they separate" (Matthiessen, 83).

17. Frank Norris, *The Octopus*, 347–60. Presley, Norris's hero and spokesman, who makes this statement is akin to Henchard in Thomas Hardy's *Mayor of Casterbridge*, who is more awed by cosmic forces than depressed by the social miseries in his surroundings.

18. William Dean Howells, *A Modern Instance*, 333.

19. How successfully Dreiser manipulates this scene can be seen by the success of his similar treatment of the subject in Clyde's drowning of Roberta in *An American Tragedy*.

20. I agree with Louis Auchincloss, who notes: "It is a curious ending, for two reasons: one, as already indicated I do not see why it is so bad to dream such happiness, and, two, it had not occurred to me that Carrie *was* that kind of dreamer. Only at the end are we given the notion that Carrie cares about beauty" (Auchincloss, x).

Dreiser, *Sister Carrie*, and Mrs. Doubleday: Gender and Social Change at the Turn of the Century

MARSHA S. MOYER

THE CENTRAL FOCUS OF THIS ESSAY IS A FAMOUS MYTHOLOGICAL CONstruct in American literary history which arose in 1900 at the beginning of the controversy surrounding the novel *Sister Carrie*. It is a myth about artistic repression which came to symbolize intense contradictions within the critical debate. This debate over the merits of Dreiser's work was part of a larger, late-nineteenth-century cultural challenge to the "official version of the whole of American history," similar in tone and concern to the recent controversy over the new American History Standards developed by UCLA.[1] The myth involves two opposing representations of the female: Dreiser made symbolic use of his publisher's wife, Mrs. Nellie Doubleday, to represent the still powerful and lingering Victorian social fabric, while the fictional Carrie Meeber of *Sister Carrie* represented an emerging new society tied to a growing presence of industrialized urban centers. This myth, which embodied current contradictions and crises over morality, sexuality, and the role of women in society, provided a gendered foundation for subsequent critical debate on the meaning and value of not only *Sister Carrie*, but also of Dreiser himself, literature, and the relationship between literature and American culture. A gendered analysis of the discourse in which this myth became embedded flows from the symbolic meaning of these feminine constructions.

The myth portrayed Mrs. Doubleday as the evil power attempting to squelch the successful reception of Dreiser's first novel. This story had actually been started by Dreiser's friend Frank Norris, a reader at the Doubleday, Page publishing company, as a plausible explanation for all the fuss over publication. Dreiser continued to use this story and it was later picked up by others as a sufficient theory for *Sister Carrie*'s troubled beginnings. Dreiser's characterization of the genteel Mrs. Doubleday defending the proper role of literature as moral instruction against the amoral threat of *Sister Carrie* symbolized for Dreiser the cultural struggle of nineteenth-century America's transformation into a twentieth-century society. But it also must have helped him to deal with the humiliation of perceived failure over his unwelcome text. Under a cloud of reluctance and animosity, *Sister Carrie* was published on 8 November 1900. Frank Norris was allowed by his boss to send out 127 review copies out of a total of 558 prints, but the publisher did nothing else to promote the book and it was a commercial failure.[2] Dreiser's further humiliation and feeling of rejection which occurred as the result of the failure of his marriage, together with a "black storm of combined ill-health and morbid depression," added to his need for an explanatory model which could encompass such multilayered failure.[3] Ellen Moers has noted that Dreiser summarized the reasons for his three-year bout with what was labeled "neurasthenia" by writing that "from me . . . a world or given order was passing."[4] This disintegration of a stable life contributed to Dreiser's desire for some kind of all-encompassing paradigmatic context in which to place himself and his troubles: so he created a cultural myth, larger than his own experience, which served as a sustaining metaphor of artistic integrity in his time. Dreiser's opposition of the two representations of the female and their contrasting moral codes exemplified the changing role expectations of women. The union of morality and sexuality within the feminine, when threatened with disassociation by compelling social forces, could create deep psychological pain within both men and women. And Dreiser seems to have suffered through such pain on several levels at once.

Dreiser's tidy provision of a mythic narrative as an explanatory model for the troubled reception of his novel provided critics with specific gendered representations through which they could organize their arguments. Alfred Kazin has noted that the legend that *Sister Carrie* had been suppressed by the publisher's wife became "so dear to the hearts of the rising generation of the twentieth century that Mrs. Doubleday became a classic character, the Carrie Nation of the American liberal epos, her ax forever lifted against the truth of American life."[5] The legend established the importance of *Sister Carrie* in American culture, referring to it as the prime example of how repressive Victorian values were continuing to thwart the efforts of serious American writers at the turn of the century.

The understanding that the Doubleday legend was unfounded has finally lessened scholarly interest in an event that produced so much emotional, at times bitter, intellectual debate. But a focus is needed on *why* the myth had such tremendous staying power, and why it gave critics, writers and historians, as well as the reading public, a way to talk about a story that was going on about *them*, an expansive historical narrative in which they were all players. The clear polarization of two symbolic women pitted against each other in a struggle for cultural supremacy suggests an obvious gendered meaning for both sides of the debate: women are viewed as cultural enemies of their own freedom, while masculine virtue remains cloistered on the sidelines, the innocent, beleaguered bystander of the fray.

Mrs. Doubleday as cultural symbol represented to Dreiser the confining genteel code held in place by the sanctity of home and virtuous womanhood, a code which shaped the cultural discourse that influenced the negative reception to his first book. The publishing industry in particular was the strong arm of the traditional cultural norms. Literature was viewed as an instructive tool of the educated classes whose audience also included the lower classes, in proper behavior and morality. Alan Trachtenberg has remarked that "the voices of gentility insisted on their view of art" in the production of readable fiction for the masses: it should "display the good taste of gentlefolk; it should 'avoid' vulgarity by the simple device of refusing to recognize it. Like the refined gentry, art should protect itself from common life, should concern itself with 'ideal' characters, pure thoughts, and noble emotions."[6]

The period between 1885 and 1905, when the number of American magazines almost doubled, was, however, a time of great change and transformation for American publishers. The post-Civil War explosion of prosperity and growth included a growing sophistication in economic regulation and advertising, forcing publishers to accommodate an old-style "courtesy system" to a demanding, competitive business atmosphere.[7] A major change in the new system revolved around the author's willingness to take part in a promotion process which would carry over from book to book. Walter Hines Page's gentlemanly pressure upon Dreiser to submit to his publisher's management of his literary career was simply an example of the Doubleday firm's successful adaptation to a modernizing trend in a new, commercialized publishing profession.[8] Dreiser rebelled and resisted this coercion upon the artist to yield to commercial tactics, and it must have gone to the core of his struggles to separate his personal sense of integrity as a creative intelligence from an overly commercialized money-hungry society. Even though Dreiser could never have been accused of being a traditionally oriented gentleman from the older "courtesy system," he nevertheless shared with that older culture a disdain for the modernizing trends rapidly taking over in many areas of American society.

One other aspect of these "modernizing trends" included a rapidly growing involvement of women readers and writers in American public discourse and a perceived sellout to a demand for romantic escapist fictions. The unwritten Protection of Young Ladies Act provided a strong and clear purpose to editors' blue pencil censoring as well as created a climate of linguistic repression which writers characteristically internalized, becoming their own, strongest censors. In 1926 Thomas Beer named this late 1800s guardian matron of literary gentility "The Titaness," a figure who had originated in the Midwest during the 1800s and "had quietly become a figure on the American social chart, a shadowy Titaness, a terror to editors. . . ."[9] Thus two related female representations were already shaping biased assumptions about the worst of the old culture and the worst of the new: the traditional role of the married woman as cultural monitor of genteel codes and behaviors, and the Titaness, intellectual guardian of a feminized literary sensibility.

The image of an authoritative Mrs. Doubleday denouncing his attempt at a masculinized realism in *Sister Carrie* not only represented to Dreiser the looming presence of oppressive female cultural guardianship, but as well encapsulated the reasons for his failing marriage to a traditional woman, and helped him formulate an alternative strategy for living. Carrie symbolized his struggle for freedom from this repressive cultural atmosphere, a battle he had to fight on a deep personal level as well as intellectually through his writings. Thus the story contained powerful mythic content for Dreiser on a psychosexual level, and also reflected an existing historical cultural context that echoed and reinforced this psychic conflict.

Carrie Meeber represented the opposite pole of the genteel woman. She challenged directly the socialization of the female that focused on a close bonding among home life, sexuality, and religion. Carrie was single, willing to live with men without marrying them, and showed no guilt over doing so. In fact, her life flowers as a result of her deviant choices and behaviors. Midway through the novel, as her lover, George Hurstwood, begins his downward slide, Carrie's life has "just begun. She did not feel herself defeated at all. . . . The great city held something, she knew not what. Possibly she would come out of bondage into freedom—who knows? Perhaps she would be happy. . . . She was saved in that she was hopeful."[10] Carrie's re-invention of herself from farm girl into successful urban dweller represents the freedom of the human spirit to pursue its own desires, and this was seen as a direct confrontation with traditional values regulating personal and social gendered relations. It went to the heart of American society's organization because the identity and life-choices of its protagonist attacked the primary institutions of marriage and family. Carrie championed the individual against the restrictions of gender role imposed upon individual expression.

Dreiser's visits to Indiana and New Jersey in the summer of 1919 reminded him of "American society's incomplete transition from a straitlaced, basically fundamentalist morality [the code of gentility] to more liberalized standards.'' He noticed how ''the lessons of the Indiana of his youth—particularly those garnered from the harsh nineteenth-century restrictions on sexual relations—were being put to the test on the national level.'' Thomas Riggio has summarized that Dreiser's observations on American culture as he aged (particularly after his move to Hollywood during the twenties) ''gave him an almost surreal vision of the times and reinforced his sense of America's living out a vast social and moral allegory.'' It is in this *evolving* cultural, historical and psychological context that *Sister Carrie*—and the myth of its repression by the puritanical Mrs. Doubleday—assumes another, larger meaning, a meaning derived not just from a quaint historical confrontation between a shocked, morally dogmatic matron and a fictional single young woman who willingly abandons her reputation for a better life, but from ''a vast social and moral allegory.''[11]

The projection of a patriarchal culture of its unresolved psychosexual conflicts onto a divisive splitting of the feminine continues today. Some of the most heated debates in America coalesce around this heavily symbolic notion of family values. Dreiser, *Sister Carrie*, and Mrs. Doubleday, though not explicitly referred to any longer, rest comfortably just beneath the surface of modern discourse on an enduring conflict in American culture. The depth and density of meaning can be found in conversations and debates involving the nature and problems of the family, and changing sex role identities common to late-twentieth-century America. For instance, when Betty Ford, the spouse of ex-President Gerald Ford, appeared on a television program on 16 July 1993 to discuss the renowned substance abuse center named after her, she noted that women have a worse time struggling through their rehabilitation process because there seems to be a greater amount of guilt, shame, anger, resentment—''somehow they're supposed to be the models for the world, the nurturers and the caretakers. . . .'' Ford went on to discuss how women feel particularly guilty when coping mechanisms they have employed to deal with the heavy responsibility of being a ''model for the world'' break down and they can no longer function in their ''important'' role. Women tend to internalize their despair, taking longer to recover.

Social historian Joan Wallach Scott's admonition that gender ''emphasizes an entire system of relationships'' that are not necessarily sexualized, providing a ''primary way of signifying relationships of power,'' assists my attempt to trace intellectual debates flowing from *Sister Carrie* criticism.[12] Gendered meanings in Dreiser's critics and their writings flow through the decades in discussions about free will and atheistic philosophy; notions of democracy and socialist values; and struggles to define the relationship between language, style and culture. The symbolic meaning of Mrs. Doubleday conflates issues of family values and social chaos with all of the above themes.

In his 1950 doctoral dissertation, "Dreiser among the Critics," Stephen Stepanchev discussed the various critical schools and movements and their differing reactions to Dreiser, and he made a general division between schools of "impressionistic" reviewers who tended to like Dreiser's work, and genteel reviewers, who were unanimously opposed to the writer "on the ground that he failed to bring elevation to the novel and emphasized a sordid realism that was unrepresentative of American life as they knew it."[13] This opposition, although intellectually simplistic, is useful as a way of seeing how the mythic constructs of Carrie and Mrs. Doubleday represented "worlds" of meaning for their supporters and detractors. In 1915, for instance, Stuart P. Sherman noted that Dreiser demands "a moral vacuum from which the obligations of parenthood, marriage, chivalry, and citizenship have been quite withdrawn or locked in a twilight sleep"; conversely, in the thirties Dorothy Dudley, Dreiser's first biographer, wrote that such "high principled American matrons" as Mrs. Doubleday, "naively innocent in their pursuit of good works . . . hoping thereby to concoct some sort of social stability in a hit-or-miss land . . . what fine institutions they have gathered money to build up, to house the victims of their bloodless code!"[14] Dreiser critics, in fact, were entering into an ongoing, fundamental intellectual debate in American culture which had its roots in conflicting interpretations of a seventeenth century Puritan inheritance.

Warren Susman has discussed the renewal of deep concern in American intellectuals around 1890, generated by Frederick Jackson Turner's *Frontier Thesis*, about the uses of the American past. Defenders of traditional American culture and values had created a strong official creed which had become intolerable to a growing class of alienated intellectuals. Susman notes that "all through the nineteenth century there had been a rumbling of dissatisfaction with the inheritance from . . . Puritan theology and social organization and values," and that this philosophical dissatisfaction with the dominant view of the Puritan tradition had become an important part of "official American mythology." But a great explosion of critique occurred during the 1890s, and would continue into the 1940s.[15]

Dreiser's contribution of ponderous social narratives to his culture coincided with this period of intellectual foment; his overly simplistic analysis of *Sister Carrie*'s troubled publication, defined by two gendered poles of female representation, was picked up by critics as a convenient expression of the conflict between morality and immorality, cultured refinement in style and freedom of discourse, the successful, rising business class and the rapidly growing working classes, and finally, socialism and capitalism.[16]

In 1901 Dreiser tried to refute the cool reception of his critics towards *Sister Carrie* by explaining his authorial intentions in a *New York Times* interview. Although Dreiser mentions neither Mrs. Doubleday nor his protagonist, Sister Carrie, the political importance of language usage is evident and emotionally charged. To the writer, the emphasis on proper English is "silly" and "ridiculous" when compared to "tragedy." Power relations are clearly outlined in this short comment from writer to critics. It is evident that Dreiser meant to challenge and subvert the hegemonic power of the critics, who shaped the content, evaluation and dispersal of American literary expressions:

> Well, the critics have not really understood what I was trying to do. . . . [This book] is intended not as a piece of literary craftsmanship, but as a picture of conditions done as simply and effectively as the English language will permit. To sit up and criticise me for saying "vest," instead of "waistcoat"; to talk about my splitting the infinitive and using vulgar commonplaces here and there, when the tragedy of a man's life is being displayed, is silly. More, it is ridiculous.[17]

In 1903 Dreiser again tried to explain his work, and in the process elucidated the multiple levels of discourse that the Mrs. Doubleday myth would come to symbolize:

> What the so-called judges of the truth or morality are really inveighing against most of the time is not the discussion of mere sexual lewdness . . . but the disturbing and destroying of their own little theories concerning life, which in some cases may be nothing more than a quiet acceptance of things as they are. . . . It is true that the rallying cry of the critics against so-called immoral literature is that the mental virtue of the reader must be preserved; but this has become a house of refuge to which every form of social injustice hurries for protection. . . . Immoral! Immoral! Under this cloak hide the vices of wealth as well as the vast unspoken blackness of poverty and ignorance . . . a true picture of life, honestly and reverentially set down, is both moral and artistic whether it offends conditions or not.[18]

Dreiser was fighting a struggle not only against provincial moral standards, but aesthetic values, sociopolitical issues and economic injustices. But negative reviews continued to accumulate. On 27 June 1907 the Chicago *Advance* put out a review which stated that "the book is not a good or wholesome one for women to read, for Sister Carrie is not nice or clever or bright or kind-hearted or respectable . . . a volume containing a terrible warning to men and one that women had better not read is *Sister Carrie*."[19] Another critic in 1907 in the *New York Evening Sun* trivialized the myth by referring to the repressive Mrs. Doubleday as "the publisher's grandmother or maiden aunt, or somebody like that, [who thought *Sister Carrie*] was in bad taste." And then he makes the connection between bad taste and bad style: "Of course it really wasn't. It was simply crude and rough and immature . . . a powerful story badly told." Insulted by Dreiser's 1901 comments on American criticism in general as "the joke which English literary authorities maintain it to be," the reviewer continued to ridicule Dreiser by advising him that "a short course in home reading would be desirable" before he "completes his second book . . . [and that he] would learn how to do a thing 'simply and effectively'."[20] A *New York Press* review in 1907 also made connections between bad taste and bad style:

> After reading *Sister Carrie* we can understand easily the shock it gave the first publisher's relative. But we think the shock might have come from another cause than her reported objection to the moral atmosphere of this "novel with a purpose." . . . Indeed, as a picture of an actress of a certain type, a woman of little intelligence and practically no moral sense, we think Carrie Madenda may take rank with [other famous literary actresses]. But we were shocked by one element in this novel and that was the fashion of the writer's English. We cannot recall such vulgar forms of expression in any book we have ever read.[21]

The conflation between style and content, and hence style and morality, was being constructed in these early years by Dreiser and his critics alike. The myth which had centered around morality was now beginning to represent a struggle over aesthetic values.

Between 1911 and 1915 Dreiser wrote five more books. The last, *The "Genius"*, was also suppressed and revived the story of the suppression of *Sister Carrie*.[22] Both events were widely publicized by a group of radical critics as examples of the destructive force of American puritanism. But conservative critics also began to escalate their attacks upon the growing reputation for powerful expression that Dreiser was beginning to acquire. New meanings began to appear explicitly in Dreiser criticism that conflated aesthetic values, earlier connected to moral standards, with sociopolitical content.

Stuart P. Sherman's essay, "The Naturalism of Mr. Dreiser," appeared in a December issue of *The Nation* and became the official starting point for serious critical debate on the merits and faults of Dreiser's works. Noting that "a great change has rather recently taken place in the spirit of the age, in the literature which reflects it, and in the criticism which judges it," Sherman summarizes this "supposed revolution" as a turning away from an illusory view of life and toward, "for the first time in history," a facing and acceptance of the facts of life. Sherman deems it necessary to remind his readers that Dreiser, "a novelist of the new school," comes "from the 'ethnic' element . . . which, as we are assured by competent authorities, is to redeem us from Puritanism and insure our artistic salvation." Sherman suggests that a focus on "the facts of life" is "but a clever hypnotizing pass of the artist, employed to . . . evade moral responsibility for any questionable features. . . ." He characterizes the new writing as analogous to "photographing wild animals in their habitat by trap and flashlight."[23]

Refuting the claim that this naturalistic approach to writing is "scientific," Sherman is careful to point out that Charles Darwin, the most influential scientist in the cultural development of realism, "frankly declared that he could not observe without a theory." Sherman is able to dismiss any serious claims to a more scientific approach to writing in the new writers because they display no moral limits; they have no "theory" of human conduct. Dreiser's books portray society as a jungle, with men and women as sexualized, mindless animals in constant pursuit of each other after the manner of beasts in the jungle. "Mr. Dreiser's stubborn insistence upon the jungle-motif," Sherman argues, "results in a dreary monotony in the form and substance of his novels. . . . Read one of these novels, and you have read them all."[24] Sherman accuses Dreiser of simplifying American life "beyond recognition," and "whether it is because he comes from Indiana" or because of his insistence on the jungle motif Sherman cannot say. He "can only note that [Dreiser] never speaks of his men and women as 'educated' or 'brought up,' but rather as 'raised,' like stock animals."[25]

Sherman, although not specifically referring to the Mrs. Doubleday myth, calls up her image in his criticism of Dreiser's simplistic philosophical outlook, defending traditional obligations of "parenthood, marriage, chivalry, and citizenship."[26] Mrs. Doubleday's opposing force, *Sister Carrie* and now Dreiser himself, is evoked by comparisons to the jungle, the "ethnic element" in American society, animals and sex, and even by a reference to Indiana. A lack of refinement in philosophical theory cannot produce worthy literary texts; refinement and sophistication in thought and morality must subsume the literary imagination.

Supporters of Dreiser inverted Sherman's negative portrayal of Dreiser into a virtue. Sherwood Anderson wrote in 1917 that Dreiser was reflecting the prevailing "crudity of thought in America," and suggested that most writing was still done by people who "have drawn [themselves] away" from that reality:

> We have not had faith in our people and in the story of our people. . . . We are fools. We talk of writers of the old world . . . [while below] us the roaring

> city lies like a great animal on the prairies, but we do not run out to the prairies. We stay in our rooms and talk. . . . As a people we have given ourselves to industrialism, and industrialism is not lovely . . . the whole thing is as ugly as modern war. . . . The dominant note in American life today is the factory hand. When we have digested that fact, we can begin to approach the task of the present-day novelist with a new point of view.[27]

The proper behavior of Mrs. Doubleday is turned into a sterile blindness to the facts of modern America, while Carrie represents the muteness of the working classes, involved in battles of economic survival which the Mrs. Doubledays primly ignore. To defend and fight for *Sister Carrie* is to be like the great knight Frank Norris, a brave virility shining through one's every move, thought, and commitment to a noble cause.

Because *Sister Carrie* describes working class people and their struggles, Dreiser used language he considered reflective of the culture of the American working class of that time. Largely uneducated but rapidly assimilating into an industrializing economy and culture, the working classes did not speak the same language as the dominant middle and upper classes, the classes which also controlled the production of literature. Working class discourse was a threat to those levels of society characterized by established Eastern backgrounds, high levels of education and close ties to an Anglo heritage. It indicated a level of undeveloped Americanism at best; at worst, a sign of evil tendencies such as sensualism, irreligion, ethnic peasant traits, boorishness, and laziness.

Thus the linguistic analogy to the morally repressive Mrs. Doubleday was a pretentious, elitist literary discourse, while a simple direct style became equated with the simple, aesthetic desire and moral freedom of Carrie. The genderization of language usage in literary expression embodied a powerful meaning for both sides in the critical debate over Dreiser's validity as an acceptable writer. Champions of decency, morality, good family values, proper educational and religious training of the young and of society, saw in educated discourse a representation of a controlled female sexuality, a sexuality refined, contained, and properly serving the interests of society by remaining within marriage and serving the production of children. Supporters of artistic and individual freedom and hence a certain modernity, could praise the boldness and freshness of style such as Dreiser's as being representative of a new, modern attitude toward the body, with the liberated female as its symbol.

The mythic construct of the social meaning of *Sister Carrie* reappeared, full of vigor and embellishment, at the beginning of the thirties, an era which saw increasing emphasis on philosophy and politics in literary criticism. Dreiser had a decade or so of glory, in which he was hailed as "the culmination of an American progressive tradition with eighteenth-century roots."[28] He was seen as a folk-hero who wrote in plain language for the masses. *Sister Carrie* seemed victorious. This renewed effort to establish Dreiser as a serious writer in America began with a direct appeal to the Mrs. Doubleday myth and its threatening content by Dreiser himself.

In 1931 Dreiser repeated his version of the myth in a preface to a new edition of *Sister Carrie*, adding that Mrs. Frank Doubleday "was a social worker and active in moral reform." He further elaborated that because his original contract with Doubleday, Page did not include selling, only publishing, that this in fact is how Doubleday got his revenge, by no advertisement whatsoever of the book. Dreiser even suggested that all copies were thrown into a cellar, with the exception of about one hundred, which Frank Norris rescued and sent out to some reviewers. Dreiser continued his account of the difficulties in getting *Sister Carrie* properly exposed to the American public.[29]

One year later Dorothy Dudley, one of Dreiser's few female critics, attempted a biography of Dreiser called *Dreiser and the Land of the Free*, which has been characterized as a polemic against American puritanism. In her book, Dudley practices a little creative fiction herself, imagining what that original reading of *Sister Carrie* must have been like for Mrs. Doubleday, and

> again enters the villain, Propriety—this time . . . in the refined and engaging dress of Mrs. Frank Doubleday . . . it is possible to identify the enemy—according to her friends, as an almost perfect woman, wife, mother, church member, hostess, in this well-fed, well-bred apex of New York in 1900. . . . She was beautiful, she was a lovely woman, she was stately. . . . Wrap in such an aura, I imagine her now entering the study where Mr. Frank Doubleday was busy reading and possibly enjoying *Sister Carrie*.
>
> In those days the more valiant New York matrons were occupied among their good works with purity leagues for the suppression of vice, for the lapsed and lost, for the social evil. Indeed at about this time they were making a pleasant sanitary prison where wayward girls too tender in years for the jail might be agreeably locked up—the Florence Crittendon Home. And here was Doubleday, Page about to publish a book about vulgar people, a Chicago drummer and a factory girl from the country, which apparently recommended prostitution as a way of life in little tan jackets with large pearl buttons.
>
> It must have been [Mrs. Doubleday] was mortified as she went from lewd fact to fact lighted by her orthodox mind . . . why she did not feel that a precious record of the grim life on top of which she ate and slept and dressed and had her being, was in her hands, is hard to say.[30]

Dudley then attempts to analyze the original reactions to this event:

> There is an inclination, perhaps unconscious, among the men connected . . . with this publishing company to belittle the importance of Mrs. Doubleday in the suppression of a now historic book. . . . It is as if to protect her name from taint of prudery, now become unfashionable. . . . Mr. Lanier . . . volunteered that the publisher's wife was one of those deceptively beautiful characters who loved to dominate in the name of virtue.[31]

Dudley then states that she believes "the myth has legs to stand on—a symbol of the way Americans have always entrusted to women the matter of art along with the matter of society, as unworthy of [men's] important lives.[32] Dudley was attempting to clarify the social and political meanings of Mrs. Doubleday and portray her as a symbol of a still influential genteelism in American culture.

Transformations of the social behavior code that the discourse of genteelism represented appeared in overtly political discourses. The growth of the Communist Party in America after World War I and its cultivation of members from the body of sympathetic writers and intellectuals provided political fuel for critics who were unable to stem the tide of modernism in literature through traditional criticism.[33] Lionel Trilling was the most influential of these critics, who portrayed Dreiser as a naive thinker and an awkward writer because of his involvement in the Communist Party.

Trilling felt that liberal praise of Dreiser's realism for its hugely sympathetic portrayal of the victims of capitalism "ran the risk of endorsing Stalinism." To represent class difference in America, implies Trilling, is "to impose a politically dangerous . . . literary mode."[34] Trilling and others sided with their generation's disillusionment with oppositional politics, and the corresponding need to reinforce the broader intellectual consensus which held that America was a classless society without internal ideological conflicts.

Trilling accused Dreiser supporters of confusing literary crudeness with social and political virtues; he reminded readers of cultural historian Vernon L. Parrington's label of Dreiser as a noble peasant who was impatient with the "sterile literary gentility of the bourgeoisie." Trilling commented that it is as if "wit, and flexibility of mind, and perception, and knowledge were to be equated with aristocracy and political reaction, while dullness and stupidity must naturally suggest a virtuous democracy."[35] The further simplification of these two poles of argument to the symbolic representations of the matron Mrs. Doubleday and the wayward Carrie Meeber are just beneath the surface of Trilling's words. Married, virtuous women are elitist, educated, and Republicans; single, sexually active women are working-class, stupid, and always Democrats, or perhaps, socialists.

The close approximation to prostitution that Carrie represented allowed a discourse which could not only privilege lower class culture, but also could provide an opportunity to assault the economic underpinnings of a bourgeois society. This metaphoric use of prostitution as a symbol of commercialization had been developed earlier during the Jacksonian era by reform-minded women, who often expressed their ideas privately in letters and journals, as well as occasionally participating in public debates. "The friendless prostitute symbolized for [those] women their own powerlessness within the new urban economy."[36] The association of prostitution with the economic value of the female body imbued the Mrs. Doubleday story with economic and political overtones. In the myth gendered aspects of the female are used as symbols of an ideological struggle over the sexual meaning and function of a woman's body. But it is also a struggle of the middle class woman to appropriate and control the alleged sexual freedom of the lower class woman. This merging of sexual identities with class implies the importance of sex as an economy. But foregrounding issues of sexual freedom or repression of the female in the myth serve to mask economic, class, and power struggles. As Dreiser himself stated so succinctly in an essay called "Neurotic America and the Sex Impulse," "sexual repression creates a desire for material wealth and status. A search for material pleasures sublimates a desire for sexual freedom."[37]

The use of a young female to represent a search for the good life in a big city both confounds and clarifies the relationship between sex and class issues. Carrie's free association with men symbolized the underlying sexual nature of rapacious business activity. But Carrie Meeber, in her choice to live an unrepentant, sexually free single life, also became the representation of socialist and populist working class politics. Opponents often referred to any socialistic ideas as immoral, promiscuous or simple-minded—as though they were describing a working-class prostitute.[38] Arun Mukherjee, a modern Dreiserian scholar from India, represents a common perspective among non-American Dreiserian scholars on this issue. Dreiser's concern with economic power relations and the rapacious ideology of American business is viewed as central to these scholars, who seek to understand the historical origins of Anglo-American imperialistic policies and their profound impacts upon Third World societies.[39]

Trilling's influence succeeded in removing Dreiser from the literary canon for his crude style and lack of intellect. In his place Trilling inserted Henry James, a cultured, upper-class Easterner thirty years Dreiser's senior. James had always valued great literature as an indicator of the moral health of societies. According to James, the writer should maintain a disinterested view of life from an educated, critical distance. James, living at the end of an era in which his elitist values held cultural dominance, committed his life to the responsible use of the moral imagination. James's novels depicted the power of the individual to shape reality within the limits of personal moral dilemmas rather than in the field of social relations.

In the forties the growing critical movement called New Criticism reinforced Trilling's opinion because it attached supreme importance to educated, disciplined writing and sophisticated cultural themes. Separation of the literary text from historical context gave authority to the critic as the most accurate interpreter of literary works by development of a formal schematic structure. A scientific linguistic characterized the New Criticism, which privileged once again an educated, refined use of language; subtlety, sophistication and refinement became the norm, and other style of writing were either ignored or relegated to minor status in literary canons.

Dreiser's prose was seen as awkward and blunt, the antithesis of this new aesthetic view of fiction. Alfred Kazin has written of this period during the forties and fifties as a time when Dreiser's work was "a symbol of everything a superior intelligence was supposed to avoid." Again the image of the angry and educated Mrs. Doubleday condemning the working-class stupidity of *Sister Carrie* forms beneath the surface of the written words. Dreiser lost whatever status he had achieved, and was practically ignored as a serious American writer for over two decades.[40]

Those few scholars who defended Dreiser characterized the New Criticism as a sign of "a modern nervousness and irritability"; there is "a terrible hunger for conformity . . . high polish must not be marred."[41] The polished virtue of Mrs. Doubleday must be protected by an appeal to rigid categories of analysis; the New Critics appear to be sexually repressed obsessive-compulsives. These critics who insisted on relating *Sister Carrie* and other works by Dreiser to an historical context were seen by New Critics as socialistic, sloppy scholars doing unimportant work.

Joan Wallach Scott has attempted to clarify the "interesting questions" for historians as they seek to transform their discipline from a search for single origins to a concern with "processes so interconnected that they cannot be disentangled." "Of course," Scott is careful to say, "we identify problems to study, and these constitute beginnings or points of entry into complex processes. But it is the processes we must continually keep in mind. . . . We must pursue . . . meaningful explanation." To do this "we need to deal with the individual subject as well as social organization and to articulate the nature of their interrelationships."[42] Dreiser, his work, and his life are particularly well-suited to the development of "interesting questions" because, as Dorothy Dudley observed, "[Dreiser] is to this day a challenge to writers to sacrifice themselves as completely, and more intimately if they can, to our history . . . he has passages . . . of identity with the mood, moments of penetration, when he goes over from being the historian into being the poet. In him our disorderly order gleams with its mysteries . . . he has managed to get down to the floods underlying dirt and rock."[43]

A gendered analysis of the Doubleday mythic narrative discloses relationships in critical debates between ideological arguments and gendered assumptions about literature, language use, politics, economics, and art. Because Dreiser criticism through the twentieth century began with such a clearly gendered polarization of the meaning of Dreiser's first work, *Sister Carrie*, and because its dimensions of meaning were employed often by both supporters and detractors of Dreiser to elucidate complex arguments about the meaning and role of literature and artistic expression in the twentieth century, Dreiser criticism exists as a model for other intellectual debates of the twentieth century in related disciplines and over related topics. Since political and cultural debate can be shown to be gendered in Dreiser criticism, it follows that debates following the same lines of argument also have at least the potentiality to be gendered.

When Dreiser began *Sister Carrie* in 1899 at age twenty-eight, he recalled that "my mind was a blank except for the name. I had no idea who or what she was to be. I have often thought there was something mystic about it, as if I were being used, like a medium."[44] Sister Carrie, invoked by Dreiser's subconscious and fleshed out by his literary imagination, became a fictional entity that took on a life of her own, particularly when others resisted that life and Dreiser chose a real life woman as the symbol of her opposition.

NOTES

1. See Warren I. Susman, *Culture as History*, 20. A few discussions on the American History Standards include: San Diego State University Professor Ross E. Dunn, "Curriculum Critics Err"; University of California, Los Angeles Professor Joyce Appleby, *Telling the Truth about History*; Appleby was interviewed on 7 November 1994, on *Talk of the Nation* PBS radio, about her book. Appleby stressed the need to introduce students to complex interactions, the full psychosocial context of the past, the study of intellectual conflicts, including gendered analyses of intellectual "structures," as well as the understanding that historical study involves evaluation, analysis, and judgment. Dissenting opinions have been most widely put forth by Lynn Cheney, former chair of the National Endowment for the Humanities.

2. Ellen Mores, *Two Dreisers*, 173.

3. Ibid.

4. Ibid.

5. Alfred Kazin and Charles Shapiro, eds., *The Stature of Theodore Dreiser*, 7.

6. Alan Trachtenberg, *The Incorporation of America: Culture and Society in the Gilded Age*, 182.

7. Christopher P. Wilson, "*Sister Carrie* Again," 289.

8. Page was the perfect man for the job, by virtue of his lifelong inner conflict between graceful intellectual pursuit and aggressive business activity, a conflict which polarized feminine and masculine associations going back to Page's childhood. This theme of psychosexual conflict runs through John Milton Cooper's biography, *Walter Hines Page: The Southerner as American*.

9. Thomas Beer, *The Mauve Decade*, 18–32.

10. *Sister Carrie* (Philadelphia: University of Pennsylvania Press, 1981), 290.

11. Thomas P. Riggio, *Theodore Dreiser: The American Diaries, 1902–1926*, 27–31.

12. Joan Wallach Scott, *Gender and the Politics of History*, 32, 42.

13. Stephen Stepanchev, "Dreiser among the Critics," 8.

14. Stuart P. Sherman, "The Naturalism of Mr. Dreiser," 650; Dorothy Dudley, "The 'Suppression' Controversy," 171–81.

15. Susman, *Culture as History*, 18.

16. David Minter's discussion of the rising "businessman's culture" during the twenties and the direct literary response to it, particularly by Sinclair Lewis, is illuminating, providing a useful cultural backdrop to Dreiser and his critics during this huge shift from an old "work ethic" to a new "consumer" and "leisure ethic." Minter even compares Lewis's character of George Babbitt to Sister Carrie, noting Babbitt's extension of Carrie's less apparent passivity and vague yearnings. See David Minter, *A Cultural History of the American Novel: Henry James to William Faulkner*, 88–94.

17. Dreiser, ". . . the game as it is played . . . ," in Kazin and Shapiro, 60.

18. Dreiser, "True Art Speaks Plainly," 129.

19. Anon., Review of *Sister Carrie*, *Chicago Advance* (June 27, 1907), in *Theodore Dreiser: The Critical Reception*, ed. Jack Salzman, 42.

20. Anon., "Mr. Dreiser and His Critics," *New York Evening Sun* (June 18, 1907), in Kazin and Shapiro, 66–67.

21. Anon., Review of *Sister Carrie*, *New York Press* (July 3, 1907), in Kazin and Shapiro, 68.

22. Kazin, "Introduction," 7.

23. Sherman, 650.

24. Ibid.

25. Ibid.

26. Ibid.

27. Sherwood Anderson, "An Apology for Crudity," in Kazin and Shapiro, 81–83.

28. Vernon Louis Parrington, *The Beginnings of Critical Realism*, vol. 3 of *Main Currents in American Thought*, 238.

29. Dreiser, "Preface," in *Sister Carrie* (New York: Modern Library, 1932).

30. Dudley, 171–81.

31. Ibid.

32. Ibid.

33. It is tempting to note how much this early twentieth century debate resembles current attacks on the discourse of deconstruction. Lewis Lapham has remarked on conservatives' attempts to tie the "spores of Marxist ideology" to the "monster of deconstruction that devoured the arts of leaning." See Lewis Lapham, "Reactionary Chic: How the Nineties Right Recycles the Bombast of the Sixties Left," 32.

34. Amy Kaplan, *The Social Construction of American Realism*, 4.

35. Lionel Trilling, "Reality in America," in *Liberal Imagination*, 12.

36. Carroll Smith-Rosenberg, *Disorderly Conduct: Visions of Gender in Victorian America*, 46.

37. Dreiser, "Neurotic America and the Sex Impulse," in *Hey Rub-A-Dub-Dub*, chapter IX.

38. The symbol of the prostitute was also used in 1930s China during the struggle for power between Chiang Kai-shek and Mao Tse-tung. Mao's revolutionaries were ridiculed in one poster that announced solemnly: "The women's association suggests to have a naked body procession of the 1st of May, in promoting the principle of freedom. If anyone wishes to enter this naked body procession an examination of body is necessary. The choice will fall on the one who has a snow white body and a pair of swollen nipples." Quoted in Jonathan Spence, *To Change China: Western Advisers in China, 1620–1960*, 200.

39. See Arun Mukherjee, "*Sister Carrie* at Ninety: An Indian Response" and *The Gospel of Wealth in the American Novel: The Rhetoric of Dreiser and Some of His Contemporaries*. The sexual discourse for Mukherjee serves as a distorting screen to larger social structural issues. Because of the unquestioned assumptions which subsume symbolic use of gendered language, this discourse also hides the ways in which sexuality serves as an ideological tool in political debates. Sexuality represents through gendered discourse as well as limits through symbolic representation a concern with the expansive notions of individuality, freedom, and self-transformation. When these notions have been discussed through the use of female imagery, often the reaction is revulsion, disgust, or an attempt to neuter the images. Dreiser holds persistent interest for other Indian scholars as well. Among them are L. Jeganatha Raja, P. Marudanayagam, R. N. Mookerjee, and Brij Mohan Singh. Other non-American scholars include: Monica Wanambisi, "Eight Exemplars of the Twentieth-Century American Novel, 1900–1959," and Yoshitsugu Uchida, "A Conflict between Spirituality and Material Civilization in *Sister Carrie*."

40. Donald Pizer, "Introduction," in *Critical Essays on Dreiser*, ed. Pizer, xi.

41. Kazin, "Introduction" in *Stature of Dreiser*, ed. Kazin and Shapiro, 9.

42. Joan Wallach Scott, "Gender: A Useful Category of Analysis," 1067.

43. Dorothy Dudley, *Forgotten Frontiers: Dreiser and the Land of the Free*, 4.

44. Ibid., 160.

Alcohol and Drinking in *Sister Carrie*

JAMES L. W. WEST III

IS ALCOHOL A FACTOR IN *SISTER CARRIE*? IS IT IMPORTANT IN ANY OF Dreiser's writings? We don't think of alcohol as significant in his life; until his last years he drank very little. He was never able to match Mencken pilsner for pilsner, nor was he much interested in doing so. And there is the apocryphal story of F. Scott Fitzgerald's showing up one night at a Dreiser soirée with a bottle of champagne which he presented to his host, expecting the older writer to pop the cork and offer libations to those present. Instead Dreiser shoved the bottle in his icebox and saved it to drink later. This was a concept unknown to Fitzgerald.

Dreiser made no serious effort that I'm aware of in his fiction or nonfiction to explore the effects of alcohol on human behavior and personality. Perhaps he felt unqualified; probably the subject didn't interest him in the same way that it did Fitzgerald and Hemingway and Malcolm Lowry—and many other writers who have explored alcohol and alcoholism. Dreiser's characters are driven by forces and compulsions other than drink, most of them economic and social. Lester Kane, for example, dies in part from overindulgence in rich foods and wines, but there is no suggestion that he is an alcoholic. He expires more from weariness with life and bafflement over its meaning and arrangement than from any physical addiction. And no one important in the Trilogy of Desire, or in *An American Tragedy*, or in the other novels and stories, or in the nonfiction writings such as *Twelve Men*, is destroyed by drinking.

The same can be said, for the most part, of *Sister Carrie*. If ever a man had reason to turn to liquor for solace, Hurstwood would be that man, especially after he bottoms out in New York. Certainly liquor has been a part of his life; he manages two saloons in the course of the novel, and he must know that alcohol can be a soothing agent and that it can help one to forget the past. But there is no hint that Hurstwood is a drinker; he is destroyed by economic and social forces, not by bad personal habits. Likewise with Drouet, who seems to enjoy his tipple, but who is energized by the pursuit of women, not by the pursuit of the bottle.

There are, however, three appearances of alcohol in *Sister Carrie*—in the Pennsylvania text of the novel—that are important, and that I'd like to discuss in this essay. I want to argue that in Dreiser's original conception of *Sister Carrie* these three appearances constitute a pattern, a leitmotif, and that he uses these mentions of alcohol to measure the three major male characters in the novel. Two of these appearances are not present in the first edition, the 1900 Doubleday, Page & Co. text. The third is present in both texts. Dreiser removed one mention from the typescript of the novel, probably between the time he submitted it to Harpers in May 1900 and had it turned down, and the time a few weeks later when he sent it to Doubleday. The other appearance vanished between the setting-copy typescript and the first printing. In preparing the Pennsylvania text, I restored the two passages, reasoning that the cuts must have been made either to take out references to liquor, or simply to remove details so that the plot might move along more swiftly. I'd like now to reexamine my thinking in making those restorations and to speculate about how the novel is changed by the presence or absence of the passages.

All three mentions of alcohol occur within a space of about one hundred pages. The first occurs when Drouet, who has discovered that Carrie has been seeing Hurstwood in the afternoons, goes to their apartment, resolved to confront her with his new knowledge. "The drummer was flushed and excited, and full of great resolve to know all about her relations with Hurstwood," wrote Dreiser in his manuscript. Then comes this detail: "He had taken several drinks and was warm for his purpose" (223).[1]

Drouet proceeds to make a fool of himself. He tells Carrie that Hurstwood is a married man, something she has not known, and she, in a display of emotional illogic, becomes angry with him for not letting her know of Hurstwood's matrimonial status. Drouet has not meant to break off with Carrie; he has not really suspected her of serious wrongdoing. His vanity has been wounded, and he wants to reassert his control over her. But to his surprise she shows considerable spunk. "I won't talk about it," she says. "Whatever has happened is your own fault" (232). Drouet, after whining a little, packs some things in a valise and puts his hand on the doorknob. "You can go to the deuce as far as I am concerned," he tells her in his exit line. "I'm no sucker" (232).

This is an important scene; it sets in motion all else that will happen in the novel. Hurstwood, who has been observed riding in a buggy with Carrie, is facing problems of his own now—an angry, unforgiving wife who is dictating some quite severe financial terms for a divorce settlement. He will shortly steal ten thousand dollars from his employers, lure Carrie (now alone) onto the train to Montreal, and progress from there to New York with her. It is necessary, therefore, that Drouet behave foolishly in his confrontation with Carrie. Certainly those "several drinks" he had taken, in Dreiser's original conception of the scene, should have muddled his judgment. Was Dreiser trying to suggest that Drouet was not foolish enough on his own to botch this showdown with Carrie? Did he need assistance from alcohol?

It's impossible to know exactly what Dreiser thought. What we do know is that the sentence quoted above—"He had taken several drinks and was warm for his purpose."—is present in the typescript (264) but missing from the first printing (242). It must therefore have been cut in galleys or page proofs. But by whom?

Perhaps the cut was made by someone at Doubleday, Page. Perhaps it was made by Dreiser—either under pressure from the publisher, or at the suggestion of someone else, or of his own volition. We do know that Dreiser removed allusions to sex and instances of profanity from the typescript at the publisher's prompting. These passages were queried in blue pencil; Dreiser responded by making the excisions.[2] Might this process have extended into the galley and page-proof stages, where a reference to drinking was targeted? We also know that Dreiser was influenced to make cuts and changes in manuscript and typescript by Arthur Henry, his friend, and Sara White Dreiser, his wife. Some of these changes toned down sexual or otherwise "offensive" passages. Might one of these two persons have suggested that he cut the sentence about Drouet's drinking?

These are possible explanations, but let's assume for now that Dreiser made the cut himself, without pressure or prompting. Why might he have done so? Possibly he did not want Drouet to have alcohol as an excuse for his behavior. Drouet is good hearted but shallow. He is not long on intellect, nor is he the sort of man who would handle himself nimbly or cleverly in a face-off with an angry woman. Perhaps, then, Dreiser wanted to remove any excuse for Drouet. He might have wanted to take alcohol out of this equation and let Drouet make a fool of himself without the assistance of those "several drinks." That sounds plausible, but it's no more provable than the other two propositions.[3]

The next mention of alcohol in *Sister Carrie* is the one that remains unchanged from manuscript to typescript to published book. This is the pivotal scene in which Hurstwood, depressed over his problems with his wife, begins drinking with some patrons at Hannah and Hoggs—several actors, a theatrical manager, and a wealthy rounder of Chicago. In Dreiser's phrase, Hurstwood joins in the drinking "right heartily" and matches his companions "glass for glass." Dreiser notes, "It was not long before the imbibing began to tell" (266). Lubricated by liquor, the men begin telling droll stories of sexual conquests, Hurstwood contributing a few of his own, and they continue drinking.

When closing time comes, at midnight, Hurstwood is "in a very roseate state." His mind, Dreiser tells us, is "warm in its fancies" (266). He retires to his office, counts up the receipts, and discovers the ten thousand dollars in the safe. In these sections, Dreiser reminds us twice more that Hurstwood is still under the influence of drink. "Wine was in his veins," Dreiser says (268). And then, about a page further on, "The imbibation of the evening had not yet worn off. . . . [He] was still flushed with the fumes of liquor" (269). When Hurstwood takes the money, therefore, his reason is beclouded. He loses his head, puts the cash into his satchel, watches the door to the safe close and click shut, then panics and runs.

Dreiser removed none of these references to alcohol between manuscript and typescript or between typescript and print. Here he must have felt that Hurstwood, normally a man of probity (if not actual honesty), would have needed a prod from alcohol to commit an act of thievery. In this way Dreiser was giving Hurstwood, at least in part, an explanation for his bad judgment. Whatever Dreiser's apprehensions (if he had any) about including references to alcohol in his text, he must have felt that these needed to stay. It is also true, however, that these references would have been difficult to remove. There were several of them, scattered throughout a lengthy scene. They were integral to the language and motivation of the section; Dreiser would have had to rewrite from scratch in order to remove the mentions of alcohol.

The third reference to alcohol also comes in an important scene—the one in which Carrie goes to dinner at Sherry's restaurant with Mr. and Mrs. Vance and Robert Ames. This is Carrie's introduction to Ames, and ours as well. Ames will play an important part in what is to come in the novel. He will function as a tutor of sorts for Carrie; he will stand as an example that she will attempt several times to follow. The portly, prosperous Mr. Vance spreads himself in the elegant restaurant, ordering "freely of soup, oysters, roast meats and side dishes." Vance, Dreiser tells us, also has "several bottles of wine brought, which were set down beside the table in a wicker basket." Then follows this exchange:

> Young Ames volunteered the information that they knew he did not drink.
> "I don't care for wine either," said Carrie.
> "You poor things," said Mrs. Vance. "You don't know what you're missing. You ought to drink a little, anyhow."
> "No," said Carrie, "I don't believe I will." (333)

It has been made clear to us that Ames does not use alcohol; this is almost the first thing we learn about him. Carrie, watching him refuse the wine, decides on the spot to follow his lead, the first of several times she will do so in the narrative. The small exchange begs for interpretation, not least because Ames is generally thought to be Dreiser's representative in *Sister Carrie*. The exterior details of his career are probably taken from the career of the inventor Thomas Edison, but the ideas and the personality seem to be Dreiser's—as Dreiser wanted to see himself. Ames, like Dreiser, is not interested in drink. We know, then, that he will speak with a voice unbefuddled by alcohol. He will operate with reason and will speak with clarity.

About one hundred pages earlier we have seen Drouet—in the Pennsylvania text—make a fool of himself under the influence of whiskey. And about fifty pages after that, Hurstwood has made an even bigger mess of his affairs after drinking too much. Ames, it is obvious, has been placed in the novel to stand in contrast to Drouet and Hurstwood. He is more intelligent and independent than they, mush less dazzled by wealth and material display, infinitely better read and better informed, and more intuitive and sympathetic toward Carrie. In the Pennsylvania text, he has announced that he does not drink alcohol—a trait Carrie seems to like and which she mimics. Is his abstinence another instance of his superiority to Drouet and Hurstwood?

The exchange over wine at Sherry's, however, was cut from the typescript (389) by Dreiser and does not appear in the Doubleday text (355). And here we have evidence that someone, most likely Arthur Henry, suggested the cut to Dreiser, who then made it. We know from Dreiser's later testimony that Henry went through the typescript of *Sister Carrie* and marked passages that he thought could be pruned. We have evidence of Henry's work in the left-hand margins of the typescript sheets. He drew lines bracketing the passages that he recommended for excision. Dreiser came behind and made the cuts, sometimes (but not always) erasing Henry's lines. On this particular typescript sheet, Henry's marks were erased but are still easily visible around the passage in which Ames and Carrie turn down the wine. It's almost certain, then, that Henry suggested the cut.

What does this mean? One's best guess is that Arthur Henry failed to recognize the point Dreiser was making about alcohol (if indeed he was making such a point) and saw the small exchange about wine as a bit of detail that could be dispensed with. From his other work on the typescript, it appears that one of Henry's chief goals was to streamline the narrative. Dreiser went ahead and made the cut; we can only speculate about *his* motives. Perhaps he had decided that the point about alcohol was not important. Or perhaps he had forgotten the contrast that I believe he was making between Drouet and Hurstwood on the one hand and Ames on the other. Perhaps he was too trusting of Henry's judgment. (It is true that he cut virtually every passage that Henry marked for removal.) Or perhaps he had no point at all to make about the drinking habits of these three men. It is impossible finally to know.

It should be obvious what I have been doing here. I have been constructing small biographical narratives and literary interpretations that will explain the presence of alcohol in three places in *Sister Carrie* and that, more importantly, will give reasons for Dreiser's having removed two of those references. I have in fact wanted to find reasons that will justify my having restored those references to the text of the Pennsylvania edition. Perhaps I should say that *we* have been constructing such narratives, for I would guess that readers of this essay have been doing the same thing as they have followed these speculations, perhaps inventing some alternate motivations for Dreiser or constructing some other interpretations of his text. This is fun: it's what textual editors do all the time. At base it is an exercise in biography. It certainly is not a cold, logical, dispassionate consideration of dry textual evidence—not a turn-the-crank exercise in editorial method. It's a mixture of biography, textual scholarship, and literary interpretation.[4]

I won't spin out the implications of these passages any further, but I would encourage readers to do so. It seems to me, in looking back now almost twenty years to the late 1970s, when I was first trying to make decisions about what to restore to Dreiser's text and what not to restore, that my evidence for restoring the reference to Drouet's "several drinks" was thin and speculative. That doesn't mean that the decision was wrong: only that I took a leap of faith in putting the sentence back into the text. I did so because I conceived of Doubleday, Page as keen to remove as much disreputable behavior as they could from his novel, and of Dreiser as willing to go along a certain distance in order to mollify the firm. The year, after all, was 1900, and representatives of the genteel tradition were still very much in the saddle in the literary world, as editors and critics. What is more, temperance was a large issue in American public discourse of the time. Many temperance advocates watched popular literature closely and attacked authors, and their publishers, if narratives were favorable or even neutral on the subject of alcohol. Dreiser, with his experience in the magazine world, would have known this. Perhaps, in such an atmosphere, Drouet's "several drinks" could be cut from the proofs.

I also restored the reference to Drouet's drinking because I liked the three-part statement about alcohol. Drouet drinks and behaves foolishly; Hurstwood drinks and behaves irrationally; Ames does not drink and behaves well (if a bit stiffly). I thought I discerned a pattern, a statement that Dreiser wanted to make, but I could have been wrong.[5]

I was on firmer ground, I believe, in restoring the lines in which Ames turns down the wine at Sherry's and Carrie follows suit. This is just the sort of small touch that Dreiser was good at. It is also the kind of detail that Henry asked Dreiser to cut at many other points in the typescript. I'm convinced that the restoration of such material to the Pennsylvania *Sister Carrie* makes it a richer, more suggestive and allusive novel than the Doubleday text. And here I have not only my interpretation to rely on but also Henry's marks in the margins, bracketing the passage for removal.

The larger matter that needs to be emphasized is that textual editing of this kind is far from a mechanical process. That's what makes it such an intriguing business. It requires us to think of *Sister Carrie* as an unstable, unsettled text, capable of yielding many variations in interpretation, especially when one knows the origins and textual history of important passages. A game of "What if?" is instructive here. What if the reference to Drouet's drinking were absent but the reference to Ames's abstinence were present? A textual editor could justify such a course. One's opinion of Drouet might change: he might seem even more of a fool (because he is sober and still behaves in a silly way), and Ames might seem simply to be a stuffed shirt who cannot relax and enjoy himself with a little wine at dinner. Or what if, as in the Doubleday text, only Hurstwood drinks and no mention is made either of Drouet's "several drinks" or of Ames's preferences? In that case the novel might be thought to contain a veiled moral lesson: if one imbibes when one must make important decisions, one risks ruin and destruction. Or what if, as in the Pennsylvania text, alcohol is present in all three places? Here my own take is that Dreiser is asking us to judge these three men, all of whom are important in Carrie's life, in part by the ways in which they handle strong drink. Ames wins the contest.

From an editor's point of view, these are really questions of biography. One is speculating about Dreiser's motives and intentions, and about Arthur Henry's and Doubleday, Page's as well. One is constructing roles for people to play (Dreiser as realistic and blunt, though willing to compromise in order to get his novel into print; Henry as facile and shallow, interested primarily in making Dreiser's narrative move along more quickly; Doubleday, Page as keen to remove anything from the text that might cause trouble with reviewers and public moralists). The evidence upon which one is speculating is no weaker or stronger than that used by most biographers—a famously imaginative group of writers. Textual editors, we should therefore realize, are a rather imaginative crew themselves, though they often cloak their speculations and imaginative flights in technical sounding terminology, and they cover themselves with textual tables that are hard to decipher and interpret.

One can raise questions about alcohol in *Sister Carrie* (or about similar conundrums in the text) not only in published essays such as this one, but in classrooms as well, both graduate and undergraduate. In this case, the students might be encouraged to think of *Sister Carrie* as a gambling machine. Pull the lever and only one reference to alcohol appears—but which one? Pull it again, and two references appear—but which two? Pull it once more and all three appear. How does one's interpretation change after each pull? This would not simply be a literary parlor game. An editor could justify any combination in which the references to Hurstwood's drinking remained in the text—and it might be instructive to speculate about the effect on the novel if those references were cut as well.

I hope that teachers of *Sister Carrie* will engage in this kind of exercise, and that they will use the textual apparatus in the Pennsylvania text to ferret out other points at which a restoration changes one's interpretation of the novel, in a small or a large way. That's what textual editors are supposed to do: stir up the silt at the bottom of the pool. Editors shouldn't claim that the text they present is calm, shimmering, and serenely perfect. They should instead muddy things up and stimulate discussion, as I've tried to do here.

Notes

1. References to *Sister Carrie* are to the text of the Pennsylvania edition: Historical Editors, John C. Berkey and Alice M. Winters; Textual Editor, James L. W. West III; General Editor, Neda M. Westlake (Philadelphia: University of Pennsylvania Press, 1981).

2. See the Pennsylvania *Sister Carrie* 1981: 525, and West's *A "Sister Carrie" Portfolio*, 64–65.

3. An interesting side note here is that in a quite similar scene in *Jennie Gerhardt* (1911), a reference to drinking by Lester Kane was removed. See *Jennie Gerhardt* (New York: Harper and Brothers, 1911), as well as *Jennie Gerhardt*, ed. James L. W. West III. In fact, between manuscript and print, nearly all mentions of alcohol were cut from the text of the novel. In the passage in question, Lester has learned from a distraught Jennie that she has a child—little Vesta, whose existence she has been concealing from him. Vesta's caretaker, however, has come to the apartment that Jennie and Lester are sharing in Chicago and has told Jennie that Vesta is dangerously ill. Jennie rushes away to minister to the child, but not before Lester has extracted from her the information that she has a daughter. While Jennie is away, Lester meditates (rather uncharitably) on Jennie's past history. Almost his first action is to leave the apartment and stop "at the first convenient saloon" for alcohol (*JG* 1992: 208). Thus when he confronts Jennie later, after she returns, he has some of that alcohol in his bloodstream. His demeanor toward her is angry at first, but he is quickly disarmed by the simplicity and honesty of her explanations. The reference to Lester's drinking, however, was cut between manuscript and print. Since the

typescript on which the editors at Harper and Brothers worked does not survive, one cannot know certainly whether they or Dreiser removed the reference, but other mentions of drinking, by Old Gerhardt, for example (*JG* 1992: 271), were also removed before the Harpers text was published. I decided that the Harpers editors probably made the cut, and I restored Lester's visit to the saloon to the Pennsylvania *Jennie Gerhardt*.

4. For an elaboration of this idea see West, "The Scholarly Editor as Biographer."

5. See West, "Fair Copy, Authorial Intention, and 'Versioning.' "

"But a Single Point in a Long Tragedy": *Sister Carrie*'s Equivocal Style

KIYOHIKO MURAYAMA

TODAY MUCH OF THE WRITING ABOUT DREISER SUGGESTS THAT HIS greatness is simply taken for granted. "Certainly," Jack Salzman wrote in 1977, "we need no longer argue about Dreiser's position in the history of American letters; that disagreement has become a part of our past" (339). It is good that there should no longer be any doubt about his stature, but I find something disturbing in the more recent interpretations of his novels by some younger scholars. While correctly appreciating his insights into American society, they often subvert his criticisms of it.

Many critics and scholars have discussed how Dreiser is related with capitalism. Some have exposed his fascination with the materialistic dream of success as a symptom of the vulgar attachment for capitalist values. Others have praised his latent critiques of capitalism. In recent studies, Dreiser has emerged again as the most powerful writer in American literature that grasped the dynamics of American society in its capitalistic phase. Particularly Walter Benn Michaels among others maintains that *Sister Carrie* is powerful because Carrie is depicted as an embodiment of the logic of the marketplace at the turn of the century. His reading may be valuable as a corrective to the conventional humanist interpretations toward which he directs his irritation. Nevertheless, this reading is questionable in that Michaels refuses to see Dreiser's criticism of capitalism.

In *The Gold Standard and the Logic of Naturalism*, he asserts "that Carrie's economy of desire involves an unequivocal endorsement of . . . the unrestrained capitalism of the late nineteenth and early twentieth centuries." To him "[the] power of *Sister Carrie* . . . derives not from its scathing 'picture' of capitalist 'conditions' but from its unabashed and extraordinarily literal acceptance of the economy that produced those conditions" (35). Michaels dismisses as worthless any stance for or attempt at criticizing the shortcomings in capitalist society. "From this standpoint," he writes, "even Dreiser's personal hostility to capitalism comes to seem like only the first of what would be many failed attempts to make his work morally respectable" (58).

It is, however, at the least, difficult to understand that "an unequivocal endorsement of . . . the unrestrained capitalism" should be compatible with "Dreiser's personal hostility to capitalism." Rather, we can assume that Michaels grudgingly admits that there is some kind of detachment from capitalism in *Sister Carrie*, even if he dismisses it as mere "personal hostility." Such a dismissal enables him to neglect the very structure of the novel in which Carrie's discontent as well as Hurstwood's failure toward the end suggests the novel's problematics.

Rachel Bowlby, in *Just Looking*, makes her point by criticizing Michaels's one-sided picture: "the novel does not present a world in which capitalism in its hypothetical utopian form has been achieved. Behind the attractive images of consumption, it clearly shows up some of the peculiar disparities created by that institution in the form it took in the 1890s" (61). All the same, she also collapses this distinction by asserting, "The Hurstwoods of the bread line and Brooklyn strikebreaking, struggling feebly and falling, . . . act only as the backdrop" (64). As a result, she, not unlike Michaels, talks more about the indefatigable power of consumer culture than Dreiser's critique of it, and shows little interest in reflecting upon "the peculiar disparities" depicted in the novel.

For all their likemindedness, Michaels discloses uneasiness about Bowlby's comment. In the introduction to his book, he gives an explanation for including therein the article that has invited Bowlby's chiding. "Bowlby is surely right about this," he writes, "but my own unease had nothing to do with a sense that I had overstated my claim—what bothered me was the 'endorsement' itself, not whether it was 'unequivocal' " (18). In spite of this acknowledgment, Michaels keeps the phrase "an unequivocal endorsement" intact in the book, while he has dropped the passage quoted by Bowlby, "*Sister Carrie* is not anti-capitalist at all," which was found in the article he had published in *Critical Inquiry* several years earlier. Does this not make him uneasy?

Perhaps trying to justify himself, Michaels contends that "transcending your origins in order to evaluate them" is wrong, "not so much because you can't really transcend your culture but because, if you could, you wouldn't have any terms of evaluation left—except, perhaps, theological ones" (18). However, "transcending your origins in order to evaluate them" is not the only possible way for cultural criticism. You can have other "terms of evaluation" than "theological ones." Otherwise, it would be very difficult for many today to be engaged in cultural criticism, since they are usually not concerned about theology.

Michaels is unquestionably right when he argues, "It thus seems wrong to think of the culture you live in as the object of your affections: you don't like it or dislike it, you exist in it, and the things you like and dislike exist in it too" (18). All the same, it does not follow that you must like it.

Michaels talks about capitalist society as if it is a monolithic world with no residual or emergent antagonism in it. In other words, he denies the feasibility of not only Dreiser's but also of any other critique of capitalism. In any culture, some kind of conflict or division exists. It comes about as a contradiction in representation by those writers who have deeply grasped the culture. Michaels, however, is not ready to explore such a conflict. On the contrary, he cannot mention such a problem without making it seem meaningless. This is not unlike the method with which he argues in *Against Theory* that intention and meaning as well as knowledge and belief are one and the same thing. In a similar vein, he dismisses what may be in conflict with "an unequivocal endorsement of . . . the unrestrained capitalism" as products of "Dreiser's personal hostility to capitalism." His dismissal is all too easy, as facile as Bowlby's shrugging off pictures of poverty in *Sister Carrie*, "only as the backdrop."

Michaels's case may in effect come to the political message that capitalism is a total system from which no one can escape so one can only accept it to find happiness in it. This message is almost the same as Ames's view which Michaels interprets as an embodiment of the Howellsian economy of scarcity, for according to Michaels, Ames is preaching to Carrie, "you are happy if you are satisfied with what you have" (34). To Michaels, Ames is unperceptive to the truth of "the equation of power with desire" (34), holding up a false ideal.

However, when bantering "the newly politicized proponents of 'oppositional' criticism," Michaels says "[T]ransforming the moral handwringing of the fifties and sixties first into the epistemological handwringing of the seventies and now into the political handwringing of the eighties does not seem to be much of an advance" (14). While scoffing at Ames, Michaels coincides with Ames in despising "handwringing," for Ames also says, "It doesn't do us any good to wring our hands over the far-off things" (355).[1] As Michaels contends, their difference lies in what they regard as futile to seek. According to Michaels, the desire for "the far-off things" in the realm of consumption is a source of power, but to long for "the far-off things" in the political arena is a sign of impotence.

The "far-off things" in the political arena are in other words the objects of "the Utopian impulse." If so, Michaels's reading of *Sister Carrie* may well attract the attention of Fredric Jameson, who tried in *The Po-*

litical Unconscious to bring out "the Utopian impulse" (157) as the political unconscious latent in the text of important literary works.

Jameson called Dreiser "our greatest novelist" (161), and characterized the realism of Dreiser as well as Scott and Balzac "by a fundamental and exhilarating heterogeneity in their raw materials and by a corresponding versatility in their narrative apparatus" (104). "Heterogeneity" is Jameson's term for Dreiser's contradictions. If it be true, as Michaels claims, that *Sister Carrie* means "an unequivocal endorsement of . . . the unrestrained capitalism," there would be no room for "the Utopian impulse" that Jameson found in it. Then, Jameson owed it to himself to plead his own case against Michaels, whose argument may scandalize almost all of the preceding Dreiser criticisms.

In *Postmodernism*, Jameson discloses his view of Michaels's theoretical premises. Against Michaels's stipulation about the impossibility of transcending one's own culture, Jameson resorts to the basics of Marxism: "The force of Marxism as such" lies in "a demonstration of the ways in which socialism was already coming into being within capitalism" (205–6). Upon such a premise rests his criticism of Michaels: "This model of the presence of the future within the present is then clearly quite different from the attempt to 'step outside' actually existing reality into some other space" (206).

In philosophical terms, Jameson characterizes Michaels's posture as immanence which has long been set against transcendence. Abhorrence of transcendence makes Michaels an unacknowledged heir to the old New Criticism, in which what was called extrinsic criticism was denounced as a method of transcendence. And Jameson himself too, in his peculiar way, sometimes betrays a predilection for immanence, by confirming "the priority of literary and cultural analysis over philosophical and ideological investigation" (209). All the same, what he points out remains worthy of attention. The "model of the presence of the future within the present" is a dialectic solution of the contradiction between transcendence and immanence, which will allow us to have terms of evaluation other than theological ones without transcending our own cultures.

As Michaels says, Dreiser had a "personal hostility to capitalism" while he was attached to its power. Certainly, this is a contradiction, but grappling with this kind of contradiction was central in his struggle as a writer. Nobody would deny that capitalism is powerful. In *Sister Carrie* Dreiser depicts how powerful it is, but he also depicts how debilitating it is, alienating people living in it. Representing capitalism as the seducing city, he, at the same time, admires and condemns its power. It is this lack of consistency, rather than the unilateral logic of marketplace Michaels finds embodied in Carrie, that makes the novel powerful.

His contradictions have been pointed out often enough to have become familiar in the study of Dreiser, but have seldom been explored in their total significance. If his contradictory attitude to capitalism is a problem, it is rather his criticism of capitalism, to which one should now give more attention without flattening his ambivalence. The other side, namely his fascination with the power and wealth of capitalist America, has been recognized, whether it may be condemned as a symptom of his vulgarity, or admired as a bold insight into the power of capitalism. It is that very quality which both Michaels and Bowlby admire, but, by doing so, they fail to grasp Dreiser's complexity.

Difficulty may lie in Dreiser's problematic style. The position of the narrative voice is hard to locate, because at first the narrator more often sounds like a cold-hearted moralizer who looks down on Carrie as a girl "full of the illusions of ignorance and youth" (1), while he becomes more sympathetic as the book closes, so sympathetic as to call to her at the end, "Oh, Carrie, Carrie!" (369), but throughout the novel he never settles to either side, wavering all the time between the two poles.

Describing the fine figure of Hurstwood in the lobby of Avery Hall before the curtain rises on "Under the Gaslight," for instance, the narrator says, "It was greatness in a way, small as it was" (131). It is hard to determine whether Hurstwood is admired or despised. What is happening here is a clash of opposing views within one sentence. This kind of incongruity appears in many places in the novel. Not only is the narrator divided and quarreling within himself, but also he quite often addresses himself to characters as well as to undesignated opponents. On occasion, characters are even engaged in debating with the narrative voice or some unknown sage. As a result, where the author or, for that matter, the novel as a whole stands becomes unclear.

Another example is the discursive passage about the resort of which Hurstwood is the manager. "To one not inclined to drink," says the narrator, "and gifted with a more serious turn of mind, such a bubbling, chattering, glittering chamber must ever seem an anomaly, a strange commentary on nature and life" (35). This may be taken as a denunciatory judgment on the frivolity of the saloon business, but it turns out that the narrator is rather speaking in defense of it, for he continues, "Nevertheless, the fact that here men gather, here chatter, here love to pass and rub elbows, must be explained upon some grounds" (35). This passage is actually a rebutter against "one not inclined to drink." But who is this "one"? Who is it that is refuting him?

When Hurstwood is confronted with the detective who has pursued him to Montreal after the embezzled money, the following passage appears.

> He began to see the nature of that social injustice which sees but one side—often but a single point in a long tragedy. All the newspapers noted but one thing, his taking the money. How and wherefore were but indifferently dealt with. All the complications which led up to it were unknown. He was accused without being understood. (210)

The reductive ways of storytelling that permeate in journalism and the legal system must be rejected. Dreiser's equivocal style is the product of a will to refuse to have his story reduced to "but a single point in a long tragedy." This passage also entails equivocality in that who is addressing whom is ambiguous. The latter part of the passage can be regarded as a free indirect speech: it may be Hurstwood's thoughts. He is trying to protest against the world. But is he? Isn't it the narrator who is trying to vindicate Hurstwood? This kind of ambiguity often turns up throughout the novel.

When Carrie begins to waver between Drouet who is now providing for her and Hurstwood who has avowed himself to be in love with her, her situation is depicted in these terms.

> Now, she was comfortably situated, and to one who is more or less afraid of the world, this is an urgent matter, and one which puts up strange, uncanny arguments. "You do not know what will come. There are miserable things outside. People go a-begging. Women are wretched. You never can tell what will happen. Remember the time you were hungry. Stick to what you have." (160–61)

Carrie is debating in her mind with some unnamed opponent who raises the "uncanny arguments." What terms she is actually employing for the debate, however, cannot be easily determined, partly because the sentence at a halfway point switches to the present tense so that the situation is highly generalized. (Such generalizations expressed in the present tense are constantly occurring in the novel.) It remains unknown who her opponent is and how she refutes the "uncanny arguments."

This novel is full of such speech acts as refuting, deriding, chiding, preaching, protesting, or appealing, even if sometimes the addressee is hidden. The novel comes to present a series of enactments of the debates between the embattled social discourses of various positions. Sometimes, the narrative voice represents authoritative judgments as conservative moralists are likely to deliver upon the erring, which is then followed by a refuting comment which the same narrative voice offers as a direct intervention. More peculiarly, however, a protest against such a judgment is often represented by the free indirect speeches of one character or another.

Such characters as Carrie, Drouet, and Hurstwood are so inarticulate that they cannot formulate their own thoughts clearly. In a strict sense, therefore, their thoughts cannot be conveyed through free indirect speeches: what they feel must be put into shape by someone else. Through what appears to be a free indirect speech, the narrative voice has to speak for them. This limitation of theirs is explicitly pointed out a few times in the novel. About Carrie's perception of the difference between Drouet and Hurstwood, for example, the narrator says, "She could not have framed thoughts which would have expressed his defect or made clear the difference between them, but she felt it" (78). In addition, such a remark as "How true it is that words are but the vague shadows of the volumes we mean" (6), or "People in general attach too much importance to words" (88), repeatedly appears in the novel. Inadequate is not the characters' capability of using language, but the capability of language itself. In spite of these limitations, what Dreiserian characters would like to say if they could is represented through a device which may be called a free indirect speech.

Thus, *Sister Carrie* comes to take on a stylistic quality similar to "the polyphonic novel" which Mikhail Bakhtin finds in Dostoevsky's work, with rich resonance of "the hidden polemic" and "hidden dialogicality" (195–99). Making use of "the hidden polemic" and free indirect speeches, Dreiser presents quarrels between the main characters and the narrator, the world or the dominant culture. In *Problems of Dostoevsky's Poetics*, Bakhtin explains the polyphonic novel as follows:

> Not only does the novel give no firm support outside the rupture-prone world of dialogue for a third, monologically all-encompassing consciousness—but on the contrary, everything in the novel is structured to make dialogic opposition inescapable. Not a single element of the work is structured from the point of view of a nonparticipating "third person." In the novel itself, nonparticipating "third persons" are not represented in any way. There is no place for them, compositionally or in the larger meaning of the work. And this is not a weakness of the author but his greatest strength. By this means a new authorial position is won and conquered, one located above the monologic position. (18)

Sister Carrie is a novel in which the author and the characters, if not overtly, contradict themselves and each other all the time. At the end of the novel, for instance, "[a]mid the tinsel and shine" of her success, Carrie is said to be "unhappy" (368). "Sitting alone, she was now an illustration of the devious ways by which one who feels, rather than reasons, may be led in the pursuit of beauty" (369). The blame should be put on no one in the novel, but on what led Carrie by "the devious ways'' to the unhappiness at the end. At the start of the novel, however, Carrie is to blame because she is ''full of the illusions of ignorance and youth,'' so the narrator contradicts himself at the end. But what is it that ''led'' her? It is ''[t]he city [which] has its cunning wiles, no less than the infinitely smaller and more human tempter'' (1). ''[T]he devious ways'' are part and parcel of the power of capitalism, which the city embodies. Capitalism must be criticized in *Sister Carrie*, because the novel's basic task is a vindication of ''the feeling mind unused to reason'' that has been ''[allured]'' (368).

Now why must ''one who feels'' be contrasted with one who ''reasons''? This distinction has strategic significance for the vindication of Carrie and her ilk. One can find this distinction made in many places in the novel. When Hurstwood begins to go down in the world, his sense of social alienation is discussed in these terms.

> If one thinks that such thoughts do not come to so common a type of mind—that such feelings require a higher mental development—I would urge for their consideration the fact that it is the higher mental development that does away with such thoughts. It is the higher mental development which induces philosophy and that fortitude which refuses to dwell upon such things—refuses to be made to suffer by their consideration. The common type of mind is exceedingly keen on all matters which relate to its physical welfare—exceedingly keen. It is the unintellectual miser who sweats blood at the loss of a hundred dollars. It is the Epictetus who smiles when the last vestige of physical welfare is removed. (241)

Apparently this passage seems to convey intellectuals' disdain for such a ''common type of mind'' as Hurstwood's, but actually it attempts to refute the charge by ''one who reasons'' that ''such thoughts do not come to so common a type of mind.'' The high-minded are likely, it is implied, to think that the lowly tend to be, far from suffering, content with the given conditions. Against the highbrows' misunderstanding, the author is trying to vindicate such unintellectual people as Hurstwood and Carrie on the basis of the fact that they are ''keen.'' Moments like this of secret quarreling with superior people often crop up in the novel.

Practically, these passages enact the ongoing debate between the prosecutor and the advocate of unintellectual people. The lack of reasoning power, or the lack of education, in the main characters is a sign of their humble origins, which makes them vulnerable to the power of capitalism. If the victims of the power of capitalism are redeemed by virtue of the apologies for them offered by one segment of the debating narrative voice, however, it does not follow that the novel as a whole makes ''an unequivocal endorsement'' of the power of capitalism. Even if a judgmental comment on the baseness and vulgarity of the characters and their world is refuted, the comment still retains its justice: both they and their world remain vulgar. In other words, the contradictions between the prosecutor and the advocate within the novel are never resolved. In the narrative parts of the novel, the author plays both roles. One can in vain try to find a synthesis. Such is the nature of the contradictions in the novel that they bring forth Bakhtinian dialogues rather than Hegelian dialectics.

Almost every action or emotion of the main characters in the novel is depicted with implicit comments from this or that standpoint which is contradictory to the ones in other passages. This inconsistency suggests that lack of "a unified spirit" to which Bakhtin attributes the uniqueness of Dostoevsky's novels, for, as Bakhtin expounds, "[e]ach novel presents as opposition, which is never canceled out dialectically, of many consciousnesses, and they do not merge in the unity of an evolving spirit" (26).

Examples of contradiction might be multiplied indefinitely. When desire seizes Carrie, now living with Drouet, and awakened to "fortune's ways," Dreiser says. "Be it known that this is not fine feeling, it is not wisdom" (75). Again, this seems an admonishment educated people would deliver against materialistic desires. However, it is followed by this passage.

> The greatest minds are not so afflicted; and, on the contrary, the lowest order of mind is not so disturbed. Fine clothes to her were a vast persuasion; they spoke tenderly and Jesuitically for themselves. When she came within earshot of their pleading, desire in her bent a willing ear. The voice of the so-called inanimate! Who shall translate for us the language of the stones? (75)

This is a virtual negation of the preceding lesson, for Carrie is vindicated on the account of her keenness. Her capability of being afflicted by desire indicates at the same time her vulnerability and her innocence. She can plead not guilty, the author seems to imply, because "[t]he voice of the so-called inanimate" is too persuasive for her to resist.

As for desire, then, it is affirmed in *Sister Carrie*, not because Dreiser wants to extol it as a source of the power of capitalism, but because it helps to make clear what is to blame, whereas Michaels contends that "the 'disruptive' element in desire . . . is for Dreiser not subversive of the capitalist economy but constitutive of its power" (48). If we can talk about desire in such general terms as does Michaels, we might say that desire is both constitutive and subversive of the power of capitalism. Indeed, desire for the underprivileged like Carrie is a sign of the capability of "the feeling mind unused to reason," that is, the one who, being an easy victim of capitalism, nevertheless cannot help searching for a better life. "The unintellectual are not so helpless" (49), says the narrator at one place. As long as desire sustains them, there is a possibility that they can survive the many plights they undergo. In that sense, desire is rather a source of the power that may save them.

For instance, when kidnaped by Hurstwood to Montreal, Carrie does not seem to be perturbed for long.

> She did not feel herself defeated at all. Neither was she blasted in hope. The great city held much. Possibly she would come out of bondage into freedom—who knows? Perhaps she would be happy. These thoughts raised her above the level of erring. She was saved in that she was hopeful. (204)

Carrie can get through the difficulty because she retains hopes, urged by desire. In this passage, Carrie's free indirect speech gives way without any warning to the vindictive comments by the narrative voice in the last two sentences. In such a moment as this, the narrator does not hesitate to indulge in an aberration in which he discloses uncanny favoritism for a character. He becomes an interested pleader rather than a detached narrator. He cannot submit tamely to the dominant culture's expectation that Carrie would axiomatically be reduced to a mere victim. Desire is brought up to enhance the poignancy of alienation that is caused when desire is thwarted. It is not only unavoidable as fate is, but it also serves to instigate the oppressed to change their lives.

If it is unavoidable for people of ordinary minds to have desire, who can blame them? This is the logic the advocate for the victims uses for their vindication. "Not evil," says the narrator in a closing remark, "but longing for that which is better, more often directs the steps of the erring" (368). The novel is in a sense a courtroom drama in which various participants contend with each other over what is to blame. One side of the divided narrative voice, prosecuting the erring, appropriates the discourses which were prevailing in journalism, law courts, academies, and pulpits at the turn of the century. When unequivocally exteriorized as other's words, such discourses are to be located in those of "Laws" and "Convention" (368). In many cases, however, they are assimilated by the narrator to such an extent that they still show something of being other's words. The other side, trying to plead for the victims, timidly gives voice to protests against the unfair indictments.

If this novel can be looked upon as a courtroom drama, it does not reach any sort of conclusion except an ambiguous one, a kind of hung jury. It is such unresolved contradictions, which remain intact even at the last stage of the novel, that induce critics to offer such opposing interpretations. As a story of thwarted desires, it also has a propensity, if only latent, for being analogous to a tragedy. In this respect, too, it has something in common with Dostoevsky's novels, for, as Bakhtin remarks, "[i]n none of Dostoevsky's novels is there any evolution of a unified spirit; in fact there is no evolution, no growth in general, precisely to the degree that there is none in tragedy (in this sense the analogy between Dostoevsky's novels and tragedy is correct)" (26).

The tragic design of *Sister Carrie*, however, is not obvious, mainly because the novel ends with Carrie dreaming in a rocking chair. She lives in a luxurious hotel, having attained success in the world. The tragic design would become undeniable if she dies a miserable death like Lily Bart in Edith Wharton's *The House of Mirth* (as Lily, whose life traces a reverse course to that of Carrie's, can be pertinently compared with the latter), or at least, if the novel ends with the scene of Hurstwood's suicide, as it actually does in the Pennsylvania edition. "This ending is bleaker and philosophically more deterministic," as the editors of the Pennsylvania edition claim, "than the equivocal ending of the 1900 text," so that "in its purified form . . . *Sister Carrie* emerges as . . . a new and more tragic work of art" (*SC* 1981: 535).

In this regard, Michaels seems to agree with the editors, for he writes about the novel's ending:

> It could have ended with the far more dramatic scene of Hurstwood's death (as indeed, in an earlier draft, it did) or with a vision of Carrie moralized, renouncing desire in favor of an Amesian self-sufficiency. Both these alternate endings would have made the novel more genteelly anti-capitalist by bringing it to terms with the facts of physical life (death, the limits of desire) in which writers like Howells sought an ideological refuge from the new facts of economic life. (55)

While Michaels agrees to the view that the ending with Hurstwood's death would make the novel more tragic, he cannot endorse it, because it would also make the novel "more genteelly anti-capitalist." Michaels makes his argument vulnerable by turning down the Pennsylvania edition, because he cannot but admit that his scope of examination is limited to the 1900 edition. More fatally, his flat rejection of the Pennsylvania edition prevents him from inquiring into the possibility that even the ending of the 1900 edition might not cancel out the tragic design latent in the novel.

To be sure, the tragic design of *Sister Carrie* is hidden. For that matter, even in the Pennsylvania edition, the tragedy is hidden in the sense that Carrie the protagonist, at the last stage, presents a success in the world, as in the 1900 edition. In either edition, however, Carrie's unhappiness caused by disillusionment as well as Hurstwood's death toward the end of the novel suggests that the tragedy, if hidden, lies there. Whether the former scene or the latter may come last, such a difference would not change the basic nature of the story.

A more interesting question would be why the tragedy must have been hidden. For one thing, the author, who needs to protect his favored heroine, flinches from meting out a tragic fate to Carrie. On the other hand, "hidden dialogicality" in the narrative voice makes it difficult for the novel to attain relentlessness a tragedy ought to assume. The tragedy could have risen to the surface in its entirety, only if the social discourse that canonically censures the erring could have been cogently silenced. The censuring voice in the narrative parts, indeed, persists in forcing quarrels upon the vindicating voice, and then the rule of separation of styles, which such a dogmatic censor would demand, cannot be easily overcome.

As Erich Auerbach demonstrates in *Mimesis*, however, "complete emancipation from the doctrine" (554), which is the rule of separation of styles, makes possible tragedy in modern realism as a style that reveals the problematic in everyday life of the underprivileged. "The serious treatment of everyday reality, the rise of more extensive and socially inferior human groups to the position of subject matter for problematic-existential representation" is, as he accounts, one of "the foundations of modern realism" (491). "When Stendhal and Balzac took random individuals," he writes, "from daily life in their dependence upon current historical circumstances and made them the subjects of serious, problematic, and even tragic representation, they broke with the classical rule of distinct levels of style, for according to this rule, everyday practical reality could find a place in literature only within the frame of a low or intermediate kind of style, that is to say, as either grotesque comic or pleasant, light, colorful, and elegant entertainment" (554).

Sister Carrie allows us to see the opposing camps negotiating with each other, unobtrusively engaged in dialogues even within the narrative voice, over the question how to see Carrie's story, whether it should constitute a tragedy or not, as well as how to deem a lower social order. Such a "hidden dialogicality" prevents the novel from reaching a neat closure, keeping the author indeterminate about the ending.

The contradictions in the novel which resist synthesization may be traced down to Dreiser's divided allegiance. While on one hand he seeks to be assimilated with the dominant social discourse, on the other hand he wants to vindicate the victims. What is more complicating, the dominant culture itself is not homogeneous in the least. Dreiser, embodied in the narrative voice, finds himself sometimes affiliating with conservative uplifters, who are likely, for instance, to look down on Carrie as a silly girl, but, in other times, he finds himself joining up with progressive intellectuals like Ames, who are likely not only to despise the vulgar world Carrie lives in but to try to help stray sheep like Carrie to start life anew. Although, from Dreiser's point of view, both moralists and intellectuals are respectable enough to belong to the dominant culture, the conflicts between them are not to be easily resolved. Harder to be resolved, however, is the conflict between the moralists and intellectuals, on the one hand, and the underprivileged's inarticulate, protesting speeches or the vindicating narrative voice which speaks for them, on the other. Because of this divided allegiance, the style of the novel presents a seldom appreciated intricacy.

Beneath the equivocal style and ending of the novel lies Dreiser's sympathy with lower-class people. But his attitude toward them was never consistent or stable. Because of his own impoverished childhood and young manhood, he sometimes sympathized with the poor, and sometimes felt disgusted with them, wavering between hatred and pity, narcissism and self-criticism. Such irreducible contradictions shaped the structure of his writing.

At the same time, not forgetting the plight of the poor, Dreiser had to caution himself against the hardened egoism of a social climber, into which he was always on the brink of falling. There have been few critics, however, who paid much attention to his self-criticism, as Arun Mukherjee in her *The Gospel of Wealth in the American Novel* points out: "His bitter irony was probably incomprehensible to his critics as they judged the vulgarity of youthful Dreiser's aims as personal failure" (53). According to her reading of Dreiser's novels, the logic of social Darwinism or individualism apparently held up in them is nothing but parodies, that is, ironical expressions, of the rhetoric that the defenders of capitalism were using in the contemporary America of the time. Her interpretation implies that he achieved clear criticism of capitalism from the beginning of his career. So in her interpretation, she may be open to the charge of committing the error of simplifying Dreiser's ambivalence, too, though in her case, contrary to Michaels's, it is Dreiser's fascination with capitalism that is ignored. Nevertheless, Mukherjee is sensitive to Dreiser's self-criticism and his criticism of American culture, raising an important question that has seldom been considered.

The sympathy with the poor in *Sister Carrie* rests upon Dreiser's own experiences and his tenacious efforts to explore their meaning. He knew well that he was unable to express such sympathy without taking some risks and raising as implications some criticism of capitalism. He expressed it more unequivocally in his nonfiction writing like autobiographies. By taking them also into account, we can have a more detailed picture of his attempts to make sense of American society as he knew it.

In *Newspaper Days*, for example, he writes how he as a newspaperman was shocked to find many ugly aspects of society. Discrepancies between reality and professed American ideals were quite incompatible with the precept Howells had just preached about "the more smiling aspects of life, which are the more American." Among many disillusioning experiences, the most recurrent and disturbing was the labor question: workers' poverty, strife between capital and labor, and the press's cowardice about this question. When he was assigned to cover a streetcar strike in Toledo, Ohio, he wrote an article about it for the *Toledo Blade*. A part of the story, which includes an episode of a scab being attacked by the crowd, went into the strike scene in *Sister Carrie*.

The decisive moment for Dreiser, however, came when he worked in Pittsburgh. Though his stay there was relatively brief, Pittsburgh was to him an important revelation; as he recalls, "Never in my life, neither before nor since, in New York, Chicago or elsewhere, was the vast gap which divides the rich from the poor in America so vividly and forcefully brought home to me" (326). While he was fascinated with the wealth of business magnates like Andrew Carnegie, he was also much concerned about the sense of defeat and sullen despair of the workers in the town of Homestead, where the great steel strike had been bitterly fought only a year and a half before. As usual, he was not free to write about the conditions of the workers there. The city editor said to him as a new reporter; "We don't touch on labor conditions except through our labor man . . . and he knows what to say. There's nothing to be said about the rich or religious in a derogatory sense" (338).

"Our labor man" became one of the two men who were most helpful to Dreiser there. As Dreiser saw him, "[he] was an intense sympathizer with labor, but not so much with organized as with unorganized workers" (331). While he was initiated even to the ideas of socialism through this man, Dreiser says about the Pittsburgh newspapermen in general, "Never had I encountered more intelligent or helpful or companionable albeit cynical men than I found here" (330). It is from these senior colleagues that he received lessons in hard-boiled cynicism, which would later serve him as an acquired defense mechanism.

Only after criticizing his own individualism and snobbery through which he had craved for affluent status or affected Bohemianism, could Dreiser come to terms with life. The difficulty to do so had led him to his peculiar contradictions and ambivalence toward the power of capitalism. *Sister Carrie* as his first novel, captures the dialogues exchanged incessantly in the social arena through diverse discourses as they take place in each individual's mind that ruminates them. It shows in its equivocation the strained debate between the opposing parties, of which the novel is an enactment, nevertheless coming closer to a "serious, problematic, and even tragic representation" of the poor whom Dreiser was anxious to vindicate for all their unintellectual illusions.

Notes

1. Since Michaels relies on the 1900 edition of *Sister Carrie* published by W. W. Norton & Co., I cite page references to the same edition, not to the Pennsylvania Edition.

Jolly Mrs. Yerkes Is Home from Abroad: Dreiser and the Celebrity Culture

PHILIP GERBER

TO BEGIN WITH, SHE WAS ANYTHING BUT JOLLY. SHE HAD VERY LITTLE TO be jolly about. And to say that she had come "home" was to suggest that she had a "home" to come to. What she had was a house, albeit a grand one, a palace of a house, in fact, superbly situated on a northeast corner lot along Millionaires Row in Manhattan. She was childless, and her husband had long been a husband in name only. It was a second marriage for him, and Mary Adelaide, after a glorious, passionate beginning soaring with hopes for their bright future, had not been able to climb social heights for him any more adeptly than had his first wife, so her husband, being imperious as well as ambitious, was doing his best to rid himself of her. His original bride, Susanna, had been older than he and ineffective as a social hostess in Philadelphia. She had produced five children (two had survived), but aside from that her usefulness had come to an end. Now it was Mary Adelaide's turn to go—if he could manage it, if only she would be more cooperative, consider his imperative needs.

So,—no, Mrs. Yerkes could not accurately be described as a happy woman. Happy or unhappy, however, that was of small consequence to the New York newspapers (though in truth unhappy people did seem to make better copy, by and large). What did matter very much was that as surrogate for her husband Mrs. Yerkes had claim to immense wealth. It mattered also that Charles T. Yerkes, Jr., himself, had been a headline-maker for decades, more often than not as a scoundrel. For better or worse—that scarcely was the point. For he was a Celebrity. A very big one. And so was she—a Celebrity-by-Association, if you will and by virtue of that connection, eminently worth watching.

As a raw teenager during the 1880s, Theodore Dreiser was already watching. First, through the newspapers, which had paid much attention to the costly downtown tunnel on LaSalle Street through which Yerkes's streetcar lines passed; they said that in a shady political deal he had all but stolen it from the city. And then there had come the great strike against the Yerkes streetcar lines in 1888, bringing scenes of street violence which Dreiser had watched from curbside with bewildered and uncomprehending young eyes. The newspapers laid all of the fault at the doorstep of the intransigent owner, the haughty, arrogant Capitalist known as Baron Yerkes when not called a Buccaneer or simply slurred as The Philadelphian, a snide innuendo reminding readers that Yerkes in his native city had raided the treasury, been caught with his greedy hand in the till, been tried, convicted, and incarcerated there in Eastern Penitentiary for his crime.

I

By the early 1890s, while young Dreiser got his journalistic toes wet serving as a bottom-of-the-totem-pole reporter on local newspapers, it was apparent to any perceptive citizen that Charles T. Yerkes had worn out his welcome in Chicago. The financier himself expressed puzzlement. In his eyes, he had done all the right things. He had built up an imposing collection of Old Masters (thereby sending out the calculated suggestion that his personality contained another, altogether nicer and more altruistic side), and he had lent his favorite paintings, including that of his wife by Jan Van Beers, to the city for exhibition at its great fair, The World's Columbian Exposition, in 1892 and 1893. He had erected in Lincoln Park, hard by Lake Michigan, a mammoth electric fountain. A rainbow of colors played onto jets that shot fifty feet into the air before dropping back to earth in showers of diamonds. This was his magnanimous gift to the city. But—could anyone please Chicago? Apparently not. Yerkes was a plague, cried one columnist; he'd done Chicago as much harm as the cholera epidemic. The man was not well liked, no, not by businessmen, not by newspaper editors, not by the streetcar-riding public. But few denied that he possessed a certain something that made watching his every move addictive. You had to smile at the sheer effrontery with which he approached the world. He was always good for a story, and so the reporters loved him. He was charismatic in the extreme, and he lived like an emperor. He smiled enigmatically, was a master of the one-line put-down. The rapt newsmen took copious notes and hustled back to their smoke-filled newsrooms to write up their copy. For them, Charles T. Yerkes was the Celebrity par excellence.

But those with firm footholds in the Chicago social world would have none of Yerkes or of his socially ambitious wife, who quite naturally was assumed to be the man's co-conspirator and counterpart. His sharp business practices poisoned the well. He was treading on too many prominent toes. As the 1880s merged into the 1890s, anyone interested in Celebrities might notice in reading the Chicago Society pages that Mary Adelaide Yerkes's name was not likely to be listed anymore among those ladies invited to join Chicago's numerous bicycling clubs, lately the rage. Her name was conspicuously absent also from the published list of guests at the fashionable "bicycling teas" at which society ladies raised money for charity. Nor did the name of Yerkes appear among published lists of invited guests at dinners given by important Chicagoans such as the Marshall Fields, the R. S. McCormicks, the Potter Palmers, the Marvin Hughitts, the S. W. Allertons, and the Philip Armours. However much a power Charles Yerkes might be in business, he had become a social pariah, *persona non grata.*

As for Mrs. Yerkes, Chicago seemed to have tamed her since that day in 1880 when she had swept into town as the financier's second wife with a take-over manner that seemed to announce: "I'm here. Follow me!" In her staid Philadelphia neighborhood, as a girl, the fiery Mollie Moore had set tongues wagging even at age sixteen and seventeen, not long before she became infatuated with the thirty-one-year-old Yerkes. Friends of childhood days remembered Mollie's graceful figure, her raven eyes, her striking mass of black hair, but most of all they recalled the rebellious spirit that encouraged her to drive the streets of the Quaker City, not as a passenger in the usual sedate family brougham coach, but in a carriage drawn by four coal-black horses in gold harness—and in lieu of coachman, she herself controlling the reins. Disapproving voices could be heard behind the lace curtains: "There goes that wild Moore girl again, the young one, Mollie. Right up in the coachman's seat! What can her mother be thinking of? Why don't her parent *do* something about her!"

But with Mollie, passion came first, even if it meant a break with her parents and her big family of siblings (eight brothers and sisters). By the time Yerkes divorced his first wife, Susanna—anathema in the Philadelphia social set—the headstrong girl was branded in polite circles as a homebreaker. The financier, out of prison a half-dozen years, his fortunes now resurgent, suggested to his young mistress that they relocate, make a new start in Chicago. Mollie was quite prepared for the change. They would make a new beginning in the West, where so many were newcomers that to be an *arriviste* was the common and expected thing. So many had left the East under a cloud, it was considered impolite to inquire too deeply into anyone's past, for who knew when tit for tat might cause the tables to be turned? In Chicago, the family responsibilities were to be divided. Charles was to find a way of commanding a top spot in the financial world; while Mary Adelaide was to be the wedge that would break a path for them into the very best and topmost rungs of local society.

If Charles Yerkes before too long was disappointed by his second wife's inability to garner that coveted spot for him atop the Chicago social heap, he retained common sense enough not to discard her on that basis alone, for he recognized that their social *declassement* was based on jealousy and, even more than that, grounded in revenge. Who did these hypocritical meatpackers and drygoods merchants think they were? Had he not played his civic role to the hilt? Had he not presented their new University with the greatest telescope in the world—and a splendid observatory to house it? And had it not been his skill and determination and *imagination* that had built the Union Loop, ringing their downtown business area with streetcars that brought the housewives flocking in from the increasingly far-flung suburbs to shop all day for clothes and household trinkets at Carson, Pirie, and Scott, The Fair, and Marshall Field's new department stores? He couldn't figure these Chicagoans out. What did they resent? And the newspaper editors—who could please them? He'd gone to great expense to cater to the swelling rage for technological innovation, electrifying his lines, and building power plants all over the city to supply the new alternating current that ran his underground cables. But what was his thanks for getting rid of the smelly horse teams that had hitherto fouled the streets? One curt blast after another, front-page stories carping that his smokestacks rained oily black flakes of coal-snow over Chicago! And now, after everything he had done for the city, its councilmen (whose votes had cost him a good $20,000 apiece) did not find it politically expedient to grant him a lifetime monopoly. On top of this, the Illinois state legislature had had the effrontery to nix his bid for a fifty-year streetcar franchise.

Yerkes was ready by the mid-1890s to quit Chicago entirely, as soon as he could unload his well-worn equipment on the next fellow. Chicago was a big town, all right, but he was ready for the Metropolis. In fact, being usually a step or two in advance of his detractors, Yerkes by the end of the 1880s was letting it be known on visits to New York that while he considered Chicago a fine place to make money, he thought New York the best place to spend it. Early in the 1890s he began planning for his mansion on the southeast corner of Fifth Avenue and Sixty-eighth Street, just across the asphalt from Central Park. A good neighborhood, full of Astors and Vanderbilts. The Havemeyers, with a great fortune based on sugar, had built just across the street to the north. Like him, they were collectors of art, kindred spirits, it seemed, and he was planning for a spacious and up-to-the-moment gallery to be attached to his own new home, a room where his own growing collection might be displayed to guests advantageously. Who knew? Perhaps some day, if everything went right, that stone palace and gallery might preserve his name to posterity as one of the great benefactors of society by becoming the Charles T. Yerkes, Jr., Museum of Art, open to the public and second only to the Metropolitan. He'd like that.

When word of Yerkes's plans leaked back West and he was questioned by reporters, he pooh-poohed the rumors, declaring his eternal fidelity to the city that had provided his fortune, and with a straight face explaining that his place in Manhattan would never be more than a *pied a terre*, just a handy out-of-town cottage to be used on his frequent business trips or for short stays prior to or following his and his wife's trips to Europe, a continent they found it convenient to visit more and more frequently now as he built up his collection of old masters. He might have added that it gave the two of them something productive to do during their summers, when they were not welcome in most of the fashionable watering spots popular with Chicago society such as Lake Forest or Oconomowoc. Yerkes had given a good deal of thought to his eastern move and, in fact, had already built his final resting place, again in a very posh neighborhood, on Cypress Avenue in Brooklyn's Woodlawn Cemetery, not far from the tomb of the Whitney family. There he had erected a vault of white Vermont granite, in the Greek style, reminiscent of the Parthenon (but more modest in scale, of course, only 50 feet by 23). Behind its massive bronze doors he had caused to be placed, side by side, beneath an iron-grilled window of stained glass, a suitable pair of sarcophagi, outer cases of polished marble, inner of bronze.

Within these the encoffined bodies of himself and Mary Adelaide would one day be placed, there to rest side by side like some happily bonded couple, perpetually. Over the portal, among the grille work and lions' heads (his chosen totem, they would be carved into the stone of his mansion as well) the name YERKES, chiseled deep into the stone in clean-cut Roman letters that rain or storm could never obliterate. For the spot must be well marked for posterity. Again, who could say? Perhaps in some future time the mausoleum would become a shrine, visited by his admirers and honor paid, for he had made up his mind now to be remembered as a very important philanthropist, dreaming of a great charity hospital that, bearing his proud name, might, as a supplement to his art gallery, just do the trick.

To accomplish this ambitious aim, the financier needed not only to preserve his considerable fortune but see that it multiplied. And he needed to gain socially what had not been possible in that western boondock, Chicago. He had to create a lasting niche for himself in New York society. More than that, he must command a place in the hearts of New Yorkers high and low, young and old. It was love that Yerkes yearned for—the group love of the streetcar-riding populace, whose rain of nickels and dimes had filled his pockets. In seeking immortality as a philanthropist, Yerkes knew it was imperative that he avoid the many mistakes he and Mary Adelaide had made in Chicago. By the time his new home was ready, in 1894, he had determined that this time around he would take pains not to step on the toes of men who could retaliate. Power did have its privileges, he'd learned that lesson.

II

Theodore Dreiser by now was settled in New York himself. He had left Chicago during the early 1890s to begin ascending the journalistic ladder, one eye, like Yerkes's, ever on a move to the Metropolis. His big brother Paul, already in full career as a Broadway song-and-dance man, helped him to get established in Manhattan, and before long Dreiser had a position with the Joseph Pulitzer's New York *World*, ideally situated for Yerkes-watching. New York was already considerably ahead of Chicago so far as taking note of Celebrities was concerned. Nothing even vaguely approaching such modern Celebrity-driven publications as *People* magazine existed, not to mention its lower-browed counterparts *National Enquirer* or *Star*, or any of their TV avatars like *American Journal*, but a bare-bones beginning had been made in gossip publications such as *Town Topics*. Among newspapers, when it came to sensationalism, the *World* stood in the vanguard.

Dreiser, like Yerkes, was ambitious to become Somebody. His goals and methods were quite different, naturally. He was looking on the newspaper game as possibly serving for no more than a temporary haven, a fine spot in which to hone his natural talents as a writer by learning from his aspiring colleagues and by closely observing the jungle of life as it whirled on its daily course around him in all its manic phases, from politics to the morgue. New developments in high-speed printing were encouraging the growth of slick-paper monthly magazines, and he took notice that these pages were beginning to provide something resembling steady work for freelancers. Beyond all this lay areas that an untested young writer from the provinces as yet might only dream about. So many of his reporter friends were trying their hands at novels—those of Frenchman Zola, books like *Nana* and *Germinal*, scandalous though they were said to be, popped up as favorite models.

Dreiser must have felt that destiny was somehow at work when he learned that the Charles Yerkeses were abandoning Chicago for the East. He had long been fascinated by the tumultuous career of the streetcar-king and by the runaway rumors concerning the couple's precarious marriage. Yerkes himself seemed such an outrageously outsized figure, a chameleon, a cat that always landed on its feet. He was so much bigger than life, really. Dreiser had packed a thousand Yerkes items away in his memory and carried them with him to New York, and he was ever on the alert for more. From his own Chicago years he had retained scores of fresh recollections. They would provide a good foundation to build on . . . when the time came. His reportorial nose advised him to keep track of both of these Yerkeses. Meanwhile, Yerkes's reputation had preceded him. Much concerning his activities was to be found in the daily pages of the *World* itself, for while the Chicago editors had been rather highly moralistic, determined to blame Yerkes, brand him as an outlaw, and drive him from Illinois, the New York papers were considerably less attuned to making judgments, and more interested in the color of life—in Celebrity, as such.

As the Charles Yerkes mansion was readied for occupancy in 1894, Dreiser seems already to have initiated his practice of scissoring juicy items from the papers. He noted, for his own reference, that sometime around 1893, Yerkes was beginning an open campaign to establish his wife in New York society. And someone at the papers kept—or was kept—abreast on a daily basis of progress with the Fifth Avenue palace, the dollar amounts of what it was costing, with what rarities it was being furnished, and, most vital of all, what type of grand social affairs might be expected soon to occur within its walls.

Contrary to expectations, very few of these looked-for galas occurred. The New York social "400" was notoriously difficult to break into. Money by itself rarely possessed the power to purchase entry for an otherwise unsavory newcomer. As Dreiser would express it in his first book, New York was a sea full of whales, and a man who had dominated other, lesser waters might count for no more than a minnow in Manhattan. In addition, Yerkes was a divorced man, and divorce carried a powerful stigma. A twice-divorced man would be twice-damned. It might well drop him into pariah status. The upshot of this was knowledge that he badly needed Mary Adelaide to be at his side, playing her essential role as Trophy Wife, bedecked in Paris gowns, in diamond chokers and strands of pearls, in feathers and furs. She and his lavish house must become synonymous, the grandeur of one mirroring the splendor of the other. His mansion was to be a marble stage on which great social dramas might be enacted; as Hostess, Mrs. Yerkes was to be the star in these performances, charming everyone. As recompense, engraved cards surely would be delivered by private coachmen, reciprocal invitations to other great houses, other newsworthy parties, up and down the full length of Fifth Avenue.

In his mid-fifties at the time he moved East, Yerkes still stood arrow-straight, six feet tall, his dark, wavy pompadour well greyed, but his dark eyes as piercing as ever. A commanding presence. In Chicago he had been regarded as a man with phenomenal sex appeal and a legendary influence on women (a gift the self-deprecating young Dreiser would have killed for). There had been any number of women in the fellow's life. The Yerkes paramours came and they went, but always there was someone, young, beautiful, perhaps even talented—always talented, of course, in the arts of love, or if not to begin with, then mentored in them by the grand master.

As the twentieth century dawned, the New York financial world was rife with rumors that Charles Yerkes, American monopolist and creator of the Chicago Loop was conniving for control over transportation in London. It was quite true: Yerkes was planning to invade the London Underground field. But he had a second abiding interest in London, for Mrs. Yerkes, as the old century waned, was challenged by a serious new rival for her husband's affections. The ascendant was a Kentucky beauty, Emilie Grigsby, rumored (truthfully) to be the daughter of a society-whorehouse madam whom Yerkes had met at an opulent establishment in Louisville. The daughter, not yet out of her teens, was spectacular. With a cloud of auburn hair and skin like the finest alabaster, Emilie charmed Yerkes, and he fell hard. In no time at all he had brought her to New York along with her mother and her brother, Braxton, whom he employed in his enterprises. Yerkes could not bear to be parted from his new love. If he traveled to Europe, to further his Underground scheme or to visit artists' studios on a buying spree with Mary Adelaide, Emilie and her mother (acting as cover) were sure to have cabins booked for them on the next big liner setting out.

In New York, at the Hotel Grenoble, it was surmised that the Grigsby trio must have access to unlimited cash. Although no one knew quite who they were at first, they occupied an elaborate suite of rooms, staffed by their own personal servants, and kept a stable of saddlehorses and carriages at their disposal. Everyone wondered upon first seeing Emilie, "Who can she be?" Who, indeed! It came out quickly enough, although not publicly, of course. Yerkes had unloaded his rusting streetcar lines in Chicago for twenty million dollars, and a portion of this new wealth went into a place for his Emilie on Park Avenue at 67th Street, a house, if not as spacious as his own, fully as grand, and, audaciously, not more than three blocks away. Sometimes, as if relishing the risk he was taking, Yerkes arranged for the Grigsbys to be entertained at dinner in "Hotel Yerkes," as he mirthfully referred to his grand palace at 864 Fifth Avenue. Mary Adelaide was happy to have them; they were such congenial company, Emilie so strikingly pretty, for she had not had any remarkable luck at breaking into the divine circle whose circumference was both described and delimited by the *Social Register*. Even the purchase of a box at the Metropolitan Opera had not quite done the trick of throwing open the "right" doors. Because Yerkes's reputation was badly stained, and his wife was considered to be a "climber," the gates to social prominence never really opened. They found themselves relegated to a secondary position, relying more and more upon *arrivistes* like themselves or, even more so, to the not quite acceptable new stratum of Celebrities who were eagerly easing their way into notoriety by way of other venues, notably the entertainment world: singers and actors and directors and playwrights. The comic actress Ada Rehan, then at the peak of her popularity, her photograph appearing in widely circulated magazines such as *McClure's*, became one of Mary Adlaide's favorites. The pair became fast friends and, after Rehan had her portrait painted by the society painter John Singer Sargent, Mary Adelaide had her own picture done wearing the same costume in which Rehan had trod the boards in her most famous role, that of Lady Teazle in Sheridan's "A School for Scandal."

So Mrs. Yerkes was glad for the Grigsbys' company—for a time. A full year after Emilie's appearance in Manhattan, a society bachelor at a dinner party, when asked by Mrs. Yerkes whether he had managed to meet the young, pretty, and single Miss Grigsby, replied that she had been pointed out to him at the opera as a magnificent beauty, yes, but was, apparently, the kind of girl of whom everyone may be aware but whom no one should know. Mary Adelaide was aghast. Infinitely more shattering was the revelation, determined after a few inquiries, concerning the reason that Emilie was considered to be *declasse*, the crushing truth that the flow of dollars maintaining the Grigsbys in baronial splendor flowed from the open purse of her husband.

Once Mary Adelaide understood what the rest of New York had long since been aware of, the bronze doors of HOTEL YERKES snapped shut, never to reopen to her rival. No matter. Emilie was comfortably ensconced among her own Aubusson tapestries, diamonds, cameos, cabinets of jades, carved chairs, and $85,000 piano. She would not really miss her intimate little parties on Fifth Avenue all that much. But the unmasking of Emilie Grigsby did serve to snap the threadbare strands of the Yerkes marriage even though on the surface, for public consumption, the couple persisted in their loving-couple charade. On this point the newspapers were silent, perhaps recalling an oft-recounted story from Chicago days, that Yerkes had once discovered an unsavory story-in-the-making that revealed too much about his wife's past and had threatened the reporter so convincingly with death by gunfire that the story never appeared in print.

The nineteenth century passed. Charles Yerkes became a near-total stranger to his official residence. In its place, he maintained a private suite further down Fifth Avenue in the Waldorf. Defeated at heart, Mrs. Yerkes's spirit flagged, and no amount of JOLLY MRS. YERKES press notices were likely to revive her. She maintained a glacial stoicism, clinging to the only thing of real worldly value she had left, her legal status as Yerkes's wife. No more tears. Instead, she became a fury.

III

Theodore Dreiser had tracked Yerkes since the 1880s when, as a sixteen-year-old *parvenu* he had observed from the curbside with some wonderment the violence of the strike against the Yerkes streetcar companies in Chicago. By the mid-1890s both Yerkes and Dreiser had relocated to Manhattan and Dreiser, now a budding novelist, had a grandstand seat for observing Yerkes's thwarted attempts to break into New York society. When Yerkes died in December 1905, Dreiser made a note to himself concerning the ironical nature of life as he preserved his thought that Yerkes the multimillionaire had died in an ordinary hotel room. That was the artist at work, of course, altering actuality and waxing hyperbolic to suit his own purposes, for the death chamber was no ordinary hotel room at all, but the same elaborate Waldorf suite which Yerkes had occupied for some years. Bright's Disease, for which there was no cure then (or now) had made quick work of the transportation king.

But hotel bedroom or not, there were ironies aplenty for Dreiser to take note of, for Yerkes had perished while poised on the brink of carrying off the greatest financial coup of his career, control of the London Underground system, a fact that before long would lead to a carnival of lawsuits from creditors who piled in like a famished armada of buzzards ready to tear gobbets of flesh from the Yerkes estate. Another was the sudden emergence of tiny five-foot-three Mrs. Yerkes as a central actor in the unfolding drama. After 1905 Dreiser found himself—along with the rest of New York—inundated with new Yerkes stories as revelations withheld by editors out of propriety or because of the quite real fear of retaliation now became the stuff of everyday headlines—headlines that Dreiser was busily snipping out of the *World* and the *Herald* and squirreling away for future reference, because by this time Dreiser was quite certainly on the verge of beginning an important novel that would be based on Yerkes's life. With Yerkes safely deposited across the river in his magnificent tomb in Woodlawn, the newspapers felt easier about revealing such details of Yerkes-Grigsby connection as were known, including the news that as long ago as 1898 the financier had given Emilie the title to her splendid house on Park Avenue. What other private financial settlements had quietly been made for her would never be known for certain, of course, but suffice to say that the mistress was very well fixed for life, all her expensive toys intact.

Would that life were going as easily for Mary Adalaide Yerkes. During the 1905 summer, it could now be told, the financier, even though mortally ill, was in England to push his Underground scheme, doggedly determined to direct his own destiny. He had secured the services of an unnamed but prominent Manhattan attorney to approach his wife regarding the possibility of a divorce. For years and with reason aplenty, Mary Adelaide had distrusted her wayward spouse, knowing that her presence constituted a rankling obstacle to his happiness and fearful that he would make a sneak attack with some tricky legal maneuver that would oust her from her position and rob her of her legal rights. Yerkes's attorney, said the papers, had apparently been over zealous, exceeding his instructions. He had endeavored to persuade Mrs. Yerkes to vacate 864 Fifth Avenue, threatening, when she balked, to have lights and water shut off. When she stood pat, he then exacerbated the situation by causing her to believe that the financier might leave her unprovided-for in his will. In this manner, it was said, he hoped to provoke her into asking her own attorneys to file for a divorce with a satisfactory financial settlement.

During the autumn of 1905, motivated by intimidation and overweening curiosity, Mary Adelaide Yerkes summoned workmen to the mansion and put them to drilling her absent husband's private safe. Inside she found a bill of sale, dated 1896, which legally transferred to her all of the couple's household goods, furniture, paintings, and other valuables. But knowing her husband's wily nature, this discovery did little to put her mind at rest. And the huge house itself terrified her. It embodied her disastrous social failure and now was staffed by servants she suspected of being no more than her husband's minions. Amid a king's ransom in art, she became a prisoner, terrified that should she leave the house, Yerkes's spy-servants would lock the doors to prevent her return. She barred herself in. Only a small handful of trusted intimates were allowed entry. A guard was stationed outside her private quarters. Emissaries from anyone even remotely connected with Charles T. Yerkes, Jr., were shunned. Mrs. Yerkes tottered dangerously near collapse.

The metropolitan newspapers bided their time, waiting, watching, then reporting. All of this cloak-and-dagger action had the incipient signs of great drama buried in it somewhere. Readers were showing great interest. The story was growing daily more complicated with current legal developments and biographical revelations out of Yerkes's checkered past. Dreiser had been as fascinated, as any other habitue of Celebrity news, as the final chapter in Yerkes's life story approached. In

November 1905, returning from London aboard a great liner, the financier had needed to be carried by ambulance directly from the dock to his private apartments in the Waldorf Astoria. His spin doctors released a story explaining that he could not be taken to 864 Fifth Avenue because the place was undergoing extensive remodeling of the art gallery. Few were fooled, and it was noted that the revamping of the mansion in no way rendered the house uninhabitable for Mrs. Yerkes. Public curiosity was piqued by the sudden arrival of the financier's son, Charles E. Yerkes, who had been in Chicago handling what remained of his father's enterprises there. Yerkes's daughter, Mrs. Rondinella, also appeared. Clearly a vigil was underway, and the reporters gathered. The circumspect arrival at the Waldorf of Emilie Grigsby was spotted by alert journalists. But Mary Adelaide remained at home, not venturing out to the Waldorf or anywhere else. Eventually, both Yerkes's major attorney, Louis Owsley, and his financial secretary, Clarence A. Knight, called in person at 864. They struggled to convince Mrs. Yerkes that she had been the victim of a plot designed to embitter her against her husband. But she remained adamant against visiting the man whose audacious verve for life had supplied the supreme thrill of her youth. She seemed fearful now that a simple act of mercy might well prove her undoing. Owsley and Knight met the reporters who stood waiting on her pavement and gave them to understand that Mrs. Yerkes would happily have visited her husband were she not indisposed.

The financier sank rapidly. More and more, a persistent battalion of reporters besieged the mansion. Via her butler Mrs. Yerkes sent out a clarifying message to them: She had not been to the hotel; she did not intend going to the hotel; she was not indisposed; and she absolutely would not discuss her reasons for her actions. From her cunning and imperious husband she had learned a good deal about handling journalists. Soon after taking this bold stand, however, Mary Adelaide Yerkes relented in response to urgent messages from her stepson. A cab was called, and she was driven to the Waldorf posthaste. Because no one expected that Mrs. Yerkes under any circumstances would make a deathbed visit, the watchers' diligence had relaxed. Emilie Grigsby was thrown off her guard. The wife and mistress met face to face at the door of the sickroom. Mary Adelaide was infuriated, raised her voice, and the furor caused inquisitive guests in nearby suites to scurry from their rooms. Eventually, hotel detectives escorted Emilie to her carriage.

Reporters outside the Waldorf accosted Mrs. Yerkes as she left, accompanied by her sister, Mrs. Haywood. Had she seen Mr. Yerkes? Were the couple undergoing a reconciliation? Not at all, said Mary Adelaide: "He treated me shamefully." Mrs. Haywood declared that there was no reason for deathbed forgiveness. Mr. Yerkes had never known how to value his wife, and he quite obviously had learned nothing from his illness. Her sister was through with him. It was Christmas week, but Mrs. Yerkes had long since ceased being sentimental. Asked for permission to have the corpse brought to 864 Fifth Avenue to lie in state, she refused. Even so, on New Year's eve, Yerkes's bronze casket lay in the imposing two-storied reception hall of his marble palace. Friendly reporters confided to Dreiser their discovery that during the wee hours of the night servants had been bribed to open the doors for the undertaker.

Soon the papers were full of news concerning the intended bequest of the Yerkes art treasures to the city of New York. Beyond that, there was to be erected in the Bronx an immense, endowed charity hospital bearing the financier's name to posterity. So, complained the cynical, Yerkes intended to achieve the impossible dream: to pick the public's pocket and make them love him for it. As the press, during January, glutted itself on scandalous disclosures regarding Emilie Grigsby, including the revelation that her mother had been the madam of a brothel, Mrs. Yerkes's attitude took a strange turn. In an abrupt about-face, she now announced that she was seeking consolation in single-minded devotion to her late husband's plans. The idea of the Yerkes Hospital, she said, had been as much her dream as her husband's, and she intended devoting the remainder of her life to seeing that the dream was realized.

The breaking story seemed now to have reached its natural conclusion, but as January 1906 came to a close, there filtered through the news media a rumor too incredible to be believed. It tossed everyone's beliefs and expectations into a cocked hat, and Theodore Dreiser, hearing the rumor, must have wondered what could be happening to the story that had appeared to be winding down so neatly, all of its plot threads finishing, and its giant themes taking shape, including Death as the Great Leveller and the Evanescent Quality of Fame. Now it was said that the Widow Yerkes had remarried. If true, this had to be the first page in an entirely new and unexpected chapter. The precipitate haste of the wedding—supposing there had been one, cast a lurid, Hamlet-like unnaturalness over the death of the financier. But news even more bizarre lay just ahead. The wedding had been secret. What was more, the bridegroom was twenty years Mrs. Yerkes's junior, a Broadway wannabe from the Celebrity circles whose daily companionship she had relied upon in her loneliness.

To the reporters who flocked anew to 864 Fifth Avenue, following leaks from circles close to the putative groom, it all seemed too patently false, at best a sad, sorry joke, certainly not at all a funny prank to play on a poor, bereaved woman. And who was this groom, this Mr. Wilson Mizner, anyway? Mrs. Yerkes, when she eventually showed herself in answer to the newsmen's clamor, seemed near to hysteria. She branded the whole wedding story false, a malicious report advanced by her enemies. Of course she had not married Mr. Wilson Mizner—or anyone else! It was just too ridiculous. Her intention was never to marry again, had she not made the clear?

The reporters located Wilson Mizner at his Broadway digs. He laughed long and loud. Of course the wedding had taken place! In fact, the ceremony had been performed at the Yerkes mansion on 30 January, the one-month anniversary of the financier's demise, Reverend Andrew Gillies of St. Andrews officiating. Mizner was the soul of credibility as he cited times, details, names of witnesses. After the ceremony, the small wedding party had been served refreshments by the Yerkes servants. Then Mizner drove to the Seymour hotel to have sandwiches with some pals while the new bride went out to visit a friend. Later he had called for her, escorted her back to 864, and then returned to his bachelor pad at the Astor.

Word spread immediately to Chicago, where Charles E. Yerkes was initiating the probate of the Yerkes will. A telegram arrived from Mary Adelaide: STORY IS SIMPLY RIDICULOUS, and armed with this, the financier's son denied the Mizner claim. But the telegram was ambiguous. Chicago newspaper joined the New York press in pointing out that the word *ridiculous* might be an attempt to characterize the sensational headlines of recent days, nothing more. Reporters continued to dig. They located another Mizner, Addison, then an antique dealer, but soon to achieve fame as the designer of Spanish-style homes in the very newest of celebrity watering spots, Boca Raton and Miami Beach. Addison Mizner confirmed what his brother had said, and eventually, under pressure, Mary Adelaide dropped her pretense, admitting that indeed she was Mrs. Mizner. "I thought she had more sense," said Charles E. Yerkes, in a dour comment. Did he know Wilson Mizner? Yes, they had met, that was about all. What was he like? How would Charles E. Yerkes characterize him? The younger Yerkes begged off. Hadn't the fellow's own prolixity and the pressure he had put on Mrs. Yerkes stamped his character clearly enough for anyone to see? Surely, the man was a cad.

At age twenty-nine (his bride was fifty) Wilson Mizner now became an instant Celebrity, the press using his own words to dub him a "gentleman of the wide, wide world." Like many men unused to celebrity, Mizner talked altogether too much, telling long-winded stories of his adventures in Central America and the Klondike while puffing on a brown-paper cigarette, all the while nursing a drink in one of Yerkes's best silver goblets. He had come to New York with some vague ambitions to become a playwright, had struck up friendships with theatrical folk, joined the Bohemian Club, and figured in some amateur entertainments. In this company he had become acquainted with the widow Yerkes. The press pegged him "an ambitious Broadway promenader." Sensing his craving for publicity, the reporters dogged his trail, allowing him to swagger a bit and brag until his energy flagged, then writing up the story. Not too much slanting had to be employed, for Mizner, his own worst enemy, set up his own pillory.

On 2 February, on Mizner's invitation, a flock of reporters penetrated the mansion, from which Yerkes had always barred them. Mizner asked the press corps to cool their heels in the Japanese Room off the grand reception hall while he went off in search of his bride. Soon she appeared at a balcony overlooking the foyer, her hair hastily arranged, still gowned in her silk wrapper. She was nervous, her hand gripping and ungripping the marble balustrade as she braced herself to look at the heads turned upward toward her. What did she have to tell them? "All I can say is that I am married to Mr. Mizner. And I hope you will say that I am not fifty but eighty." She seemed confused, at a loss. A bit later the reporter from the *American* was able to speak with her alone and, somewhat more coherently. She told how Mizner had befriended her, supplying help and sympathy while she had lived in the mansion alone, deserted, friendless, and terrified. They had found that they shared certain interests—art, books, reading. She was certain they would be happy. Later in the day, the new master of the house escorted the parade of reporters on a tour of the Italian-garden room and the famous art gallery, where Old Masters were stacked three-deep on the walls. He stopped before a huge oil showing a group of medieval pages playing at dice: "We'd say 'newsboys shootin' crap,' wouldn't we?" Giggles arose from the circled men. The press played up the balcony scene, calling Mizner Romeo and former Mrs. Yerkes a balcony Juliet with a good-looking bank account. Charles T. Yerkes would have known how to handle such brazen audacity from reporters, but he was in his grave. With no protector, his widow was at their mercy. And the presses were hungry.

Reviewing materials for what he now thought held the fine potential for the final pages of his novel-to-be, Theodore Dreiser wrote another note to himself reflecting his dismay at the nastiness overwhelming the journalistic world: "It should be noted in speaking of Mrs. Yerkes the flippant, shameless newspaper accounts—coarse and vulgar." Dreiser's surprise may have sprung from the fact that for so many years the press had handled the Yerkes story with kid gloves. He knew, of course, that a good deal of that reticence had stemmed from fear of massive retaliation. But with the financier safely out of the way, his widow and Mizner seemed literally to beg for it. Of course, the yellow sheets and the tabloids could be expected to exploit this idiotic behavior. But only a few years in the past, when the theft of Mrs. Yerkes's calling-card case and purse had served as a trigger for questionable stories, the staid New York *Times* had rushed to her defense, declaring that a paper that printed gossip without the consent of the victim should be ready to face charges of invasion of privacy. The *Times* itself had been the soul of restraint on the subject of Emilie Grigsby, as an example, although the mistress's story had long been known. But this sad Yerkes-Mizner affair! Even the *Times* was impelled to hoot.

IV

From 1906 onward Mrs. Yerkes-Mizner knew little peace. Within three weeks rumors spread that the newlyweds had quarreled and separated. On a tip, reporters flocked to Coney Island and dug like dachshunds in the sands of that seaside resort until they located Mizner sparring with boxer Jimmy Britt in an effort, he told them, to regain his lost strength and repair his wasted features. Questioned about a potential reconciliation, Mizner said that he had "slung the slumber mitt" on his dreams of bliss and, gave an answer in two words: "Nothin' doin'." This prognosis notwithstanding, when Mary Adalaide in June 1906 reopened her Chicago house, ostensibly to be available during probate of her dead husband's will, Mizner followed, registered at the Auditorium Hotel, and called on her, offering a spin in an automobile. Instead, Mary Adelaide remained in Chicago to establish legal residence for a divorce, her attorney (who formerly had guided the financier) gathering evidence to prove that his client had been drugged at the time of the marriage and remembered nothing of the ceremony but what other had told her about it. Mizner countered by producing the Reverend Gillies, who would testify that Mrs. Yerkes had been rational, sufficiently to pledge him to keeping the marriage secret for as long as he could manage. In May 1907 an amicable divorce was granted, Mary Adalaide resuming the name of Yerkes, and Mizner withdrawing from her life. Reports of a million-dollar settlement were denied.

Dreiser wondered how any such settlement could have been possible, given the sad shape in which the Yerkes estate found itself, besieged by creditors. Yerkes's wealth had been estimated at some twenty million dollars (perhaps two hundred million in 1998 dollars), but some months after his death no more than eight million could be located, and his debts amounted to at least five million. Maintenance of the mansion and the army of servants who staffed it cost a small fortune, and the house was still under mortgage. Yerkes's wealth existed primarily in shares of the Chicago Traction Company and the London Underground Railway.

But the London subway had not yet been completed; Yerkes's plan to monopolize the Underground still hung precariously in the balance at the time of his death. A plague of lawsuits followed, four years of litigation and legal warfare. Disgusted with the Mizner debacle, Charles E. Yerkes attempted to oust Mary Adelaide from 864 Fifth Avenue, and she in turn attempted to dismiss Louis Owsley as executor of the will, he opposing her wish to claim her dower rights. The dower rights would give her a third of all property; her alternative was to wait for a full share upon eventual settlement of the estate, a prospect that appeared more and more to exist far off in the dim future. The longer she waited, the less worthwhile it seemed, and finally she sued for the dower rights and they were granted.

The implications were immense. For one thing, the Yerkes possessions had to be liquidated in order to determine the dower rights and produce the cash to satisfy them. In consequence, Mary Adelaide must forfeit her right to occupy 864 Fifth Avenue. Plans proceeded rapidly to sell the house and its contents. Everything in Mrs. Yerkes's room was to remain hers, as well as certain canvases from the collection. Otherwise, all personal effects were to go on the auctioneer's block. In December 1909 everything was transferred to the Receiver, Mr. Burlingame: mansion, stables, art gallery, paintings, sculptures, and the famed collection of oriental carpets. Mrs. Yerkes naively had relied to the end on the bill of sale she had found in her husband's private safe, and when the courts finally declared it to be invalid, she was dazed to learn that she would in fact be dispossessed. Guards were stationed in the mansion to prevent her removing so much as a vase; they wore rubber-soled sneakers to protect floors, stairs, and carpets, and this made Mrs. Yerkes ill at ease, despite the fact that the 24-hour surveillance supposedly was designed so as not to interfere with her leaving or entering the home.

The newspapers offered their readers a running account of events, allowing the public to "eavesdrop" while agents of the auction company entered 864 at will. The house that had lacked for visitors was now overrun with men tagging hundreds of paintings, bronzes, and rare carpets according to their placement in the elaborate catalog that was being readied. Collectors, art experts, and dealers joined them, sauntering about the mansion as if they owned it, openly speculating upon values, eyes alert for potential bargains. Even Mrs. Yerkes's boudoir was invaded, and, suffering from neuralgia, she was in a gloomy mood as the work progressed. Theodore Dreiser just then was a busy man, running the Butterick magazines from a limed-oak office and preoccupied with his attempted seduction of eighteen-year-old Thelma Cudlipp, daughter of an employee. But the onrushing show on Fifth Avenue captivated him as well, and he followed the spectacle day by day, learning when the wagons arrived to begin the task of carting three hundred paintings by such as Rembrandt, Hals, Corot, Watteau, Van Dyck, Holbein, Turner, and Rubens to the American Galleries on 23rd Street. Eventually, followed by sixty trunks and a retinue of servants, Mary Adelaide Yerkes left Fifth Avenue for temporary quarters at the new Plaza Hotel before moving to a more permanent home she was leasing at 861 Madison Avenue. Learning from the papers that her new house was considered to be puny compared with the mansion she was leaving, Dreiser jotted down the appropriate thematic comment, in line with the ironic cast that was to characterize the closing pages of his novel-to-be: "And that, after her $50,000 pink marble bath!"

Then, on 5 April 1910, the great Yerkes sale opened to overflow crowds. A $1.00 admission charge during the pre-auction exhibition had not dissuaded many, but only served to whet the appetites of those who wanted to attend the auction and, if not to bid, certainly to be there, to occupy a seat where they might see and be seen. The fact that his copy of the auction catalog was saved among his papers suggests strongly that Theodore Dreiser was among that crowd—and who had a better right or more pressing motive than the man who was now planning somehow to cram all of this American spectacle between the covers of a novel? What an unexpected bonanza this was! What unlooked-for drama was unfolding in this plot that Life was laying out before him? It was like some grand, appetizing buffet of delicacies! On the first evening of the sale, paintings by Innes, Bouguereau, Israel, Burne-Jones, and Alma-Tadema were knocked down for $162,225. That this sale was going to set an American record seemed certain. On the second evening, any doubts were dispelled as the total ran well past the $400,000 brought by the record-making Mary J. Morgan sale. On the third evening another half million was added to the take with the sale of pictures such as Rembrandt's "Portrait of a Rabbi" and Frans Hals's "Portrait of a Woman" (now in New York's Frick Collection). By the end of the evening the receipts had marched past the two-million-dollar mark.

The auctioneer paused for the weekend. On Monday the auction moved to the mansion, which was to be sold along with the remaining treasures it housed, such as Mrs. Yerkes's Louis XV bedstead of palisander, ormolu, and bronze, and Rodin's marble "Cupid and Psyche." The Celebrity-adoring public at last were enabled to enter the great double bronze doors, free to wander at will up and down the grand central staircase, through the library, into the conservatory, the Japanese Room, the Italian Gardens, to marvel for themselves at the panoply of Success in America, perhaps even to bid on some of the 1300 items tagged for auction—chairs the great Celebrity may have sat in, lamps that had lighted his dinner table. Outside the mansion, on the pavement of Fifth Avenue, a perceptive reporter from the *World* spied a carriage passing slowly, a number of times, the horse pacing first north, then south. He recognized the lone passenger. It was Mary Adelaide Yerkes. When he wrote up his minor scoop, the headline attached to it read: IN BROUGHAM, MRS. YERKES SEES CROWD THRONG HOME. Mary Adelaide Moore Yerkes Mizner Yerkes, the life-hungry girl who so long ago had run in company with her Titan husband like a pair of leopards intent on subduing Chicago and the world, now had little left to live for. Her husband was lost, irretrievably, his fabled wealth vanished like a mirage, her own money melting away by the minute. Expecting many millions, she realized a paltry $163,362 after the lucrative sale and the payment of debts. Her health failed along with her expectations. During the fall of 1910 she suffered badly from an attack of grippe; another attack, in February of 1911, finished her off. She died in her rented house on Madison Avenue.

Mary Adelaide had never canceled her plan to rest beside Yerkes in his marble mausoleum out at Greenwood. One final irony—as her funeral cortege wound its slow way through Manhattan toward the Brooklyn Bridge, it was bound to skirt the Forty-Second-Street neighborhood where the Lyric Theatre was presenting *The Deep Purple*, the first smash hit by the heralded new Broadway playwright Wilson Mizner.

By the time that Mrs. Yerkes was laid in the mausoleum at Greenwood, Theodore Dreiser was anticipating publication of his second novel, *Jennie Gerhardt*. The manuscript had been completed in the aftermath of the great auction of Yerkes's art collection, and the subsequent sale of the mansion. (The man who bought it denied that he intended tearing it down in order to build a huge apartment building on the site—but of course, New York being what it is, he did precisely that, and as soon as possible.) In *Jennie Gerhardt* Dreiser accelerated his use of urban newspapers as plot devices, intensifying his focus upon reporters driven by an ardor for Celebrities. In these pages he made immediate practical use of much that he had learned about current journalistic practices from his attention to the coverage given Mrs. Yerkes's troubles, and in his new novel, reporters, sniffing out a scandal surrounding the love nest that Lester Kane has set up for Jennie Gerhardt and himself, lie in wait for the girl. They stalk her, really, dodging behind shrubbery in order to shoot clandestine film of her daily comings and goings; and newspapers then run soap-opera headlines such as: SACRIFICES MILLIONS FOR HIS SERVANT-GIRL LOVE and THIS MILLIONAIRE FELL IN LOVE WITH THIS LADY'S MAID, headlines which are directly reminiscent of those run in New York during the revelations concerning Yerkes and Emilie Grigsby. These intrusions add immeasurably to Jennie's misery, and Dreiser's criticism of them reflects his own sympathetic response to Mrs.

Yerkes in her time of trial, as well as his disgust with intrusive reporters out to "get the story" whatever the cost.

Dreiser was only about twenty years older than the brash young newsmongers of the post-1910 era, but he felt himself to be of another and distant generation entirely, so fast was social change occurring in America. He thought himself to have been bold and even aggressive in tracking down reluctant interviewees during the years surrounding the turn of the century, but his methods could in no way be compared with the voracity of the bloodthirsty young men who had hounded the widow of the financier. Dreiser's reticence was out of date. There were old-fashioned limits beyond which he would not transgress, and these included attacks upon the living. So long as Yerkes lived and his wife survived, Dreiser contented himself with piling up data against the day when he might be freed legitimately to begin composing his epic story. He lived in a muckraking era but was not at heart a member of that clan. He was a novelist. It was strange, though. He'd never written a novel in this manner. Data was accumulating on a daily basis, it seemed, a new surprise arriving with each dawn. He didn't know anyone else who may have composed a novel in his manner, either. It was all quite peculiar, but extremely exciting.

When both of his principals were safely in their graves, even then the Yerkes saga refused to bring itself to an easy finish. In some ways it appeared only to be getting a good start, for legal hyenas descended upon the scene with a series of lawsuits filed by late-coming creditors and would-be creditors who were intent upon chewing what bones of the estate were left to be gnawed on. These developments, as engrossing as they were appalling, underscored for Dreiser the deep irony of the financier's life and the bubble quality of all of his dreams and brave endeavors. But Dreiser had to move on, because others besides himself were captivated by the story, and it would not wait long for a teller. Already, one of the great new slick magazines, *Everybody's*, had run a summary piece entitled "What Availeth It?" and told much of the tale, complete with photographs. But before he published, Dreiser felt that he needed to do more in site investigation of Yerkes's origins in Philadelphia, read more books on that amazing era in American finance (crib from them if it came to that), and, best of all, take to the road in search of the mysterious essence of his financier. Arguing that he couldn't very well write about a millionaire without learning first-hand how a millionaire had lived, he proposed to sail for Europe and dog Yerkes's footsteps until he came to a full comprehension of what his man's life had been like when he had bulled his way through Paris and London as a famous American Celebrity, gambled for big stakes at Monte Carlo, and purchased expensive art directly from the studios of famous painters. Late in 1911, temporarily setting aside the pages that were fast accumulating for the big novel he was now calling *The Financier*, Dreiser boarded the princely liner *Mauretania* in search of the data that would allow him to sail with confidence through Yerkes's later years. Coming home, in April 1912, Dreiser would argue strongly for permission to arrange westbound passage on the maiden voyage of the fabled new liner *Titanic*, the ship he felt sure that Yerkes would have taken, given opportunity. Fortuitously, as it turned out, his impatient publisher refused to support the extravagance.

Meanwhile, the third point of the Yerkes love triangle, the principal figure that Dreiser sometimes lost sight of, had complicated the tale by making her reappearance in New York and moving to center stage. Emilie Grigsby, now popular in exclusive circles in London, where she was rumored to have been the guest of Princess Mary during the coronation of Edward VII, walked down the gangplank of *Titanic*'s sister ship, *Olympic*, in September 1911, dressed elegantly in black (with a white veil blurring her features) and carrying a bouquet of fresh flowers from a new admirer. Customs officials showed little interest in Emilie's ten trunks, but the man from the *Herald* saw them concentrating instead on the leather bag entrusted to one of her maids. It was opened before the eyes of passengers. Inside, her jewels glittered in the light: diamond tiaras, emerald brooches, a pendant ruby of great size, chokers and ropes of perfectly matched pearls. $800,000 was the value attached. Emilie was disdainful. She invited the officials to examine the settings with care. They would see that her treasures were of *American* design and workmanship, thus not subject to a single red cent of import duty. This was the kind of news that was making the headlines now. Emilie was taking her turn as The Celebrity.

V

When Dreiser returned to New York, Harper and Brothers were screaming for his manuscript, promised so long ago. Dreiser envisioned his fictional account of the Yerkes story as a single volume, admittedly a pretty thick one. He already had written more than a thousand pages, yet his manuscript went no further so far than the Philadelphia years of Frank Algernon Cowperwood, which was the name that he had conjured up for the Yerkes persona. That part of the story had been simple, adhering at most points to the framework established by Yerkes's life and activities. But the parallel account of Mary Adalaide Moore Yerkes required a good deal more work and imagination. Dreiser could have followed either of two paths. He might have cast the second Mrs. Yerkes in a distinctly minor role, obscured by her husbands's gigantic shadow. That would have been advantageous, perhaps, in highlighting the titanic figure of Cowperwood as Dreiser envisioned him, for he surely was to be the motivating center upon whom the plot turned. Another path—the path Dreiser chose—would throw the spotlight upon Mrs. Cowperwood as well and provide her character with a role almost as large and significant as her husband's.

The danger lay in diluting the attention paid to Cowperwood, in possibly creating a second and competing center of dramatic interest. In choosing to go this direction, Dreiser increased his work significantly, for relatively little ready-made material existed concerning the family of Mollie Moore. They were not public figures on whom the newspapers kept tabs. But in a burst of inventiveness that gave the lie to those who carped that he could only report, never invent, Dreiser managed to conjure up for Mollie Moore a celebrity background that rivaled Cowperwood's own. He gave her a wholly new Philadelphia family: two brothers, a sister, an acquiescent mother, and a powerful civic-leader father. It was fictional family cut from whole cloth, yet suggested strongly enough by the mid-nineteenth-century American-big-city milieu as not to violate the sense of actuality that was the lifeblood of Dreiser's story. The family would be headed by Edward Malia Butler, a Philadelphia garbage collector whose shrewdness has assisted him toward a power position in Philadelphia and who works in cahoots with Cowperwood as he bilks Philadelphia of millions.

The Butler character is one of Dreiser's most significant additions to the Yerkes record, a major creation in its own right. But Dreiser's eye is on Butler's daughter, Aileen, the persona through whom Mary Adelaide Moore is reincarnated as a beautiful and headstrong girl whose position as a Butler allows for a convenient and convincing method for her and Cowperwood to become acquainted. Cowperwood first visits the Butler home when Aileen is fifteen. Dreiser has given her a full cosmetic makeover, abolishing Mollie Moore's dark hair and eyes and substituting in their place red-gold locks and blue eyes. Cowperwood is struck by her beauty and her outgoing personality but regards her as a child. Over the next three years Aileen matures, Dreiser introducing another and highly significant physical alteration; rather than remain at Mollie Moore's height of five-foot-three, Aileen has grown to be "nearly" the same height as Cowperwood (who stands five-foot-ten). There is no doubt in my mind that Dreiser here was vitally affected by the publicity given to Mrs. Yerkes after her husband's death; the time period of composition coincides with the years during which the novelist was formulating definite plans to transmute the Yerkes story into fiction. Knowing that in the pages of his novel Mrs. Yerkes-Copwewood must become something of her husband's equal—in the aftermath of his demise she must stand alone at the center of the action—he took the steps that seemed essential to writing an effective conclusion for his story. Readers have generally assumed that the title of that eventual third portion of the trilogy, *The Stoic*, refers to Cowperwood. But it is Aileen Butler Cowperwood who is the stoic forced to endure silently whatever blows her unkind destiny rains down upon her.

Frank and Aileen Cowperwood are birds of a feather, ideally mated, rather equally ambitious, handsome, amoral creatures of passion. Dreiser in describing Aileen employs terminology that otherwise would be reserved for his hero. She is "vigorously young," "intensely alive," full of "raw, dynamic energy" and "burning vitality," both "fiery" and "intense." At the grand ball celebrating the opening of new side-by-side houses for Cowperwood and his father, the sparks of romance are first struck, Cowperwood crying out, "You're like fire and song." In dramatic terms, these early scenes set the stage appropriately for the future and for its ironic aftermath. At times, in his own rush of enthusiasm for the reified Aileen character (perhaps also to relieve himself of excessive direct authorial adulation of his financier), Dreiser adopts Aileen's point of view, allowing her to depict the Frank Cowperwood she is smitten by. She has been searching for a man whose "love of life" tallies with her own, and in Frank she finds him: "Love! Love! That was the greatest thing in the world. And Frank Cowperwood was the loveliest, most wonderful, most beautiful man that ever was." The lovers do not hesitate at duplicity. As a practical solution to the question of a trysting place, they meet in suburban parks. Here Dreiser expanded inventively upon the single source-note he possessed concerning Mollie Moore's passion for horses. Against tradition, Aileen drives her own pair of spirited bays to the rendezvous, or else dons a riding skirt and rides western style. She averts suspicion for the simple reason that for years she has habitually driven or ridden during her afternoons. The neighbors are accustomed to it. Later, as the love affair matures, Cowperwood sets up a house for clandestine meetings in Tenth Street, furnishing it with treasures from his expanding collection of art works and antique furniture.

Dreiser's plot is served well by this alliance. He arranges for Edward Malia Butler to become a major backer of Cowperwood, supporting him in his risky maneuver to profit (along with the Philadelphia city treasurer) while he uses city funds for his own speculative purposes during interim periods. When the rug is pulled from beneath Cowperwood's feet by the sudden economic crunch that follows the great Chicago fire of 1871, Butler is persuaded by political cronies—but even more so by an anonymous letter exposing Cowperwood's seduction of his beloved daughter—to let the financier twist in the wind. Thus Cowperwood's ruination is linked intimately with the love affair. And following Frank's pardon and release from Eastern Penitentiary, Dreiser again tampers with the actual record as he eliminates the half-dozen and more years during which Yerkes had unsuccessfully attempted to reestablish his reputation in Philadelphia; instead, he causes his locally disgraced lovers to depart for Chicago within six months. One result of these changes in the record is to bind Frank and Aileen together more strongly, to influence the reader to see them as necessary partners in a common fate. Their subsequent social failure, then, and Aileen's predicament when ultimately she is abandoned by Frank, are rendered all the more poignant.

There were many decisions yet to be made by Dreiser. Clearly, the role played by Emilie Grigsby (whom he would dub Berenice Fleming) was going to be a large and important one, how much so was not clear even in 1910 and 1911, for many revelations were yet to come, including the sale of Emilie's Park Avenue home and her quite improbable (but factually accurate) conversion to the simple life through a trip to India. He hardly dared allow Emilie to become as significant in fiction as she had become in life. But at least, once the financier was dead, the way had been cleared for Aileen to emerge as a believable replacement for Frank at the center of the novel. What to do about the Widow Yerkes's marriage to Mizner was a real puzzle. Its inherent flamboyance held the potential for wrecking Dreiser's otherwise rather neat plot-from-life. Was his story of the financier to be outdone, perhaps swamped, by the outrageous color of that affair? It was a point for serious consideration.

As it happened, such decisions did not need to be made at once, for Harpers, concerned over Dreiser's continual delays in delivering a finished manuscript, acted aggressively. The argument was put to him that his Cowperwood story would never fit between the covers of a single novel. A thousand pages of manuscript had already been examined at the publisher's offices, and it appeared that, with the lovers' departure from Philadelphia, one discrete action had been completed. How would Dreiser feel about allowing Harpers to publish this section under his original title for the whole saga, *The Financier*, both for its own sake and as a drumbeater for two sequels? *The Financier* could be advertised as the opening portion of a trilogy. Three books for one! Dreiser bought the argument. Happily. He gained time; Harpers gained a Dreiser novel for their fall 1912 list. Dreiser then cut his manuscript at the appropriate spot, added a coda which he larded with hints of what was to come, and on 15 October of that year, bulking up at 780 pages and dressed in the same mottled blue binding used in 1911 for *Jennie Gerhardt*, Dreiser's huge story of a businessman as American Celebrity was officially released for sale.

Immediate reactions were mixed; that was not unexpected, given the unorthodoxy of the novel's central players and their deviation from the prevailing social proprieties. But over the long haul, after critical passions had cooled, the novel would be recognized as constituting a superior piece of fiction. In 1959 Ellen Moers declared that *The Financier* and its sequels constituted the best fiction about the world of business that had been published in America;[1] and Maxwell Geismar, in his *Rebels and Ancestors*, confirmed the rightness of Dreiser's decision regarding Aileen, declaring it a "brilliant accomplishment" and saying further that eventually "it was Aileen, the suffering woman, rather than Cowperwood, the perfect operator, who became the central figure in the story of their growing estrangement."[2]

Notes

Most of the data in the essay rely upon the thousands of manuscript notes that Dreiser compiled as he prepared to write *The Financier*. These are preserved in the Dreiser collection, University of Pennsylvania.

1. Ellen Moers, *Two Dreisers*, xii.
2. See Maxwell Geismar, *Rebels and Ancestors*.

Men Strike, Women Sew: Gendered Labor Worlds in Dreiser's Social Protest Art

LAURA HAPKE

THEODORE DREISER WAS AS APT A STUDENT OF THE LITERARY MARKETplace as Carrie Meeber was of fortune's ways.[1] Yet he deplored the sanitizing of women wage earners central to virtually every popular tale of urban tenement life excepting Stephen Crane's explosive *Maggie: A Girl of the Streets* (1893), which he praised for its realism. While steering clear of the issue of streetwalking, his own "kept woman" novels, *Sister Carrie* (1900) and *Jennie Gerhardt* (1911), subverted the cultural fantasy of proletarian womanhood promulgated in the Laura Jean Libbey dime-novel mode, in which the virtuous lower-class girl is rewarded by marriage to a merchant prince.

Yet Dreiser's ability to transcend the gender discourse of his time was mired in a lingering Victorianism. Astute critical labels such as "Victorian vamp" and "purified fallen woman" suggest the compromised radicalism of his invented narratives of blue-collar female sexuality. Within the cultural parameters available to one who so craved success, the creator of Carrie and Jennie articulated as detailed an analysis of the intersection of labor-class women and capitalism as the era's most "proletarian" text, Upton Sinclair's *The Jungle* (1906). Dreiser's "saving hands" (*SC* 1981: 3) approach to feminine economic exploitation, however, reveals the strengths and limitations of his gendered labor vision.

To examine his representation of labor-class women, it is necessary to understand Dreiser's disappointing male proletarians, personified in his novels by the sullenly ambitious stockyard railway worker Hanson in *Sister Carrie* and in his prose writings by the mindless coworkers of his unfinished, autobiographical *An Amateur Laborer* (1904). Working-class men appear in his nonfiction more often than their female counterparts, though rarely as organized-labor militants. Perhaps this ambiguous vision of the masculine worker is the reason little attention has been paid to his gendered approach to class struggle (although, as an author who was fascinated by supermen capitalists and the seductions of upward mobility, class struggle is not a term he would have employed.) In this essay I argue that the sexual segregation in the labor worlds of Dreiser's art and the full extent to which he mirrored his era's prejudices about wage-earning women are illuminated by a look at the connections between Dreiser's journalism and fiction on labor. I thus urge a careful rereading of *An Amateur Laborer*; "Fall River," his unpublished 1899 account of New England loom workers; his assorted articles on factory work, from pieces in the mainstream magazine *Cosmopolitan* to those in the short-lived little magazine *1910* and in the socialist *New York Call*; his retrospective *Newspaper Days* (1922), a description of a mid-1890s visit to a crushed, post-steel strike Homestead, Pennsylvania; and his 1894 *Toledo Blade* piece on a violent local railway strike. Not only does he draw on the beliefs informing the above pieces in the labor-protest section of *Sister Carrie*, but such journalism is crucial for a comprehension of why, for instance, Hurstwood is thrust into the era's real labor turmoil, albeit as a strikebreaker, and Carrie and Jennie are not.

In the labor writings noted above, Dreiser routinely laments the passivity of a lumpenproletariat and occasionally associates embattled working-class manhood with industrial anger. Most often he constructs a work world of men for whom his sympathy is diluted by a certain scorn. As a class-conscious "amateur" in this blue-collar world, he admires the skill involved in some of the most menial construction work. Yet he characterizes his fellow workers as "dull to the ordinary matters of importance in life."[2] He underscores the point in a portion of the manuscript later published in *McClure's* as "The Mighty Burke" (1911), in which he praises a foreman at the expense of his crew. Nor can he defend hands at a cotton sheeting plant—"these people are human beings" (177)—without maligning them as "hopeless inadequate to the task of living well" (176).[3] It is true that in "Three Sketches of the Poor" (1913), the socialistic Dreiser of the *New York Call* preaches to the converted that the baker's day is one of working hard for little. Yet, returning to a more characteristic stance in his "Transmigration of the Sweatshop" (1900), he finds a solution to labor exploitation in enlightened if paternalistic employers who design villages to "rid . . . industry of the smirch of the sweat shop" (499). Curiously, his *Cosmopolitan* piece on the female-fueled workplace bypasses work conditions entirely in favor of the fascinations of the mechanized assembly line.[4]

In his most extended journalistic sortie into a company town, Dreiser's unpublished Fall River essay pinions the mill workforce as "deadly poor in body and soul" ("Fall River," 5). The men and—described more cursorily, the women—depress him by their ill health, mechanical movements, and air of defeat. Cruder than the vulgar shoe-factory workforce that so repels Carrie Meeber, the population is reminiscent of Crane's bellicose Bowery, where drink, profanity, dirt, and family rows prevail. As a major Massachusetts textile town, Fall River was the site of much trade unionism among the more skilled weavers in the years prior to the Dreiser visit; yet he chose to visit the poorest tenement districts, where militance was less visible. There, as at the mills, he deplores the area's spineless workingmen. In the kind of bi-gender approach to workers that he employs in his two classic working-girl novels, he stresses how unattractive the workingwomen are. They are at best, in his important words, "shapeless" and "colorless" ("Fall River," 2). At their worst, they are "slatterns" (6).

Dreiser does give male proletarians respect when they rise up against an oppressive corporate structure. Visiting the Pennsylvania company town of Homestead two years after a momentous, if failed, strike against the Carnegie steel mills, he deplores the crushing defeat. Homestead was one of the most dramatic in a lengthy series of violent confrontations between business and the organized labor movement, and the defeat of the Amalgamated Association of Iron, Steel, and Tin Workers (AAISW) sent shock waves through the American Federation of Labor (AFL), forcing a new policy of pragmatic business unionism and marking relations in basic industry for a decade.[5] While Dreiser focuses on the lowest rung of workers affected by the strike rather than the skilled workers, he does ask whether a democratic nation can suppress its workforce, deny them decent wages, and, by implication, crush the union activity that was at the core of the Homestead experience.[6] Furthermore, he finds legitimate class rage in the violence of urban Ohio workers following the hiring of streetcar scabs. Interestingly, his *Toledo Blade* piece paints the union men in a positive light, downplaying the tumultuous nature of the protest and focusing on their inability to reclaim their jobs after the strike was settled.

As James L. W. West III notes, Dreiser could sympathize but not identify with workingmen (*SC* 1981: xxx). In *Sister Carrie*, this ambivalence about labor-class effectiveness complicates the portrait of an unwilling proletarian, Hurstwood. In the novel's revised strike scenes, the understandable anger of the Toledo protesters (and, notes Donald Pizer, that of Brooklyn streetcar workers who went on strike in 1895) is now blind, unreasoning fury, disturbing but powerful enough.[7] Yet the energetic wrath of the strikers only makes a scab more sympathetic. Dreiser's journalistic empathy for the played-out Homestead steelmen, who rose but to be crushed by the forces of Carnegie and Frick, is now displaced onto the strikebreaking Hurstwood, a fallen bourgeois morally superior to the working mass in general and Carrie's psychically shrunken brother-in-law, Hanson, in particular. Moreover, little of Dreiser's later compassion for the used-up Harlan County coal miners emerges in the martyrdom of the once-entrepreneurial Hurstwood. Rather, in the scab scenes the potentially anarchic anger of thwarted breadwinners coexists uneasily with the equally thwarted bourgeois individualism of Carrie's downwardly mobile lover. The very drama of Hurstwood's downward trajectory to mendicancy and suicide seems more filled with passion than the Fall Riverite loomworkers' listless anonymity.

Looking at Dreiser's work in the light of women's position in the turn-of-the-century workforce, though, his divided attitude toward collective protest against blue-collar passivity acquires a quite different meaning. In his two "fallen woman" novels that most directly protest inequitable wages and labor-class exploitation, feminine economic oppression, which was far greater than men's, fuels none of the real-life laborite rage evident, for example, among the decade's female textile, clothing trades, and shoe-stitching workers in upstate New York, in New England, or on the Lower East Side. The Fall River Young Ladies' Union of Spoolers, Warper-Tenders, and Drawing-in Girls, prominent in Fall River's 1889 and 1894 strikes, have no more part in his two novels than in his article on his visit there,[8] or than his 1906 *Broadway* magazine interview with firebrand Elizabeth Gurley Flynn in the eponymous *Jennie Gerhardt*, completed a few years after he met with Flynn.[9]

Dreiser knowingly chronicles the twined urban industrial dangers of women's sexual harassment or their dubious "escape" from sweated work through sexual favors to middle- or upper-class men. In his careful attention to the factual realities of salary, work conditions, restrictions, and social relations, as well as to Drouet, Hurstwood, and Lester Kane, men who pay for sex and live with women outside of wedlock, his novels provide fictive counterparts of key sections of Progressive-era documentary classics like the economist Elizabeth Beardsley Butler's *Women and the Trades: Pittsburgh, 1907–1908* (1909). That work appeared under the aegis of the ambitious Pittsburgh Survey, the first systematic effort in the United States to analyze industrial life, including the inequities of sex segregation. Butler's massive industrial study "virtually documented the absence of [non-sex-trade] occupational mobility among wage-earning women" in an early-twentieth-century city comparable to Chicago and New York.[10] Her ambitious examination ranges from scrutinizing the physical characteristics of factories to detailing the laundress's tasks, the sexual division of labor in leading industries, and the health conditions of workingwomen, all subjects treated in the Dreiser novels, taken together. Butler matter-of-factly provides many capsule case histories of women who bartered sexual services for the possibility of ascension. Butler includes her own "Jennie," a small-town Akron girl unable to ascend as a Pittsburgh salesgirl, who "consented to be kept in an apartment" (306). A number of her other subjects even send money home from their new jobs in houses of prostitution (304–6).

What is implicit in Butler is explicit in Dreiser, for he mounts a situational ethics argument that all but transforms the sexual "falls" of Carrie Meeber and Jennie Gerhardt into self-protective feminine economic activity. Yet in a symbolic attempt to shield the labor-class woman from another form of cultural behavior deemed unfeminine, he removes working-class womanhood from the labor fray, and thus from the possibility of a political culture with feminine institutions and networks.

It could certainly be argued that laboring women's actual militance prior to the Depression era was circumscribed indeed, though there was an added erasure of such protest by both the wider culture and unenlightened male trade unionists. Yet the years roughly between the publication of *Sister Carrie* and *Jennie Gerhardt* saw a period in American labor history in which more women engaged in or spearheaded strikes than at any earlier time. However, only three percent of working women, at most, actually belonged to unions, owing in part to discouragement from male trade unionists fearful of female competition for jobs. Certainly those women who were active were visibly so. In 1903, a few years before Dreiser interviewed Flynn, 35,000 women marched in the Labor Day parade in Chicago—the city where the task of organizing women was taken up more successfully than in any other American city, and where large portions of *Jennie Gerhardt*, which ignored events of this nature, were set. Also in 1903, the Women's Trade Union League, the first national body dedicated to organizing women workers, began its operations in Chicago and New York. Between 1905 and 1915, 100,000 women in the clothing factories of those cities joined workers in Philadelphia, Rochester, and Cleveland and walked off their jobs. Massachusetts textile workers, San Francisco tobacco strippers, Boston telephone operators, and collar starchers in Troy, New York, all agitated for improved working conditions in the face of, at best, lukewarm AFL support and a publics perception of them as the most unwomanly of women.[11]

Carrie Meeber's experiences among female sewing machine operators in a Chicago shoe factory mirror those of the women who created political cultures out of sweatshop toil. But her response to these experiences reasserts Dreiser's need to gentrify her in order to justify her presence in the workplace. From the moment she enters that sex-segregated work site—the skilled male workers are spatially separated from the unskilled females—Dreiser focuses on her revulsion at the "common" women (*SC* 1981: 53) she meets there. To her eyes, they are too familiar with the men, who joke and even touch them playfully. Indeed, these implicitly promiscuous women realize the period's worst fears about the workplace, for they are "free with the fellows . . . and [exchange] banter in rude phrases which at first shocked her" (53). Certainly their manners and language are worlds away from her own, as Dreiser is at pains to emphasize. He deplores the fact that the workmate at her right speaks to Carrie "without any form of introduction" (37). Through the bad grammar of the girl at her left, also unnamed, he suggests that she too is vulgar and uncouth. The implication is that these girls are members of an army of women, not worth dignifying by name, who inhabit a verbal world characterized by questions like "Say . . . what jeh think he said?" (38). Sexual innuendo and the rowdy giggling with which it is received further brand Carrie's work peers as part of a community of women she does not wish to join. Dreiser summarizes Carrie's response sympathetically: she "felt bad to have to listen to the girl next to her, who was slangy and rather hardened by experience" (53).

Had Carrie met these women's overtures of friendliness with anything more than aloofness, they might well have included her in the jaunts to dance halls and saloons of which they gossiped and which, as Kathy Peiss tells us in *Cheap Amusements*, their real-life counterparts certainly frequented (89–93). Insisting on her separateness from the brazen workplace women, who personify something "hard and low" (*SC* 1981: 40), he casts her as a princess among the serfs.

Even if he makes no link to reactive trade unionism, Dreiser is too much the realist to deny that these women's behavior is an adaptation to the grueling conditions of the workplace. Acknowledging that "[n]ot the slightest provision had been made for the comfort of the employés" (*SC* 1981: 39), Dreiser suggests that the women, routinely addressed by the foreman as "you," must endlessly repeat mechanical movements in a stifling atmosphere at a pace directed by the owner. Dreiser's observation that the work speed turned men and women alike into "clattering automatons" (36)—a term he uses for the machines of Fall River, incidentally—is borne out by autobiographies by garment-trades women such as Elisabeth Hasanovitz and Rose Cohen.

As in many actual factories of the period, the women are used routinely to train apprentices like Carrie, an assignment that takes unpaid time from their own work; they are also denied access to skilled "men's jobs" and treated rudely by bosses and male workers. They are even forbidden to talk on the job because it was believed to lower feminine productivity. Given this dehumanizing taboo against conversing, like their real-life counterparts, they band together to circumvent both ruling and punishment by talking animatedly about their recreational activities and warning one another when the foreman is in listening range. Their work culture, as described by one modern historian of women's work, this fashion, "organize[s] workroom social life around the interests and experiences shared by most young women."[12] Although part of his scorned the low intellectual level on which these women functioned, Dreiser knew that such gossip reflected the interests of young working-women. When in a reminiscence he recalled his own sisters, who worked in low-paying jobs in Chicago in the 1880s, he said they talked constantly of "[c]lothes and men."[13]

Furthermore, if the shoe factory women are attuned to the sexuality of their male coworkers' familiarities, much like the rather wayward Dreiser girls themselves, they also exemplify a consideration for one another, including newcomers like Carrie. The historian Leslie Tentler finds in the turn-of-the-century feminine workplace countless instances of a "supportive work group . . . embodying an oblique protest" (66) against the demands of incessant productivity. So too among the women Carrie encounters. The very girl whom Dreiser brands as unmannerly for not introducing herself also gives Carrie tips on conserving her energy for the afternoon's sewing. All try to slow up their work so that the inexperienced new girl can better learn her machine. And they try to initiate her into workplace mores. "Don't you mind. . . . He's too fresh" (*SC* 1981: 40), one says to comfort her when a young man prods a mortified Carrie in the ribs.

Yet in the end Dreiser still buries the issue of their hard, unremunerative work by decoupling women and work. He uses the providential male rescue to separate his atypical shop girl from the toughened types who try to befriend her. Carrie, it is true, is not able to marry the free-wheeling Drouet, and Hurstwood's union with her, though she cultivates ignorance about it, is a bigamous one. But unlike the average lower-class woman of the time, who could expect to work seven years before marriage, Carrie enters a series of semimarital relationships that provide her with much greater economic and emotional rewards than a Hanson for a mate.

Carrie's male protector, however, is not the final resolution of her problems. First one man then another supports her financially. But by encouraging her early attempts at acting and not meeting her needs or insuring her security, both plant the seeds of interest in a career. Her fairly rapid rise to theater fame and financial independence is both her escape from working-girl status and the moral compromises that tarnish her for middlebrow audiences. Even her new work has little to do with the shoe-factory drudges of her erasable past. No arduous climb that involves learning her craft or engaging in endless chorus-line work, Carrie's overnight success is that lucky accident, largely independent of her own efforts, for which she had wished. For, having left Hurstwood and returned to the ranks of wage earners, Carrie does not really reenter the workforce. Just as when she left the vulgar women of the shoe factory, Dreiser undercuts her identity as a working girl. Indeed, given his prejudice against unchaste workingwomen, his refusal to include Carrie, "fallen" or not, in that morally suspect group is a way of defending her innate purity. Sheldon Grebstein, analyzing Carrie's sexual relationships, argues convincingly that Dreiser sanitizes her by playing on associations with "innocence, purity and helplessness" (545). Thus, Dreiser depicts a Carrie, ever demure and wistful, who "sins chastely" (551), quite unlike the brazen women of the city workplace.

A decade later, Dreiser again quickly removed a labor heroine from a worker's life and a Flynn-like militancy. To do so, *Jennie Gerhardt* chronicles a cross-class love affair in which a toiling protagonist, remarkable for beauty and family self-sacrifice, escapes waged work through rescue by a romantic capitalist. In many ways, Dreiser offers the same fairy tale as do the more conservative authors of female labor novels of the 1900s, which replaced the tenement story as the favored working-girl fiction of middlebrow audiences. Unlike these writers, Dreiser criticizes the snobbery that prevents Jennie from marrying Lester Kane. Yet if the plutocratic Lester is unwilling to marry a working woman, Dreiser, ever protective of his heroines, demonstrates his own kind of condescension toward laboring women: he is reluctant to permit his heroine even a transient identification with consciousness of her class situation, and thus with workers' militance.

As early as 1906, laundresses in San Francisco, rebelling against their notoriously ill-paid work, successfully struck for overtime and reduction of the workweek (Foner, 309). Although their striking counterparts in other cities, such as New York, were less successful, the image of the militant laundress had established itself to a certain extent. So, by the time of *Jennie Gerhardt*, had the woman who sewed the clothes that a Senator Brander might send for Jennie to launder. Addressing readers for whom Dreiser himself sometimes wrote, Theresa Serber Malkiel's *Diary of a Shirtwaist Striker* (1910), first serialized in the 1910 *New York Call*, acquainted that audience with the convictions fueling Uprising of the 20,000, as the 1909–10 New York City Shirtwaist Strike was called: "[W]orking people won't be ground to dust much longer. . . . [T]heir ever rising fury is bound to break out any day" (204–5).

Dreiser's vision of the female worker, in contrast, is one of complete self-containment. He keeps her from contact with women in the trade, dissatisfied or otherwise. To demonstrate her probity (and thus bolstering his defense of her later dealings with Senator Brander and Lester Kane), Dreiser focuses on Jennie's gratitude for the work. Historian Meredith Tax observes that immigrant and first-generation women often expressed appreciation for the most wretched sweatshop work, comparing it with the poverty of their European lives (28–29). But in distinct contrast to the unreflective Jennie, these women at least had a work consciousness, a sense of what Tax calls "their money-earning capacity" (29). Furthermore, by the second decade of the twentieth century, these were the women who would transform passive gratitude into solidarity and even revolt.

When, early in *Jennie Gerhardt*, Dreiser comments that his title character is too beautiful to have to work with her hands, he both reflects the curiously antilabor bias of the labor romance and demonstrates the impulse to protect his working heroine that characterizes *Sister Carrie*. Like Carrie, Jennie enters the world of work as if she had just come to the city. Both are vulnerable—unused to the splendor of urban places patronized by the affluent, given to blushing when interested men stare, and easily manipulated by ostentatiously successful men who act kindly and press money into their hands. But in his later novel Dreiser seems even less interested in locating his heroine in a work milieu. Though the Gerhardt women are city dwellers at least seasoned enough to take on cleaning work outside the home at an opulent Columbus hotel, Jennie soon settles for piecework at home, a throwback to women's tasks in the domestic economy of a preindustrial age. She apparently does not think to seek permanent wage-earning work as a hotel laundress. Women routinely held such full-time jobs in large urban centers, as Dreiser, a laundry-wagon driver attracted by the women he worked with in 1890s Chicago, well knew.[14] But his very awareness of the public perception of these women may have prompted him to keep Jennie apart from them.

In her study of laundresses in nineteenth-century French culture, Eunice Lipton argues that middle-class culture insisted on seeing such women "in exclusively sexual . . . terms" (302). The fantasy, which bore some relation to reality, was that women who worked in intense heat in semiclothed conditions, who reinforced each other's need for alcohol to cope with their work, and who delivered men's garments to them in their rooms, were among the most immoral of the female working class. In 1904, Dorothy Richardson, who worked for a time in a New York laundry, gave a less racy description of American laundresses, but one that emphasized their slovenliness, their love of drink, and, to her unsympathetic eyes, a work culture characterized by slang, shouting, and complaints (229–49).

Although he uses Jennie's laundry work as a symbol of the fate of unskilled, impoverished women like her mother and herself, Dreiser censors Jennie's involvement in it. He does not even give it the few pages of description allotted to Carrie's shoe-factory labors. Rather than dignifying Jennie's work, her creator almost calls up the fantasy of the sexually available laundress. To soften the harsh truth that, to make any money, Jennie has only herself to sell, Dreiser emphasizes that she is "barren of the art of the coquette."[15] She does not "fully understand [Senator Brander's] meaning" (37) when he proposes a liaison, and though she accepts his proposal, "enjoy[s] it all innocently" (43)—the second of Dreiser's chaste Chicago sinners.

The dominant late-Victorian trope of the sexually vulnerable woman needing protection against a predatory economic world and her own frailties generated images of deserted streetwalkers in the works of writers even less involved in labor issues than Dreiser, such as Crane's title character in *Maggie* and Frank Norris's Trina in *McTeague* (1899). Lacking male protectors, these working-class women die, it could be argued, of carnal knowledge. (Trina's greed and masochistic sexuality are frequently linked in the Norris text.) Yet whether they perish or, like Carrie and Jennie, endure and ascend, immersion in what the labor historian Francis Couvares calls the "plebeian sea" of worker culture is denied them (36).

Given the real but circumscribed feminine working-class protest during the 1890s and early 1900s, Dreiser's placement of men only in the dialectic between collectivity and competitive individualism compromises the otherwise ardent defense of breadwinning womanhood at the core of *Sister Carrie* and *Jennie Gerhardt*. Consciously or not, he distances himself from what the new labor historians term "woman's work culture," the workingwoman's response both to her female peers and her employer's rules and strictures.[16] Divided between compassion for and condescension toward the typical working woman, between locating their heroines in the feminine workplace and rescuing them from its coarsening influence, Dreiser's novels illustrate his ambivalence about wage-earning women. He has a profound vision of the economic, social, and psychological forces shaping them. But like the sentimental slum tales and romantic labor novels that "explained" working women to middle-class America, Dreiser's fiction draws back from exploring the feminine work experience. If to a certain extent he transcends such fiction, he also shares the prejudices that permeate it. The shelter from female proletarianism he offers is removal from both the industrial working class and the labor movement that rose to defend its interests.

Notes

1. Dreiser, "The Literary Shower," *Ev'ry Month* (February 1, 1896): 10.
2. Dreiser, *An Amateur Laborer*, 1904, ed. Richard W. Dowell and James L. W. West III, 117.
3. Dreiser, "The Factory," 1910, rpt. in *Theodore Dreiser: A Selection of Uncollected Prose*, ed. Donald Pizer, 175–80.
4. Dreiser, "Scenes in a Cartridge Factory," 322.

5. Ronald L. Filippelli, "Homestead Strike," in *Labor Conflict in the United States: An Encyclopedia*, ed. Filippelli, 241.

6. Dreiser, *Newspaper Days*, ed. T. D. Nostwich, 500.

7. Donald Pizer, "The Strike," in *Sister Carrie*, ed. Pizer (New York: Norton, 1970), 416.

8. Filippelli, "Fall River Textile Strikes," in *Labor Conflict*, 176–77.

9. Hapke, *Tales of the Working Girl: Wage-Earning Women in American Literature, 1890–1925*, 88.

10. Maurine Weiner Greenwald, "Introduction: Women at Work through the Eyes of Elizabeth Beardsley Butler and Lewis Hine," in Butler, *Women and the Trades: Pittsburgh, 1907–1908*, ix.

11. See Philip S. Foner, *Women and the American Labor Movement from Colonial Times to the Eve of World War I*, ch. 17; and Meredith Tax, *The Rising of the Women: Feminist Solidarity and Class Conflict, 1880–1917*, ch. 1.

12. Leslie Woodcock Tentler, *Wage-Earning Women: Industrial Work and Family Life in the United States, 1900–1930*, 69.

13. Dreiser, *Dawn*, 69.

14. Richard Lingeman, *Theodore Dreiser: At the Gates of the City, 1871–1907*, 86.

15. *Jennie Gerhardt*, 1911, (New York: Penguin, 1989), 35.

16. Patricia A. Cooper, *Once a Cigar Maker: Men, Women, and Work Culture in American Cigar Factories, 1900–1919*, 2.

Working Out to Work Through: Dreiser in Muldoon's Body Shop of Shame

KATHY FREDERICKSON

IF FRANK COWPERWOOD IS DREISER'S "INCARNATION OF THE LIFE FORCE,"[1] William Muldoon is its maintenance man. The Ur-man of Dreiser's narrative was a figure of a popular 1870s ditty: "Go with me and I'll trate [sic] you decent. / I'll set you drunk and I'll fill the can. / As I walk the street, each friend I meet / Says: 'There goes Muldoon, he's a solid man' " that Muldoon's biographer provides in his 1928 text.[2] But this "solid man" who values spirits and animated conviviality (if, in fact, the "I" pronoun is read as Muldoon's own self-referentiality) seems hardly the same "solid man" of Dreiser's text. The historical Muldoon (1845–1933), a he-man of Arnold Schwarzeneggerian body building, subject of Dreiser's "Muldoon, the Solid Man," was a champion wrestler and professional health manager who acquired the sobriquet and image of "solid man" for his athletic prowess while an 1876 member of New York City's Police Department. But since his "real life work was the operation of an establishment of physical hygiene" (Van Every, 83–84), he opened a paramilitary sanatorium, "Olympia," three miles north of White Plains, New York in 1900 to a clientele of unfit and neurasthenic men, and Dreiser is supposed to have stayed from 21 April to 2 June 1903.[3]

Robert Coltrane notes that Dreiser's first account of his stay at Muldoon's institute appeared as a sketch entitled "Scared Back to Nature" published 16 May 1903 in *Harper's Weekly*. In 1904, Dreiser again chronicled his experience in *An Amateur Laborer*, which Tom Lutz calls "an autobiographical novel" (38), but the 1919 sketch disguised the identity of his subject, since Muldoon was still alive, and renamed him "Culhane, the Solid Man" in *Twelve Men*, published by Boni and Liveright, April 1919. Though Coltrane acknowledges that criticism of *Twelve Men* is scant,[4] the 1919 collection was not, according to Richard Lingeman, "the big novel [Dreiser's] publisher was hoping for, but it was vintage Dreiser . . . a return to his earlier style and to turn-of-the-century America . . . [with Muldoon portrayed] as a . . . likable character, whose gruff, bullying ways mark the benevolent heart of a healer'' (Lingeman, 174). Van Every's biography supports Lingeman's summation and offers abundant anecdotal evidence of Muldoon's tough but humane treatment of clients. He assists, for example, a young clerk, a ''poor little sickly shrimp of a chap from Georgia.'' Lacking the funds to invest in a six-week stay at the institute, the young man is not only allowed to remain, but is not charged. Having received a check sent from his employers to cover the cost of treatment, Muldoon insists the young man take it instead (Van Every, 290).

Though ''vividly drawn,'' Dreiser's profile, Van Every writes, ''was inaccurate . . . no one can know [Muldoon] at all intimately and make out the virility of the man as uncouth . . . as has been the case in the Dreiser article, which is so resented by the friends of Muldoon'' (26). Having been advised by others of Dreiser's alleged misrepresentations, Muldoon had not bothered to read the piece. Van Every quotes Muldoon's response to Dreiser:

> Paul [Dreiser/Dresser] spoke to me about his half-brother [sic], Theodore, and how the latter might have in him the makings of a genius. Paul asked me to take his brother up to my place and I agreed. The morning after his arrival Theodore Dreiser came to me and secured permission to return to New York for the purpose of bringing back some additional clothing. He never came back. Just one night was all he could stand. So that is as far as his study of myself, my place and my system went in his personal observation. And yet in his article . . . he deliberately sets out to give the reader the impression that he has endured all of the hardships (such as they are) of my course through its entire six weeks (265–66).

It is not my intention to interrogate contesting accounts of either Dreiserian biography or Dreiserian mimesis,[5] but rather to explore his representation of remasculinization as process and performance, particularly as it is conjoined with the function of shame—shame that is not so much a neurotic affliction as a generator of transformative self construction, or as Carl Schneider describes it, ''a guide to a more authentic form of self-realization.''[6] As a participatory observer or an ''observant outsider'' to use Neda Westlake's label (*AAL* viii), Dreiser creates a text, or a work(out), that enables a renarrativization of the spectacle of the male body. What may be the source of the ''convincing characterization'' Nostwich finds in *all* of Dreiser's short fiction and semi-fictional ''tales'' is in ''Muldoon, the Solid Man,'' the author's (and his contemporary readers') fascination with Muldoon's ability to recreate men and manliness. Like Twain's Hank Morgan, Muldoon runs a man-making factory where he ''turn[s] groping and grubbing automata into *men* . . .''[7] Like the frontier Frederick Jackson Turner celebrates for its dialectical role in remasculinization/Americanization—the individual man "transforms the wilderness" only after, David Leverenz reminds us, "the wilderness has transformed him"—Muldoon's institute is a "crucible of man-making."[8]

Several turn-of-the-twentieth-century discursive fields intersect in "Muldoon, the Solid Man"—the rhetoric of neurasthenia, of nativism and nationalism, of fraternalism and brotherhood, and of Rooseveltian strenuosity, what critics have dubbed the "cult of masculinity," or "virility impulse"[9]—but the supporting axis which all ideological formations adhere to is a psychosocial dynamic that hinges on shame and shame anxiety. Muldoon's theater of the male body creates what Bette London calls "the structure of spectacle,"[10] and in each client's participation in the intensely regimented physical shape-up plan, "the Muldoon system" as Van Every calls it, is also a mandatory public exposure of weakness, inadequacy, failure. Repairing the physically weakened male body reinscribes and is underwritten by a concomitant act of collective reparation.[11] Muldoon forces his clients to transform personal irresponsibility—"[t]hey had no understanding of the most important of their possessions, their bodies" (351)—into social responsibility. His institute is a site for the psychosocial mechanism of restoration: individual bodily transformation is a compensatory action mandated by an ideology of adherence to a collective identification of performatively constructed American white manhood. As a cultural worker, Muldoon participates in contemporary health reform activism[12] that capitalizes on consumers' shame of corporeal lack that precipitates secondary shame, feeling ashamed of shame.

The opening sentence of "Muldoon, the Solid Man" links the physical and the psychological: Dreiser writes, "I met him in connection with a psychic depression which only partially reflected itself in my physical condition" (341). In need of a curative for both body *and* mind, Dreiser claims to have invested $600 for six weeks' stay at Muldoon's "repair shop" expecting to restore waning strength and fitness as well as rejuvenate a compatible ego ideal. The second sentence, "I might almost say that I was sick spiritually" (341–42), repeats the neurasthenia theme but also suggests another link between the spiritual and social: Dreiser is ashamed. He knew first hand the pain of failed material and social fulfillment. Critics have chronicled his severely debilitating emotional collapse following the market failure of *Sister Carrie*, published in 1900, and the abandonment of *Jennie Gerhardt* during the winter of 1902 and Dreiser himself relates his neurasthenic experience a year later in *An Amateur Laborer*. So too does *The "Genius"* (1915), considered the "most autobiographical of the novels," record protagonist Eugene Witla's nervous collapse and recovery through physical labor.[13] As far back as 1899, Dreiser felt qualms and embarrassment over his ability to write short fiction. Joseph Griffin quotes Dreiser to Mencken: "And after every paragraph I blushed for my folly—it seemed so asinine. [Arthur Henry] insisted on my going on . . . and I thought he was kidding me, that it was rotten. . . ."[14] His trials in the literary arena activated his deep fears of personal and professional failure, of humiliation, of shame, what Gershen Kaufman calls "a sickness of the soul."[15]

It is the third sentence of "Muldoon, the Solid Man," though, that further reveals Dreiser's disillusionment and despair for what it really is, shame: "At the same time I was rather strongly imbued with a contempt for [Muldoon] and his cure" (341). Contempt wards off fear of being considered contempt*ible* (and abandoned). According to William Morrison, contempt is a displaced manifestation of shame, an "attempt to 'relocate' the shame experience from within the self into another person and . . . attempt to rid the self of shame" (14). Leon Wurmser labels this action of shielding against internalized shame as "reexternalization," a means of "turn[ing] shame from a passive experience of humiliation into the active form of humiliating others" (46–47).[16] Dreiser's disavowal tries to make Muldoon a "container" by focusing on Muldoon's working class origin, but Muldoon counterprojects and, in what Richard Dowell calls "savage attacks" ("Introduction," *AAL* xxi), mercilessly shames all of his clients. Clients arrive, like Dreiser, with the intent to restore self, but also to conceal from the public gaze their neurasthenic bodies, to render invisible from the public sphere the private work of solidifying softness.

The current literature on shame, rapidly filling a gap created by the scarcity of its treatment in psychoanalytic literature—Robert Karen calls shame "psychology's stepchild"[17]—stresses both the inter- and intrapsychic features of shame and its affects. A bedrock text, *Shame and Guilt: A Psychoanalytic and a Cultural Study* by Piers and Singer, published in 1953, posits the paradigmatic conceptualization of the shame/guilt differentiation elaborated upon twenty years later by Helen B. Lewis in her landmark book *Shame and Guilt in Neurosis* and by others in the 70s.[18] Piers and Singer see shame as originating in the tension between ego and ego ideal, not between ego and superego, which they see as characteristic of guilt. "Whereas guilt is generated whenever a boundary (set by the superego) is touched or transgressed," Piers writes, "shame occurs when a goal (presented by the ego ideal) is not being reached. It thus indicates a real 'shortcoming.' Guilt anxiety accompanies transgression; shame, failure" (24).

Helen B. Lewis notes that "shame is about the self" (passim) and her discussion of the "shame family" (humiliation, chagrin, mortification, ridicule, dishonor, and embarrassment, which overlap with Wurmser's list of affective states to include "embarrassment, shyness, humiliation, inferiority feelings and low self-esteem, a sense of degradation, and narcissistic mortification" [*The Mask*, 51]) stresses the interactive nature of shame. Kaufman, in agreement, writes, "Interpersonally induced shame develops into internally induced shame" (7). Theorists discuss ideals and identification: failing to live up to beloved ideals, being discovered as something other than what we wish to be provoked shame. Which is not to say shame functions only in limiting or repressive ways. Carl Schneider believes "[S]hame raises consciousness" and "[T]o extirpate shame is to cripple our humanity."[19]

Muldoon makes his fortune subscribing to that notion and his primary modality for instigating clients' self-objectification and defensive maneuvers is sight, and through sight, vision. Vision, writes Francis Broucek, is "informed seeing that penetrates mere appearance"[20] and Muldoon masters the *look* of the Other.[21] Gary Thrane reminds us that shame "dwells in the eye"[22] and Leon Wurmser that "the eye is the organ of shame par excellence," that "[L]ove and power are vested in the gaze; but that also means that there will be exposure and rejection because of this 'hungry look' and this 'craving eye' " (*The Mask*, 84, 94). Muldoon's objectifying gaze, which the men try to hide from—Dreiser's medicine ball partner says most pathetically, "Come on, let's play fast so he won't notice us" (350),—establishes a scopic economy of shame and shame anxiety.[23] Shames's aim is "disappearance," Wursmer notes (*The Mask*, 84), but clients have no refuge from Muldoon's watchful eye. Who looks exerts power over those looked *at* and those gazed upon cannot question the authority of the gazer: "It is impossible to see the eye that is seeing."[24] Theorists agree that shame, though afflicting an individual possibly independently of social context, usually involves exposure of a self believed to be defective in some way. The affect is usually global—R. D. Laing calls it an "implosion" of the self (qtd. in Lewis, 37)—and the autonomic response of blushing, bowing head, wishing to flee is often accompanied by averted eyes.

Muldoon is impossible to escape and his omnipresent roving eye, creating what Lewis might call "shame ideation"[25] has its vantage point everywhere, even in the dining quarters. The social aspect of sharing meals is all but removed and the men are reduced to a mechanical function; neither can food be used as a defense against shame. Since Muldoon has full control over what he considers calorically correct dietary consumption, the men cannot indulge themselves, cannot "counter-devour" his "devouring" looks, nor can they hide their oral anxieties. The "all but drooling creatures" are constantly denigrated as "poor, fallible, shabby, petty" (369). Dreiser experiences first hand a scathing put down when Muldoon discovers Dreiser and his tablemate have exchanged potato portions. Ever aware of his "steely-eyed host" (346), Dreiser had suggested to his colleague, "He isn't always looking, and we can fix it. You mash up your big potato and put butter and salt on it, and I'll do the same with my little one. Then when he's not looking we'll shift" (372). Muldoon's derisive response globalizes the transgression into a self entirely flawed:

> "This big boob here" (he was referring to my esteemed self) "who hasn't strength of will or character enough to keep himself in good health and has to be brought up here by his brother, hasn't brains enough to see that when I plan a thing for his benefit it is for his benefit, and not mine. Like most of the other damned fools that come up here and waste their money and my time, he thinks I'm playing some cute game with him—tag or something that will let him show how much cuter he is than I am. And he's supposed to be a writer and have a little horse-sense! His brother claims it, anyhow. And as for this other simp here," and now he was addressing the assembled diners while nodding toward my friend, "it hasn't been three weeks since he was begging to know what I could do for him. And now look at him—entering into a petty little game of potato-cheating!" (372–73)

And to the client who refuses to eat carrots Muldoon clarifies the distinction between inside/outside selves. Within the boundary lines of Muldoon's sanatorium, one is subjected to his rules and fiats: "No, not outside perhaps, but here you do. You eat carrots here, see?" (371). His tag question, "see?" further reinforces the link between the always-in-play dynamic of seeing/exposing/understanding/understanding one is seen and exposed.

Muldoon presides over a "small private table, which stood in the center of the dining room and far apart from the others" (356). Strategically placed, "eyeing [clients] with a look of infinite and weary contempt" (360), he literalizes the function of Jeremy Bentham's Panopticon: his observation post creates the surveillance system Foucault describes in *Discipline and Punish: The Birth of the Prison*. His chapter, "Panopticism," elaborates on the prison model which employs a central tower and "arranges spatial unities that make it possible to see constantly and recognize immediately"; such an architectural apparatus reverses two functions of the dungeon—deprivation both of light and of refuge—to create a mode of discipline that relies not on external authority, but on internalized restraints, constraints, and norms.[26] Though Bentham's supervisor remains invisible to the inmates, Muldoon is *on* exhibit, forcing clients *to* exhibit/ expose their "puffy, gelatinous" (368) bodies which Muldoon singles out one at a time because he "could not resist the temptation to make a show of [each], to picture him as the more or less pathetic example that he was, in order perhaps that he,

Muldoon, might shine by contrast" (356). Forced visibility in the dining quarters denies clients any escape from the loss of face created by the face-to-face encounter with Muldoon that targets and exposes each man's oral anxiety and lack of bodily integrity. Each client becomes, like the inmates Foucault describes, "the object of information, never a subject in communication" ("Panopticism," 200).

Destabilizing customers' socially constructed gendered identities, Muldoon violates their self-images: They "were all children, weaklings, failures, numbskulls, no matter what they might be in the world outside" (351). Divested of the "best of clothes, . . . cars, servants, city and country houses perhaps, their factories, employees, institutions . . . [they were] as lymphatic and flabby as oysters without their shells, myself included. It was really painful" (348). Daily harangues, what Dreiser calls "table speeches" (364), on what Muldoon perceives as the evils of professional occupations target perfomatively constituted identity as masquerade.[27] Muldoon recognizes no vocation, validates no occupation held by a man whose body is, at its core, still in a "baby-class" (361): "You call yourself an editor! Why you couldn't edit a handbill! You can't even throw a ball straight!" (348). Lawyers, Muldoon assumes, are "little more than sharper crooks than the crooks they have to deal with" (368). Merchants, he believes, suffer from middle-class conformity: "And then when they're just like everyone else, they think they're somebody" (369–70). But doctors he can barely tolerate since they "came to steal his theory and start a shabby grafting sanitarium of their own. He knew them" (370). Victims of generalized degradation, the speechless men would "gaze at [their] plate[s] or out the window" (368) oppressed by the wordless state the shamer induces for the shamed.

Insults directed to specific individuals are just as wounding. Dreiser experiences acute anticipatory shame thinking he may singled out by Muldoon: "I was fairly stirred up as to the probabilities of the situation. He might call me!" But escape can be only a temporary respite. Dreiser falls to the floor during an exercise and is sent "drooping back to the sidelines to recover while [Muldoon] tortured someone else. But the names he called me! The comments on my none too smoothly articulated bones—and my alleged mind! As in my schooldays when, a laggard in the fierce and seemingly malevolent atmosphere in which I was taught my A B C's, I crept shamefacedly and beaten from the scene" (350). Acknowledging shame allows Dreiser and others to avoid becoming completely engulfed by Muldoon's persecutory tactics. Eliciting what Robert Karen calls "situational shame" (58) is here a temporary strategy to expose and repair individual weakness and thus enforce adherence to a collective strength and strength of character. After all,

Muldoon is trying not to debilitate men but renew them. And he succeeds.

For six weeks Muldoon's "guests" agree to allow themselves to be objects in a paradoxical attempt to eliminate the shame of objectification. Muldoon's presence mirrors the absence of his clients' self control and further incites their narcissistic identification—on two levels. Shame evokes some "restitution within the domain of the self, some narcissistic affirmation," (Lewis, 89), the hope that they can remake their bodies and emulate Muldoon. Secondly, they must repress any homoeroticism and thereby bypass the shame of homosexual panic.[28] What is on the face of things a fraternal organization/club, and bears some resemblance, albeit limited and inverted, to the secret ritual described by Mark Carnes,[29] is both a homosocial and homo-*nonsocial* gathering of men whose leader is trying to produce men fit enough to contribute to and benefit from homosocial arrangements. Dreiser is awed by both Muldoon's "lithe and lion-like," perfectly sculpted displayed body, his bared chest (348) and by the lack of such muscular definition in himself and his colleagues. Muldoon's ageless, sixty-year-old, flawless, *whole* body, "that mount of brawn" (348) stands in stark contrast to his clients' defective impoverished grotesque body *parts*: Dreiser sees assembled in the gym, "[t]he leanness! the osseosity! the grandiloquent whiskers parted in the middle! the mustachios! the goatees! the fat, Hoti-like stomachs! the protuberant knees! the thin arms!" (347).

That clients are "obviously drawn" to Muldoon because "there was something about him which *gave* [them] *confidence*" attests to both his image of unconflicted man-beast and his ability, his "iron power" to push his clients to new levels of physical achievement. Their performance anxiety (Broucek claims performance anxiety, in general, is more accurately viewed as shame anxiety [70]) is always high, and, often, like the distraught manufacturer who complains that his heart "flutter[s] so" as he jogs, but is ordered to carry on, men aren't sure whether to be "overawed or reassured" (362). Intrigued by and attracted to Muldoon, Dreiser, as spokesman for his peer, is willing to idealize Muldoon and confer upon him a new world-historical status:

> It was a blazing material world of which he was the center, the sun, and yet always I had the sense of very great life. With no knowledge of or interest in the superior mental sciences or arts or philosophies, still he seemed to suggest and even live them. He was in his way an exemplification of that ancient Greek regimen and stark thought which brought back the Ten Thousand from Cunaxa. He seemed even to suggest in his rough way historical perspective and balance. He knew men, and apparently he sensed how at best and at bottom life was to be lived. (362–63)

According to Wurmser, "[I]dealization is a device to endow the object with that omnipotence that the [individual] wants to possess himself and in which he hopes to partake. It is perhaps the most widespread and resilient defense against nagging envy" (*The Mask*, 64). Dreiser's wish to recast Muldoon from the humiliating personal trainer into cultural hero confirms not only the interplay of the individual and the social nexus, but also Dreiser's need/desire for authorship; he authorizes Muldoon's popular image and inverts the act of concealment. Having been objectified by Muldoon's violating gaze, he can now, in composing the portrait, position himself as subject and (re)create his "screen memories." His meaning-making narrative, as both reaction and drive, brings closure to the experience and affords him some mastery over it by (re)-perceiving/(re)seeing its linear evolution and situating its personal significance in a social context.

Appended to the short story are two reflections spaced two years apart. In the first, Dreiser claims to have been passing through the New York area and desired "to see my liege once more and also to learn whether he would remember me at all," to "have a look at him once more, great lion that he was" (381). Dreiser's wish to *see* Muldoon reflects his underlying desire to *be seen* by Muldoon and to be, this time, not a "humble [slave]" (381) but a validated subject. Sitting in a green and white striped marquee tent, Muldoon reminds Dreiser of a "latter-day Stoic and Spartan in his tent" (382); the connotations too of both field-officer *and* circus performer contribute to the sense of spectacle that "fascinate[s]" Dreiser so (382). Treated "as courteously and formally as though he had never browbeaten me in the least" (382), Dreiser feels ego-enriched by Muldoon's courteous demeanor and notes Muldoon's reading selection, Lecky's *History of European Morals*, a text which concerns not the physical, but the abstract. Dreiser's response, "Now! Well!" (382) indicates a new appreciation for what may be, to Dreiser, proof of a more complex Muldoonian weltanschauung than Dreiser had imagined. That surprise is, two years later, in an attempt "to set down what I really did think of him" (382), transformed into an understanding that Muldoon's mission is moral and reformist. As Dreiser sees it, what partially constitutes Muldoon's effectiveness is his radical separatism:

> As the Church and society view Muldoon, so they view all life outside their own immediate circles. Muldoon is in fact a conspicuous figure among the semi-taboo. He has been referred to in many an argument and platform and pulpit and in the press as a type of man whose influence is supposed to be vitiating. Now a minister enters the sanatorium, broken down by his habits of life, and this same Muldoon is able to penetrate him, to see that his dog-

> matic and dictatorial mental habits are the cause of his ailment, and he has the moral courage to shock him, to drag him by the apparently brutal processes out of his rut. He reads the man accurately, he knows him better than he knows himself, and he effects a cure. (383)

According to Muldoon, a man's body should be dominated by his will and become the *em*bodiment of self-discipline, self-control and self-reliance. While the turn of twentieth century saw some relaxation in the ideology of a "spermatic economy"—the idea of a closed-energy system that considered nonreproductive intercourse wasteful and potentially debilitating—Muldoon recalls nineteenth-century admonitory discourse on "the secret vice" and establishes an ethos of "sexual penury" by stressing continence, control, and healthful living.[30] He reminds men that his institute is not "a hospital attached to a whorehouse or a saloon" (367). He prohibits gambling and campaigned to make smoking history: "[smoking] sets a bad example to a lot of young wasters who come here and who ought to be broken of the vice" (373). The client who is seen drinking one night in New York City while having claimed a need to tend to "urgent business" is humiliated the next day at lunch with, "A dog . . . is so much better than the average man that it's an insult to the dog to compare them. . . . A dog doesn't get a red nose from drinking too much. . . . He doesn't get gonorrhea or syphilis" (366).

Horses and dogs may be more manly than men, but women are not. Feminizing his insult—"Say, you're not an actor—you're a woman! You're a stewed onion!" (350); "What do you think you're doing—drinking tea?" (348)—*ef*feminizes (domesticates in its alignment with a vegetable and beverage) thus rendering as shameful, nonaggression. Like Freud, Muldoon would consider shame the "feminine" character trait "par excellence,"[31] particularly for "sissies and mamma's boys and pet heirs" (373). And the connotations of what E. James Anthony calls a feminine "pseudoidentity" characterized by "masochism, self-denial, self-abasement, submissiveness, nonassertiveness, servility, undue deference, shyness, oversensitivity, undue modesty, shamefulness, and frailty ('Frailty, thy name is woman')"[32] would be easily suggested to Dreiser's 1919 audience still somewhat anxious about turn of the twentieth century New Women and the emerging 20s relaxation of rigid sexual mores.[33] Feminization degrades his clients but not him: Muldoon does not so much discard as re-encode anything signed as feminine.

In Muldoon's cosmology, the function of Other (Woman) is not erased. Muldoon is not only masculine Self; he is not only a powerful agent of control whose subjectivity rules, but he also simultaneously occupies and appropriates *to-be-looked-at-ness* usually coded as feminine. He enacts both gendered positions described by John Berger: "A man's presence is dependent upon the promise of power which he embodies. . . . [While a woman's] sense of being in herself is supplanted by a sense of being appreciated as herself by another."[34] The degree of power Muldoon's body emblematizes pressures clients into a constant action of surveying self which, Berger notes, is what women do. Feminized clients can be only surveyed while Muldoon the surveyor is likewise surveyed. His body is both the object of the gaze (feminine) *and* the representation of the more perfect ego ideal (masculine) that his clients both feel alienated from and long for.[35] Occupying these polarized positions, Muldoon does not so much neutralize or collapse the split as aestheticize his body which reinscribes both hypermasculinity (subject) and his appropriation of the feminine (object) position.[36] It is not so much that he is sexually pure (though he is) or androgynous (though he may be interpreted to be so) as he is freed from constricted sex roles while powered by them. He both represses and expresses, appropriates and expropriates a fleshed out model of an integrated, "unconflicted egotistical type" who exhibits "a seemingly total lack of tension between the idealized self and the realistic self."[37] Public and private selves merged into a display of aggrandizement that dissolves any tension between being a body and transcending that body, he employs a shaming technique that deploys an invasively penetrating gaze.

Not one of Muldoon's patrons can disavow his shame, not in the gym, not in the dining room, certainly not in the shower room: "Here a goodly portion of the force of his method was his skill in removing any sense of ability, agility, authority or worth from those with whom he dealt" (350–51). Nothing as basic as washing oneself is conducted in privacy. Muldoon prescribes a one-minuite-or-less system of showering and seizes the opportunity to demean anyone who exceeds his time limit. A "noble jurist" who can only remain "huddled . . . in a shivering position under the water . . . [and becomes] quite undone by his efforts" is singled out as a "particular specimen" abused to the point of utter confusion: "watching him as might a hawk," Muldoon verbally attacks "the stalky, bony affair" and causes him to appear "as though his body were some vast complex machine which he had never rightly understood before" (351–52). Though the "distinguished victim[s]" (353) protest, Muldoon exposes not only their "mental inadequacy and feebleness which he displayed before all the others" (352) for a specific task failure, but also exposes the self to the self: "And here again, even more than in the gymnasium, they were at the disadvantage of feeling themselves spectacles, for here they were naked" (351). The *real* body is a foul dis-smelling, disgusting site of weakness and exposed genitals amplify the origin of the shame experience.[38]

In Freud's 1930 discussion of primitive family configurations, he notes that "[man's] assumption of an upright gait . . . [m]ade his genitals, which were previously concealed, visible and in need of protection, and so provoked feelings of shame in him." Stripped of any outward signifiers, Muldoon's clientele, like the primitives Freud describes, experience regressive archaic anxieties over visibility and vulnerability. Like Oedipal boys Freud analyzed in 1924, clientele long for identification with the father (and all the priviliges masculine identification assumes over the feminine, including, as Freud noted in 1925, "the contempt felt by men for a sex which is the lesser") and must work out/work through a reactivated fear of castration—here the complete social negation of manhood affected by physical feminization. In 1933, Freud claimed that women were more prone to shame since women were physically and psychically mutilated men, whose development required "concealment of genital deficiency."[39] Muldoon discovers/sees his clients' genital anxieties, and "all but despise[d] weakness and had apparently a thousand disagreeable ways of showing it" (355). What he sees is lack—lack of strength and stamina in "solid" bodies. Such deficient virility translates to "womanized" men whose lingering castration anxiety further contributes to their shame anxiety. Since shame is "contagious," ([Broucek, 4]; he also claims that castration is "usually a code word for shame" [18]), Dreiser and his peer are each forced to become aware of their selves as feminized objects for Muldoon, thus confirming the shame dynamic described by Wurmser: "To be seen means to be overwhelmed; to see means to exert horrendous power."[40] Self objectification, then, precipitates each man's view of himself as delimited, inferior and incompetent.

Calling into question the very essence of their being—their sex—Muldoon defines what a man is *not*:

> "I say that the word *man* ought to be modified or changed in some way so that when we use it we would mean something more definite than we mean now. That thing you see sitting up on that wagon seat there—call that a man? And then call me one? Or a man like Charles A. Dana? Or a man like General Grant? Hell! Look at him! Look at his shape! Look at that stomach! You think a thing like that—call it a man if you want to—has any brains or that he's really any better than a pig in a sty? . . . A thing like that connects himself with one end of a beer hose and then he thinks he's all right. He gets enough guts to start a sausage factory, and then he blows up, I suppose, or rots. Think of it! And we call him a man—or some do!" (376)

Dreiser may be unsure of what to call Muldoon—"host or manager or trainer" (343)—but Muldoon has no doubts about his role or his image. He projects "brute" courage (341), a "wolfish attitude" (356), an "air of savage strength" and "tiger-like eyes" (347), an animal-man form

(Buck's true father?) whose "tiger-like mien [created] the feeling that . . . you would get a physical rip which would leave you bleeding for days" (369). Evocative of what Leverenz calls the myth of the "beast-patrician," Muldoon dramatizes the "civilized and savage" figure whose "downward mobility . . . save[s] the manhood of upwardly mobile men" (*The Last Real Man* 29). Muldoon's mission, to "rebuild all these men and wastrels and to control this great institution" (356) saves by metamorphosing, what might be considered regeneration through psychological violence. Dreiser's description of Muldoon, though lengthy, is worth quoting in full since it conflates all of the images that constitute what Dreiser perceives as the more perfect ego ideal worth emulating:

> a more savage and yet gentlemanly-looking animal in clothes *de rigueur* I have never seen. He was really very princely in build and manner, shapely and grand, like those portraits that have come down to us of Richelieu and the Duc de Guise—fawn-colored riding trousers, bright red waistcoat, black-and-white check riding coat, brown leather riding boots and leggings with the essential spurs, and a riding quirt. And yet really, at that moment he reminded me not so much of a man, in his supremely well-tailored riding costume, as of a tiger or a very ferocious and yet at times purring cat, beautifully dressed, as in our children's storybooks, a kind of tiger in collar and boots. He was so lithe, silent, cat-like in his tread. In his hard, clear, gray animal eyes was that swift, incisive, restless, searching glance which sometimes troubles us in the presence of animals. It was hard to believe that he was all of sixty, as I had been told. He looked the very well-preserved man of fifty or less. The short trimmed mustache and goatee which he wore were gray and added to his grand air. His hair, cut a close pompadour, the ends of his heavy eyebrow hairs turned upward, gave him a still more distinguished air. He looked very virile, very intelligent, very indifferent, intolerant and even threatening. (344)

As disciplinarian, Muldoon assumes both a paternal function and a role in what Mark Seltzer calls the "topography of masculinity in American at the turn of the century" (141). As father figure and source of reason, Muldoon's authority, as Victor Seidler writes about patriarchal authority generally, is "based on the capacity . . . to discern what is morally right."[41] Self-control follows discipline and Muldoon, seemingly aware of the Kantian notion that "[U]ndisciplined men are apt to follow every caprice" (*Education* qtd. in Seidler, 274–75), produces moral as well as bodily reform by prescribing and overseeing all remedial activities. Clients' telltale bodies announce the folly of having followed "every caprice" and must bear/bare the shame of exposure. In his discussion of the American turn of the century "body-machine complex" (141), Seltzer describes the technologies of man-making as consisting of "flow and continuous movement'' (153). Anxieties about agency, consumption, identity, he notes, are quelled by the belief that ''bodies and persons are things that can be made'' (142), hence the systematic management of labor, the work process and production. Rigid and precise in his demands for a routinized program, Muldoon understands Seltzer's observation that ''corporeal discipline appear[s] at once a violation of the natural body and its transcendence'' (149). Extremist in his diatribes and denigrations, he affects change: his clients produce new bodily selves. Made to feel ashamed of what Muldoon considers personally incorrect consumption, men must compensate by following laborious, mechanized activities. The incorrigible man who ''swills around at hotel bars, stays with some of his lady whores, and then comes back here and expects me to pull him into shape again, to make his nose a little less red. . . . [Who] thinks he can use my place to fall back on when he can't go on any longer, to fix him up to do some more swilling later on'' (367) Muldoon considers most pathetic since such an individual does not recognize consumption—conspicuous or concealed—as disease.

That his institute, his ''healthatorium'' or what Dreiser calls a ''sporting sanitarium'' that evolved into a ''decidedly fashionable institution'' (341), is a country retreat suggests parallels with moral regeneration, the ''antidote to consumption'' (Seltzer, 143) and mimics the jaunt out west for neurasthenic men. The original title, ''Scared Back to Nature,'' carries both Emersonian/Thoreauvian associations of redemption in/by nature, what Leo Marx calls a ''temporary return to first things. . . . [To] regain contact with essentials''[42] and a turn of the century ideology of muscle and phallus (muscular phallus?) also associated with the purifying, that is, man-making, power of nature. But Dreiser also implies that a man must be ''scared'' and scared ''back'' to the state of nature, that only in regression (from the demands of modern society) prompted by fear of a loss of bodily control, could he restore personal productivity. The very American disease of the nerves, neurasthenia, was, according to the ''father'' of neurasthenia, George M. Beard, an affliction of the most highly civilized society. The stresses of modernity, he claimed, were contributing factors to the onset of nervous collapse: ''The modern differ from the ancient civilizations mainly in these five elements—steam power, the periodical press, the telegraph, the sciences, and the mental activity of women. When civilization, plus these five factors, invades any nation, it must carry nervousness and nervous disease along with it.''[43] E. Anthony Rotundo notes that by the 1880s neurasthenia reached epidemic proportions and not until 1910 did occurrences of the disease begin to wane. He further notes that neurasthenia ''did not become a badge of shame until the very turn of the century.''[44]

Roosevelt's *The Strenuous Life* (1900) marks the high point of a growing concern with exercise and the benefits of physical culture. Though gymnastics and calisthenics had been popular forms of ensuring health since the 1850s, the relaxation and moderate exercise therapy advised by physicians for neurasthenic men became supplanted by an increasingly mass marketed ideology of rejuvenation through strenuous activity. Sport, Green writes, "was, in effect, Roosevelt's model for life" (236) and his advocacy of countering the debilitating effects of urban life by physical labor, athletic prowess, and immersion in woods and streams contributed to a growing political alliance of virility and conquest.[45] Chapter One of *The Strenuous Life* addresses "you men of Chicago" to "bring up your sons to work . . . [because] we admire the man who embodies victorious effort . . . who has those virile qualities necessary to win in the stern strife of actual life" (3–4). His earlier *Ranch Life and the Hunting-Trail* (1888) claims the "West is no place for men who lack the ruder, coarser virtues and physical qualities, no matter how intellectual or how refined and delicate their sensibilities."[46] His own self restoration and regeneration as well as his influence on Owen Wister and Frederick Remington has been detailed by historians.[47] while Van Every chronicles Roosevelt's advocacy of Muldoon. Van Every also describes Secretary of State Elihu Root's recuperation effected by Muldoon's regimen (284–88).

Removed from urban contamination, Olympia is physically located in a privileged purified realm. An "institute on a hill," Olympia is Muldoon's scaled down version of Mount Olympus—he the only god in residence—and Dreiser sees Olympia as the apotheosis of an idyllic space that mediates mainstream culture:

> It was spring and quite warm and bright. The cropped enclosure which surrounded it, a great square of green fenced with high, well-trimmed privet, was good to look upon, level and smooth. The house, standing in the center of this, was large and oblong and gray, with very simple French windows reaching to the floor and great wide balustraded balconies reaching out from the second floor, shaded with awnings and set with rockers. The land on which this inn stood sloped very gradually to the Sound, miles away to the southeast, and the spires of churches and the gables of villages rising in between, as well as various toy-like sails upon the water, were no small portions of its charm. To the west for a score of miles the green-covered earth rose and fell in undulating beauty, and here again the roofs and spires of nearby villages might in fair weather be seen nestling peacefully among the trees. Due south there was a suggestion of water and some peculiar configuration, which by day seemed to have no significance other than that which attached to the vague outlines of a distant landscape. By night, however, the soft glow emanating from myriads of lights identified it as the body and length of the

> merry, night-reveling New York. Northward the green waves repeated themselves unendingly until they passed into a dim green-blue haze. (342–43)

But it is Van Every who describes how the area is mediat*ed* and deliberately constructed: "When Muldoon first acquired this beautiful terrain it still presented a primeval aspect. There are still evidences in the close vicinity of the days when the Indians roamed its wilds and found habitation. It took a considerable expenditure of money and months of labor before the scene took on its sylvan charm" (251).

Though Muldoon's clients are situated in an eastern environ, they act out/work out western roles. Yet unlike the rough riders of Rooseveltian aplomb, these men are made to feel their shortcomings and weaknesses. Recapitulative of cowboy ruggedness, horseback riding is barely managed by the crew and Dreiser undercuts militaristic equestrianism in an anecdote that sets Muldoon fuming over the inability of every man in the group to blow a trumpet (378–80).

Olympia's locale suggests another function that Philip Fisher describes in his discussion of *An American Tragedy*: "setting enforce[s] a set," that is, "[E]xperiencing oneself as 'one of' this or 'one of' that is the primary way of constituting a self in the novel."[48] Identity for Dreiser and his peers is based upon both an individual and collective experience of bodily lack emphasized by public exposure and recognized by a set uniform: "Guests must be dressed in running trunks, shoes and sweater, and appear in the gymnasium by six sharp!" (347). Uniformed bodies signify uniform behavior, but for Muldoon, attire marks difference:

> In his cowled dressing gown he looked more like some great monk or fighting abbot of the medieval years than a trainer. He walked to the center, hung up his cowl and revealed himself lithe and lion-like and costumed like ourselves. But how much more attractive as he strode about, his legs lean and sturdy, his chest full, his arms powerful and graceful. (348)

Unlike the variety of uniforms Clyde Griffiths wears—as bellboy, servant, businessman, and inmate to connote a "set" identity—Muldoon's clients don only workout attire and street clothes. Their identity does not shift; they subscribe to a "set" routine of daily exercises and activities.

All of this is not to suggest that Muldoon is shame free or totally shameless. His contempt for his clients is rooted in his superior physical condition and also in his defensiveness. Having origins in the Irish working class,[49] Muldoon, Dreiser claims, resents his clients' class status and social ascriptions. Dreiser write, "He felt, and I think in the main that he was right, that [his clients] looked down on him because of his lowly birth and purely material and mechanical career" (355). Try as he may to discount Muldoon's agency—"he was not the creator of his own great strength, by any means, impulses and tendencies over which he had no control having arranged for that" (356)—Dreiser cannot deny Muldoon's success and perhaps projects his own shame of working class, immigrant origins onto Muldoon.

The self-made man, the "completely individualistic man" (Coltrane 194), Muldoon plays out the success story of the ambitious, virtuous poor man whose vertical mobility testifies to his strength of character. Muldoon embodies the Alger hero, whose "great attainment," John Cawelti notes, "is to leave the ranks of the 'working-class' and become owner or partner in a business of his own." (120)[50] But, Cawelti also notes, the Irish play a "distinctly inferior role in Alger's version of America" (113). Muldoon both preserves and disrupts that pattern: unlike the Alger hero who finds a fortune, he makes one. He is sole owner of his spa because he has practical skills and knowledge lacking in his professionalized clients. Dreiser specifies Muldoon's trajectory from a variety of obscure working class jobs to famous grandstanding entrepreneur, the "lord of the manor" (345):

> from youth up, he had been a peasant farmer's son in Ireland, a scullion in a ship's kitchen earning his way to America, a "beef slinger" for a packing company, a cooks' assistant and waiter in a Bowery restaurant, a bouncer in a saloon, a rubber-down at prize fights, a policeman, a private in the army during the Civil War, a ticket-taker, exhibition wrestler . . . of the world . . . and . . . trainer of John L. Sullivan. (341)

Having climbed the ladder of success, Muldoon resents those who didn't. Particularly offensive to him are heirs of conspicuous leisure:

> take a man—more especially a gentleman—one of these fellows who is always very pointed in emphasizing that he is a gentleman. . . . Let him inherit eight or ten millions, give him a college education, let him be socially well connected, and what does he do? Not a damned thing if he can help it except contract vices—run from one saloon to another, one gambling house to another, one girl to another, one meal to another. He doesn't need to know anything necessarily. He may be the lowest dog physically and in every other way, and still he's a gentleman—because he has money, wears spats and a high hat. (366–67)

His class biases are further compounded by a collective antisemitism; Dreiser claims Muldoon has an especially "wolfish and savage idea" in admitting Mr. Itzky, a "stout and mushy-looking Hebrew, with a semi-bald pate, protruding paunch and fat arms and legs." Muldoon's desire is to "torture this particular specimen" for whom Dreiser and his peers feel "no particular sympathy." Itzky has difficulty horseback riding and when he falls off his horse injuring his foot (Dreiser isn't sure if he rolled off, implying Itzky may be feigning injury to escape the work-[out]), he is left, miles from Olympia, to walk his horse back to the stable and may not be guaranteed any lunch if he takes too long. Singled out for his class privilege as well as his Jewishness, Itzky maintains a fringe position in the group: Dreiser feels Itzky should be shamed for being "a fat stuff, a sweat-shop manufacturer . . . let him walk and sweat" (358–61).

Re-presenting the drama of the survival of the fittest, Muldoon's body emblematizes the racial superiority so dear to Roosevelt's anxieties about race suicide.[51] Van Every's defense of Muldoon's birth right attests to the cultural valorization of nativist hegemony and though Dreiser upholds *and* denigrates Muldoon's image as a popular culture hero—"It has always been interesting to me to see in what awe men of this type or profession are held by many in the more intellectual walks of life as well as by those whose respectful worship is less surprising" (341)—he recognizes Muldoon's success. Along with the other profiles of *Twelve Men*, Muldoon's "reflects the concern of nearly all of Dreiser's fiction—his fascination with the question of how one defines success" (Coltrane, 193).

Muldoon is "solid," physically dense, and "solid" in the sense Nostwich suggests was associated with the 1870s song—"staunch, reliable, or unbreakable" (407). Yet Muldoon transcends materiality because his hard body symbolically galvanizes the dialectic of male national identity—the social imperative to be "fit for America"—to a male subjectivity ashamed of its dubious masculinity. When Richard Dowell labels Muldoon a "sadistic brute" (xliv), he may be cuing in on Muldoon's talent for shaming, which does, on the surface, appear excessively unrelentingly savage; yet, paradoxically, healing since clients are "cured." What appears to be a constant barrage of toxic "shock[s] to one's dignity" (352) has, for its ultimate goal, redemptive transformation. Carl Schneider's title, *Shame: The Power of Caring*, is an apt moniker for the dynamics of Muldoon's "repair shop." And former Senate Majority Leader Bob Dole's comment, "[M]y view is that shame is still an important tool in America,"[52] is, nearly one hundred years after the fact(icity) of Muldoon, a testimony to the socio-political uses of the shame experience.

Notes

1. Richard Lingeman, *Theodore Dreiser: An American Journey, 1908–1945*, 100.

2. Edward Van Every, *Muldoon the Solid Man of Sport: His Amazing Story as Related for the First Time by Him to His Friend*, 45.

3. The text of "Muldoon, the Solid Man" is reprinted in T. D. Nostwich, ed., *Fulfilment and Other Tales of Women and Men*, 341–84. Nostwich claims Dreiser stayed at Olympia from 21 April to 2 June 1903. Nostwich may be relying on information obtained from Dreiser's firsthand account in *An Amateur Laborer*, ed. Richard W. Dowell et al, which reproduces Dreiser's bill for his stay at the institute. The bill is dated 13 June 1903 for the period 21 April to 2 June, and payment "in full" is listed as $256.75, not the $600 Dreiser claims in the text of the story (Dowell et al, 196). Lingeman also cites Dreiser's stay with Muldoon in 1903 (174). See also Tom Lutz, *American Nervousness, 1903: An Anecdotal History*, whose chapter, "Making It Big: Theodore Dreiser, Sex, and Success," describes Dreiser's neurasthenia as "both a tactic in his career of conquest and a response to temporary setbacks in that career" (39) and connects Dreiser's condition to a cultural ethos linking "nervousness" with social mobility and success (38–62).

4. Robert Coltrane, "The Crafting of Dreiser's *Twelve Men*," esp. 201.

5. Like "Muldoon, the Solid Man," *An Amateur Laborer* details Dreiser's experience at the institute as an extended six-week period. Several anecdotes recur in each piece; for example, the toe-washing scene in "Muldoon, the Solid Man" depicts a merciless Muldoon ordering a client (called "patients" in *An Amateur Laborer*) to scrub his toes in the shower ("Muldoon," 353–54; *AAL*, 81).

6. Carl Schneider, *Shame, Exposure and Privacy*, xvii.

7. Mark Twain, *A Connecticut Yankee in King Arthur's Court*, 112. A comparison of the two texts may reveal similar thematic concerns with masculinity even though Dreiser is typically considered an apolitical novelist while *Yankee* may be read as a critique of contemporary imperialism.

8. Frederick Jackson Turner, "The Frontier in American History" (1920), his expanded version of "The Significance of the Frontier in American History" (1893), rpt. in *The Historians' History of the United States*, 1: 463. See David Leverenz, "The Last Real Man in America: From Natty Bumppo to Batman," in *Fictions of Masculinity*, ed. Peter F. Murphy, 32. See also David Leverenz, *Manhood and the American Renaissance* for an elaboration of his "most basic thesis, that any intensified ideology of manhood is a compensatory response to fears of humiliation" (4) also personalized and dramatized in his "Manhood, Humiliation and Public Life: Some Stories."

9. "Virility impulse" is James McGovern's label. See his "David Graham Philips and the Virility Impulse of Progressives." See also, for example, Mark Carnes and Clyde Griffen, eds., *Meanings for Manhood: Constructions of Masculinity in Victorian America*; E. Anthony Rotundo, "Body and Soul: Changing Ideals of American Middle-Class Manhood, 1770–1920"; Mark Seltzer, "The Love Master"; Kevin Mumford, " 'Lost Manhood' Found: Male Sexual Impotence and Victorian Culture in the United States"; Amy Kaplan, "Romancing the Empire: The Embodiment of American Masculinity in the Popular Historical Novel of the 1890s."

10. Bette London, "Mary Shelley, *Frankenstein*, and the Spectacle of Masculinity." See also Steve Neal, "Masculinity as Spectacle: Reflections on Men and Mainstream Cinema."

11. The Kleinian usage of "reparation" is analogous to what I see Dreiser and his peers acting out. Melanie Klein defines the psychological need to "mak[e] reparation" as a response to repressed guilt evoked by aggressive, hostile fantasy toward a loved object: "[s]ide by side with the destructive impulses in the unconscious mind both of the child and the adult, there exists a profound urge to make sacrifices, in order to help and to put right loved people who in fantasy have been harmed or destroyed." See Klein, "Love, Guilt and Reparation," 65–66. Muldoon's men are attempting to redress their corporeal deficits for which they feel not so much guilty as ashamed; and though Dreiser denigrates the persecutory Muldoon, he reveals an underlying awe of the man and desires his approval.

12. See Harvey Green, *Fit for America: Health, Fitness, Sport and American Society*, esp. "Living the Strenuous Life," "Old-Time Quiet in a Breathless Age," and "Dietetic Righteousness," 219–317. For a recent parody of the nutrition craze dominated by J. Harvey Kellogg see T. Coraghessan Boyle's *The Road to Wellville* and the movie adaptation.

13. For biographical information see, for example, Richard W. Dowell, "Introduction," *An Amateur Laborer*; Thomas P. Riggio, "Introduction," *Theodore Dreiser: The American Diaries, 1902–1926*, ed. Riggio; Richard Lingeman, *Theodore Dreiser: At the Gates of the City, 1871–1907* (New York: Putnam, 1986) and *Theodore Dreiser: An American Journey, 1908–1945*; Richard Lehan, *Theodore Dreiser: His World and His Novels*; Yoshinobu Hakutani, *Young Dreiser: A Critical Study*, esp. 43–66; and Dreiser's autobiographies, *Dawn: A History of Myself* and *A Book about Myself*. The quote is taken from Richard B. Hovey and Ruth S. Ralph, "Dreiser's *The 'Genius'*: Motivation and Structure." See also Miriam Gogol, "*The 'Genius'*: Dreiser's Testament to Convention."

14. Joseph Griffin, *The Small Canvas: An Introduction to Dreiser's Short Stories*, 17.

15. Gershen Kaufman, *Shame: The Power of Caring*, 2d ed., ix.

16. Andrew P. Morrison, *Shame: The Underside of Narcissism*, 14; Leon Wurmser, *The Mask of Shame*, 46–47.

17. Robert Karen, "Shame," 40.

18. Gerhart Piers and Milton Singer, *Shame and Guilt: A Psychoanalytic and a Cultural Study*; Helen B. Lewis, *Shame and Guilt in Neurosis*; Carl Schneider, *Shame, Exposure and Privacy*; Gary Thrane, "Shame and the Construction of the Self."

19. Carl Schneider, *Shame, Exposure and Privacy*, xiv–xv. Andrew P. Morrison rewrites the tension of ego and ego ideal (which Leon Wurmser's comprehensive *The Mask of Shame* discusses) as tension between self and ideal self in *Shame: The Underside of Narcissism*.

20. Francis J. Broucek, *Shame and the Self*, 142.

21. Jean Paul Satre writes, "Shame . . . is the recognition of the fact that I am indeed that object which the Other is looking at and judging" in *Being and Nothingness: An Essay on Phenomenological Ontology*, 261. He further equates positions of vulnerability with positions of visibility: walking through the park (254), peeking through a key-hole (259); "What I apprehend immediately when I hear the branches crackling behind me is . . . that I occupy a place and that I cannot in any case escape from the space in which I am without defense—in

short, that I *am seen*" (259). See Part Three, Chapter I, Section IV, "The Look," 252–302.

22. Gary Thrane, "Shame and the Construction of the Self," 323.

23. Wurmser differentiates between shame and shame anxiety: "Shame clearly is an affective state, either short-lived or enduring. It may be so enduring that becomes an affective attitude. A special form of anxiety is an inherent part of this affect, but shame and anxiety cannot simply be equated, nor can one be subsumed under the other. If shame assumes the typical stereotyped, compulsive quality of a neurotic phenomenon, appearing without due regard for external reality, it is a symptom. Furthermore, if it is analyzed according to the structural theory, shame, like other affects, reflects a tension between distinct structural elements, between the ego ideal (what one wants to be) and the ego (what one perceives one is)" (*The Mask of Shame*, 49).

24. Philip Cushman, *The Construction of the Self, Constructing America: A Cultural History of Psychotherapy*, 260. Darwin refers to the "surveying eye of the unmerciful spectator" which prompts "not the simple act of reflecting on our own appearance, but the thinking what others think of us which excites a blush." See "The Expression of the Emotions in Man Animals" (1872), rpt. in *The Portable Darwin*, ed. Duncan Porter and Peter Graham, 368–93.

25. Lewis defines "shame ideation" as "[o]bserving oneself from one's own or another's point of view as one is experiencing a state" (111). In *An Amateur Laborer*, Dreiser writes, "All the time I was wondering what so strong a man should think of so weak a body as mine. Anyone with so much strength must have a royal contempt for physical weakness" (74).

26. Michel Foucault, "Panopticism," in *Discipline and Punish: The Birth of the Prison*, trans. Alan Sheridan, 220.

27. I use "masquerade" in its denotative sense not in relation to the complex Lacanian sense of women's position of "appearing" to be the Phallus while men "have" the Phallus. See "The Meaning of the Phallus" in *Feminine Sexuality: Jacques Lacan and the Ecole Freudienne*, ed. Juliet Mitchell and Jacqueline Rose, 83–85.

28. Eva Kosofsky Sedgwick analyzes "homosocial desire" in her *Between Men: English Literature and Male Homosocial Desire*; "Introduction" and "Gender Asymmetry and Erotic Triangles," rpt. in *Feminisms: An Anthology of Literary Theory and Criticism*, ed. Robyn Warhol and Diane Price Herndl, 463–86. Sedgwick writes, "To draw the 'homosocial' back into the orbit of 'desire,' of the potentially erotic, then, is to hypothesize the potential unbrokenness of a continuum between homosocial and homosexual—a continuum whose visibility, for men, in our society, is radically disrupted" (463).

29. Mark Carnes, *Secret Ritual and Manhood in Victorian America*. Of the father-son dynamic inherent in fraternal ritual, Carnes writes, "The rituals affirmed that, although woman gave birth to man's body, initiation gave birth to his soul, surrounding him with brothers who would lavish on him the 'utmost affection and kindness' " (121). A stay at Olympia, though, is an affirmation that its leader can conflate a paternal, authoritative, directive role with an appropriated maternal role in giving *re*-birth to men's bodies. And though men are individually targeted and isolated in their humiliation, they share some degree of brotherly support and solace.

30. See G. J. Barker-Benfield, *Horrors of the Half-Known Life: Male Attitudes toward Women and Sexuality in Nineteenth-Century America*, esp. 175–88; Peter Filene, "Men and Manliness," in *Him/ Her/ Self: Sex Roles in Modern*

America; Carroll Smith-Rosenberg, *Disorderly Conduct: Visions of Gender in Victorian America*. See also Charles E. Rosenberg's widely referenced essay, "Sexuality, Class and Role in 19th-Century America" in *The American Man*, [selected by] Elizabeth Pleck and Joseph Pleck, for a discussion of male sex role conflict.

31. Sigmund Freud, "Femininity," Lecture XXXIII, *New Introductory Lectures on Psychoanalysis*, 132.

32. E. James Anthony, "Shame, Guilt, and the Feminine Self in Psychoanalysis," 207–8.

33. See Smith-Rosenberg (note 30 above), esp. "The New Woman as Androgyne: Social Disorder and Gender Crisis, 1870–1936," 245–96. See also Elaine Showalter, *Sexual Anarchy: Gender and Culture at the Fin de Siecle*.

34. John Berger, *Ways of Seeing*, 46–47.

35. Laura Mulvey's classic essay, "Visual Pleasure and Narrative Cinema," discusses the dynamics of projective identification: male subjectivity as structuring norm invites narcissistic male fantasies of mastery over/of women who are represented as objects of desire.

36. Van Every reproduces two photos from the Albert Davis Collection depicting Muldoon in poses imitative of "Famous Greek statues" (159). Alasdair Foster, in *Behold the Man: The Male Nude in Photography*, notes that "male nudes should be smooth" and thus connote "associations with marble" (43).

37. Broucek, 59–60.

38. In his study of human emotions, Silvan Tomkins's "affect theory," in *Affect/ Imagery/ Consciousness*, equates nine innate positive and negative affects as mainly facial responses. Dissmell and disgust are two negatives responding to offensive smell and a "bad other." See Tomkin's discussion of affects as related to shame in "Shame" in *The Many Faces of Shame*, 133–61. I use "dissmell" and "disgust" to suggest Muldoon's clients *evoke* these negative affects in Muldoon.

39. See Sigmund Freud, *Civilization and Its Discontents*, 1930, trans. and ed. James Strachey, 54; "The Dissolution of the Oedipus Complex," 1924; "Some Psychical Consequences of the Anatomical Distinction Between the Sexes," 1925; "Femininity," 1933.

40. Leon Wurmser, "Shame: The Veiled Companion of Narcissism," 79.

41. Mark Seltzer, "The Love-Master," 141 Victor Seidler, "Fathering, Authority and Masculinity." See also note 29 above. A Lacanian interpretation of Muldoon's signification of the "law of the father" is, perhaps, suggested by the text(ure) of the narrative and assumes a reading not too far afield from my own.

42. Leo Marx, *The Machine in the Garden: Technology and the Pastoral Ideal in America*, 69.

43. George Beard, *American Nervousness*, qtd. in Lutz, *American Nervousness*, 4.

44. E. Anthony Rotundo, *American Manhood: Transformations in Masculinity from the Revolution to the Modern Era*, 186–88.

45. See Amy Kaplan (note 9 above); also Lora Romero, "Vanishing American: Gender, Empire, and New Historicism." Also of note is the comparison between the masculine "activity" cure for regeneration and the feminine "rest cure" advocated by S. Weir Mitchell. That women, including Edith Wharton, Charlotte Perkins Gilman, Jane Addams, Winifred Howells (daughter of William Dean) and Virginia Woolf, were subjected to nearly total infantilization speaks to the sexual politics underlying the medico-cultural constructions of gender and gen-

der roles. For a historical overview, see Ellen Bassuk, "The Rest Cure: Repetition or Resolution of Victorian Women's Conflicts?" in *The Female Body in Western Culture*, ed. Susan Rubin Suleiman, 139–51.

46. See Theodore Roosevelt, *Ranch Life and the Hunting-Trail*, qtd. in Leverenz, "Last Real Man," 34.

47. See David McCullough's biography of Roosevelt, *Mornings on Horseback* qtd. in Leverenz, "Last Real Man," 51.

48. Philip Fisher, *Hard Facts: Setting and Form in the American Novel*, ch. 3, "The Life History of Objects: The Naturalist Novel and the City," 128–78, 143–44.

49. Defending Muldoon's claim to a native birthright, Van Every claims Muldoon was born "May 25, 1845, in a little farm settlement in the Genesee Valley district of the state of New York which later came to be known as Belfast" (13).

50. John Cawelti, *Apostles of the Self-Made Man*; see also Irvin Wyllie, *The Self-Made Man in America* and Richard Weiss, *The American Myth of Success: From Horatio Alger to Norman Vincent Peale*, 97–194.

51. Roosevelt's letter to Mrs. Van Vorst explicitly voices the rhetoric used to discourage childless marriages of the white middle-class: "But the man or woman who deliberately avoids marriage and has a heart so cold as to know no passion and a brain so shallow and selfish as to dislike having children, is in effect a criminal against the race and should be an object of contemptuous abhorrence by all healthy people." See letter 2482 in *The Letters of Theodore Roosevelt*, 3: 355.

52. Kevin Galvin, "Dole Hints of Blocking Vote on Foster." Referring to the movie "Priest," Dole appears to gear his remarks to "conservatives who are angered by what they see as America's moral decline."

This Sex Which Is One: Language and the Masculine Self in *Jennie Gerhardt*

STEPHEN C. BRENNAN

"THE ENGLISHMAN JEFFERIES HAS TOLD US THAT IT REQUIRES A HUNdred and fifty years to make a perfect maiden."[1] With these words, Dreiser introduces an extended quotation from the English nature mystic Richard Jefferies at the moment Jennie Gerhardt yields her virtue to Senator Brander. Identifying the "perfect maiden" with the beauty of a world evolving through endless cycles of death and regeneration, the quotation most obviously suggests that Jennie, like Hardy's Tess, remains a pure child of nature despite her sexual fall. Jefferies, however, sounds a darker note as well. Beneath the beautiful surface, nature is in his account a highly sexualized, secret space in which "yellowing wheatstalks crowd up under the shadow of green firs" and "devious" brooks emit their "sweetness" (73). As a passing phase of an evolutionary process, beauty is the ephemeral embodied, and so the maiden produces not joy but romantic melancholy: "the world yearns towards her beauty as to flowers that are past. The loveliness of seventeen is centuries old. That is why passion is almost sad" (74).

It is this sadness that Dreiser emphasizes, when, immediately following the Jefferies quotation, he poses a question to those whose hearts have responded to natural loveliness: "if all beauty were passing, and you were given these things to hold in your arms before the world slipped away, would you give them up?" (74). While the question invites us to understand why the aging Brander needs Jennie, it also suggests the danger of grasping at what, in its deceptiveness and inevitable passing, can produce only a painful sense of loss. As a forty-year-old man who had recently lost his head, and his job as magazine editor, over eighteen-year-old Thelma Cudlipp, Dreiser knew all about that kind of pain, as he did the disappointment Lester feels when, while attempting to hold "the most perfect thing under the sun" (338), he discovers beneath Jennie's beautiful surface a more disturbing sexuality and sadder history than he has suspected.[2]

Dreiser, however, only partly identifies with Lester. As Donald Pizer has noted, Dreiser was able to turn his own past into unified works of art when, as in *Dawn* and *A Book about Myself*, he maintained a tension between lyric identification with and a "wry detachment" from his own youthful "fatuousness."[3] He keeps the same ironic distance from Lester, whose desire to live with Jennie in the perpetual "light atmosphere which is of childhood" (270) is but one fatuous desire shared with the protagonist of the autobiographies. The young Theo of *Dawn*, Richard Lingeman points out, is "a scopophiliac child—always looking."[4] Scopophilia, the desire to look, derives, Freud argues, from the infant's pleasure from gazing at his own penis; it resembles fetishism since the fetish object stands for the penis the man, fearful of castration, refuses to admit the woman lacks.[5] It is not surprising, then, that Theo's childhood scopophilia develops into fetishism. In one of the autobiography's most significant scenes, the boy digs up a salamander from its hole and feels "a kind of horror of unlikeness, strangeness" that causes him to smash the animal to a bloody mass. Filled with thoughts of "death and mud-holes and left-over specimens of saurian life," he enjoys gazing at a comet "with a great, flaring tail," a "great red stranger, sharply outlined against a silver and lemon sea of space." This horror of a formless otherness lurking beneath the surface of things anticipates the castration anxiety that dominates Theo's later relations with girls, and his pleasure at looking at the phallic comet anticipates his defense against that anxiety. Girls create in him a "blood and brain fury" and threaten to reduce him to a humiliating state of impotence unless he remains at a safe distance gazing on their beauty. By the time he enters college, he is so terrified of sexual failure that he worships feminine beauty as "a kind of fetich."[6]

As fetish, the female body has phallic integrity. Enclosed within "an ever-moving line of beauty," it possesses a "seeming subtlety which was not unlike that which veils the chalice to a Greek or Roman believer" in Aphrodite. Just as he builds up girls in his mind as "absolute paragons"—that is, perfect maidens—so does he imagine the chalice "glitteringly" and "inviolably enshrined," its recesses hidden behind the veil.[7]

What seems in *Dawn* the neurotic defense of an outsider, a poor, insecure "mother child,"[8] is in *Jennie Gerhardt* characteristic of an entire male-dominated society. Dreiser thus anticipates much recent theorizing about gender differences. In *This Sex Which Is Not One*, to take perhaps the most striking example, Luce Irigaray virtually identifies scopophilia with Western patriarchal culture. Because female genitals are invisible as well as dual, she writes, men respond to them as "*the horror of nothing to see*," preferring to gaze on the female form as "beautiful object of contemplation." Because the penis is visible and singular, a society ruled by men (the sex which *is* one) "privileges phallomorphism"; it values "the *one* of form, of the individual, of the (male) sexual organ, of the proper name, of the proper meaning." As a consequence, men create "systems that are self-representative of a 'masculine subject.' " Discourse becomes dominated by linear logic and univocality, and sexual relations become a "reign of hom(m)o-sexuality"[9] in which female otherness is reduced to a masculine sameness.

Lester is the product of such a society. When confronted with the generative power of the "All-mother" working "in silence and darkness," most men, Dreiser writes, follow the "ridiculous tendency to close the eyes and turn away the head as if there were something unclean in the method of nature" (92). When a woman violates sexual norms, she is no longer perceived in her integral connection with nature's beauty but becomes subject to the "scornful gaze of men" (94). Lester is thus typical in feeling threatened by Jennie's seemingly indiscriminate sexuality. Although he possesses the wealth and sexual prowess Theo envies, he, too, tries to keep the veiled chalice in its shrine as beautiful object of contemplation. Having accepted his father's ideal of a personal integrity identified with the univocal written word, he can live only so long with a duplicitous woman whose spirit overflows language and all the other forms within which he tries to contain her. Preferring sameness to difference, he returns to a comfortable, explicable—and deathly—world that, like Theo's fetish, glitters with reflections of his own masculine oneness.

I

In an often-quoted passage near the end of the novel, Lester comes back to comfort Jennie after her daughter Vesta dies but manages only some disquieting observations on human beings as "pawns" in a cosmic chess game. "The best we can do," he concludes, "is to hold our personalities intact. It doesn't even appear that integrity has much to do with it" (392). We might almost take this statement as a heroic assertion of human dignity in an absurd universe if it were not part of a weak effort to maintain a manly image in Jennie's eyes ("I'm pretty bad," he tells her a moment later, "but I'm not all bad" [393]). Far from being a self-reliant individualist, Lester is typically male in valuing integrity—Irigaray's phallomorphism—above all else.

This is not to say that he actually possesses integrity, at least not the kind that would bring success in the masculine sphere of business. His "trouble," Dreiser specifically indicates, is that he lacks the "ruthless, narrow-minded insistence on his individual superiority" that would make him a "forceful figure" (305). Usually driven by poverty, a forceful figure is "an individual of one idea largely" whose obsession is "a raging flame" that becomes "the be-all and end-all of . . . existence" (305). Despite his privileged early life, Lester's brother Robert is apparently such a figure, for he is "on fire with his ideas" about monopolizing carriage manufacturing and is therefore "a happy man" (323).

In contrast with Robert's passionate commitment to his own idea, Lester's integrity owes much to the "theory" (137) of his father, who represents an older, more paternalistic economic system than the one Robert operates in.[10] While Robert creates a monopoly by cutting costs and consolidating companies, Old Archibald Kane has grown rich by generously "filling" a great public need. Himself a "big man," Archibald naturally prefers the "bigger," "softer, more human" Lester to the "spare," "hard" Robert (137). Yet, Dreiser implies, adherence to any single theory tends to harden and narrow the personality. In his old age, Archibald has become "keen, single of mind and unsullied of commercial honor" (127), a fact which bodes ill for Lester, who has probed "the whole gamut of things material, social, spiritual" only to be so baffled by life's complexity that he has fallen back on his father's single-minded belief: "Not a single idea of his, unless it were the need of being honest, was finally settled" (126). Too much remains unsettled for Lester to be happy like Robert, but even in his most cynical moods he ominously holds on to "a right method of living," a "theory of life" that makes the "intact" (128) personality the still point in the turning world.

This kind of integrity requires not only honesty but visibility, as Archibald Kane makes clear in his frequent advice to Lester:

> "Never try to make a thing look different from what it is to you. It's the breath of life—truth—it's the basis of real worth . . . it will make a notable character of any one who will stick to it." (293)

For the Kanes, a true thing must not "look" different from what it "is." When Archibald asserts that Jennie's gold-digging motives are "as plain as the nose on your face," Lester naturally counters with the only argument that could have much meaning for his father: "Father . . . why do you talk like that? You never *saw* the woman. You wouldn't know her from Adam's off ox" (275, emphasis added). This is, to be sure, an admirable plea for fairness, but the emphasis on appearance suggests that Lester's own knowledge of Jennie is hardly a profound understanding of her individuality.

The invisible, Lester and other men fear, is either a void or a principle of decay. The earth itself is hollow, a scientist at one of Letty's parties tells Lester, and so in "old age" its "perfect molten sphere" will collapse into "a sunken, bony remnant of itself to be destroyed, possibly by collision or entombment in the sun" (371). Lester, himself a container of "molten forces" (127), fears a similar fate, for while he responds to "the wealth of affection" (269) Jennie bestows, he values "above all her youth and beauty" because it keeps him from "drying up," like the earth, "into an aimless old age" (270). Old Gerhardt, returning home with hands burned by molten glass and cheeks "slightly sunken" (150), has already become an aimless old man who hates the fact that all beauty is passing. "We want to be careful now not to break anything," he cautions his family after Lester sets them up in a spic-and-span house in Cleveland. "It's so easy to scratch things up, and then it's all over" (177). Despite feeling intellectually superior to the superstitious old German immigrant, Lester shares this attitude. Fearing that the world is "apt to be brought back to its chemical constituents" (270) at any time, he does all he can to hold things together. "You're the first one to insist on perfection," Letty Pace chides him, "—to quarrel if there is any flaw in the order of things" (406).

It follows from this attitude that perfection is not Jefferies' evolving mysterious essence, a "preciousness" (73); rather, it is an unbroken surface, a static picture revealing that beauty is truth, truth beauty. When Lester discovers a rupture—Jennie's "divided" love—he pieces together the clues about her illicit relations with Brander until "they fitted together perfectly" and Jennie "stood before him beautifully convicted" (207). Forcing Jennie to tell all her past, he holds her to the "ideal that a woman should reveal herself to a man in love, perfectly" (208). Vesta herself begins to win him over when, "plainly seen," she appears framed in a doorway as a complete "picture" (217) of youthful innocence.

Dreiser's men seem to feel most secure against the forces of change when confronting the unbroken surface of the printed text, as when Old Gerhardt, Hurstwood-like, goes "back to his newspaper reading and brooding" when life seems "a complete failure" (174). Lester is "quietly enjoying his cigar and his newspaper" (200) when he accidentally finds the toy lamb that reveals Vesta's existence, and he pulls "an evening newspaper out of his pocket" (215) and returns to his "lounge" to mark the restoration of his "decently organized" (216) world. Old Gerhardt later takes Lester's accumulation of old newspapers as an indication of wastefulness when it more likely suggests his tendency to live in a perpetual present in which nothing is lost.

Absorbed in reading, Lester is safe from emotional intimacy. Significantly, Jennie experiences a "premonitory wave of terror" when, while she is with him on the train to New York for their first sexual encounter, her tears hardly disturb the "imposing and comfort-loving soul quietly reading his letters" (165). Jennie apparently learns she cannot speak her mind to Lester, for after Louise Kane's discovery of the ménage on the North Side of Chicago, she feels she must write him a letter explaining why she wants to leave him.

In a world of readers, authority means power and self-esteem. Letters, notes, telegrams, and other written documents, in fact, constitute the primary means for men to act in the world. Senator Brander sends letters to procure a job for Old Gerhardt in a local mill and to revoke Jennie's brother Bass's fine for stealing coal. Lester summons Jennie on many "hurried trips" around the country "in answer to telegraph messages" (178), and after his father dies and Robert forces him out of the family business, he feels strangely disoriented because he is no longer "definitely connected up with his father's enterprise by letter and telegraph" (307). The most important written document in the novel is, of course, Archibald Kane's will, which forces Lester to choose between Jennie and his old life.

Authority, however, depends on a vehicle that carries what the author puts in it. In despising romantic lovemaking as a "hollow proposition" (130), Lester reveals his belief in such a vehicle, a language that is not formulaic and empty but sincere and filled with authorial meaning. He is mistaken, especially about written language. "The written word and the hidden thought," Dreiser ejaculates, "—how they conflict!" (380). Newspaper reporters uncover many facts about Lester and Jennie, but even when the "whole story [is] rather nicely pieced together," the meaning is not *in* the text. The Sunday editor prints the story with the "idea" of being "complimentary" (285); the story, "in spite of itself" (286), produces in Lester only a profound embarrassment.

Rather than revealing the meanings in the depths of things, words often point outward to other words. The speculator Samuel E. Ross has "impressed" (327) Lester with a real estate scheme, but when Lester seeks certainty he finds only shifting meaning and value within a closed system of signifiers. The "character" of the land they invest in has a potential for appreciation that can be "judged" only "by the land adjacent" (329). Lester thinks it "easy to verify his [Ross's] statements" but finds himself caught in a system in which words—Ross's "propositions"—are verified only by other equally ambiguous words—"his signs out on the prairie stretches" and "his ads in the daily papers" (331). When newspapers print other untrustworthy words without "verifying" (333) them—rumors that a meat-packing plant is moving next to the proposed development—no amount of counteradvertising can convince buyers that the property would make an "ideal residence section" (334). In Ross's mind, the property becomes "a hoo doo—a black shadow'' (335) as its value plummets and Lester, ''greatly disheartened'' (334), suffers a heavy financial loss.

The shadow metaphor in this last passage is reminiscent of the first meeting of Carrie and Drouet in *Sister Carrie*, when neither can express or understand a clear intention because ''words are but the vague shadows of the volumes we mean.''[11] In using similar imagery in *Jennie Gerhardt*, Dreiser suggests that the world, like the word, is a text that defies reductive interpretation. He thus reverses the Platonic parable that treats the phenomenal world as the play of shadows cast by the light of eternal truth. If there is a universal truth, he wrote at about this time in ''A Confession of Faith,'' it has nothing to do with a realm of changeless forms. The material world is ''past all understanding'' and perhaps is only a ''dream,'' but even if it is not, ''the first and cardinal principle of life is change.''[12] Thus, true meaning is to words and things as the mutability, color, and three-dimensionality of objects are to the flat shadows they cast.

Most of us, Dreiser believed, could not accept change as life's first principle. Phenomena rise mysteriously from ''the well-springs of the deep,'' he writes in *Hey Rub-A-Dub-Dub*, and ''all names and fames and blames by which we qualify it [nature's power] are as nothing, save that they brighten the face of its one outstanding tendency, which we must accept whether we will or not—change.'' The language of abstractions and morality, in other words, reveals human subjectivity; it expresses a need to contain an intolerable mutability and to hide the truth ''written large over everything''—that man's knowledge is as ''the veriest gnat or leaf'' in relation to the vast unknowable.[13] When ''superstitious'' (335) Ross, for instance, names the property a ''hoo doo'' and blames it for his and Lester's failure, he brightens the face of change by eliminating the kind of uncertainty that leads to his bankruptcy three years later in another venture.

As Donald Pizer argues, Lester's own reading of the shadows tells us more about his character than about Dreiser's pessimistic determinism.[14] In that scene of consolation after Vesta's death, Lester retreats into a ''fit of abstraction,'' gazing through the window of a Chicago hotel room at the masses of traffic and ''counter-streams'' of hurrying people, which he perceives as ''shadows march[ing] in a dream'' (392). The *marching* shadows recall the much earlier account of Lester's confusion by the ''vast army of facts and impressions'' that overflow his ''cup-big'' mind (125). An army marches to the beat of another's drum; in using the military metaphor, Lester is thus projecting onto the streams of people the same passiveness he feels when he calls himself a pawn. But even while finding his own insignificance written large on the world, he, like Ross, brightens the face of things by shifting the blame for his own failures onto a superior power, in this case a cosmic commander or chess master. He perhaps finds solace as well in the fact that even cosmic chess masters have to play by the rules.

More often, however, he thinks that life follows the generic rules of written texts. As soon as he takes up the chess metaphor he drops it for one even more congenial to his cast of mind: "After all, life is more or less of a farce. . . . It's a silly show" (392). Perhaps Lester is not being entirely pessimistic here, for even a farcical, silly show follows a script that affirms the existence of the social forms it mocks.

But Dreiser himself perceived a more satisfying principle of order in the flux. Early in *A Hoosier Holiday*, the accounts of his 1915 automobile trip to Indiana, he at first draws from his observation of American industrial life in Paterson, New Jersey, conclusions very like Lester's: human beings are either "atoms" being used by some higher power for some unknown purpose or clownish characters in a "mad, aimless farce." As he travels west towards the Delaware River, however, the sights and sounds of rural life mingle in the gloom of approaching evening and even the terrifying "deep shadows" of the forest become part of a moving aesthetic experience: "Life orchestrates itself at times so perfectly. It sings like a prima donna of humble joys, and happy homes and simple tasks."[15] Lester's real problem, we can reasonably conclude, is not the absence of a single burning idea but an insensitibity to the symphonic or operatic form that evolves out of what Jefferies calls "the rhythm of time unrolling" (73) and that finds expression in Jennie's innocent "song of goodness" (16). Always subject to "the peculiar stratification of life . . . which fixes the lives of people almost beyond their volition" (263), he illustrates what Dreiser in *Hey Rub-A-Dub-Dub* calls the "most inartistic and discouraging phase" of human existence, the "tendency to stratification, stagnation and rigidity."[16]

Lester is therefore incapable of fully appreciating a beauty associated with ambiguity and hidden meanings, Jefferies' beauty as "chronicle unwritten and past all power of writing" (73). Perhaps because he has grown up with the "standard" (139) books in his father's library, he can conceive of nothing beyond the power of writing. Even absurdity must fall within the conventional irrationality of farce and "all the darksome chapters" (209) of Jennie's past must make up a conventional cautionary tale, a "fine tragedy of low life" in which Brander is the "undoer" of a "self-confessed washer-woman's daughter" (210). Life itself becomes like Ross's propositions, a text verified only by other texts.

In creating a world in which things reflect words, words reflect other words, and both words and things reflect the subjective light that brightens the face of change, Dreiser has created a hall of glittering mirrors. In the disturbing newspaper story, journalists have used "the dark, sad facts" (286) of Lester's and Jennie's lives to construct "glittering social figures" in a tale "*reflecting* the romance of the time and of life" (284, emphasis added). In Dreiser's "competent analysis," which attempts to elevate Lester from sexual predator to frustrated metaphysician, Lester is one who has tried to "see into things" only to encounter a confusing "kaleidoscopic glitter." Radically different ideas and things have become radically alike in their inability to reveal the infinite complexity and mutability of truth. Multiplicity disappears in the uniformity of that "vast army of facts"; words merge in the "white light of publicity" that "is too white" for human understanding (125). The shadow world has, for "agnostic" (382) Lester, become a meaningless blank, Melville's "colorless, all-color of atheism."

Yet, as in Irigaray's phallocracy, Lester and other men persist in treating language as a system "self-representative" of masculine unity. They want to be a "forceful figure" expressing a single idea or, like Archibald Kane, a "notable character." They want authority, and what they want to author above all is themselves. In leaving Jennie, Lester seems to have achieved this ideal, for he impresses her as a "solid conservative figure" with a "sense of self-reliance and prosperity written anew all over his frame" (367). Even ineffectual Old Gerhardt aspires to be "as good as his word" (81) in carrying out his threats against Jennie. The irony is that as long as he lives up to his word, which is merely a reflection of conventional morality, he is less a self-authored individual than "an image jerked by a string" (83). Language indeed reflects masculine integrity, but only the superficial integrity of an image helpless to express its deepest meanings.

II

While Lester has inherited his father's impoverished shadow world—"It was to him that Lester owed his instincts for plain speech and direct statement of fact" (292)—Jennie's "inheritance" is the plenitude of "a conformable and perfect world. Trees, flowers, the world of sound and the world of color" (16). As part of this world, Jennie's "spirit," like Jefferies' "chronicle unwritten and past all power of writing," transcends language, for it is a "mellowness . . . words can but vaguely suggest" (16). It is not surprising, then, that Jennie's written words often do not communicate. Her first letter agreeing to meet Lester fails to reach him in time, her farewell letter after Louise's surprise visit is quickly dismissed by Lester, and her telegrams fail to bring any of her brothers and sisters to their father's funeral or to reach Lester when Vesta dies. She does communicate her pain at Lester's marriage, but only because Lester "could read between the lines" (382) of her congratulatory letter. This power in Jennie that transgresses the lines of writing and other boundaries endures despite the efforts of men to contain it within a system of stable signifiers.

These efforts link *Jennie Gerhardt* with many modern narratives that, as Peter Brooks argues, associate the body with "the mysteries of life" and try to make it "semiotic, to mark or imprint it as a linguistic and narrative sign." Equating realism's emphasis on the visual surface of things with scopophilia and fetishism, Brooks finds the realistic plot frequently a "process of undressing" that stops short of revealing what may be a fearsome vision of the castrated body without meaning—"that final object of sight that cannot be contemplated."[17] Dreiser also treats the body as a sign of life's mystery, though in his typical balancing of opposites he offers two simultaneously possible readings. In his extended attack on the "unnatural interpretation" (92) of sexuality, he not only denies that the body is fearsome but calls on man to "read a wondrous plea for closer fellowship" (93) in the bounty and procreative force of nature. In the novel's last scene, however, he suggests that the body may indeed contain a mystery best left shrouded, for Jennie is both baffled by life and cut off from the sight of Lester's corpse, "that last shadow of his substance" (416) inside a coffin inside a box inside a freight car under "a great black plume of smoke" (417) cast up by the locomotive taking him home for burial. Jennie herself is "a woman in black, heavily veiled" (414), suggesting that, for the Kanes, at least, she remains a "marked example of the result of evil-doing" (94) rather than a sign revealing nature's generosity.

Men especially must make Jennie's sexualized body signify some single thing. "I think it will be a girl," the doctor tells the Gerhardts after examining the pregnant Jennie. "He was judging by a peculiar conformation of the muscles of the back which at this period was to him an invariable sign" (96). Since at some other period than *this* period the doctor presumably reads women's bodies differently, his interpretation of Jennie becomes like Ross's reading of the "hoo doo" property, a futile effort to reduce mystery to certainty.

Jennie is from the start frequently connected with the shadows upon which men read their own meanings. The book opens with Jennie and her mother viewed through the eyes of a Columbus hotel clerk, who, "manlike," responds to the "shadow of distress" in Mrs. Gerhardt's eyes by seeing the two women as an intensely "appealing . . . picture of honest necessity" (3). The night she and the other Gerhardt children steal coal from the railroad cars, Brander responds to her much as he might to a written character. She appears as a "form [that] came shadow-like" across a background of "white snow" (30). At this moment, she has no meaning in herself; she is the lack, the nothing, that allows him to recognize in "the far cry between her estate and his" that "it was something to be a senator tonight" (29). Jennie is always what he needs her to be—"the essence of human comfort" (34) or a projection onto a shadow of "what he most desired": "In the glow of the shaded lamp she seemed a figure of marvelous potentiality" (73). Perceived as the potentiality to signify, to be a "figure" of male desire, she cannot be loved for herself.

Lester would make Jennie a visible representation of his own ideal integrity, what Lacan terms the "phallus." The phallus is "a signifier" whose function is "to designate as a whole the effect of there being a signified, inasmuch as it conditions any such effect by its presence as signifier."[18] That is to say, the inchoate subject manifests itself externally in a signifier, which in turn seems to structure the subject, the signified. Lester, "an essentially animal man, pleasantly veneered by the social opportunities which the family's position afforded him" (126), lacks inner stability: "There were molten forces in him, flames which burst forth now and then in spite of the fact that he was sure that he had them under control" (127). He surrounds himself, however, with "appointments . . . which . . . were always simple and elegant" (166), as if both to signify and condition his own simplicity and elegance. Jennie becomes one of these appointments: "It was Lester's pleasure in these days to see what he could do with her to make her look like someone truly worthy of him." Given his growing sense of inferiority in his competition with his brother, it would perhaps be more accurate to say that, when others turn to gaze at this "stunning woman" (167), he derives a pleasurable sense that *he* is worthy of *her*.

To the extent that Jennie is the Lacanian phallus, her relationship with Lester is doomed. Lying "at the heart of all the mishaps of sexual life" is the fact that each partner must be more than a subject who needs an object of love; each "must stand as the cause of desire." In Lacan's definition, desire is the demand for love that remains after all possible satisfactions of need, a "residue" experienced with "the force of pure loss." For the woman, causing desire means *being* the phallus, rejecting "an essential part of her femininity" and entering into a "masquerade": "It is for what she is not that she expects to be desired as well as loved."[19] Even when the move to Hyde Park allows Jennie for a time to masquerade as Mrs. Kane—"the role she so much craved" (254)—Jennie can never make Lester "see her as a good wife and an ideal companion" (257). Always realizing that he is only "half-persuaded that he really, truly loved her" (167), she has become an "appetite" (213) that satisfies his need but not his demands for significance and the adulation of the world at large. Desiring the desire of the Other, seeking her own happiness in signifying what Lester wants but she can never be, she tragically makes herself the cause of endless dissatisfaction.

Despite her unhappiness, Jennie's spirit—her "mellowness"—escapes signification. It can be only vaguely suggested in what Irigaray terms a "female imaginary" appropriate to a woman's intuitive relationship with her body, a fact that probably explains why for many readers she never develops, as Pizer argues she does, from "a symbolic equivalent of nature's generosity to a figure of some complexity."[20] In Irigaray's view, even traditional yonic imagery—Theo's veiled chalice comes to mind—is phallic because it identifies women with a closed form, the virgin's unruptured surface. A woman in tune with her sexualized body, Irigaray argues, would discover herself in the "*nonsuture of her lips*"; she would know the joy "*of never being simply one*" and would enter into "a ceaseless exchange of herself with the other."[21]

Dreiser attributes to Jennie a similar mysterious—and invisible—power released by the rupturing of her integrity, a power that counters Archibald Kane's notion that self-evident truth is the "breath of life." "What is the breath of life?" Dreiser asks in *Notes on Life*. It is, he responds, "a constant interflowing exchange" of energy that can occur only when the "totality" of the universe is "broken up"; otherwise, there could be "no life, no individuality, no thought, no beauty, no love, no hate, no pleasure, no pain—nothing."[22] Life is continually assaulting Jennie's own totality, as when Lester's sister Louise discovers the ménage in the Chicago apartment and destroys Jennie's plans "to rehabilitate herself in the eyes of the world":

> It cut her as nothing that had ever happened before in her life had. It tore a great, gaping wound in her sensibilities. She was really low and vile in her—Louise's—eyes, in the world's eyes, basically so in Lester's eyes. (228)

While Lester is a static "figure," a "personage" (259), Jennie becomes "a personality" because she enjoys "that quiet interchange of neighborly ideas and feelings which go to make up the substance and backbone of true social life" (258). Like Irigaray's overflowing feminine self, this interchange is not incoherence but a structural principle, the "backbone" not of static truth but of "true social life" and, paradoxically, the source of Jennie's personality, or individuality.

Sometimes communicating itself as a form of "telepathy" (268), her personality more often flows like water or sound. Cast out by her father, Jennie momentarily feels on the "outside" but, "brimming with unutterable feeling," she experiences a "vast truth . . . the last essence of knowledge," which is that "in nature there is no outside" (88). Even though she herself is essentially "a silent spirit" (258), she penetrates others the way sound does, especially music. In Walter J. Ong's words, "Sight isolates, sound incorporates. Whereas sight situates the observer outside what he views, at a distance, sound pours into the hearer," who is established "at a kind of core of sensation and existence."[23] Although pregnant Jennie may have become a "mark for the wit and a butt for the scorn of men," Dreiser explains, she is "filled" not with sorrow but with a spirit answering to nature's "heavenly call for color" and, as the breath of life, manifesting itself in song: "like the wood-dove she was a voice of sweetness in the summertime" (94). Her surging emotions thus affect Lester as would "an undertone of natural force that was like an organ-tone heard afar off" (264). As musical tone, Jennie is present even in her absence, inside even while outside.

Because her spirit is dynamic, Jennie can never be one thing, at least not for long. At first, Lester assumes that she can give herself to the "one man" who would be "something like her" (136), and for years he takes her to be "Jennie! The white-faced! The simple!" (204), but he eventually discovers the "truth" that she has been "living a lie" (206) and that her love has been "divided" (207). However, this "truth" is itself inadequate, for if at one moment she conceals an emotion "behind the surface" (22) at another she shows an "inability to conceal" (80). Alternately shadowy and white faced, she is like the words and things that make up the "kaleidoscopic glitter" of life. She also anticipates Dreiser's meditation on the Black Grouper at the end of *The Financier*, published the year after *Jennie Gerhardt*. Able to change instantly from black to white, from earth colored to water colored, this more disturbing symbol of delusive beauty is, "like the light itself," a "living lie" whose surface appearance has "nothing in common" with its inner reality. Because its "business" is to lure other fish to their destruction,[24] the Black Grouper is a fitting symbol for the world of high finance that lures Cowperwood on his endless quest for power, love, and happiness.

Jennie, however, suggests a doubling of life's duplicity itself, for hers is a duplicity with no "taint of selfishness" (364). She lures Lester away from the world of high finance towards life, not death. If she is not what she appears, it is because her inner life—with its "barometric temperament" (386) responding to the suffering of others—is not so much different in kind as richer in quality than her outward appearance ever reveals.

Jennie's secrecy and duplicity are not only selfless but the necessary conditions for her growth from perfect maiden to perfect woman. "[A]ll Nature is working in shadow," Dreiser writes in an expanded meditation of the Black Grouper in *Hey-Rub-A-Dub-Dub*, and "secrecy" is the source of life's "charm," as well as "the condition for the development of quite everything."[25] Not being one thing, Jennie, like Jefferies' beauty, evolves in time, as her spirit works, in shadow, through a series of incarnations; she begins as her father's Geneviève, then becomes in turn the Americanized Jennie Gerhardt, Lester's Miss Gerhardt and Mrs. Kane, and finally the independent Mrs. Stover. Each disruption of one life merely brings a new one. Her seduction by Brander makes her life "radically different" (74), and his death leads her father to drive her "into the shadow" to take up a "new life" (87) as social outcast, which ends with the "new one" (175) as Lester's mistress. Lester permits her to play the role of wife and mother, and his departure forces her into "a markedly different world" (377) in which she loses Vesta but establishes a new family by adopting two orphans.

Herself an orphan by novel's end, she thus works towards restoring that "perfect world" (16) from which she has fallen in the only way Dreiser thought possible for man. Rejecting all theories, Dreiser writes in "A Counsel to Perfection" in *Hey-Rub-A-Dub-Dub*, man should "think of himself . . . as a waif, an unloved orphan in space, who must nevertheless and by his own effort make his own pathetic way in the world," finding personal "joy" in "joy in others."[26] Continuously outgrowing the names and identities imposed on her, Jennie makes her own way in a hostile universe by helping other waifs to do the same.

III

"He sits down there and reads," Old Gerhardt tells Jennie late in the novel, "and then he forgets what the fire is doing until it is almost out. . . . If you don't watch him he will be just like the others, no good" (342–43). Gerhardt is complaining about Lester's handyman Henry Weeds, but the comic digression also reflects on Lester's inattention to his own homefires, coming as it does shortly after a scene in which no-good Lester enters into serious negotiations with Letty. When he is not actually reading, he is often more concerned with following social prescriptions than with Jennie's feelings. Even when he steps outside his "own circle" to take up with her, he follows the "unsocial code" that permits philandering without suffering the usual penalties of "his own plane" (129). In the midst of his reading, he can only occasionally respond to her presence with "strange sympathies" (164). He can recognize emotions in her "so deep, so real" but finally has to confess that "There's no explaining a good woman" (347). Needing a woman and a life he can explain, he deserts Jennie for Letty. In so doing, he demonstrates that if the spirit creates a living lie, the letter that becomes a static truth means death.

Lester's death is implicit in the book's first description of him, by Mr.

Bracebridge: "I like Lester. He's the biggest one in that family. But he's too indifferent. He doesn't care enough" (120). With great economy, Dreiser in this one speech gives Lester potential for a tragic fall and defines his flaw, an emotional poverty combined with a resistance to difference, to change. While social and family pressure sometimes makes him feel moved about like a pawn, most of the time he remains motionless within what Irigaray calls "*the economy of the Same*."[27] He tours the world with Jennie to see what it "had to show" but all the while thinks the "world was much the same everywhere" (306). He points out moral "differences" between ancient and modern civilizations, only to conclude how "pointless" the individual's beliefs and problems are in "light of the sum of things" (307–8), the same light, apparently, that glitters on the surface of the world and absorbs difference.

Fear of difference eventually drives Lester away from Jennie to Letty. If he stays with Jennie, his father threatens, "it will make a difference in my will." If he leaves her, Archibald continues, "We'll forget the past. . . . There will be no difference in my attitude one way or the other" (277). In taking up with Letty, he thus returns to the comfortable world he has known all his life and misses the chance for deeper, more aesthetic existence than he has ever known. With Jennie in Egypt, he momentarily feels the beauty and ugliness of evening mingling "like an undertone . . . in a symphonic composition," but when Letty intrudes wearing "glistening black beads" and a huge "flashing diamond" (316) and Jennie sends him off with a casual "Take him, Mrs. Gerald" (316), it is clear he will return to the silly superficial show of life on his and Letty's familiar plane.

We are not, however, to take Lester's decision to leave Jennie as a tragic error, for the road not taken would have led to virtually the same place he finds himself at book's end. Even had he settled down with Jennie on a "meagre" income of ten thousand a year, Dreiser explains, he "would have maintained this very same attitude to the end"—a "stolid indifference to the social world" he inhabits with Letty. Like Hurstwood in his days as a saloon manager drinking and backslapping with celebrities and his fellow Elks, he would have been a "good fellow" among "compatible cronies" and would have left Jennie "not . . . so much better off than she was not" (405). Not even Jennie's spirit, it seems, would have prevented Lester from settling into a comfortable and stable existence among men like himself.[28]

With Letty, however, he does not have to seek out other men. As Theo does in *Dawn*, he denies female otherness by seeking to possess the veiled chalice, to fulfill the impossible fantasy of having a beautiful woman who yet remains an "absolute paragon." He has what Lacan terms the "centrifugal tendency" of the male who "constitutes" the woman "as giving in love what she does not have" and who out of "his own desire for the phallus will throw up its signifier in the form of a persistent divergence towards 'another woman' who can signify this phallus under various guises, whether as a virgin or a prostitute."[29] And so when it becomes clear that duplicitous Jennie, whom he once thought would make "an excellent Mary Magdalene" (165), can never be the signifier of his wholeness, his old ideal gives way "in the background of his mind" to "the shadowy, tenuous figure of Mrs. Gerald" (361), who thus corresponds to the "ideal" of womanhood "located fixedly in the back of his brain" (124). Despite being a widow, Letty seems virginal, for she is "shapely as Diana" and possesses a "smooth body" (318) seemingly unruptured by sexuality. Because this fantasy makes Letty a reflection of his own ideal integrity, the two relate to one another "like two old comrades among men" (313). Their marriage thus expresses the "hom(m)o-sexuality" Irigaray attributes to sexual relations in patriarchal cultures.

Much more than Jennie, Letty is at home in Lester's static textualized world. When he finally speaks of their "silent understanding" about marriage, the direct communication surprises her: " 'Do you really mean that, sweet?' she exclaimed, looking over at him from her chair, where she had been reading. They had been spending the evening together" (377). They are thus "together" only when mediated by a written text, and Letty becomes so like a text herself that her embrace "*spelled* a form of delight to him" (376, emphasis added). Letty possesses the "vocabulary" (313) to relate to Lester on an intellectual level and believes that she is the "kind" of woman Lester needs, one who has never changed from the "Letty Pace that was" (319) in their earlier years, as opposed to the dynamic, deeply emotional Jennie, who is inept "in light conversation" because she is "living the thing she was" (314). Lester finds no "basis in fact" to support a belief in "one, divine far-off event"; Letty consoles him by indicating that she is "of very much the same opinion" (395) and thus becomes the mirror of his pessimistic worldview.

A life without difference must endlessly repeat itself, and so after the "perfect smoothness" (382–83) of their wedding ceremony, Lester and Letty settle into a "pyrotechnic succession" (394) of parties that "glittered with a perfection of appointments" (370). Lester's decline is especially evident in his verbal repetitions, which make his spoken words more like mass produced texts than like Jennie's song. He first enters Jennie's life as "a deep resonant voice that carried clearly everywhere and bespoke a presence, whether you saw him or not" (212). Yet he has all his life been subjected to Archibald Kane's "constant, reiterated" (292) admonitions to tell the truth, so he himself speaks in formulas. He impresses others as "a man of affairs" because of the way he pronounces " 'Business is business,' a favorite axiom with him" (127), and he gives Jennie a false impression of his courage in repeating his "pet motto, 'Hew to the line, let the chips fall where they will' " (194). In seducing her, he repeatedly falls back on his "favorite expression": "Listen to me, Jennie . . . I tell you you belong to me" (134). As Dreiser writes in *A Hoosier Holiday*, the self is a "delicious presence" of impressions, but each transfer of impressions in language, painting, or music is, by the "law . . . of the transmutation of energy," a little death, a sagging of the soul towards a "thin and pathetic end."[30] Lester's favorite expression may at one time have sprung from an original impulse, but with each repetition his spiritual presence fades into absence even while his corporeal presence grows.

As Lester prepares to abandon Jennie, he moves fatally towards the repetitiveness, integrity, and materiality of the ideal written word, the invariable sign. He wants, but cannot find, a conventional literary form that would validate his relationship with Jennie. He is neither the "hunter and destroyer of undefended virtue" (125)—the conventional "undoer" he takes Brander to be—nor is he the adolescent hero in the "more or less Romeo and Juliet story" (286) concocted by newspaper reporters. Because his society authorizes only these two roles, he does not know how to feel or act. "I don't know whether I'd be able to discuss that divine afflatus with you or not," he jokes when Robert asks if he is in love with Jennie. "I have never experienced its *prescribed* sensations myself. All I know is that in the present case the lady is very pleasing to me" (232, emphasis added). Far from being the "centralized authority in himself" (230) his parents take him to be, Lester is a character in search of an author.

In marrying Letty Pace, he becomes a "significant figure" (376), and what he primarily signifies is the wealth and social standing of his wife, "one of the most significant and interesting figures on the social horizon" (375). When he returns to business late in the novel he prefers "to be represented by counsel" (394) rather than to deal directly with others, but he cannot be anything more than one link in a chain of signifiers.

As signifier of his wife's status and wealth, Lester has assumed the function Veblen attributed to women in a culture of conspicuous consumption; he has also undergone another gender-role reversal, becoming a text read by the women he once presumed to read. In seducing Jennie, he professes to read on her body the truth she does not recognize within herself: "You'll have to come to me eventually. Don't you know you will? Your own attitude shows that" (134). A few years later, when asked what he is going to do about her, he honestly can't say. "Now you explain me to myself, if you can!'' (340), he tells Letty on one such occasion. Although she professes that she wants to love him, not explain him, explain him she does. ''You need another type,'' she insists, someone ''on our plane'' (341). Once capable of taking ''a geometrician's straight line to a woman's heart'' (130), he finds his mind ''working in a circle'' (361) and requires Jennie to translate into words his own desire to desert her without guilt:

> ''You must let me go. What difference does it make? I will be all right. Maybe, when this thing is all over some time you might want to come back to me. If you do, I will be there.'' (360)

When she implies that he can leave without making any ''difference,'' she enables him to shatter their lives while deluding himself into thinking that little has changed at all.

Living a life without depth on Letty's plane, Lester tries to express his ''temperament'' in a ''solid, material manifestation'' (404), but he has nothing of his own to manifest. Accepting his life as ''prescribed'' (403) at three-score and ten, he makes himself a material manifestation of a mere ''biblical formula'' (402) by stuffing his gullet with rich food and drink. There is something potentially heroic in a man who has ''refused to budge'' from his beliefs and resists doing anything except, ''as he always said, 'Look the facts in the face,' and fight'' (403). But Lester has become frozen in a static posture, his beliefs always merely negating what others think and facts always merely reflecting his own hostility. His ''expression was unchanged'' (412), Dreiser writes of Lester's corpse, as if to signify that a man who expresses himself only by what ''he always said'' has been as good as dead all the while. Finally, it seems, Lester has fulfilled Dreiser's dictum that the single idea of a forceful figure is the ''be all and *end all*'' of existence.

Notes

1. *Jennie Gerhardt*, ed. James L. W. West III, 73. All citations of the novel are from this edition; page numbers will henceforth be included parenthetically in the text. I use this eclectic text largely for convenience. Based upon Dreiser's original complete typescript, it contains passages relevant to my concerns that did not appear in the 1911 Harper's first edition. My reading, however, applies essentially to both versions of the novel.

2. This is not to say that Jennie is a thinly disguised Thelma, who apparently was totally inexperienced before taking up with Dreiser and who never did more than kiss him. But, as Richard Lingeman points out in *Theodore Dreiser: An American Journey 1908–1945*, 37–38, ''Some of the grief he felt [over the loss of Thelma] had added a somber music to the passages on love and sorrow

in *Jennie Gerhardt.*" According to his wife Jug, even before the affair, Dreiser, projected his own tendencies on others and "had no confidence in the fidelity of any woman or man" (qtd. in Lingeman, 2:25). On leaving *The Delineator* because of the Thelma scandal, he wrote Mencken in words resembling Jefferies': "I have just discovered that this is a very sad world" (qtd. in Lingeman, 2:29).

3. Donald Pizer, *The Novels of Theodore Dreiser: A Critical Study*, 143.

4. Lingeman, *Theodore Dreiser: At the Gates of the City 1871–1907*, 31.

5. Freud, *Three Contributions to the Theory of Sex*, in *The Basic Writings of Sigmund Freud*, trans. and ed. A. A. Brill, 567–68 n. 3, 593. I cite this edition rather than the Standard Edition because it represents the ideas as Dreiser himself would have encountered them years later when he read Freud in the Brill translations.

6. *Dawn*, 62, 202, 380.

7. Ibid., 380.

8. Ibid., 19.

9. Luce Irigaray, *This Sex Which Is Not One*, trans. Catherine Porter and Carolyn Burke, 26, 74, 171.

10. Christopher P. Wilson, "Labor and Capital in *Jennie Gerhardt*," in *Dreiser's Jennie Gerhardt: New Essays on the Restored Text*, ed. James L. W. West III, 107–8. Wilson argues persuasively that the novel criticizes both the older and newer forms of industrial capitalism, the older, paternalistic system run by artisans like Old Archibald producing in laborers a dependency not much different from that under the seemingly more cold-blooded system headed by capitalists like Robert.

11. *Sister Carrie*, 2d ed., ed. Pizer, 6.

12. Dreiser, "A Confession of Faith," in *Theodore Dreiser: A Selection of Uncollected Prose*, ed. Pizer, 181.

13. Dreiser, *Hey Rub-A-Dub-Dub*, 19, 23, 119.

14. Pizer, 119–20.

15. Dreiser, *A Hoosier Holiday*, 17, 28, 38.

16. *Hey Rub-A-Dub-Dub*, 19.

17. Peter Brooks, *Body Work: Objects of Desire in Modern Narrative*, 8, 103.

18. Jacques Lacan, "The Meaning of the Phallus," in *Feminine Sexuality: Jacques Lacan and the Ecole Freudienne*, ed. Juliet Mitchell and Jacqueline Rose, trans, Jacqueline Rose, 79–80. Lacan strongly influenced Irigaray, who was once a member of his school. Irigaray, however, implicates Lacan in the phallocentrism she attacks in the name of a feminine nature that exists prior to language, while Lacan argues for the construction in language of both genders. For a discussion of these issues, see Rose's introduction to the above collection, esp. 53–57.

19. Ibid., 80–81, 84.

20. Pizer, 114.

21. Irigaray, 30, 31.

22. Dreiser, *Notes on Life*, ed. Marguerite Tjader and John J. McAleer, 14–15.

23. Walter J. Ong, *Orality and Literacy: The Technologizing of the Word*, 72.

24. *The Financier* (New York: Harper and Brothers, 1912), 779.

25. *Hey Rub-A-Dub-Dub*, 145, 147.

26. Ibid., 123, 125.

27. Irigaray, 74.

28. For a discussion of similar male relations in *Sister Carrie*, see Scott Zaluda, "The Secrets of Fraternity: Men and Friendship in *Sister Carrie*," in *The-*

odore Dreiser: Beyond Naturalism, ed. Miriam Gogol, 77–94. In Zaluda's reading, *Sister Carrie* anticipates many of the themes I find in *Jennie Gerhardt*. Dreiser, he argues, revealed the eroticized "homosocial" basis of male friendship and criticized the tendency of men in the late nineteenth century to frequent saloons and join fraternal organizations as a defense against social change and female influence.

29. Lacan, 84.

30. *A Hoosier Holiday*, 29.

Part II
Essays of Intertexuality and Interauthoriality

Obscuring the Home: Textual Editing and Dreiser's *Jennie Gerhardt*

ANNEMARIE KONING WHALEY

SINCE THE PUBLICATION OF *JEANNIE GERHARDT* IN 1911, SCHOLARS HAVE continued to battle over its place within the Dreiser cannon. With the publication of the Pennsylvania edition by James L. W. West III, however, a whole new set of problems has been introduced into the literary equation, and the issue of the novel's place within the cannon has taken a new direction. Scholars are now finding themselves reevaluating the text based on what Dreiser's intent may have been for the novel. In order to do this, though, they must first wade through the mounting primary material that is now beginning to make its way into the scholarly arena and then not only pinpoint the thousands of changes made to the novel before and after its publication but come to some conclusion concerning the necessity of those changes within the scope of the novel's larger thematic concerns. This does not mean, however, that scholars should toss aside all editorial changes simply because they do not constitute the author's original language; instead, we must examine the way in which these changes reshaped the novel as a whole. This essay will begin this critical process by looking at how certain textual changes made during the editorial process, whether by the editors or Dreiser himself, obscure the author's image of home as a place where parents and siblings are genuinely concerned for one another, acting in a sacrificial manner to sustain the health and welfare of the family unit.

The issue of finding authorial intent in *Jennie Gerhardt* is a slippery one for Dreiser scholars. Not only did Dreiser extensively revise the novel before submitting it to Harpers, but he also relied heavily on outside editorial advice from friends and family. In addition, when he finally turned the novel over to Harpers Publishers for editing, they cut some 26,000 words, of which Dreiser restored 9,000 to the manuscript, and heavily emended his style.[1] Although we can argue that Dreiser was probably forced into accepting many changes to his text, we must also remember that he did approve the negotiated edited text, even though his contract stipulated that he could take the manuscript to another publisher if he were unhappy with the end product (West, *Pennsylvania Edition*, 435). On the other hand, Dreiser was also under a great deal of financial pressure to publish something that would make money, especially after the commercial failure of *Sister Carrie*. What all of this means is that although we know what changes were made, we do not always know exactly who made them or why Dreiser approved them. In considering authorial intent, then, we must come to terms with the way in which the editorial process both helped and hindered the creative process.

In examining the differences between the Harpers edition and the original manuscript, West argues that the changes made to Dreiser's submitted text are so substantive as to dramatically alter the reader's perception of Jennie. In his introduction to *Dreiser's Jennie Gerhardt: New Essays on the Restored Text*, he argues that the novel has not been as "important historically" as other Dreiser novels, most notably *Sister Carrie*, because in the Harpers version, Jennie "seems overly pliant and malleable, with no coherent approach to the living of human life" (vii). In his "historical commentary" on the Pennsylvania edition, he adds that the textual cuts and emendations change the story from "a blunt, carefully documented piece of social analysis to a love story merely set against a social background" (442). Richard Lingeman agrees, adding that "Hitchcock and his subeditors tarted up Dreiser's plain style with rewriting that made it closer to that of what was current popular fiction."[2] Few critics who reviewed the 1911 version immediately after its publication, however, saw it as either a romance or a "tarted-up" version of the original text. The critic for the Newark *Evening News*, for instance, writes that the novel deals with "[t]he side of life . . . [which] is, very emphatically, not a pleasant one" and that "the novelist is under no illusions, nor does he wish his readers to be" (91). H. L. Mencken states that it is "a novel that depicts the life we Americans are living with extreme accuracy and criticizes that life with extraordinary insight."[3] And as Richard Lehan writes in his 1969 analysis of the novel: "We move in *Jennie Gerhardt* from the level of the individual, to the level of society, to the level of metaphysics, seeing man in one larger vortex after another, spinning like chips of wood in a whirlpool toward a center that can best be described with a question mark."[4]

Although I do not believe that editorial changes made to Dreiser's manuscript radically alter it, they do, as West later suggests, "put the book out of balance" (*Pennsylvania Edition* 447). This is especially evident when we examine Dreiser's original conception of the Gerhardt home. Although poverty-stricken and oftentimes desperate, the Gerhardts are somewhat of an ideal and, in the Pennsylvania edition, become the family upon which all other familial relationships are measured. Perhaps this is because Dreiser was writing during a time of great mobility when children began moving farther and farther from their families in search of a more financially secure life. As a result of such migration, the traditional notion of the extended family was fast becoming a thing of the past. This type of fragmentation is clearly seen in Dreiser's depiction of the Kane family, whose members form relationships based on commercial rather than emotional needs and, as a result, end up completely alienated from each other: " 'It's quite plain,' " states Lester's sister, Louise, " 'that your family means nothing to you' " (P227).[5] Even Lester's relationship with his mother, he states, "had not so much to do with real love as with ambition" (P214). It is this type of fragmentation that Dreiser rails against in his depiction of the Gerhardt family, wherein members rely heavily on their connections with each other and work hard to provide as comfortable an environment for each other as they can. This stability, though, is not always easily maintained, for it is constantly threatened by Mrs. Gerhardt's nervous timidity and overwhelming naivete, Gerhardt's rigid social and religious sense, and Jennie's moral indiscretions.

One of the most important relationships in the Pennsylvania edition, and to some extent in the Harpers text, is that of Jennie and Mrs. Gerhardt, whose relationship is one of mutual love and sacrifice. Although Jennie's actions are often motivated by her concern for her family, she is specifically interested in providing some sense of security for her mother. As a child, Dreiser writes, she had been "the right hand of her mother" (P17), and "She of all the children fully understood her. . . . She alone of all of them grieved for her" (P108). When Senator Brander proposes, Jennie's first motivation for accepting is her feelings for her mother: "Her mother came into her mind. Maybe she could help the family" (P49). And eventually, when Jennie agrees to go away with Lester Kane, it is, again, an attempt to provide her mother with a stable home. As she makes her decision, "[s]he thought . . . while her mother sat there looking haggard, distraught, weary of life. What a pity . . . that her mother must always suffer! Wasn't it a shame that she could never have any real happiness" (P149). Jennie's emotional connection with her mother, though, is clearly mutual. When Jennie and Brander begin to court, for instance, Mrs. Gerhardt risks the anger of her husband by keeping it a secret, hoping that in the process she can somehow ensure Jennie's chance at a decent life. When Gerhardt finally finds out about the affair, she, in "tears" confronts him crying, " 'You know whether she is a good girl or not. Why should they say such things?' " (P56). In addition, despite the insults of a gossiping community, Mrs. Gerhardt never wavers from her belief that Jennie is good and moral and is always quick to defend her against the onslaught of insults that come as the result of her relationship with Brander. When the hotel housekeeper speaks to her about the inappropriateness of Jennie's gold watch, for instance, Mrs. Gerhardt's reaction is characteristic of her confidence concerning Jennie's behavior: "Mrs. Gerhardt was too astonished and hurt for utterance. Jennie had told her nothing, but even now she did not believe there was anything to tell" (P42). Unable to bear the thought of Jennie's reputation being slandered, however, she opts to "get the wash herself" thereafter (P42).

In the Pennsylvania text, their relationship is set up in such a way that their intimacy and trust is intensified and strengthened through their common struggles and sacrifices. Their priority is always to give of themselves in order to provide the family with the necessities of life. This is specifically seen in the opening chapter, when Gerhardt becomes too sick to work and Jennie and her mother must apply at the local hotel, the most public of places, for positions as maids. Despite their old-world pride, they embrace their new position, placing the needs of the family above themselves: "When it came to scrubbing the steps, and polishing the brass work of the splendid stairs, both needed to steel themselves, the mother against her timidity, the daughter against her shame at so public an exposure" (P7). Despite their shame, they not only scrub the stairs of the hotel but take in washing from Senator Brander. Miriam Gogol argues that such activities help reveal a type of "shame dynamics" within the Gerhardt family, which in turn fosters and perpetuates Jennie's feelings of inadequacy, forcing her to strive for perfection in an effort to deal with her shame (140). Although shame is a force that shapes certain behavioral patterns in the Gerhardt home, it is also, at least in this opening scene, a force that draws Jennie and her mother to each other, further strengthening their close and intimate relationship.[6] This strategic placing of the hotel scene at the beginning of the novel is important in setting the foundation for the tension Jennie later feels between her love for her family and her need to leave them in order to ensure their financial survival. In this scene, two substantive changes were made to the copy text, both of which the Pennsylvania edition restores.

In the opening scene of the original manuscript, Jennie's and Mrs. Gerhardt's sense of shame is most clearly emphasized when they are contrasted to the beauty and opulence of the hotel itself, a place where Jennie and her mother are clearly outsiders. In the revised text, part of the description of the hotel that best articulates the distinction between those who stay there and those who work there is cut. The beginning of the passage in both texts read, "The structure, five stories in height, and of imposing proportions, stood at one corner of the central public square, where were the Capitol building and principal stores" (P6,

H462). In Dreiser's original manuscript, the passage continued with "and, naturally, the crowd and hurry of life, which, to those who had never seen anything better, seemed wondrously gay and inspiriting. Large plateglass windows looked out upon both the main and side streets, through which could be seen many comfortable chairs scattered about for those who cared to occupy them" (P6). In addition, once Dreiser completes his elaborate description of the hotel, he adds that "[m]other and daughter, brought into this realm of brightness, saw only that which was far off and immensely superior" (P7). The words "far off," however, were cut in the Harpers text, which is problematic because both passages, in their entirety, function together to emphasize the awkward duality of Jennie's and Mrs. Gerhardt's position at the Columbus Hotel. The barrier that exists between these women and the world of the hotel is as contradictory as the "large plate-glass windows" that separate the street people from the hotel guests. Mother and daughter are a physical part of the opulent, comfortable lifestyle of the upper class, yet they are cut off from it, separated from a world they can easily see but which is "far off" from them. It is a world they must function in continuously, but one which makes them "too timid to touch anything" (P7).

Their awkward situation is a microcosm for the larger thematic concern of the novel, that being the problematic effect of allowing abstract class distinctions to dictate personal concerns. Virtually everyone in the novel is on one side of the "large plate-glass windows," and although complete happiness seems within reach, it can never be realized. Lester, for instance, despite the fact that he loves Jennie, must leave her for Letty or lose his fortune: "It seems strange," he tells Jennie on his death bed, "but you're the only woman I ever did love truly. We should never have parted" (P410). And even though Jennie gives herself completely to Lester, she is always on the outside of his world looking in. In the end when Lester marries Letty, Jennie "followed it all hopelessly—like a child, hungry and forlorn, looking into a lighted window at Christmas time" (P383). The cut passage also emphasizes the comfort and ease of the wealth as opposed to the harsh world of the Gerhardt women—a world where hard physical labor renders few monetary rewards. Not everyone, for instance, can occupy the *comfortable* chairs alongside the window, those physical objects symbolizing rest and comfort. Unlike the financially secure patrons of the hotel, Jennie and her mother will "kneel" on the stairs, working at "the feet" of its patrons (P8). The richness of the hotel only serves to make them that much more conscious of their social position, which in turn intensifies their shame at having to do their work in the "bright" public halls of the building (P7). Although the passage was probably cut to tighten up

Dreiser's prose, its absence obscures an otherwise sharp visual image of a society that is incapable of seeing beyond its created materialism, cutting itself off from that which it needs most to function effectively—intimate human connections, such as that between Jennie and her mother.

In the Pennsylvania edition, the bond between the Gerhardt women is further emphasized several paragraphs later. As Jennie and her mother scrub the hotel staircase, mother tells Jennie not to "forget to rub into these little corners. . . ." In turn, Jennie, is "reassured" by her comments and falls "earnestly to her task" (P7). The use of the term "reassured" emphasizes the intimacy and admiration Jennie has for her mother, in addition to establishing the traditional work ethic that the family has internalized.[7] Jennie and her mother wish not only to do an honest day's work but will work together to complete the task at hand. Moreover, Jennie's reassurance at her mother's comments seems appropriate when we consider that Jennie, a young girl of eighteen, would have little experience doing such work and would therefore need her mother's direction. After all Mrs. Gerhardt has spent many more years than Jennie scrubbing floors and washing clothes.[8]

In the Harpers edition, however, the term "reassured" is replaced with "mortified" (H463), which dramatically alters the nature of the relationship. This change becomes even more significant when placed alongside the scene that follows, wherein Jennie becomes allied with Brander rather than her mother. In this scene, Brander is forced to walk around the two women as they scrub the floors of the hotel. Instantly, Jennie "caught his eye," and he "carr[ied] her impression with him" (P8). Within moments, Jennie almost forgets "the troubled mother" working beside her, thinking, rather, of "the fineries of the world" (P9). By the time Jennie and her mother leave the hotel that night, Jennie has taken specific notice of the opulent world in which she works, "wish[ing] that a portion of it might come to her" (P9). With little thought, she tells her poverty-stricken mother, "I wish we were rich" (P9). The simple act of replacing the word "reassured" with "mortified" serves to create a tension between Jennie and her mother that does not exist anywhere else in the novel. This tension then becomes more powerful when juxtaposed against Jennie's seemingly insensitive comments to her mother concerning their lack of finances. Because this emendation alters the nature of their relationship, it is unlikely that Dreiser would have overlooked it during the editorial process. He may have even made the emendation himself in an attempt to subtly separate Jennie from her mother, therefore allowing him room to maneuver Jennie into a somewhat reciprocal relationship with George Brander. As a result, however, the relationship between Jennie and her mother at the beginning of the novel is inconsistent with what appears later. In addition, the change alters our perception of Jennie as a selfless, devoted daughter who is not easily swayed by the trappings of the rich. As Dreiser himself explains, "Jennie had not sought to hold herself dear. Innate feeling in her made for self-sacrifice. She could not be readily corrupted by the world's selfish lessons on how to preserve oneself from the evil to come" (P88). Although Harpers', or perhaps even Dreiser's, intent was to sharpen the text through these cuts and emendations, the result is a somewhat murky vision of Jennie and her relationship with her mother.

Unfortunately, Gerhardt's characterization suffers from the same type of ambiguity in the Harpers edition. By restoring many of these cuts and emendations, however, the Pennsylvania edition has recast Gerhardt in a more sympathetic light which, in turn, lends itself to a more realistic reading of his eventual reunion with Jennie and his intimate relationship with Vesta. Despite Gerhardt's tyrannical outbursts and his rigid religiosity, he is, in the Pennsylvania text at least, also a sympathetic father and grandfather who has some very clear moments of honest emotion and concern for his family, and for this reason he is eventually able to experience such convincing familial connections. For these intimate relationships to be realistic, however, the reader, like Jennie, must be able to see him "in his true perspective, a hard-working, honest, sincere old German who had done his best to raise a troublesome family and lead an honest life" (P346). At the same time that we are to be sympathetic towards him, though, his moral rigidity must be obvious because through it we are better able to fully realize Jennie's all-giving qualities. This, then, is the intricate balance that must be maintained.

Dreiser initially establishes Gerhardt's connection with rather than disconnection from his family by placing many of Gerhardt's most touching moments at the beginning of the novel. At Christmas time, for instance, "when the fulness of their large family affection manifest[s] itself," Gerhardt mourns for the gifts his children will not get:

> What would little Veronica not deserve after her long illness? How he would have liked to give each of the children a stout pair of shoes, the boys a warm cap, the girls a pretty hood. . . . He hated to think of the snow-covered Christmas morning, and no table richly piled with what their young hearts would most desire. (P25)

And when Bass is put in jail for stealing coal, Gerhardt "shook with grief" and "broke down and began to cry. No word could cross his lips, because of his emotion." Despite the fact that his son has attacked a policeman, Gerhardt cried, "It is my fault that I should let you do that" (P64). Once Gerhardt has seen Bass locked away, he is led away "shaking" (P65). Valerie Ross cites this specific scene as an example of Dreiser's attempt to keep Jennie from being seen as the only character to have "affective displays (the show of emotion) and affective responsibilities . . ." (32).

In this strategic opening chapter, however, several large cuts were made to the original manuscript which in their entirety obscure the careful depiction of Gerhardt as a sympathetic character. In this chapter, for instance, we are made aware that the desperate situation of the Gerhardt family is due largely to Gerhardt's illness and the state of affairs in the glass-blowing industry. He is, in other words, a victim of circumstance, placed in an impossible situation that is out of his control. Each day he is forced to swallow his old-world pride and rely on the generosity of other people and the hard work of his wife and oldest daughter. As Dreiser writes, "[T]hey lived from day to day, each hour hoping that the father would get well and that the glass-works would soon start up. But as the winter approached Gerhardt began to feel desperate" (H461). In the copy-text this passage is followed by, " 'George,' he would say, when the oldest of those attending school would come home at four o'clock, 'we must have some more coal,' and seeing Martha, William, and Veronica unwillingly gather up their baskets, would hide his face and wring his hands" (P5).

In the Harpers text, this passage is cut, the next paragraph beginning with Gerhardt's thoughts, "I must get out of this now pretty soon" (H461). Seemingly repetitious and wordy, the passage was probably cut because it directs the reader away from Gerhardt, therefore subtly subverting the sympathy intended for him in this scene. This passage, however, is part of the intricate balance Dreiser was trying to achieve between the love Gerhardt feels for his children and the authority he must exercise over them. Although the passage is tighter and Gerhardt's desperation is intensified, the removal of the children's names somewhat obscures the familial connection and emphasizes his emotional disconnection from the family. In this passage it is clear that Gerhardt is ashamed at having to send his children out into the cold to steal coal for the family fire, even though it is a necessity. This shame forces him to react to his own authority by "hid[ing] his face and wring[ing] his hands." The restored passage demonstrates that Gerhardt's desperation is a direct result of his family's suffering, not his own, and that his role as patriarch does not come without an emotional price.

The sympathetic image of Gerhardt is, in the Pennsylvania text, extended to his relationship with Jennie, whom he sees as more than a piece of property to be bartered to the highest bidder. His relationship with her, however, is difficult to define because his love for her is constantly threatened by his stern religious beliefs. It therefore becomes important to examine the way in which his religiosity motivates him. Few scholars would argue that the pattern of his existence has been defined by Lutheran doctrine, which he has been reared to believe is the standard by which all people should be measured. As Dreiser describes, "His Lutheran proclivities had been strengthened by years of church-going and home religious service . . . and from that situation he inherited the feeling that the Lutheran Church was a perfect institution, and its teachings of all-importance when it came to the matter of future life" (P50–51). It is important to recognize, however, that Gerhardt's tyrannical reaction to his family's behavior is not as a much a reflection of them as it is of himself. Accordingly, Gerhardt honestly feels that it is his responsibility to ensure his family's salvation and that if he fails in his task, he will surely be held accountable for it in the afterlife. His salvation, therefore, is as dependent on their behavior as it is on his own: "He trembled not only for himself, but for his wife and children. Would he not some day be held responsible for them? Would not his own laxity and lack of system in inculcating the laws of eternal life to them end in his and their damnation?" (P53). Although he reasons that his religion "was a consuming thing with him" and that "God was a person, a dominant reality" (P117), his "dread of the icy marvel [hell]" makes him obsessively conscious of other people's opinions. Their verbal judgments becomes a reminder of the eternal judgment that will one day be made against him: "Oh, if he could only be so honest and upright, he thought, that the Lord would have no excuse for ruling him out" (P52–53). Such fear makes it difficult for him to differentiate between social judgment and spiritual judgment and the result is his unreasonable actions concerning issues of morality, such as when he cruelly ostracizes his own daughter from the family home when she is pregnant and alone: "I will not let her enter my door again! I will show her whether *she will disgrace me* or not. . . . Let her get out now. We will see how the world treats her" (P84, emphasis added). Even after Bass pleads with him to let her stay even one night, arguing that "[t]his is no time to send a girl out on the streets," Gerhardt will not relent: " 'She goes now,' " he said " 'Let that be an end of it' " (P86). At the same time, however, such excessive behavior is tempered by his condemnation of himself for allowing Jennie's moral downfall. Had he been a better parent, she might not have gotten pregnant. Such feelings are clearly articulated in the Pennsylvania edition when Gerhardt tells his wife, "If I had not let her alone, she would be a better woman today" (P182). Gerhardt's words clearly extend the blame of Jennie's immorality to himself and further clarifies his motivation for acting so cruelly.

This important passage, however, was cut in the Harpers edition, which make Gerhardt's actions towards Jennie seem not only insensitive but egocentric and irrational, when in fact they are as much a judgment against himself as they are against Jennie.

In addition to accepting partial blame for Jennie's predicament, Gerhardt also, in the original manuscript, acknowledges the role poverty has played in bringing about their tragic circumstances. This is seen in his reaction to the fact that Jennie must hide her child from Lester: "[T]here was nothing to do except wait . . . ," he thinks to himself; "He wanted to get out of this mess of poverty and earn something" (P174). In the Pennsylvania text, then, it is clear that the Gerhardts suffer not simply because she gives birth to an illegitimate child, but because they cannot break through their walls of poverty despite the fact that they are honest and hard-working. Their efforts are futile in a world that recognizes only those at the top of the social ladder. However, the revised text is changed to read "deception and dishonesty" rather than "poverty" (H611), which, in turn, shifts the blame from an uncontrollable social force back to Jennie herself.

Further weakening the Harpers depiction of Gerhardt is a large cut made to Dreiser's extensive introduction to Gerhardt that appears in chapter VI of the Harpers text, our first intimate look at the old patriarch. Although the opening pages concern themselves specifically with Gerhardt's religiosity, Dreiser, in the original manuscript, carefully balances it with the following passage:

> Gerhardt felt, rather than reasoned. He had always done so. A slap on the back, accompanied by enthusiastic protestations of affection or regard, was always worth more to him than mere cold propositions concerning his own individual advancement. He loved companionship, and was easily persuaded by it, but never beyond the limit of honesty. (P50)

This passage was cut from the Harpers text, and was replaced with "Gerhardt was an honest man, and he liked to think that others appreciated his integrity" (H503). Although the basic tenets of Gerhardt's honest nature are still intact, the revision omits any reference to Gerhardt's understanding of relationships—an important point when we consider his eventual intimate connection with his daughter and his granddaughter. The restored passage reminds the reader that Gerhardt is a human being who longs for companionship much like any one else, and that companionship is more important to him than personal advancement. Gerhardt's values extend beyond the religious, encompassing a strong belief that money should never have the power to redefine traditional values, especially those that function to protect his family against predators. Despite his desperate financial situation, for instance, Gerhardt refuses to place Jennie in a compromising situation with Senator Brander, even though it would ensure the family's financial survival. Although Brander has been generous to the family, Gerhardt fully understands that because he is too old for Jennie, his motivation is probably based on self-interest, which it is: "He [Brander] had not so very many more years to live. Why die unsatisfied?" he thinks (P40). Interestingly enough, Gerhardt's worst fears about Brander are realized. He takes advantage of Jennie's naivete and her desperation, ultimately leaving her, albeit accidentally, pregnant, unwed, and poverty-stricken. When juxtaposed against the long narration concerning Gerhardt's religiosity, therefore, the restored passage serves to create a balance in Gerhardt's characterization that is lost in the Harpers text.

This pattern of cuts and emendations made to Gerhardt's intimate relationship with his children also concerns Vesta, an extension of Jennie, who becomes the avenue by which Gerhardt is reunited with his banished daughter. When Gerhardt accepts Vesta as a member of the family, Dreiser attempts to reemphasize his position as the moral and spiritual head of his home. Because Vesta has no immediate father figure, Gerhardt is moved into the role, and immediately begins connecting with her in the same way he connected with his own children:

> It was during this most halcyon period, which now ensued after they moved into the new house, that Gerhardt showed his finest traits of fatherhood toward the little outcast. "He is trying to teach her to say her prayers," Mrs. Gerhardt had once informed Jennie after she had privately noted his progress in that direction with the lisping child for some little time. (P183)

In creating Gerhardt's relationship with Vesta, Dreiser was careful to ensure that Gerhardt's rigid religiosity does not overshadow the honest feelings he has toward the child. This was not, however, an easy task. After all, Vesta is illegitimate, a fact that does not easily reconcile itself with Gerhardt's morality. In both the Harpers and Pennsylvania texts, the pivotal scene establishing their relationship is, ironically, the baptismal scene, a scene wherein Gerhardt's stern Lutheran faith is directly challenged by his deep, honest familial feelings for the "little outcast." It is a time when "[a]ll the forces of his conventional understanding of morality and his naturally sympathetic and fatherly disposition were battling within him . . ." (P112). In order for this scene to work, his religious beliefs, a stumbling block to his relationship with Jennie, must become the avenue by which he will bring this "outcast" back into the family fold.

In examining the changes made to this scene, it is important to recognize that certain emendations made by the Harpers editors helped rather than hindered the careful balance Dreiser was attempting to create between Gerhardt's religious intentions and his fatherly feelings for his grandchild. These are changes that West maintained in the Pennsylvania edition. Although Gerhardt begins the baptismal ritual "satisfied . . . that he had done his duty" (P115), his religious feelings soon give way to those of "natural affection," not just once, but twice (P114, 117). Although it is only an intimation of his strong emotion for the little girl, it is all the reader needs to understand that Gerhardt is not completely controlled by "[t]he stern religion with which he was enraptured . . ." (P115). However, Dreiser's original phraseology for the second emendation, which emphatically ends the chapter in both the original and revised texts, was "necessary kindliness" rather than "natural affection," a term denoting little more than a perfunctory duty (West Table, P507). Dreiser's use of this term at such a crucial place in the chapter seems oddly out-of-place, especially considering that he has already introduced Gerhardt's feelings as those of "natural affection." The emendation, which was first adopted in the Harpers edition (H562), makes the text consistent with what Dreiser originally intended for the scene—a balance between Gerhardt's religiosity and his familial feelings for Vesta. There were also other slight changes to this scene in the Harpers text, which West adopts. In both texts, when Gerhardt is asked to stand as "godfather to the child" (P113; H558), the affinity between Gerhardt and this new member of the family is somewhat ensured. According to West's tables, however, Dreiser originally referred to "the child" as "it," an ambiguous pronoun, normally used to refer to inanimate objects (P507). The juxtaposition of the terms "godfather" and "it" represent a relationship devoid of feeling and intimacy, and Gerhardt is perceived as merely performing a religious duty rather than forming an emotional bond with the little girl who "twine[s] its helpless baby fingers about the tendons of his heart" (P183). The emendation ensures that his particular scene is read in a way that is consistent with what we eventually come to know about their relationship.

According to West's tables, there are also other instances where Dreiser refers to the child by the ambiguous pronoun "it" (P539). Although one could argue that Dreiser was trying to avoid being repetitious, the choice of the term "it" over a variety of other more personal pronouns seems a poor choice. Emending them to read either "the child," "she," or "Vesta," restores the familial intimacy between the old man and his granddaughter and infuses the scenes with a subtle, more powerful sympathy.

Although in revising Dreiser's manuscript the editors at Harpers seem to have made, at times, a concerted effort to reconcile familial relationships within the Gerhardt home, it is often thwarted by cuts and emendations that cancel out previous changes. A clear and intimate portrait of the Gerhardt family is important to maintain, though, because it is Jennie's familial background that shapes her into the giving woman that she becomes and renders her final decision to leave them for Lester Kane emotionally heart-wrenching. Although we understand that Jennie finds Lester Kane attractive, her connection to her family is significantly greater than any feelings she has toward him, especially when we consider the touching reunion between her and her father that occurs upon his return home. Although few words are spoken, Jennie's "feeling of affection and sorrow" is "now so overwhelmingly strong in her" (P152), and when she speaks to him for the first time in months, Gerhardt "broke down again and cried helplessly. . . . he thought he could forgive, and did" (P152).

The gradual "readjusting" of "this affectional relationship" (P152), makes it increasing difficult for Jennie to leave her family. Although her decision to answer Lester's letter is tangled with antithetical desires that push and pull her toward her final answer, her basic instinct is to stay at home, for there is where she finds her most honest relationships. Although life in the Gerhardt home is not perfect, she is not forced to lie to those she loves about her past, nor does she have to keep her child a secret. All of these issues are on her mind as she contemplates her life with Lester: "She had told him that she did not wish to do wrong. Must she tell him that she had a child and beg him not to come any more?" (P147). When her father sends word that he has burned his hands and must return home, though, Jennie's hand is forced: " 'I don't see what's to become of us, now,' said Mrs. Gerhardt at last, completely exhausted by this new financial complication, which this calamity had wrought" (P150). Jennie knows that if her family is to survive she must go away with Lester; she knows that she must answer Lester's letter in the affirmative, even though it is not what she wants: "Should she write? He would help them. Had he not tried to force money on her?" (P152). But she does not have to be with Lester long to realize that her decision was a mistake and that her life with him will, more than likely, have tragic consequences: "What was this thing she was doing? What other wretched relationship was she allowing herself to slip into? How was she to explain to this man, if at all, why she did not want to have anything to do with him—could not" (P130).

It would therefore seem appropriate that once she has committed herself to a future with Lester, she waits on the day with "a sort of soul dread" (P153). The revised text, however, emends this last line to read that once the letter is sent, she would await the day with "mingled feelings of trepidation and thrilling expectancy," thus giving equal weight to Jennie's feelings for her family and those for Lester (H592). Although it is clear that Jennie is attracted to him, she also feels "horrified, stunned" by his advances, and looks at him "with a growing terror" when he attempts to hold her (P123). Nowhere in the previous text are we led to believe that she loves Lester with the same passion that she has for her family, and therefore I would agree with West, who states that the rewriting changes the tone of the scene, allowing "[t]he reader . . . to escape Dreiser's implications more easily" (P449). If we accept Jennie's decision to leave as an anticipated event, the sacrificial nature of her decision is diffused and she is more easily seen by the reader as one who was easily lured away from her family and her child. In coupling her dread with "thrilling expectancy," then, Jennie's "sacrifice" becomes little more than an exercise in self-proclaimed martyrdom.

Her "sacrifice" and subsequent "soul dread" are also important within the larger thematic concerns of the novel. Jennie leaves a home where she has her mother and father, her siblings, and her child. All secrets are out in the open and all relationships are honest. Once she leaves them, she never again experiences such completeness. Although she eventually reasons that she is happy with Lester and that he loves her, he refuses to make her his wife, and this leaves her desperate for some sense of individual validation: "For her it [marriage] meant an opportunity to justify her claim to wifehood—to strengthen the bonds of affection which bound them, to appear more conspicuously, if not legally, in the role she so much craved" (P254). To make their relationship legal would once and for all legitimize her existence and help wipe away years of shame and guilt. But this never happens, and as always she is left disillusioned and alone: "Jennie was depressed to the point of despair. She was tremendously lonely. This home had meant so much to her. . . . [S]he had imagined . . . that some day, possibly Lester would marry her. Now, blow after blow had been delivered, and the home and the dream were a ruin" (P366). This is, however, the pattern of her existence. Once she leaves the Gerhardt home, there is always one part of the familial equation missing, and although at one point she has Vesta, her father, and Lester, she does not have her mother, and eventually she loses everyone. This constant sense of loss is most clearly articulated in the dream she has towards the end of the novel wherein she sees, coming out of a "pall of smoke or haze," a small "oarless" boat containing her mother, Vesta, and Lester. As soon as she recognizes the occupants, they are taken away, and she watches them vanish while feeling "a great sense of loss" (P408). The vision, like her relationships with others, is unclear to her at first, and when she finally understands its significance, it is snatched from her. Likewise, she seldom receives the same type of love that she so freely gives away. As soon as she is given the opportunity to experience an intimate, whole connection with someone she loves, that person is suddenly taken away, and she is left, as she is in the dream, with "a great sense of depression" (P408). Vesta, for instance, dies in childhood, only a few years after Jennie has brought her into the home she has built with Lester, and once she is fully reconciled to her father, he too is taken away. Most significantly, though, Lester dies only moments after finally confessing his love for her, leaving her to contemplate the agony of her existence: "Now what? She was not so old yet. There were these two orphan children to raise. They would marry and leave after awhile, and then what?" (P418).[9]

Because Jennie's life consists of a pattern of losses, I would agree with West in assuming that the final coda seems out of place within the context of Jennie's experiences in the Pennsylvania edition. Although the coda was a part of the revised text for over ten years, its disappearance from later versions could indicate Dreiser's intent to leave Jennie as she is in the original manuscript—unfulfilled. After all, once Jennie leaves her family, she never receives the one thing she wants most—a home, one that is honest, complete, and secure, a place where family members love each other fully and completely. Because her need is never realized, it is both appropriate and consistent that Jennie, upon Lester's death, feels that her life will never be fulfilled, and although she pushed him to leave her, it was only because she knew he would be miserable as a poor man. Her insistence that he leave, however, does not mean that the break was any less painful, and to assume that she is satisfied with merely having had the opportunity to love him, is to underestimate Jennie's emotional nature. If Dreiser truly intended to write the realistic novel, it would stand to reason that Jennie's experiences would tell her that there is little to life but "endless reiteration" (P418).

In the original manuscript, then, the issue of home, and all that the word represents, is an important thematic concern. Jennie is reared in a home where members interact in a loving, sacrificial manner. Parents are deeply concerned for their children, and children are concerned for their parents. Although the Gerhardt family is not perfect, it is intimately connected, unlike Lester Kane's, and Jennie is a product of this experience. Although Dreiser's sense of home is still intact in the 1911 version, it is not as strong as in the Pennsylvania edition. Dreiser conceived of the Gerhardt family as somewhat idyllic in a world that was fast becoming transient and fragmented, as was Dreiser's own. The restoration of Dreiser's original language to the Pennsylvania text creates a more balanced image of the Gerhardt family, which in turn, confirms our image of Jennie as a woman wholly "sacrificial."

Notes

1. For a more detailed analysis of Dreiser's revisions to the text, see West's "The Composition and Publication of *Jennie Gerhardt*" in the Pennsylvania edition of *Jennie Gerhardt*, 421–56. Also see Donald Pizer's discussion of this issue in *The Novels of Theodore Dreiser: A Critical Study*, 96–105.

2. "The Biographical Significance of *Jennie Gerhardt*," 13.

3. See Mencken's review, "A Novel of the First Rank," 64.

4. *Theodore Dreiser: His World and His Novels*, 96.

5. Unless otherwise noted, page references denoting only a "P" (*Pennsylvania Edition*) are for those passages that are identical or not significantly different from those of the Harpers edition, referred to as "H."

6. Susan Albertine, in "Triangulating Desire in *Jennie Gerhardt*," 63, also notes the importance of this scene in emphasizing the nature of the mother/daughter relationship, stating that "[t]he opening of *Jennie Gerhardt* projects the unity of the two women in their climb and in their sacrifice."

7. For a detailed discussion of this work ethic, see Christopher Wilson's essay, "Labor and Capitalism in *Jennie Gerhardt*," 103–14, as well as Clare Virginia Eby's "Jennie Through the Eyes of Thorstein Veblen," 91–102.

8. For a full analysis of the way in which women during this century relied on each other to teach such skills as the Gerhardt women have, see Nancy Warner Barrineau's "Housework Is Never Done: Domestic Labor in *Jennie Gerhardt*," 127–35.

9. James M. Hutchisson also notes the importance of the dream sequence on Jennie's consciousness. In his essay, "Death and Dying in *Jennie Gerhardt*," 210, he states that "[b]ecause these various people die, Jennie for a time has no financial stability and no one to love (except her adopted child), no respectable status in society, and sometimes no home to go to. She is at the mercy of those who die, a victim of the forces of death."

From Travel Guide to Autobiography: Recovering the Original of *A Traveler at Forty*

RENATE VON BARDELEBEN

IN 1921 A LETTER WAS FORWARDED FROM NEW YORK TO LOS ANGELES, IN which a war veteran demonstrated his familiarity with Dreiser's first travel book. He proudly announced:

> I have read your "Traveler at Forty" more times than once. The mention of the town of Mayen immediately brought back to my mind your tale of search in Mayen and I told the story to the Captain Gordon, with whom I was talking, and who is the friend mentioned above.[1]

These few lines surviving in the archives of the University of Pennsylvania flesh out the meager record of the annual sales figures and are a living testimony to the brief statement of the publishing firm in 1923, a decade after the first printing, that they had "no desire to give up the publication of *A Traveler at Forty*," since "[t]he book has had a very steady sale" and, so they think, "will continue to have for some years."[2] Apparently the nationwide reviews that are documented in the scrapbook preserved in the Dreiser Collection at Van Pelt, a good deal of which has been reprinted in Jack Salzman's reception study of 1972, adequately reflects the positive acclaim. The book went into six printings between 1913 and 1930 and was among the items Horace Liveright was keenly interested in and had considerable difficulty in taking over from Century.[3] Chances are high that it was among the staple items on the shelves of the reading rooms of the major ocean liners and that, together with the popular travel guides, it helped to prepare the comfortable tourist for his first encounter with Europe.

A Traveler at Forty is the only book Dreiser ever published with the Century Company. The plan for the book was born when in November 1911, Dreiser, who had rejected similar invitations in the past,[4] decided to accept the offer of the English publisher Grant Richards to accompany him back home. However, Dreiser was not motivated by the mere wish to travel in Europe. Having recently published *Jennie Gerhardt* and become a fulltime writer, he had to consider his next novel in which he intended to recapture the life of Frank Cowperwood alias Charles T. Yerkes and for which he needed to investigate his hero's life abroad.[5] As is well known from the first chapter of the published book, Dreiser's lack of travel funds was overcome in a manner reminiscent of Mark Twain's deal with the *Alta California*: by a contract for three articles and possibly a book containing his impressions of Europe.[6]

While Dreiser signals to the reader that he will produce an open-minded, unprejudiced account that is free from genteel restrictions and proceeds to write accordingly, his authorial intention was severely marred by the editorial process, during which he had to sacrifice more than half of his original text. Out of a total of 103 chapters, only 53 survived the cutting process and went into print. The number of pages decreased from 1,165 in the "1st Typescript" to 525 in the "Revised Typescript," the new numbering in red arriving at 562 pages and the printed copy totaling 526 pages. As may be seen from the evidence of the revised typescript, Dreiser, though compliant and cooperative, made desperate attempts to rescue and reinsert canceled passages and patched the gaps by providing new, smooth transitions. A week before the publication of *A Traveler at Forty*, the frustrated author voiced his dissatisfaction with the book in print and asked his friend Henry L. Mencken for posthumous help:

> After I am dead please take up my mss of The Financier, Titan & Travel book & restore some of the woman stuff—or suggest that it be done. I am afraid I shall have to go to Doran on a try for freedom.[7]

The reference to the "woman stuff" reduces the complex nature of the changes to which the manuscript was exposed. Mencken sensed that something was amiss when he criticized: "You start up affairs which come to nothing."[8] What originally had seemed a "propitious" arrangement and unexpected good fortune turned out to be a hampering situation for the author. The wording of the original agreement "embodying your personal impressions of Europe," "growing out of your journey" provided an attractive loose frame that neither narrowly defined the material to be incorporated nor prescribed the exact manner of the articles and the book. Under the impression of comparative freedom, the author felt—as he states in the beginning—that his main obligation to the reader is to give a truthful and unrestricted account of his wanderings in Europe.

As traceable in the Diary Notes, the surviving versions of *A Traveler at Forty* and the correspondence with the Century Company and Grant

Richards, these hopes were gradually shattered. As James West pointed out in his observations on "Editorial Theory and the Act of Submission," the moment when the author places a copy of his text into the publisher's hands is an act of symbolic significance; the author "is releasing much of his control over the text and watching it enter the 'publication process.' "[9] West also stresses an obvious, yet frequently neglected point in editorial theory, where much is said and can be read about author's intentions—the *publisher's* intentions.[10] In the case of *A Traveler at Forty* the situation is further complicated by the fact that Dreiser was dealing with two publishers, the Century Company in New York and Grant Richards in London. While this is by no means uncommon for American or British authors, and Dreiser himself had dealt with both American and British publishing houses before, he was in a new and, as he was to discover, exceptional quandary: the person that had procured the opportunity for the writing of the book also suggested the nature of the literary product and, moreover, directly controlled the process of composition for some time. Dreiser was literally writing the first chapters under his publisher's supervision:

> Every evening he wanted to take my hastily scribbled notes and read them, and doing so was anxious to have me do them all just that way, that is, day by day as I experienced them. I found that quite impossible, however. (*ATF* 150)

Dreiser's moving out of his publisher-friend's country home and taking up residence in a London hotel marks an act of self-determination which is reflected by the end of the diaristic mode. As of 4 December 1911, Dreiser starts to keep a journal which he will work up only after his return to America and the finishing of *The Financier*. By this act he frees himself momentarily for the creative process but voluntarily risks disapproval. One year later in November 1912 Richards, during his customary stay in New York, had the chance to peruse the recently completed manuscript of *Traveler*. He later reports in his autobiography:

> It made extraordinarily good reading, but what would have happened to me if Dreiser's frank descriptions of my friends . . . had been permitted to stand, I tremble to think! . . Luckily Doty allowed me, encouraged even, to cut and cut. I did.[11]

Ostensibly shifting the responsibility and sharing it with the editor of Century for what is probably the worst cutting history on record for the Dreiser publications, Richards here makes a vain attempt at whitewashing his efforts to preserve his personal interests. It is difficult to establish Doty's part; he seems to have been torn among a courageous author desirous to have as much text see light as possible, Richards's strict commands, and the unease of his own publishing house that had a name to protect and a refined audience to serve. Lingeman, who is the first to have explored the circumstances of the publication of *Traveler*, quotes from a reassuring letter from Doty to Robert Underwood Johnson: "I'm cutting the Dreiser copy from 500,000 down to 100,000 and then [there] won't be anything left that is unprintable."[12] This drastic cure was partly reversed when the management of the firm had been reorganized after the resignation of Johnson. Richard Ellsworth was impressed with the book, called it a classic, and allowed several of the abolished chapters to be restored. While the publishing house relented, Grant Richards, who in a letter to Douglas Z. Doty of 12 December 1912, had threatened a lawsuit in case of noncompliance,[13] continued to exert pressure and had to be appeased. It was only at the end of September 1913 that Richards finally signaled his approval of the first nineteen galleys.[14]

The publication history provides some general idea of the type of changes to be expected. They can be summarized under the categories of expurgation and protection of the interests of persons still living and likely to be hurt. Besides the use of fictitious names, the strategy adopted to accomplish these ends was mainly cutting. The extent of the changes varies from the removal of complete chapters to the suppression of specific paragraphs and passages or the deletion of certain words and phrases. A further problem is the subtle rearrangement of the actual journey, shifts in the chronological sequence, the disguise of factual details, and the fictionalization of real persons like Grant Richards or Sir Hugh Lane. All these changes alter the very character of the book and produce a text which is substantially different from the original.

The extensive cuts were also encouraged by the fact that the book exceeded an accepted marketable length. Some of the changes serve to bring the book back in line with contemporary expectations about the subject matter to be treated in a transatlantic travelogue. Despite these adjustments, reviewers are quick to notice that Dreiser's creation "differ[s] from the customary travel book."[15] Most critics seem to agree on the formula that it is a travel book "dealing with people rather than places,"[16] which is a kind way of saying that it runs counter to ordinary readers' expectations. Some even come away with the impression that "[t]here is as much about Theodore Dreiser in this book as about Europe—perhaps more."[17]

Although there is hardly a chapter of the original *Traveler* that was not affected in more ways than one and very few escaped the process of reduction and restriction, I will, for the purpose of this essay, limit my analysis to a few crucial instances.

In opening the book, one is struck by the swift arrangement of the voyage which is magically performed and arranged solely by a *deus ex machina* who enters the scene on the third page in the guise of Grant Richards. On the fourth page of the printed version, the reader already is led on board the ship. The immediacy of the opening scene matches the novelistic style of *Sister Carrie* and *Jennie Gerhardt*, and readers may have credited Dreiser with this stage setting. Though the words are of course Dreiser's, the first chapter labeled "Barfleur Takes Me in Hand" is misleading in important ways.

A close reading of the "1st Typescript," which Dreiser himself had inscribed: "Typewritten copy of the original and unedited pen copy. It contains much material not in the published book,"[18] reveals a different pace, a different presentation of the protagonists and a different set of factual details. The pace, though not lagging, is slower, more reflective. The narrator gives a fuller picture of himself and introduces major leading motifs of the book. And he does not hesitate to inform the reader about his private circumstances by furnishing his address and his financial situation. By being reduced from the forty-eight pages of the first three chapters to a mere three pages, the original structure of *A Traveler at Forty* is severely crippled. Dreiser had chosen a leisurely pace for the unfolding of his story allowing enough space for the reader to comprehend his motivation and decision to travel in Europe and to follow him during his travel preparations. The arrangement he had chosen for his travel record is that of the traditional quest narrative, consisting of the setting out on the journey, the journey itself, and the homecoming. Meaning is created in each of the three stages, and each stage depends on the preceding stage for its essential meaning. Removing the first section almost entirely must produce disastrous effects for the rest.

The book as we read it now shows us an author at odds with the situation of American Letters and the prospects of a writer who intends to present a "straightforward, plainspoken" unadorned account of American life. Here enters the literary friend from England who invites the writer to come to England and to travel to Rome and the French Riviera. While the author is still full of misgivings, the omnipotent Englishman brushes away all doubts and arranges the financial side of the projected voyage. Dreiser provides this fairytale impression, which emphasizes the turning-point quality of his decision, when he writes:

> It [Life] walks in and says, "Here! I want you to do a certain thing," and it proceeds to arrange all your affairs for you. I felt curiously at this time as though I was on the edge of a great change. When one turns forty and faces one's first transatlantic voyage, it is a more portentous event than when it comes at twenty. (*ATF* 5–6)

But in the original he also furnishes the reader with the precise details of his situation and a description of the unexpectedly generous deal with Harper's, an advance on *The Financier*, which guaranteed him a considerable amount of personal freedom. At the same time it surprised and thwarted the plans of the Century Company and Grant Richards, who had also bargained for the forthcoming novel by offering the publication of the travel articles and book and by asking stiff terms from the rival firm they did not expect it would meet.

Though both Century and Richards can hardly be blamed for desiring to eliminate the story of the failure of their strategy, the omission serves to cast the image of a much more dependent and indebted writer, and it enhances the figure of Barfleur alias Grant Richards. The effect which is created is that the narrative will center on the character traits of the narrator-traveler (who also figures in the title) and on his English friend to whom the book is dedicated. This impression is reinforced by the voyage and the English and French chapters. Not being referred to by a mere initial but by the aptly chosen Francophile name *Barfleur* increases the status of the English publisher. While it has been assumed that the cutting was done to protect Richards and, by implication, that passages on this person were removed, the evidence of the "1st Typescript" bears out that many pages on Dreiser himself were not admitted, that numerous paragraphs and occasionally entire chapters on Richards's friends were edited out, but hardly any material on Richards himself was withdrawn. The result was that Richards grew in importance, while Dreiser and the other figures in the narrative dwindled in proportion.

The perhaps unwanted but unavoidable effect of centering the reader's interest so much around Dreiser and Richards and their amiable playful banter is an immediate loss of literary interest when Barfleur is no longer present in the Italian, Swiss, German and Dutch chapters. A shrewd reader like Mencken therefore complains:

> The whole Italian section is dragging in tempo: you have got in a lot of stuff that is unimportant, and you have put little of yourself into the rest. After all it is nothing new to praise Rome and the hill towns: the thing has been done before. . . . The defect here, I believe, lies in the fact that there is more description than narration.[19]

Mencken is dissatisfied with the travel guide character to which the book is reduced in these portions of the account. Always in need of company, Dreiser here relates his encounters with a number of female friends through whom he arrives at a deeper understanding of the respective countries. Travelmate, lover, kindly advisor, or all three, these interesting, carefully drawn portraits add the dimension Mencken asks for, but the publishers lack courage to offer to their audience. Since these passages have been edited out for the most part, the reader is unable to understand what made the traveler linger in one place or, obversely, why the traveler will speed on to the next. Thus Dreiser prolongs his stay in Rome, hoping that his friend—she is called Mrs. Vallon in the "1st Typescript" and Mrs. Q. in the 1913 edition—will accompany him to Assissi, Perugia, and Florence.[20] In Mayen, on the other hand, he hardly stays long enough to see the sights of his father's home town, and certainly not long enough to discover his cousins living there, because he has arranged to meet with Mrs. C——, the singer, in Frankfort.[21]

The gallery of women that Dreiser paints in his travelogue is motivated in three ways, none of which is intelligible to the reader of the abbreviated version. In the first chapter of the original, Dreiser explains his need to go to London in order to research the final years of Charles T. Yerkes, the prototype for his hero Frank Cowperwood. Both the chapter entitled "A London Drawing-Room," which offers a description of the small talk and tastes of English upper class ladies, and the chapter on "Lilly: A Girl of the Streets" have their direct origin in Dreiser's Zolaesque method of collecting the material for his novel.

In an old-fashioned sense, Dreiser's course of travel is a sentimental journey. The quest for the ever-vanishing lady is a leading motif which is obscured by the numerous block cuts. In the original, the traveler is frequently motivated to travel in search of the lady of his heart. In autobiographical terms, a slight hope to find his lost love, Thelma, seems to have been an unconscious additional motivation to cross the ocean. A need to replace her causes him to engage in affairs that usually end when the traveler moves on to another country; examples are Marcelle in France and Maria Bastida in Italy. When Mencken says to Dreiser: "I note an effect of reticence,"[22] he touches the editorial dilemma that did not allow Dreiser to present these adventures fully.

Better known is the complete deletion of the Hanscha Jower chapters in Berlin, which Thomas P. Riggio unearthed in 1977. In this case the omission is paralleled by the removal of all the passages on Mrs. C——, who was a strong reason and perhaps even the true cause for his visit to Berlin. The intimate picture of the singer's upper-class home in the Berlin suburb of Zehlendorf is missing, as is that of the typical working girl and near-prostitute who lives in the vicinity of the Alexanderplatz. It is Mrs. C—— who had lured him on and will even entice him further with vague promises to follow him to her sister living in Amsterdam and thus adds to the string of countries and the episodic character of the narrative. The acquaintance formed in London is continued in Frankfort, where the lady proves herself a *belle dame sans merci*, but still exerts enough fascination to have Dreiser overcome his doubts and establish himself in her home during his visit to Berlin; the latter detail was wisely corrected into a hotel stay by the editorial pen. The description of the parallel affairs on two different social planes furnishes an important comment on the pre-World War I era and the final years of the Kaiserreich. But this intimate experience and insight into the society of Berlin is sacrificed for reasons of editorial prudence, if not pusillanimity.

As printed, the Berlin presented is a city seen exclusively from the male viewpoint. After the rigorous cutting—out of the original eleven chapters only two were permitted to remain—the figure acting as a companion to Dreiser is Mr. A., the singer's husband, who, in the printed version, enters the scene out of the blue,[23] while in the original he and the housekeeper are introduced as substitute companions who welcome and cheer along Dreiser until the arrival of Mrs. C——. The Berlin chapters form another outstanding example of the alterations to which the original was subjected. As in the previous cases, the editorial strategy is clear-cut: the process of selection opposes the personal, often intimate material and instead focuses on the interests of the average male tourist. In the case of Berlin, the two chapters concentrate on the well-known public places, depict the night-life, and include a few random observations on the Prussian character—a potpourri one might expect from any run-of-the-mill guidebook.[24]

The book as originally written follows an entirely different course. In the very first chapter, Dreiser begins in the immediate present on 4 November with a description of his actual living conditions and introduces himself with his true address. He adds a brief retrospective account of his personal career and then starts an autobiographical narrative by reporting about his parents and early youth in the traditional manner of the genre. It is, in fact, the first detailed autobiographical statement extant.[25] Dreiser sees a necessity for the reader to be familiar with his personal background, "particularly," as he stresses, "if you intend to follow this record."[26]

Thus, from the very beginning, travel writing and autobiography are firmly linked in the writer's mind. The book therefore corresponds precisely to Paul Fussell's definition of the travel book as a subspecies of memoir.[27] Autobiography is not merely a formal mode here, but in the sense argued by Paul John Eakin becomes the principal large-scale metaphor:

> the self and its story, play a primary role in the conduct of experience before they ever come to serve, secondarily and derivatively, as representations of experience in texts.[28]

When organizing the experience of the recollected self, Dreiser, the recollecting self, structures it according to the categories and values he identifies with and discusses in his first chapters: truth, beauty and death. The *memento mori* of the end of the third chapter is one of the basic motifs which recurs in many chapters and is highlighted by the reference to his friend's suicide, his symbolic encounter with death in the Mayen cemetery, the funearal in Berlin, and the final escape from drowning as a potential passenger of the Titanic.

While these narrative strands at least partly survive, other themes unrelated to the "woman stuff," have been completely abolished. A case in point is the subversive pattern of disagreement with the authority of his publishers, which, from the outset, forms a subtle subtext to *Traveler*. A deterioration of the book has resulted from the editorial butchery, and the surviving torso (to use Lingeman's image) is so badly scarred that the original intention is no longer evident in many places.

Dreiser agreed to have his book turned into a convenient manual for the transatlantic tourist's preparation for Europe so as to market a book the publishers considered a literary time bomb.[29] This can be accepted in terms of Michael Hancher's final intention[30] as Dreiser's wish to see his book published at all cost. Interpretation of the original, though, shows that the 1913 edition fails in many significant ways to do justice to Dreiser's active intention, that is, the author's intended meaning. Choosing the "1st Typescript" as a copy-text and studying the variants approved by the author will produce a different *Traveler at Forty* that, as a travel memoir, will be closer to *Dawn* and *Newspaper Days* and reflect the attempt of the author at self-portraiture, in fact the first *Book about Myself*.[31]

Notes

Grateful acknowledgment is made to the University of Pennsylvania for the use of copyrighted unpublished writings by Theodore Dreiser. I wish to thank the staff of the Van Pelt Library at the University of Pennsylvania, especially Daniel Traister and Nancy M. Shawcross, for their generous assistance.

The following abbreviations are used: *ATF* = *A Traveler at Forty*; 1TS = "1st Typescript."

1. Letter of 9 February 1921, by Herbert Feis, University of Pennsylvania.
2. Letter of 12 March 1923, by Geo. L. Wheelock, University of Pennsylvania.
3. There is a handwritten note by Horace Liveright to Theodore Dreiser on the same letter: "After *long* discussions, this is the best T. R. Smith could get—I think it's a hold-up."
4. For more details see von Bardeleben, "Dreiser's English Virgil."
5. The book eventually was arranged as a trilogy, the last portion, *The*

Titan, centering on the European, London, experience to be written only much later after a second stay in England in 1926.

6. See also letter of 18 November 1911, by Frank H. Scott, University of Pennsylvania. In addition, Dreiser negotiated an advance on *The Financier*.

7. Letter of 18 November 1913, in *Dreiser-Mencken Letters*, ed. Thomas P. Riggio, 1: 127.

8. Letter of 16 November 1913, ibid., 1: 125.

9. West, "Editorial Theory and the Act of Submission," 169.

10. Ibid., 173.

11. See Grant Richards, *Author Hunting by an Old Literary Sportsman*, 186.

12. New York Public Library, n. d. See Richard Lingeman, *Theodore Dreiser: An American Journey, 1908–1945*, 86.

13. Theodore Dreiser Collection, University of Texas at Austin.

14. Letter from Douglas Z. Doty to Dreiser on 24 September 1913, University of Pennsylvania.

15. *Theodore Dreiser: The Critical Reception*, ed. Jack Salzman, 160.

16. Ibid., 147.

17. Ibid., 151.

18. Dreiser Collection, Van Pelt Library, University of Pennsylvania.

19. Letter of 16 November 1913, in *Dreiser-Mencken Letters*, 1: 125.

20. 1TS: 685, 691.

21. Dreiser wrote: "My return to Frankfort was swift and straight. . . . I was concerned with the arrival of Madame C—— the next afternoon, and the significance of her letter" (1TS 885). See also von Bardeleben, "Dreiser on the European Continent," Part I and "Personal, Ethnic, and National Identity: Theodore Dreiser's Difficult Heritage."

22. Letter of 16 November 1913, in *Dreiser-Mencken Letters*, 1: 125.

23. See ch. XLVIII.

24. For more details on the Berlin chapters see von Bardeleben, "Central Europe in Travelogues by Theodore Dreiser."

25. The twenty-two holograph pages listed as "Autobiographical Attack on Grant Richards" in the Dreiser Collection of the Alderman Library at the University of Virginia are a surviving first draft of *Traveler*. See Riggio, "Dreiser: Autobiographical Fragment, 1911."

26. 1TS, 3.

27. Fussell, 203.

28. Eakin, 181.

29. See Geismar, *Rebels and Ancestors*, 305, with reference to the Lilly Edwards chapter.

30. Tanselle, 174–75, 181; Hancher, 827–51.

31. It should be noted here that *A Traveler at Forty*, *A Book about Myself* and the 1931 impression of *Dawn* have a uniform appearance: Red cloth, lettering on front in blind within a gold box, lettering on spine in gold. This is an important device to mark all these publications as parts of Dreiser's autobiography.

Interlocking, Intermeshing Fantasies: Dreiser and *Dearest Wilding*

MIRIAM GOGOL

IN JULY 1945, WHEN HE WAS NEAR THE END OF HIS CELEBRATED LITERARY career, Theodore Dreiser wrote a letter to a young woman urging her to compose a memoir in which you "have your say concerning all the things you have had to endure and . . . what you think of life. It would be colorful and . . . dramatic and I feel it would sell . . ." (211).[1] The woman to whom Dreiser wrote this letter was Yvette Szekely, later to become the wife of Max Eastman.[2] In giving her this advice, Dreiser was no doubt thinking of Yvette Eastman's childhood in Budapest, her early separation from her father, her subsequent emigration to America, and her difficult life with her sister and stepmother.[3]

Dreiser was surely not thinking that, when she came to write her book, Eastman would describe her long relationship with Dreiser as one of the most difficult things she ever had to endure. Or that in her book he would emerge as someone whose feelings of inadequacy drove him to the company of younger and younger women. Nor did he ever think she would describe a relationship in which the celebrated author of *An American Tragedy* was guilty of statutory rape.[4]

In 1929, when Dreiser began his long campaign of seduction, Eastman was sixteen years old. When they consummated their relationship, she was seventeen, Dreiser was fifty-nine. Eastman's memoir, titled *Dearest Wilding* (1995), describes this sixteen-year relationship. It provides intimate disclosures of Dreiser's private life and actions—actions that raise serious, even legal, questions about his life. Why did Dreiser have an abiding interest in very young girls? Why was he a womanizer, a fact extensively documented by Richard Lingeman and many biographers before him?[5] We might also ask, conversely, what is the value of such intimate biographical revelations? Isn't this precisely what Joyce Carol Oates labeled "pathography" in a 1993 issue of *The Chronicle of Higher Education*?[6] Perhaps, but the value of such explorations to scholars, critics, and readers alike is that these disclosures help us understand who the real Dreiser was. The memoir tells why it was to women that Dreiser discloses many of his most private thoughts about his emotional state, physical health, feats and concerns. These revelations give us clues not only about how Dreiser saw himself and others but also about the relationships he forged. Furthermore, we come to see how many of his everyday choices, quirks, and characteristics and ultimately his unconscious mind were fantasy-driven, that is, that there was a core unconscious fantasy being repeatedly acted out[7] that led him into numerous relationships, including relationships with adolescent girls. Such revelations, I contend, can only help us better explain the themes of Dreiser's life as well as the themes of his works.

It is hard not to believe that, when he began his affair with Eastman, he was preying on a naive, defenseless girl.[8] As Eastman tells her story, Dreiser was forty-two years her senior when he began the relationship: clearly old enough to be not her *father*, but to be her *grand*father. There is no question that Eastman was in search of the "giant father" (95) to compensate for the loss of her own father at an early age. In her *Memoir*, she plaintively records her early separation from her biological father in Budapest when she, her stepmother, and her younger sister emigrated to America in 1921. She relays the disturbing molestations that began by two different men within months of her emigration, at age eight. Because her stepmother was repeatedly hospitalized for mental breakdowns, Yvette was left alone and vulnerable to predatory males. As Eastman portrays her stepmother (the only mother she had ever known), she was largely a destructive force, when she was available to Yvette, pathologically jealous and denigrative, especially in the presence of the young men who courted her daughter.

Enter Dreiser, when Eastman is sixteen. Having sensed that she was in search of an affectionate father, he then donned a supportive and encouraging persona, as shown in his early correspondence with Yvette and *her fourteen-year-old sister Sue* (more later on Sue): He was "supportive and encouraging [of] our youthful discoveries, [he] liked kidding us, and . . . was playfully teasing" (38). "I'd like to keep an eye on you, as it were," Dreiser days. "Your [sic] my *Babes in Joyland*. I like to think of you both as young and strong and happy. And I want you to think of me as one who wants you to be that way"—again, answering Yvette's call by being very paternalistic (5 February 1930).

One year later, when she was seventeen, Dreiser was able to seduce the young Yvette. According to Eastman, she "was flattered by this famous man's special interest" (44). Although she didn't reciprocate his sexual interest, she did have a deep-seated need for a father. It led her into this relationship in which she sought "the romance, the poetry, the admiration, the support, but not the physical fondling . . ." (44) of this old man.

Dreiser, according to Eastman, fulfilled her "father complex" (44): "As I gratefully responded to his fatherly interest in my young life and aspirations and his confident, cheering encouragement about meeting it, *he became intensely, desperately important to me*. It was the first time a commanding someone had focused exclusively on me: how did I feel, what did I think, what did I want, where was I going? . . . He told me that for him I was 'youth,' 'poetry,' 'gaiety,' 'understanding,' that my warmth aroused his mind and heart and all his sensual desire" (45, emphasis mine). "The seventeen-year-old me relished this—all except the pressure he began to apply with increasing frequency to go to bed with him. In a small and far-away corner of my mind, I suspected this possibility loomed larger in his thought than my 'poetry' and 'wisdom.' I kept putting the event off with excuses like having to cram for midterm exams . . ." (45).

Eastman dreads this " 'all the way' first-time great event" (45), as she later sarcastically calls their first sexual intercourse, and associates it in her mind with a "scheduled session with the dentist to have a wisdom tooth pulled" (45). Dreiser arrives for this occasion carrying a black leather satchel, like a doctor's bag. "It made me uneasy" (47), she says. "It contained a rubber sheet, some lysol" (47). "Visions of accident victims being wheeled to surgery flashed" through her mind (47).

What is apparent is Eastman's vulnerability and her felt need to sacrifice herself to Dreiser: "The bed part of it I accepted as something I had to do, like washing my hair or brushing my teeth, if I wanted to be wanted and loved . . ." (49). She is never sure of Dreiser's motives: "Going to bed, having sex—not specifically for its physical pleasures, to which I had not yet awaked—continued to be so easy, a 'natural,' 'no problem' activity if I thought I was cared about and taken as a person rather than as a sex object. But I was never quite sure" (58). Tragically, she is "mortally afraid of losing him" (64), "the illusory father" (65).

In the *Memoir*'s "Afterword," Eastman makes her darkest charge: "I came to realize that if I had never known TD, I might have gone to college, married, had children. He pushed me at that malleable age out of what might have been a conventional life into an often choppy sea that cast me on to uncharted shores where the choices I made were ruled by emotion rather than by reason. In part, at least, I thought that my quest toward being taken as a person rather than as a sex object was impeded by TD's influence" (112–13).

We know that her stepmother, Margaret Menahan, wanted Eastman to press criminal charges against Dreiser for statutory rape (203). Contributing to her distaste for Dreiser was the knowledge (in all likelihood) that he had begun to pursue Yvette's fourteen-year-old sister, Suzanne, as well, as I discovered (with the help of Nancy Shawcross, the

Curator of Manuscripts in the Special Collections of the University of Pennsylvania Library).[9] The twenty-seven letters to Suzanne that exist, heretofore undisclosed (that is, never published, never cited) in the University of Pennsylvania Library, were written by Dreiser from 1929 to 1930. These letters to "Sue" are clearly love letters, attempting to be seductive and persuasive—signed "love" and pursuing "Suzie Sweet" with "easter eggs," invitations to soirees, etc. This is verging on pedophilia.[10]

During the period of his relationship with Eastman (1929–1945), Dreiser was involved with scores of women and with girls, with Eastman being only the youngest *on record* with whom he consummated a relationship. In attempting to put this in perspective, it is useful to consider what recent psychoanalytic theory has to say about "fantasy," given the "fantastical" nature of this relationship. Psychoanalytically defined, fantasy is an internal narrative, "an imaginative story . . . that generally serves . . . a wish-fulfilling function, gratifying sexual, aggressive, or self-aggrandizing wishes . . . symptoms [that] all look backward: they all express unfinished business" (Person 7, 60). [11]

Contemporary psychoanalysis is directing increasing attention to repeating fantasies such as we see here. While Eastman was involved in a recurring search for a father (through Dreiser, her own stepfather, and Max Eastman), Dreiser was carrying on his own repeated search for very young girls and fulfilling his own fantasy of being this adored, powerful, macho figure. In Dreiser's case, this was a search for sexual pleasure and emotional relief. Psychiatrist Ethel Person discusses "organizing fantasies" in her highly acclaimed 1995 psychoanalytic study, *By Force of Fantasy*. According to Person, these organizing fantasies "play an essential role in solving the central unconscious conflicts and problems that each of us carries with us from infantile life." As such they can become integral to our sense of identity. They are often adaptive, but, and this is the important part vis-á-vis Dreiser, "they may be *maladaptive* as well—associated with neurotic symptoms or character disturbances" (74, emphasis mine).[12]

The latest paradigm of psychoanalytic theory, relational psychoanalysis, which comes out of the British School of Object Relations,[13] may be particularly helpful here. The shift is away from the classical, psychoanalytic model that focuses on the psychopathology of one singular boundaried individual. There is increasing recognition that "the individual discovers [her]/himself within an interpersonal field of interactions in which [she]/he has participated" (Mitchell 132). Relational psychoanalysis charges that acting out (that is, the playing out of unfinished business [a script form your past], restoring yourself, revenging yourself, etc.), is not done in a vacuum, that, in effect, we need a partner, that everything is reciprocal, everything is complementary in a dialectical way. Eastman is looking for an idealized father figure. That's clear to see. But Dreiser is looking for that in himself too, that heightened manliness, adequacy, effectualness of an idealized figure. To establish his own deep feelings of virility, he has to act out with multiplicities of women and girls—and, as we have seen in Dreiser's case, the younger the better. Because the younger they are, the more they adulate him—which is what he most desires. The problem is that unless these unconscious fantasies are dredged up and explored as unrealistic or destructive they are compulsively repeated. That's why even Dreiser described himself as driven in his search for "not one but three or four, even five women at once" (*This Madness*, "Sidonie," 85).[14] Dreiser knows *that* he is driven and he knows *what* he is driven for (very young, very beautiful girls). But he doesn't know *why*. He doesn't know the origins; he doesn't know the roots.[15]

An insight into Dreiser's fantasy life is provided by Dreiser's narrator in a little-known semi-autobiographical serial he sold to *Cosmopolitan* in 1929 (the same year that he met Eastman). Appropriately named *This Madness*, Dreiser shows that he had a lot of self-awareness and perhaps he even unconsciously had a sense of humor. It told of the "love affairs of a famous novelist who goes by the nicknames 'Dodar' and 'T' and whose books include *The Financier* and *The Titan*" (Lingeman 2:323). Dreiser informed the *Cosmopolitan* editors: "You people may not realize it, but in 'This Madness' you are publishing the most intimate and important work so far achieved by me" (Lingeman 2:323). This series, which was greatly censored by its editors, was very frank and honest, and revered by Dreiser as such.[16]

In *This Madness*, three elements of Dreiser's personality emerge that intriguingly reflect those captured by Eastman in her *Memoir*, but this time—reciprocally, interlockingly—the voice relating the narrative is Dreiser's own. The first characteristic is his tendency to see women interchangeably, as evidenced by Dreiser's courting Yvette while sending torrid letters to her fourteen-year-old sister. In one episode of *This Madness*, Dodar becomes simultaneously enamored of a mother and daughter.[17] Finding it impossible to choose between them,[18] Dodar exclaims: "How shall I say it? Two vases, or two graven images, of different materials, different times, moods, traditions, stand side by side. One has this. The other has that. This one is exquisite in form and coloring; that one in coloring and grace. *Yet, there is scarcely the possibility of choice between them*" ("Aglaia," typescript A [folder 1] [37]: 35).

A second behavioral element is detachment. In one of Eastman's most interesting observations, she speaks of being in awe of "that impenetrable detachment [Dreiser] emanated, as if nothing could touch him" (93).

This element appears again and again in the three episodes. In "Elizabeth," which is about Anna Tatum, another of Dreiser's young lovers, Elizabeth describes Dreiser's remoteness as a reason for leaving him for another: "I know I can't stand this any longer. I'm lonely. I like him [this other man, not Dreiser]. At least he's kindly and tender. He's not a remote, snow-covered peak" (65). In "Aglaia," although she is madly in love with him, Aglaia aborts Dodar's child. His response is detachment: "yet, . . . as strange as it may seem to some—so much having been said of her lure for me—when she was actually away from me at this time. . . . I was not so conscious of her and her absence as one might imagine . . . I was scarcely conscious of Aglaia or any human being—even Lenore—when I was thus alone" (60). It may be that the attention he manifested with these young women that made him become "intensely, desperately important" to them (Eastman 45), to quote Eastman, was a "pseudo attentiveness" as evidenced by their interchangeability to him.

A third trait is the need for adulation, the adulation that comes with such nonlateral relationships as those he pursued with very young girls or young women throughout his life. The striking examples before us are Yvette and her sister. But also striking is Eastman's description in the *Memoir* of Helen Richardson, his best-known and longest female companion, whom Dreiser met when she was twenty-five, and he forty-eight. (Dreiser thought she was nineteen or twenty). Years later, Eastman describes Richardson's demeanor around Dreiser in the following way: "her characteristic expression was either a seeking one—seeking TD's approval—or a hairbreadth anxious one, which seemed to inquire, 'Is everything all right?' " (32).

All of the women in this serial enter Dreiser's life revering his literary stature and become sexually involved with him in the process. In terms of reciprocal fantasies there seem to be unconscious interlocking attractions: Dreiser's need to be "gigantized" and their need for "gigantic" fathers. These reciprocal needs play out most dramatically in the age differential. This repetition compulsion is acted out in the women, too. They think they are reversing their own fear (by finding the father), but they are repeating it (attaching to a figure who will predictably detach from them).

It would appear that the internal fantasy image of the woman in Dreiser's unconscious is more powerful, stronger than the external reality of any given woman, thus making the women transferable objects. His desire and wish were to overcome early feelings that he was unlovable, unattractive, and puny, which is how he describes himself in his autobiography *Dawn* and in his unpublished essay about his mother, "Sarah Schanab." Implicit in the core fantasy is Dreiser's wish to prove that he is the most attractive, desirable giant figure, esteemed by all. At the same time, he banishes the fear that he will be bypassed, dismissed, rejected.[19]

Eastman's *Memoir* raises intriguing questions about patterns in Dreiser's psyche: What is the force driving someone to act out a core fantasy? Is there a connection between this acting out and Dreiser's chronic depressions? Dreiser tells us of his "five to nine a.m. horrors . . . I never get a break. They never take a holiday. Actually I consider myself an iron man to have stood it since 16—and not crashed" (99) from "this almost crushing despair" (159). By acting out his fantasies of perpetual change, he may have, in effect, created his own antidepressant. Dreiser, who struggled all his life with feelings of inadequacy may well have used his writing as a phallic compensation. Eastman, who was his youngest known lover, chosen when he was advanced in years, may be the most dramatic revelation of his own self-doubts. This relationship may uncover deeper layers of inadequacy feelings in Dreiser's self-image as a man. Especially in his declining years, the wish to revive the adolescent man in himself was intensified. His relationship with Eastman which began, legally speaking, as statutory rape, may confirm most strikingly this phenomenon on its grandest scale.

Dreiser's conduct illustrates the turmoil at the heart of his personality. Although it's difficult to sympathize with him, one can see that his literary genius lay in his ability to honestly communicate his neuroses throughout his books to his readers.[20] It is his honesty that draws readers and outweighs the unsavory, even repulsive, qualities in his personality.

Notes

1. Yvette Eastman, *Dearest Wilding: A Memoir*, ed., Thomas P. Riggio. All subsequent references to the text will appear parenthetically in the body of the essay. This memoir of Eastman's relationship with Dreiser is followed by 115 of the 229 love letters Dreiser wrote to her, love letters which commenced shortly after they met in 1929.

2. Very little of Dreiser's correspondence with women has been published. The other exception that comes to mind is *Theodore Dreiser's Letters to Louise Campbell*, ed. with commentary by Louise Campbell.

3. Special thanks to Albert Ashforth for his significant contributions to the shaping of this essay. Also, gratitude to Florian Stuber, Stephen Brennan, and Madelyn Larsen for their editorial suggestions, and to Zanvel A. Liff, past President, Division of Psychoanalysis of the American Psychological Association, for several interviews on the nature of psychic fantasy and promiscuity.

4. According to McKinney's *Consolidated Laws of New York Annotated, 1930 Cumulative Supplement*, Penal Law, Section 2010, III, until the age of 18

has been reached a woman is incapable of legal consent to sexual intercourse. Therefore, under those circumstances, intercourse is considered rape in the second degree in the State of New York.

5. Richard Lingeman, *Theodore Dreiser: At the Gate of the City, 1871–1907* and *Theodore Dreiser: An American Journey, 1908–1945*; W. A. Swanberg, *Dreiser*. For other sources and further discussion, see note 7.

6. Karen J. Winkler, "Seductions of Biography," A6. In defense of the search into a writer's private life, one must ask, does it make sense to write a biography without telling as much of the truth as can be determined? Also, see note 8 for an ongoing discussion of this issue of exploring Dreiser's "private" life.

7. Ethel S. Person, M. D., *By Force of Fantasy: How We Make Our Lives*, 74.

8. We owe a great debt to Dreiser biographers and to the editors of Dreiser's primary materials for bringing such reminiscences to press. Special gratitude should be expressed to Thomas P. Riggio, editor of *Dearest Wilding*, for his masterful and sensitive editing of this memoir. In his Introduction, Riggio raises the perplexing question that he rightfully feels biographers eventually must explain: why did Dreiser, "for all his unsavory reputation as a careless philanderer, . . . inspire . . . more such reminiscences [by women about Dreiser] than any other American writer" (ix). I would suggest that the best answer lies in the psychoanalytic realm—that all these women are still caught up in a transferential, propelling wish for an idealized father figure. Dreiser often picked women with detached fathers, or abandoned women, as highlighted in the case of the young Yvette: Dreiser was the first "commanding someone [who] had focused exclusively on me" (45), but then he abandoned her, too.

His philandering and the ensuing unhappiness of many of the women he rejected has already been documented. See *Theodore Dreiser: Beyond Naturalism*, ed. Miriam Gogol. Particularly see the Introduction: vii–xvii, and essays by Shelley Fisher Fishkin: 1–30, and by Irene Gammel, 31–54. To cite a few women, Anna Tatum took to drink shortly after becoming involved with him. Louise Campbell wanted to marry him but knew that he never would. Kirah Markham, whom some have argued wanted her freedom, said "What's the good of a freedom I don't want and can't use?" Estelle Kubitz's hysterics at finding traces of other women led her to cry in her sleep. She said she could not live with those unknown rivals whose letters she occasionally discovered and whom Dreiser could not give up.

9. Nancy Shawcross, Curator of Manuscripts, Department of Special Collections, University of Pennsylvania. The twenty-seven letters exist undisclosed in the University of Pennsylvania Library. They were written by Dreiser to Suzanne Menahan Sekey, as she is listed on the folder, from 1929 to 1930. See Theodore Dreiser Letters to Yvette Szekely and others, ms. coll. 114.

10. Following this essay are copies of four of the twenty-seven letters that Dreiser wrote to Suzanne Menahan Sekey from 1929 to 1930.

11. Unconscious fantasy by definition is an inferred construct: for what is unconscious cannot be directly observed. Nonetheless, it is valuable in understanding the way the mind works (Person, 60–61).

12. Given their connection to the central issues of our psychic lives, "repeating fantasies have special interest for psychoanalysts, who primarily view them as signposts to the mysterious world of the unconscious, as superego- and ego-edited derivatives of unconscious fantasies. Always the ultimate goal of analyzing them is to decipher *the [core] unconscious fantasy*, the key to understanding character traits and neurotic symptoms, to resolving unconscious conflict. . . ."

Repeating fantasies, according to the psychoanalyst Harold Bloom, whom Person quotes, are "linked to elusive but important aspects of self, identity, and character." Because they are integral to our conscious sense of pleasure, we cannot abandon such fantasies at will. According to Person, considerable evidence indicates that "many people spend much of their lives consciously attempting to enact their repeating fantasies or to live them out in slightly disguised forms—or, alternately, to protect themselves from the negative implications of realizing those fantasies. Moreover, such fantasies are often enacted in ways that the fantisizer does not perceive, because the enactment is such a heavily disguised version of the daydream's script" (Person, 74).

Fantasy and reality are not opposites: "rather, the former is a significant factor in our mental construction of the latter. The centrality of unconscious fantasy to mental life—its influence on thoughts, intentions, and feelings—is generally acknowledged by all contemporary schools of psychoanalytic thinking. A guiding force in motivating us, unconscious fantasy is also the headwater from which flows the rivers of neuroses and other symbolic mental products, including dreams, daydreams, and artistic productions" (Person, 65).

13. Stephen A. Mitchell, *Hope and Dread in Psychoanalysis*.

14. Gender plays a distinctive role in sexual fantasy: "The cultural stereotype of male sexuality depicts phallic omnipotence and supremacy and invests the phallus with the power of mastery. At the very least, this view of male sexuality depicts a large, powerful, and untiring phallus attached to a man who is long on self-control, experienced, competent, and knowledgeable enough to make women crazy with desire. As the psychologist Bernard Zilbergeld has described it, 'It's two feet long, hard as steel, and can go all night.' In the shared cultural fantasy, even the normally reticent female is utterly powerless and receptive when she confronts pure macho sexuality. Yet this fantasy conceals and reverses males anxieties."

"Short of violence, many men embrace some version of macho sexuality (especially the belief that *other* men are truly in possession of it). On one level, 'macho' fantasies are adaptive, counteracting underlying fears and resentments and simultaneously incorporating and neutralizing hostile impulses. At the same time they may aggravate a preexisting sexual anxiety, since many men literally believe other men are doing better, 'getting more,' and so forth" (Person, 168–69).

15. Dreiser describes himself repeatedly as a "varietist," someone in need of constant change, in his case, constant change of women: "I am driven by an *insatiable hunger for change*, like the desire of a suffering person for a drug—and yet, so often, the change, once made, is worth almost nothing to me—a few hours of conversation, a few intimate contacts, and then I see what I could not see at first—that I am not truly and really interested—even bored at times" (emphasis mine; "This Madness," "Aglaia," ms. coll. 30, box 351, Typescript A, folder 2, [37]: 85).

16. *This Madness*, an "honest novel about love," tells the story of a male character who is unable to remain faithful to one woman. The novel is subdivided into three episodes entitled "Aglaia," "Elizabeth," and "Sidonie." Although some of the events are changed, these three portraits are largely based on women in Dreiser's own life. Each episode ends in grief, the abandoned woman mourning her loss (Lingeman, 2:323).

17. We see this in the first episode of *This Madness*, which is called "Aglaia." It is based on Lillian Rosenthal, a twenty-year-old woman with whom Dreiser became intimate in 1911 while he was writing *Jennie Gerhardt*.

18. In another passage in "Aglaia," Dreiser says that "in spite of [the mother's] forty-five years and her extreme devotion to her husband she was able to evoke in me an interest which was far from platonic" ("Aglaia," Typescript A, folder 1 [37], 19).

19. Ego psychologists (but not all contemporary analysts) believe that "fantasy encompasses not only the original wish but the defenses erected against it. All fantasies show the mark of the ego's synthesizing function and, therefore, are more or less composites of wishes, defenses against them, superego directive, and reality consideration. In this view, an unconscious fantasy is not just a wish but a compromise formation, the result of a struggle between mutually exclusive wishes (contradictory drives and impulses simultaneously striving for expression) or between wishes and the opposition mounted by either internal (psychic) reality or external reality" (Person, 63).

20. An exploration of Dreiser's life vis-á-vis these women can help us more fully understand the nonlateral relationships consistently appearing in his fiction. Characters who most immediately come to mind include the autobiographical Eugene Witla in *The "Genius"* who is in chronic pursuit of younger and younger women. (Eugene's last love affair is with the eighteen-year-old Suzanne Dale.) Other notable examples are Jennie Gerhardt (age 18) with Senator Brander (50) and a few years later with Lester Kane (36), Cowperwood with the young Aileen Butler and with the many other women he pursued, and most strikingly, Carrie Meeber with the middle-aged George Hurstwood.

[March 11 1930]

Susie Sweet:

Is this anything you want?

Or do I have to do

letter?

Keep straight

And don't swear.

T. D

On this and the following pages appear four letters Dreiser wrote to Suzanne Menahan Sekey on 11, 18, 30 March and 18 July 1930. Thedore Drieser Letters to Yvette Szekely, Rare Book and Manuscript Library, University of Pennsylvania.

Thursday - Mch 18 - 1930

Dear Sus:

I'm off today - sure - for Arizona. 6 P.M. In one way I wish I didn't have to go. In another it seems that it ought to be interesting. One thing I do wish is that I might tuck you in my pocket and take you along. We'd discuss everything and you could sing me there and back. In fact you might even do a rhymed history of the trip - with music - all by Suzanne. And I'll miss coming up to 9 West 91st and being in on all the cute goings on. One thing though - no two. You're to stand straight and cut out swearing - you agreed you know. - and then you'll be perfect - that is if you don't

Letter of Drieser to Sekey, 18 March 1930, p. 1.

forget me — and write me once in awhile.

Love from

T. D.

You'll get a book from Boni & Liveright

Letter of Dreiser to Sekey, 18 March 1930, p. 2.

TUCSON, ARIZ. Mch 30 – [1930]

Dear Sue: Thanks a lot for the nice homey letter. It came just at a moment when I was tired and a bit lonely and cheered me up. Only if you think a French harp – or is it "mouth harp" could substitute for you, singing me on my way – you don't know what I think of you. You too retiring by $99\frac{99}{100}$ ct. But just the same I have some nice names for your German pup. Here they are.

1. Schmaltzhausen, 2. Dudenhausen.
3. Knochenschlager 4 Von Hindenburg.

Or if you want to give him a three part name I suggest.

Knochenschlager Von Dudenhausen Hindenburg

Its a little long but you could call him Nochy.

Letter of Dreiser to Sekey, 30 March 1930, p. 1.

or Indie or Hindi for short. But
his proper name would remain as above
and be explained - where you had the
time.

As for the 3 books sent me, - I
never received same. Maybe they're
wandering around somewhere in
an envelope, or lying on my desk
at 200 West, or passing as currency
God knows where - distributed free
by whoever got them. Too bad
you didn't hang on to them.

I found in a fair and in here
two strings of small wooden colored
beads - made in Germany. Am
mailing them to you. Wrapped three
or four times around your wrist
they'll make a gay bracelet. Or
you could wear them over the red
socks as anklets - when you
dance.

Bye bye Ina. And write me
again to Phoenix - General Delivery

Letter of Dreiser to Sekey, 30 March 1930, p. 2.

[July 18 1930]

Friday.

Dear Sue:

Heres a few trips to the Soda Fountain in these hot days. Keep up your spirit, make a real try at this art work & one day you'll be glad of it I'm sure

T. D

Letter of Dreiser to Sekey, 18 July 1930.

Dreiser and American Literary Paganism: A Reading of the Trilogy of Desire

SHAWN ST. JEAN

THE PENULTIMATE PARAGRAPH OF *THE TITAN* (1914) IS DREISER'S PROSE-poetic tribute to the tradition of bards who had before him pondered the questions of human existence:

> What thought engendered the spirit of Circe, or gave to a Helen the lust of tragedy? What lit the walls of Troy? Or prepared the woes of an Andromache? By what demon counsel was the fate of Hamlet prepared? And why did the weird sisters plan ruin to the murderous Scot? (552)

That the incantation of *Macbeth*'s weird sisters, "Double, double toil and trouble, / Fire burn and cauldron bubble" which Dreiser further quotes may itself be an allusion to Homer, "Greed and folly double the suffering in the lot of man" (*Odyssey* I. 50–51), demonstrates the eternal nature of such questions. What are the true relationships of fate to free will, suffering to desire?

Like so many American writers who came of age in the nineteenth century, Dreiser drew on a ranging classical education that provided him with both the standards and the perspective with which to interrogate modern humankind.[1] *The Titan*'s final pages are the culmination of a sustained, modern narrative relying extensively on allusive systems based in Greek mythology, Shakespeare's canon, and the Bible. Not only are allusions used as passing literary devices designed to align the author with a tradition of literary philosophy, but they reveal something of the deep structure of Dreiser's novels.

These allusive systems have not yet been adequately explored by Dreiser scholars (or Emerson or Thoreau scholars) for the insight they lend readings of the American masterworks. Reasons for this neglect may include the seeming datedness of the approach in the face of twentieth-century shifts in reading strategies and the rise of literary theory, or what might be hastily judged as the superficiality of the systems themselves or the traditional method of explication. Whatever the objection, I hope to help set it to rest by demonstrating how well consideration of some major works (in this case Dreiser's *Trilogy of Desire*) through the lens of one body of sources, Greek tragedy, functions to clarify one of the most problematic issues in Dreiser studies.

This issue has been blanketed by the term *literary naturalism*. For nearly a century critics have complained that Dreiser's leanings toward the "school" of naturalism have been heavy-handed embarrassments, detracting from the better features of his works and showing little evidence of coherence or consistency. But a more considered position would be that this "school" meets under a house of cards, that authors like Crane, Norris, Dreiser, and Wright do not share enough philosophy or technique to be heaped together in an attempt to ignore the complex questions they raise and relegate them to an eccentric corner of the canon.

Let us begin to navigate this mire in a new way first by considering the broadest definition of (Dreiser's) naturalism and some compelling specific charges by critics. We can then discover how well these sub-issues can be recontextualized by Dreiser's "pagan" view of the world.

Naturalism is the embodiment of a theory which holds that the lives of human beings are determined by forces external to themselves. Specifics have been appended to this broad definition, such as the extent of determination and naming of forces (heredity and environment are the most popular.) I use the most liberal definition in order to be fair to Dreiser, and yet some would still contend that elements of his works cannot be contained within it and that his system breaks down. For example, Lee Clark Mitchell asserted in 1989 that

> voluntarism and determinism are opposed metaphysical systems that depend upon mutually exclusive categories. When we act as if they are not—assuming for instance, that people are determined yet free, or that some people are determined while others are not—we simply show how powerful are projective moral attitudes. (137)

This charge of inconsistency undoubtedly refers, at least generally, to what has become one of the most-quoted, notorious, and yet ill-considered passages in Dreiser's canon: the opening of *Sister Carrie*'s Chapter VIII, in which man is equated with "a wisp in the wind" and "wavers" in a "jangle of free will and instinct" (*SC* 1981: 73). In 1970 Donald Pizer cited the same passage as evidence of Dreiser's "false or superficial discursive grasp of the meaning of [the] events" in his own novel, "an apology for Carrie's impending choice of an immoral life with Drouet."[2] Both of these critics represent a host of others who would prefer to read the passage as "part of Dreiser's characterization of Carrie" than as "relevant to the themes of the novel as a whole."[3] A converse critical move (but similar in its implications) is to invest such passages as above, those that contain narrative philosophy, with total overriding thematic significance, as Walter Benn Michaels does with a famous scene from *The Financier*:

> Nothing about Dreiser is better known than his susceptibility to Spenserian "physico-chemical" explanations of human behavior. And nothing in Dreiser's work provides a better example of this susceptibility than the allegory of the lobster and the squid. . . . The moral of this story, as Cowperwood and Dreiser come to see it, is the irrelevance of anything but strength in a world "organized" so that the strong feed on the weak. Such a moral is . . . curiously inapplicable to the events of *The Financier* itself, which persistently exhibit nature not primarily as an organizing force dedicated to survival of the fittest, but as the ultimate measure of life's instability. . . .[4]

These three critics, while pursuing different agendas of their own, share preconceived notions about the way literature should work that Dreiser did not. He was trained in an older system that had many congruities to his beliefs and that he readily adapted for his own purposes. These congruities are easily demonstrated. William Chase Greene, in an Aristotelian vein, declared in 1944, just a year before Dreiser's death, that

> It is often asserted that Greek tragedy is fatalistic,—that all events are predestined, that the characters are helpless in the grip of fate, . . . [but] any sweeping statement of this sort is fallacious. . . . What is true is that a part, great or small, of the action in most of the plays is considered to proceed from cause beyond the control of the characters. . . . Conversely, as fate sinks into the background, human character emerges and controls, or seems to control, the situation; in such a case, the struggle of a will to overcome obstacles, or a struggle between two or more wills, provides the chief interest. But the finest and most profound tragic effect comes when the poet is not content merely to set forth external events, nor even the fact of guilt, but exhibits also the moral attitude of his protagonist toward events and toward his own action. He answers the call of honor, come what may; he endures what fate or the gods send. His act may have caused his downfall, but his will remains noble; he learns by suffering; and there may be a final vindication of the sufferer, though of an unexpected kind.[5]

This statement provides some invaluable standards by which to evaluate literary naturalism in general and Dreiser's novels in particular. But for the moment, it helps us take the long view of the previous critical assessments of Dreiser's shortcomings.

Greene claims that the tragic work presents a continuum between fate and character on which the actions shift. Logically, the strength of a character's reactions will effect the force of fate upon him or her in such a model. Just such an insight must have prompted Heraclitus's famous adage (repeated by Emerson) "A man's character determines his fate." As I will show, Dreiser's characters behave according to this model, explaining precisely *how*, in Mitchell's terms, "people [can be] determined yet free," and how "some people are determined yet others are not." Far from being inconsistent, Dreiser's naturalism revives an ancient ideology that explained human existence for a millennia.

Meanwhile, Pizer's reaction to Dreiser as trying to excuse Carrie's immoral behavior is shown to be, in light of Greene's commentary, an importation of ethical standards foreign to those by which the work was created.

Finally, Michaels's astute observation that nature is "unstable" in *The Financier* is voided by his assertion that Dreiser failed to recognize the world he himself created, and that the author discerned no different a "moral" from the lobster and squids' battle than his own preteen character. To lump Dreiser's and young Cowperwood's powers of moral insight together is a fatal error, and can only lead to an erroneous conclusion: that the author has failed to match the events of his novel with his intended theme. The problem is that the theme has been decided beforehand by the critic, not Dreiser, who maintains a varying detachment from his characters and the (at times) philosophic narrator. Failure to employ the basic reading strategy of recognizing this disparity of author, narrator, and character has continued to mar what otherwise might be productive Dreiser criticism.

What is notable about Greene's observations on tragedy is that they could almost as well describe Dreiser's fiction. Many of his characters operate on a sliding scale between free will and total determinism, and, as with tragedy, this crucial insight is easily overlooked even by sharp-eyed critics who have been reared amidst modernist notions of consistency engendered by the scientific and industrial revolutions.[6] However, Greene and Dreiser would seem to part company when Greene speaks of the profoundest spectacle showing characters who endure what fate sends. But Greene is for the moment referring only to characters like Orestes. Equally profound in interest, and more plentiful, are those like the title characters of *Agamemnon* and *Oedipus Rex* who resist rather than endure fate and suffer doubly for it.[7]

This distinction brings us to the key connection between Dreiser and the Greeks, one far more useful than simple surveying of allusions. It is concerned rather with structural and thematic alignments. And when we realize that, just as much as Dreiser, the fifth-century tragedians were social critics, all the pieces fit together. Dreiser's novels are loosely based on the model of Greek tragedy with regard to dramatic movement and character exploration, but they adapt and incorporate a mode of social criticism suited to turn of the century *American* culture. This agenda is readily seen in the title of Dreiser's great work, *An American Tragedy*, the implications of which have been ignored or blurred by critics who insist on defining tragedy in American terms instead of vice versa.[8] Dreiser, throughout his canon, defines America in tragedic terms.

Tracing the manifestations of this agenda is a messy business, bearing in mind that the author discursively drew on other, equally strong models like Shakespeare. But a clear example of structural alignment should demonstrate my point.

Dreiser's so-called *Trilogy of Desire* examines the life of Frank Cowperwood, his rises and falls. Not only does this trilogy emulate Greek tragedy in general, but it is based on the specific myth of Prometheus and on Aeschylus's trilogy in particular. Greene succinctly outlines those works:

> The *Prometheus Bound*, probably the first part of the trilogy, shows us the punishment of Prometheus for having raised man from brutishness to civilization by the gift of fire and the arts, in defiance of Zeus. The *Prometheus Unbound*, of which scanty fragments remain, must have shown the reconciliation of Prometheus and Zeus and the setting free of the Titan. In *Prometheus the Firebringer*, of which hardly more than the title is preserved, and which probably came last, it is likely that the poet dealt with the introduction into Attic cult of the festival of Prometheus, as a fire god . . . (117)

Now beyond the obvious reference of the titles *The Titan* to Prometheus and *The Stoic* to that group of Greek philosophers, what is the structural connection? If Greene is correct in his assignment of chronology, and if Dreiser shared similar knowledge, then *The Financier* (1912) would roughly correspond to *Prometheus Bound*. Of course, the two other source texts were lost long before the nineteenth century and it makes sense that Dreiser would choose the extant drama on which to base his new novel. Notably, the first edition of *The Financier* does not contain any reference to a *Trilogy*, as that of *The Titan* does. The first part may have been conceived as a stand-alone narrative, and it is that. Similarly, the *Prometheus Bound* flashes back and forward, sketching the entire Prometheus myth. The final pages of *The Financier* allude to the rest of Cowperwood's life, leaving a sense of closure in case the other parts were never written. Aeschylus probably saw value in a similar approach: even though tragedies were performed in threes, there is no evidence that any of the trilogies (the *Oresteia*, the *Oedipus* plays) were composed or performed together, and much that suggests otherwise.

In effect, Dreiser's *Trilogy* tells the story of a man who rises, through being the underling of others more powerful, to Titan-like status (critics have been fond of calling Cowperwood a Nietzschian "superman"). When he begins to usurp the power of other financial giants, and, refusing to bow to their efforts to keep him "in his place," threatens them, he is imprisoned and stripped of all power. After regaining his freedom through compromise, he embarks on a career to regain power in another land. His efforts to do so meet with resistance everywhere.

The Prometheus myth has all of these elements. After turning against his fellow Titans and assisting Zeus in ascension over his father Chronos, Prometheus is cast aside by the new regime. The Titan, fearing that Zeus will make good on his threat to destroy flawed humankind and replace them with a more perfect race, steals fire and the arts and gives them to humanity, assisting with their survival by practical means and simultaneously enabling them to act. For this he is chained to a mountain peak and tortured daily. Eventually he is freed by Heracles acting under Zeus's orders.

More interesting than the parallels here are the ways in which Dreiser transforms them to suit his critique of American culture and society. Most notably, Cowperwood's philanthropy is more Machiavellian than Promethean: he maintains its *appearance*, but his services to humanity (street railway systems, the gift of a $300,000 telescope to a local university, and, ironically, orchestration of the failure of the monopolistic American Match Company) mask an anti-promethean lust for personal power:

> The thing for him to do was to get rich and hold his own—to build up a seeming of virtue and dignity which would pass muster for the genuine thing. Force would do that. Quickness of wit. And he had these. Let the world wag. "I satisfy myself," was his motto. . . . (*F*, 244)

Of course, the passage also demonstrates Cowperwood's closest tie to the Titan: his self-characterized "Promethean defiance" to the power and opinions of his society (*T*, 528). Unfortunately, this trait is the source of downfall for both characters. A Titan is something less than a god and more than a man, and Prometheus's refusal to divulge information about Zeus's demise to his punisher, coupled with the original bestowal of divine gifts on humankind, represents a double impiety amounting to *hybris*. He insists upon reaching beyond his sphere. Cowperwood, a man, is guilty of the same crime against society. His actions, incidentally, endear him to women, as represented in these reflections by Berenice Fleming:

> As she thought of him—waging his terrific contests, hurrying to and fro between New York and Chicago, building his splendid mansion, collecting his pictures, quarreling with Aileen—he came by degrees to take on the outlines of a superman, a half-god or demi-gorgon. How could the ordinary rules of life or the accustomed paths of men be expected to control him? They could not and did not. (*T*, 527)

Instead of gods, other financial "Titans" are the figures who undertake the duty of checking Cowperwood. In a chapter significantly titled "Mount Olympus," they confer together and summon Cowperwood to appear. They intend on calling Cowperwood's loans, thereby ruining him for his manipulation of American Match, an endeavor that threatens to make him richer at their expense. Cowperwood responds to the summons, and after hearing out Hosmer Hand's and others' polite overtures to eviscerate his career, he responds plainly:

> "I know why this meeting was called. I know that these gentlemen here, who are not saying a word, are mere catspaws and rubber stamps for you and Mr. Schryhart and Mr. Arneel and Mr. Merrill. . . . You can't make me your catspaw to pull your chestnuts out of the fire, and no rubber-stamp conference can make any such attempt successful. . . . If you open the day by calling a single one of my loans before I am ready to pay it, I'll gut every bank from here to the river. You'll have panic, all the panic you want. Good evening, gentlemen." (*T*, 434)[9]

He leaves the others enraged but intimidated by his bluff, and escapes only for a greater eventual fall. Compare the scene to one in *Prometheus Bound*, in which the Titan is confronted by Zeus's agent Hermes:

> *Pr:* Do I seem to thee
> To fear and shrink from the new gods?
> Nay, much and wholly I fall short of this.
> The way thou cam'st go through the dust again;
> For thou wilt learn nought which thou ask'st of me.
>
> *Her:* Aye, by such insolence before
> You brought yourself into these woes.
>
> *Pr:* Plainly know, I would not change
> My ill fortune for thy servitude,
> For better, I think, to serve this rock
> Than be the faithful messenger of Father Zeus.
> Thus to insult the insulting it is fit.
>
> *Her:* Thou seem'st to enjoy thy present state.

> *Pr:* I enjoy? Enjoying thus my enemies
> Would I see; and thee 'mong them I count.
>
> (959–73)

Refusal to act as underling and declaration of open hostility mark the speeches of both protagonists. In both cases this is taken for insolence by superior-positioned opponents. And both encounters degenerate into veiled threats on each side. These are contests that can at best be only temporarily won by the protagonists against overwhelming odds.

Greene hypothesizes that a kind of reconciliation is reached, after due punishment, between Prometheus and Zeus in a later part of the trilogy. Cowperwood also manages a kind of alignment with the "powers that be" in the third city to which he visits his financial wizardry, London. Despite resistance to American influence over their public utilities, Cowperwood befriends (as opposed to bribes) the right people, notably Johnson and Lord Stane, and smoothes the way. Instead of fighting the forces arrayed against him, he attempts to join with them. This would appear to be a change in Cowperwood's philosophy key to the themes of *The Stoic*: "Take things as they come and make the best of them," he reminds himself in various ways (*S*, 20, 47, 94, 148, 224, 228). In Greene's words:

> What must be, must be; but man, by his insight, may will to do what must be done, and so may act in harmony with nature; or, again, he may resist. The result, considered externally, will be the same in either case, for man cannot overrule Nature, or Fate; but by willing cooperation, by making its law his law, he can find happiness, or by resignation he can at least find peace. . . . To live "according to nature": that is the phrase, often repeated by the Stoics, which sums up their ethical ideal. . . . This is man's whole business; it leads to self-preservation; it involves action, not mere contemplation; it is attended by pleasure, though that is a by-product, not in itself the goal. (340–41)

Prometheus himself adopts an attitude of stoicism. Enchained by Zeus's agent Hephaistos, he declares "The destined fate / As easily as possible it behoves [me] to bear, knowing / Necessity's is a resistless strength" (103–5). Through this same philosophy Cowperwood comes as close to happiness as the *Trilogy* ever takes him: so far that "I satisfy myself" transforms into real philanthropy, such as plans for endowments of a public art museum and a free hospital for the poor after his death (*S*, 256).

However, tragedy dictates that wisdom is never unaccompanied by loss, and Cowperwood has learned his lessons too late. His estate is plundered after his death and the great bequests fail to materialize because in life he had failed to meet contemplation with action, or at least the right kind of action. The denouement of the *Trilogy* approximates only in sadly parodic fashion *Prometheus the Firebringer*: no cult or worship grows up around the figure of Cowperwood; indeed, the newspapers question the worth of all his endeavors in the face of the posthumous dissipation of his fortune (*S*, 303).

The Prometheus myth shows that everyone—god and man—has limits that are imposed by more powerful forces rarely understood. Rex Warner, a modern translator, explains

> that nature, and what the Greeks called 'necessity,' do not proceed in accordance with human standards of justice and morality and, so Aeschylus seems to suggest, a failure to recognise this is a dangerous and unjustifiable form of pride. (*Prometheus Bound*, 4)

Cowperwood's attempts to transcend his own limits by undermining external forces must fail regardless of the morality of his intentions (which improves with time), just as the Titan's do. After creating (and in a sense relating, since Cowperwood's life was so closely modeled on that of Charles Tyson Yerkes) these events, themes emerge *from* them,[10] one of which Dreiser's narrator ponders:

> IN RETROSPECT
>
> The world is dosed with too much religion. Life is to be learned from life, and the professional moralist is at best but a manufacturer of shoddy wares. At the ultimate remove, God or the life force, if anything, is an equation, and at its nearest expression for man—the contract social—it is that also. Its method of expression appears to be that of generating the individual, in all his glittering variety and scope, and through him progressing to the mass with its problems. In the end a balance is invariably struck wherein the mass subdues the individual or the individual the mass—for the time being. For, behold, the sea is ever dancing or raging.
>
> In the mean time there have sprung up social words and phrases expressing a need of balance—of equation. These are right, justice, truth, morality, an honest mind, a pure heart—all words meaning: a balance must be struck. The strong must not be too strong; the weak not too weak. But without variation how could the balance be maintained? Nirvana! Nirvana! The ultimate, still, equation. (*T*, 550–51)

Dreiser is not interested in chasing down the true source of this "ultimate equation," whether it be morality in a Christian God, feuding among the pagan gods, consciousless Fate, or balance in nature. He is concerned, rather, with tracing its effects in individual human lives throughout his work. Variation and individualism are necessary components for the growth of the world, yet their transformative powers are meager in themselves and can only work slowly and in concert with the world. Different characters are worth examining to see this dynamic at work. The theory also goes far in explaining what might be called variable determinism throughout his novels.[11] Characters who steadfastly refuse to act for themselves, like Lester Kane and Clyde Griffiths, are acted upon or for by the forces of balance. Conversely, Frank Cowperwood attempts to act with too much force of his own and is checked by "Fate." Whatever its name, this cosmic power operates according to a sole principle which, from the perspective of people caught up in their own lives and ambitions, is unfathomable. And because we cannot understand even the standards of "balance" by which this force operates according to human terms, stoicism (an attitude Carrie Meeber, Jennie Gerhardt, and the older Cowperwood seem to share) seems the only viable option. Even the vantage point of auditor of the literary work seems no protection. We see characters as free as any of us bowed under the same pressures we seek to evade in our own lives. Dreiser's fiction is thus rightly experienced as untidy and unpredictable, and so discomforting to readers and critics.

Henry James argued in "The Art of Fiction" (1884) that "The only reason for the existence of a novel is that it does attempt to represent life" (166).[12] If life for the realist writer is what he can observe, then life for his "naturalist" counterpart might include speculations about those observations. But such distinctions as these obviously involve a great deal of fluidity, and as time continues to pass, the critical constructs of romanticism, realism, and naturalism may become more important as icons of critical history than as functioning critical tools. Dreiser seems to be a writer on whom these convenient terms are already well-exhausted. His novels represent life alternately as he saw it, read about it, deplored it, wished it could be. He imported to American life the moral and theological perspective of a past civilization, abandoning those of his own milieu. The apparent disjunction of all this will certainly fail "to represent life" for many, who, like the fell sergeant who came for dying Hamlet, are strict in their arrest. Yet we must try to understand, as James says, "the truth . . . that *he* [not the critic] assumes, the premises that we must grant him, whatever they may be" (167, emphasis added) of a writer, if, like Horatio, we are to report him and his cause aright to the unsatisfied.

Notes

1. I have not determined the formality of this education as yet, though the internal evidence is overwhelming.

2. See *Sister Carrie*, ed. Donald Pizer, 583–85.

3. Ibid., 586–87.

4. See Walter Benn Michaels, "Dreiser's *Financier*: The Man of Business as a Man of Letters," 288–89.

5. See William Chase Greene, *Moira: Fate, Good, and Evil in Greek Thought*, 91.

6. For a pertinent example of how scientific criteria can come to dominate the thinking of humanists, see Emile Zola, *The Experimental Novel*. This important work has had a long-range influence on naturalist criticism, with the unfortunate side effect of shutting down avenues such as the one pursued in the present investigation. For example, Zola makes a distinction between determinism and fate: the former is limited to observable criteria like heredity and environment, while fate cannot be contained in such ways and is thus beyond the province of the novelist. Definitions like this one have served to devalue the work of those "naturalists," like Dreiser, whose characters are acted upon by less quantifiable forces.

7. These characters may or may not ultimately learn from their suffering. Dreiser, undoubtedly in the service of his social criticism, often dramatized the contrast between both types. For example, Carrie Meeber perseveres while George Hurstwood ends his life in despair, murmuring "What's the use" (*SC* 1981: 499).

8. Philip Gerber relates, in *Theodore Dreiser*, that consternation [engendered by misunderstanding, in my view] about the title began before the book even saw publication:

> Sections of the book were already being set up in type and proofs circulated privately among selected readers. Opinions began coming in. Some damned, some praised. Some questioned the title, which Dreiser had changed from *Mirage* to *An American Tragedy*. How arrogant! Pompous, really. "How in the world can Dreiser call a book *An American Tragedy*?" asked Thomas Smith, Liveright's closest literary adviser. The author held firm. (132)

Although Gerber does not speculate as to Dreiser's insistence, I believe it must have been to preserve the mythic dimension he was, by then, intentionally crafting into his canon.

9. Gerber has shown that this scene occurred in the real life of Charles Tyson Yerkes, the Chicago street-railway magnate whom Dreiser used as a source for Cowperwood (105).

10. A key to Dreiser's realism is his extensive borrowing from the events of real lives like Yerkes's and Chester Gillette's. It seems strange that critics have widely recognized the author's genius in doing this, but in general have resisted his interpretations of what those events mean to the human condition.

11. See my article, "Social Deconstruction and *An American Tragedy*," for a full explication of the term.

12. See Henry James, "The Art of Fiction."

Expansive and Unnameable Desire in American Fiction: From "Naturalism" to Postmodernism

LAWRENCE E. HUSSMAN

I

BY THE FINAL DECADE OF THE NINETEENTH CENTURY, THE NEW, MATERIALIST science, philosophy, and fiction had made their way from intellectual circles in Europe and England to America. Thinkers such as Charles Darwin, Herbert Spencer, John Tyndall, and T. H. Huxley, as well as novelists like Emile Zola and Thomas Hardy, had, by then, helped describe a discrepant world in which "God" had become at most a questionable concept, and humans were victims of heredity and environment, so diminished in cosmic stature as to appear virtually meaningless. The only verities recognizable in this new world were ineluctable permutation and a succession of random events.

In United States fiction, these ideas were first dramatized by the "naturalist" school, and most notably by its three great pioneers, Stephen Crane, Frank Norris, and Theodore Dreiser. It is no exaggeration to say that, cumulatively, these three worked an enormous influence on the mindset of their own and succeeding generations of this country's major writers. As most of their successors up to World War II and beyond produced fiction, they steadily established mechanistic thinking as something of a literary norm. And the work of our received postmodernists, created in the context of an ever more certain science, has been characterized by deepened determinism and increasing angst.

Crane, Norris, and Dreiser are regarded as revolutionaries, of course, because they wrote their stories and novels in an intellectual culture still dominated by Christian thought. Not only were Christian moral principles taken to be timeless, but also assumed was the idea that the travails of our "veil of tears" could be transcended, given only upright conduct, in an afterlife of eternal bliss. For nearly two millennia in the Western World, this promise of perfection in perpetuity had fed an expectation of final fulfillment. By the time of its influence on the United States' founding fathers, Christianity was wedded to the *Enlightenment*'s expectation of material progress, so that the "pursuit of happiness" was added to the other constitutional guarantees. As the new scientific skepticism gained prominence at the turn of the last century, Crane, Norris, and Dreiser, whose religious upbringings were, respectively, Methodist, Episcopalian, and Roman Catholic, became converts to "naturalist" disbelief. Crane expressed his new outlook in an epigrammatic poem in which an "Everyperson" informs the universe of human existence only to encounter indifference. Norris's novels variously equate humans with a meaningless mass ground down by a cosmic engine, or as mere "motes in the sunshine," among other reductive metaphors. To Dreiser, persons were "chemisms" and "expiring beetles." In the fictional worlds that the "naturalists" created, the fulfillment imagined through humanity's expansive desire must be found, if at all, in this world. During the twentieth century, the American novel has been in large part characterized by the anguished yearning for some substance capable of delivering secular salvation, some worthy channel toward which to direct the desire for the ultimate. And that characteristic grew out of the example set by Crane, Norris, and Dreiser.

The first of these three writers to dramatize humanity's longing for transcendence in a post-religious setting was Crane in his privately published novella of 1893, *Maggie: A Girl of the Streets*. The church reveals itself to be irrelevant to the lives of the two principal players, the Bowery brawler Jimmie Johnson and his sister Maggie. Neither pays particular attention to Christian precepts. But even in this brutalized neighborhood of "gruesome doorways," each displays an inchoate longing for some measure of bliss. This yearning sets a precedent for even the most inarticulate characters in modern and postmodern American fiction. Jimmie effects and develops a shielding "chronic sneer," believes in "nothing," and takes pathetic satisfaction in his existence so long as he has "a dollar in his pocket." But at moments he imagines a beckoning "beyond." He sometimes stands on the Bowery streets, observing city scenes and "dreaming blood-red dreams at the passing of pretty women" (11). As we will see, in evoking the idea of secular fulfillment since the turn of the last century, American writers have given it a strong sexual component. Jimmie indulges as well, however, an undifferentiated emotion that will also prove endemic to later American fiction. After he manages to secure a job as the driver of a horse-drawn truck, he takes to bettering his rounds by "fixing his eye on a high and distant object," and "going into a sort of trance of observation" (12). This kind of vague signal that there must be more to reality than our senses can locate colors Norris's and Dreiser's novels as well. Indeed, nearly all of the these writers' successors have noted humanity's failure to find satisfying ends, its penchant for indulging extravagant expectation completely out of sync with its limited, apparent objects. In *Maggie: A Girl of the Streets*, Jimmie's generalized longing never focuses beyond his libidinous thoughts and actions.

Even though the young ruffian's presence is ubiquitous enough in the novella to warrant our wondering why it wasn't called *Jimmie: A Boy of the Streets*, Crane shifts his emphasis in the middle section to Maggie. Her generic hunger for fulfillment is as strong as her brother's. She is given to "dim thoughts [that] were always searching for lands far away, where, as God says, the little hills sing together in the morning." But Crane reminds us that, despite Maggie's invocation of God, hers is a secular vision. He adds a telling sentence: "Under the trees of her dream gardens there had always walked a lover" (15). The personification of her fancy turns out to be the neighborhood bartender Pete, introduced to her by Jimmie. Maggie views this tinhorn "somebody" with his flashy clothes (by Bowery standards) and ingratiating patter as a "golden sun" (23). During their brief time together, Pete's relatively elevated "taste" spurs Maggie's intense dislike for all of her [own] dresses and quickens her appreciation of the costly "silks and laces" she sees modeled on the city streets (20, 21).

Her beau introduces her to the theater, and she begins to wonder whether she could achieve through Pete "the culture and refinement she had seen imitated" on stage (25). Soon she is contemplating "a future, rose-tinted, because of its distance from all that she had previously experienced" (35). That beckoning tomorrow, conspicuously undetailed like the many other American writers' characters' to follow, never dawns, of course, because Maggie is abandoned by Pete and forced to take up a life of prostitution (or at least we are asked to take Crane's word for it that she is forced to do so). That profession will initiate her in the truism that the real and the ideal are always hopelessly disparate. Crane climaxes Maggie's short journey from desire to disillusionment when he sends her to her suicide, appropriately chaperoned at the end by "the varied sounds of life, made joyous by distance and seeming unapproachableness" (50). Implicit in *Maggie* and in Crane's other novels and stories is an existential commitment to an ethic of compassion and human solidarity, a gratuitous moral dimension that also sets a precedent for even the most nihilistic of American fiction writers who followed.

Some six years after the appearance of *Maggie*, Norris published *McTeague*, a semi-documentary saga about a dentist somewhat higher on the social ladder than Crane's Johnson family, but with an even lower IQ. This "docile draught horse" also has longings that surpass his imperfect surroundings. Early on, these desires are symbolized by an enormous golden molar that serves as an advertisement for a rival dentist. But when he marries his lust object Trina Sieppe, he begins his own education in deception and disenchantment. His disappointment is foreshadowed in a premarriage scene in which he dimly realizes that were he to win Trina "she would never be the same to him, never so radiant, so sweet, so adorable; her charm for him would vanish in an instant" (27). Despite this isolated insight, however, he continues to invest his anticipation with a highly charged element of sentimental fantasy. He hopes to carry his love off "by main strength" to some "vague country, some undiscovered place where every day was Sunday," a wish through which Norris neatly encapsulates the dentist's mixture of testosterone and tenderness (35). But a bit later, during love making, he experiences "a slight, a barely perceptible, revulsion of feeling" (73). After the couple's love life has become routine we learn that, for McTeague, "the very act of submission that bound the woman to him forever had made her seem less desirable in his eyes" (78).

McTeague also demonstrates, like *Maggie*, that the capacity to crave the infinite is not limited to the young. In Crane's novel, only Jimmie, his sister, and, to a certain extent, Pete, display expansive longing. The brutal Bowery environment has long since stripped Maggie's parents and the novella's other older adults of any capacity for hope, the lack a measure of their dehumanization. In one of the two major subplots of *McTeague*, on the other hand, Norris establishes that even seniors in normal circumstances retain a residue of infinite desire. Old Grannis and Miss Baker, residents of McTeague's apartment house, "keep company" through the wall of their adjoining rooms, unaware of their mutual infatuation. Grannis fantasizes a meeting "in the evening somewhere, withdrawn from the world, very calm, very quiet, and peaceful." Each conjures up a "little Elysium" together, a "delicious garden where it was always autumn" (148–49), a cousin to McTeague's place of perpetual Sunday and Maggie's singing hills. But Norris grants the older couple a more favorable denouement. Once they meet they manage, thanks to long lives that have inured them to disappointment, to downsize their dreams and create an "Elysium" within the world. In his later novels, culminating in *The Octopus* (1901) and *The Pit* (1902), Norris would extrapolate from cases like Grannis's and Miss Baker's that secular fulfillment was approachable only through relationship with another and, by extension, with all others.

The heroine of Dreiser's *Sister Carrie*, which appeared the year after *McTeague*, emerges as a languid captive of her craving. In the opening scene she journeys from a small Wisconsin town to Chicago, "dreaming wild dreams of some vague, far-off supremacy" (4). The great midwestern metropolis of the 1880s functions in the novel as a symbol of human desire destinations, with its alluring profusion of possibilities and its testimony to the truth that, of all the world's viable venues, the United States offers the material resources, theoretically, to deliver secular salvation. Along Dreiser's narrative way, Carrie shows a limitless capacity to long, to covet things and people and success. And Dreiser always attributes this drive for specific ends to a generalized need that transcends the tangible. Late in the novel, for example, during a discussion with Bob Ames, the third man in her life and a partial spokesperson for the author, Carrie responds with suggestive emotion to a fragment of sentimental music played by an ensemble at a dinner party: " 'I don't know what it is about music,' she started to say, moved to explain the inexplicable longings which surged within her, 'but it always makes me feel as if I wanted something—I—' " (649). Dreiser himself as much as admits to a similar inability to describe the vagrant emotions that characterize his own, often bewildered intrusions into the novels narrative. At one point for instance, he laments the weakness of words enlisted to describe humanity's aching urges:

> People in general attach too much importance to words. They are under the illusion that talking effects great results. As a matter of fact, words are as a rule the shallowest portion of all the argument. They but dimly represent the great surging feelings and desires that lie behind. When the distraction of the tongue is removed, the heart listens. (118)

As but a bit of testimony to the continuing relevance of Dreiser's message in the two passages quoted above, we might consider why even today's classical music concertgoers, far more sophisticated than Carrie both musically and philosophically, subjected to nearly a full century of additional evidence of humanity's dead-end destiny, should have made Gustav Mahler such a postmodern icon. Surely the answer lies in the composer's uncanny ability to articulate musically "the great surging feelings and desires" for the infinite that rack so many in the destination-deficient twentieth century.

Unlike Crane and Norris, who tragically died at twenty-eight and thirty-two respectively, Dreiser lived for nearly a half century beyond the publication of his first novel. In that time he worked his way tortuously toward the spiritual affirmation of his last years. His artistic and intellectual journey produced among other novels, *The "Genius"*, a long autobiographical exploration of the possibility of achieving fulfillment through the perfect bedmate, the soon to be ubiquitous "impossible she" of later writers such as Fitzgerald. Dreiser's *The Financier* and *The Titan* proved that even monied moguls like Frank Cowperwood must confront "the pathos of the discovery even giants are pygmies" (551) when their successes are measured against their endeavors. Finally, the posthumously published novels *The Bulwark* and *The Stoic* revealed Dreiser's final conclusion, a somewhat resigned version of Norris's recommendation of a path to salvation that led away from the self. The principal bearer of this message of regard for "the other" is Etta Barnes, the prodigal daughter of Quaker protagonist Solon Barnes in *The Bulwark*. When she gives up her self-indulgent (in Quaker context) quest for personal priorities and returns home to devote herself to her dying father, she locates in the "constant" of love and service the psychic reward that had previously eluded her.

Most of the major United States fiction writers published between the turn of the century and World War II frequently addressed the anguish of modern life in terms of the distance between humanity's reach and grasp in the absence of a heaven. Among novelists, for necessarily limited example here, the phenomenon fascinated Fitzgerald, Willa Cather, Thomas Wolfe, Richard Wright, and John Steinbeck. Fitzgerald, who numbered Norris and Dreiser among his favorite authors, gave perhaps the most familiar reprise to the theme of desire and disillusionment. In his quintessentially American novels Fitzgerald limns a landscape "commensurate to [humanity's] capacity for wonder" at a time when he finds "all Gods dead, all wars fought, all faiths in man shaken."[1] Until he wins Daisy Buchanon, Jay Gatsby lacks only this golden girl to satisfy his own wonderful capacity for wanting. But he ultimately discovers that his emotional investment has been far greater than his reward.

The psychology of Fitzgerald's male characters, those sensitive souls captive to the generic promise of existence, gets its sharpest delineation in his short stories, especially in "Absolution." Fitzgerald wrote that story, a seminal tale of a youthful imagination inflamed by the world's promise, in order to document his protagonist's past in *The Great Gatsby*. After he decided instead to eliminate Gatsby's youthful background from the novel to invest him with a kind of mythical mystery, he reworked the material and published it as a short story. The result was "Absolution," the tale of eleven-year-old Rudolph Miller, whose mundane middle class existence spurs surpassing ambitions and sexual yearnings, channeled through a fantasy persona he calls by the highly evocative name Blatchford Sarnemington. The plot of this most Joycean and Yeatsian of Fitzgerald's stories turns on Rudolph's intermittently scrupulous conscience and a lie told in the confessional. Its climax comes in its fifth segment, when Rudolph tries to confess his previous confession to a priest who is himself driven by what he regards as dark desires of the flesh. The anguished Father Schwartz ministers to the boy through a rambling allegorical narrative that articulates Fitzgerald's own spiritual vexation. He asks Rudolph if he has ever been to a party and describes a tableau in which everything is perfect, "everybody . . . properly dressed" and there are "bowls around full of flowers." But the problem is, the priest indicates, eventually "even in the best places things go glimmering all the time" (149). Thus he puts Rudolph on notice that no matter how enticing worldly beauties become, their centers will not hold. The reason clarifies in a later part of Father Schwartz's allegorical monologue, when the priest conjures up the vision of an alluring amusement park with a "big wheel made of lights," and "a band playing somewhere," the whole scene one in which "everything will twinkle." But then comes the moral. Father Schwartz warns Rudolph never to "get up close" to such a park "hanging out there like a colored balloon," because proximity would only reveal "the heat and the sweat and the life" (150). Perhaps the most tragic fact of our existence, the knowledge that not even the most promising of the world's offerings can ultimately deliver, has never been more succinctly dramatized than by Father Schwartz in "Absolution."

Untrammeled longing racks Willa Cather's fictional folk as well. The pathologically wishful title character of "Paul's Case" remains her best known exemplar, but her novels are also replete with dreamers of impossible dreams. Though Cather exemplifies the several American writers whose customary response to twentieth-century anxiety was to retreat in fiction to a more palatable past, she could not resist transferring her own underfulfillment to her character. She prefaced *O Pioneers!*, for instance, with a poem called "Prairie Spring" that pits the novel's young people's "sharp desire" against "the eternal, unresponsive sky." *O Pioneers!* teems with images of thwarted yearning, its Scandinavian and Bohemian immigrants "always think[ing] the bread of another country . . . better than their own" (24). The novel's primary player, Alexandra Bergson, even rhapsodizes over an "impossible he," warming to "an illusion of being lifted up bodily and carried lightly by . . . a man like no man she knew . . . larger and stronger and swifter" and carried across the cornfields and away (80). He even wears a cloak of white, the clothing color most often associated with "impossible shes." But at novel's end Alexandra has settled for her returned girlhood interest Carl Lindstrum, and she has come to realize that only the land "belongs to the future."

Jim Burden, the narrator of *My Ántonia*, defines human desire as the wish to "become a part of something entire" and to be "dissolved into something complete and great" (18). The transplanted Bohemians of the novel constantly contrast an exaggeratedly idyllic European past with a fantasy future leading from Nebraska's "sunflower-bordered roads" to "freedom," though they must make do in the present with spring smells, "getting warm and keeping warm, dinner and supper" (29, 66). Even Father Latour of *Death Comes for the Archbishop* carries Cather's virus of regret for the lack of something more. Just before his death he contrasts Europe and America in a way that foresees the spoilage of the land he has come to love: "He had noticed that this peculiar quality in the air of new countries vanished after they were tamed by man and made to bear harvests" (273).

The American need for some inexact augmentation in the face of a depleted destiny has received no fuller treatment than that given it by Thomas Wolfe. His heroes, thinly veiled representations of himself, are forever convulsed and tormented by wants that cannot be assuaged. Typical among them are Eugene Gant in *Look Homeward Angel* and George Webber in *The Web and the Rock*. Men of enormous appetite for the world's wonders, they invariably find those treasures finally incapable of providing satisfaction. Gant, nearly seven-hundred pages but only sixteen years into his search for substance, disputes the claim of his dead brother Ben who appears to him in a vision. Ben tries to tell Eugene that "an end to hunger" is impossible and that the "happy land" he seeks is a figment of his imagination. But there is no convincing Eugene. In the novel's final lines, he fixes his eyes on the "distant soaring ranges" of his desire (693). By the time Wolfe himself had acquired enough fiction fodder through his own experience to write *The Web and the Rock* less than a decade later, however, he had come to see the crux of modern humanity's predicament even more clearly. In one of the novel's waning scenes, George Webber muses that humanity's aspirations collide with limitation, since men and women possess "but the pinion of a broken wing to soar half-heavenward" (693).

Flight metaphors also provided Richard Wright with a means of conveying African Americans' longing for transcendence beyond the social justice denied them. In *Native Son*, Bigger Thomas fantasizes about a life wrought up beyond its highest possible pitch, as seen especially in Hollywood films. Wright also signals, through Bigger's envy of flight, that all races share a generic hunger for the "yonder." In an early scene, Bigger and his friend Gus watch a sky-writing plane "so far away that at times the strong glare of the sun blanked it from sight" (14). A little later the two watch a pigeon take flight "on wings stretched so taut and sheer that Bigger could see the gold of the sun through their translucent tips" (18). These symbols of limitless aspiration form an important leitmotif in *Native Son*.

John Steinbeck's novels and stories allude again and again to their characters' overreaching hunger for indefectibility, from the Joad family's vision of California as a Paradise of orange "bushes," to Kino's discovery that worldly riches are counterfeit in *The Pearl*. "The Leader of the People," a story Steinbeck added after the fact to *The Long Valley*, puts the United States' westward movement in the perspective of humanity's quest for the infinite. In the story, the grandfather of the maturing Jody from "The Red Pony" lectures his grandson on the meaning of the movement, emotionally invoking not the west itself, but rather "the westering" (302), blocked only by the Pacific, a powerful proof for what C. S. Lewis called the "Sweet Desire" that invariably calls us from further and further to furthest and the limits of wordly possibility.[2] Illustrations of desire that leaps beyond the finite abound in most of the other major modern American writers, far more pervasively, in fact, than allow allusion in this essay. Before turning to examples from the postmodern period, however, a word about its differences from modernist age and a look at a transitional work may be in order.

II

Locating the turning point between modernism and postmodernism has always been a hazardous undertaking. One more or less accepted definition of postmodernism breaks the two "movements" at 1939, the year William Butler Yeats died and World War II began. These markers would indicate the passing of the old modernist icons and the source of a significant intensification of nihilism, alienation, and fragmentation. Another view separates the two in the 1960s, when according to the authors of one respected guide to literary terms, writers like Pynchon, Barthelme, and others began to "carry modernist assumptions about the world into the very realm of art itself."[3] Up to this point, however, a single work has not been widely recognized as a transitional text, in the way that, say, Wordsworth's "Preface" to the *Lyrical Ballads* splits English "pre-romanticism" from its full "romantic" flowering, while at the same time admitting to historical continuity. I would like to suggest such a work and provide a close analysis of it, though with little hope of winning its broad acceptance as pivotal. It is sometimes anthologized, but it has seldom been analyzed. Although it was once called "a representative anecdote for our time," it remains relatively obscure story of only six pages by a writer not considered major by any means, one in fact seemingly unqualified for serious consideration as an important modern or postmodern pessimist.[4] It has the advantage, however, of cataloguing much modernist thought, including especially its emphasis on the doomed desire for transcendence that has been the subject of this essay. And it incorporates that thought into the story's very structure and style, considered by some the essence of postmodern practice as, they believe, it dawned in the sixties. Moreover, presumably satisfying those for whom postmodernism made its appearance in the earlier era, the story was written and published in 1939.

On 15 March of that year, *The New Yorker* published the work in question, E. B. White's "The Door," later collected with some of his other stories and essays in *The Second Tree from the Corner*. The immediate inspiration for the story was a *Life* magazine article, published a few weeks earlier, about the work of a University of Michigan experimental psychologist named Norman R. F. Maier. Maier drove laboratory rats to frustrated spasms and then paralysis by running them at a series of tiny cardboard doors leading through an elaborate maze to a reward of food pellets. After hundreds of trips through the labyrinth, the rats found the final door locked, triggering their frenzied frustration and eventual torpor.[5]

White's story opens with a generic protagonist, simply referred to here and throughout as "he," describing his surroundings in a frenetically confused style. The urban setting overflows with modern synthetic bearing scientific prefixes and suffixes like "tex," "koid," "sani," and "duro." All of the familiar objects of the past are now made with these new plastics, bringing about the protagonist's confusion and prompting him to protest: "Everything is something it isn't" (77). When he approaches what seems to be a wall but turns out to be a door and then what seems to be a door but turns out to be a wall, he experiences a dizziness that he attributes to food poisoning.

As "The Door" proceeds, White develops the central analogy between contemporary humanity and those laboratory rats, the "he" character catching sight of his own eyes reflected in the "thrutex," and seeing the same expression there as in the rats' eyes. Here White relies on the favorite simile of the "naturalist" novelists, the linkage of humanity and the animal world. Like the rats, he concludes that he is "confronted by a problem which is incapable of solution" and one that leads inevitably to weariness from "the convulsions" (78). "He" believes he is sinking into madness because of his certainty that, even if he chooses "the right door," there will be no food behind it.

White's character points out that his syndrome "wouldn't be so bad if only you could read a sentence through without jumping (your eye) to something else on the same page" (79). Thus, the story's readers are asked to recognize in themselves the same pattern of compulsive anticipation and lack of sufficiency that plagues "he." At another juncture in "The Door," White seems to address the reader again when he asks: "What are you following these days, old friend, after your recovery from the last bump?" (81). Adding to these attempts at enlisting his readers in his agenda, White introduces a "subplot" about a "man out in Jersey'' who had mysteriously begun tearing his house apart brick by brick, linking his state of mind to the ''frantic racing around'' (79–80) of the professor's rats in their convulsive stage.[6]

In the deceptively garbled narrative of ''The Door,'' ''he'' frames his problem as a widespread human condition and so begins to play the role of modern (and postmodern?) Everyperson. His own compulsive ''jumping at doors'' that prove ultimately ungiving has brought him to the point where he realizes he must not let his frustrations ''unsettle the mind.''[7] But he also knows that with humans ''there will be no not jumping'' because of a mysterious ''they'' (a cruel God, determinism, modern advertizing?) who answer any and all attempts to resist by ''ruffling'' the shirker ''in the rump with a blast of air'' (79, 80).

''He'' also reveals that his twenty years of jumping at various ''doors'' that turned out to be walls may have nearly extinguished his ability to go on. At this point, White introduces the items that will stand for the major desire objects of modern/postmodern humanity, four specific passageways that finally deny access: ''First they would teach you the Psalms, and that would be the right door . . . and the long sweet words with the holy sound, and that would be the one to jump at to get where the food was.'' But religion's door had closed, of course, on a great many of White's friends and acquaintances among the American intelligentsia.[8]

The second door that has opened onto a blind alley has an ''equation on it and the picture of an amoeba reproducing itself by division.'' By 1939 it had become clear that science could not provide satisfying answers either, a realization that hits most college students today when they try to sell their used biology or chemistry textbooks back to the campus bookstore. White's third door, however, tends to deceive many Americans longer. It has a ''photostatic copy of a check for thirty-two dollars and fifty cents'' pictured on it (79). The knowledge that money can buy material treasures but not the consummation we covet has, of course, become a cliché of United States life and literature.

The fourth door/wall pictures a woman with ''arms outstretched in loveliness,'' wearing an ''uncaught'' dress (80). In a piece called ''Notes on Our Times'' in *The Second Tree from the Corner*, White identifies the Hollywood starlet Dorothy Lamour in ''moonlight and shadows'' as his masculine contemporaries' favorite version of the ''impossible she'' and ''the source of [their] common unfulfillment'' (107–8). The discovery that the door once seemingly leading to the crowning life experience has turned into yet another blocking wall becomes the most painful of all disappointments for ''he.'' It makes his nose bleed ''for a hundred hours,'' an appropriate suffering since it derives from frustration with what Schopenhauer identified as humanity's elemental drive.[9]

"He" attempts an intriguing description of the infinite longing that subsumes the differentiated desires symbolized by the closing doors in the story. Defining the mysterious object of our untargeted anticipation, he calls it "plexicoid and it comes in sheets, something like insulating board, unattainable and ugli-proof." Few attempts at isolating the aim of theologically deprived twentieth-century desire have been more successful than this one that calls attention to the insufficiency of any single, realizable, imperfect entity to assuage human hunger.

The final paragraph of "The Door" builds to a provocative conclusion. "He," having rejected the idea of ending his frustration by getting a brain operation, walks to a door that opens. He sees through it, not the girl with outstretched arms he half expects, but an escalator that will take him toward a street and people below.[10] Only with others of his kind, White implies, can "he" possibly find his way through the maze of twentieth-century life. White's insight here relates to those of Crane in "The Open Boat," Norris in *The Octopus* and *The Pit*, and Dreiser in *The Bulwark*, early and later works among many modern texts that predicate the possibility for some measure of meaning on interaction with "the other," also a common belief among postmodern American writers.

When "he" steps off the escalator and walks toward the street in the final line of "The Door," the ground comes up slightly to meet his foot. This is an allusion to a previous idea in the story. "He" had earlier mused that all of the disillusionment he had been remarking and the kind of craziness it breeds wouldn't be so bad "if only when you put your foot forward to take a step the ground wouldn't come up to meet your foot the way it does" (79). Edward Sampson, in his book on White, argues that the ground meeting the foot represents "mad nature" and "the symptom of his [the 'he' character's] tension, the projection of his inner turmoil." But it could also be read quite differently. Since it appears both in the middle of White's story and again at its conclusion, it likely carries more meaning than Sampson allows. In fact, there is a way to gloss the line that meshes more logically with Sampson's judgment that "The Door" ends with "he" achieving "a kind of victory," a reading with which William Steinhoff essentially agrees.[11] One could (should?) take the ground meeting the foot as an indication that nature may actually be ordered, as the sun's rising in the east and setting in the west, or the presence of the precise mixture of constituent ingredients in the air to sustain life would seem to argue. Read this way, the apparent chaos around us, the failure of our modern/postmodern experiences to provide satisfaction causes even greater distress ("It wouldn't be so bad if only . . .") than would be the case if we could be sure of meaninglessness. Certainly the repetition of the line at the story's conclusion appears to be more than a simple reiteration of the protagonist's dizziness.

White himself never provided much help in deciding how to read his story's final line, or any of its other lines for that matter. He talked about the "meaning" of "The Door" only once, in a letter answering an inquiry about it. His response, written nearly a quarter of a century after the story's appearance, cannot be trusted as an explanation. After dismissing his correspondent's interpretation that he had meant to reject religion as the answer to "the big questions of existence," White points out that he wrote a dizzying piece because he was literally ill with fever at the time. The idea of the street coming up to meet the foot, he says, was a transcription of what literally happened to him. But earlier in the letter he also rejects the idea that there is any specific symbolism in "The Door." To accept that patently disingenuous statement is to reduce the story to gibberish. In the letter answering the inquiry, he describes the composition procedure for the story by recalling that "a lot of things got thrown in as [he] went along."[12] But everything that "got thrown in," as we have seen, fits a pattern that, in describing the incoherence of life, is in itself highly logical and consistent. And we know from a comment in a later letter to a friend that White was quite proud of the story, a proprietorship that certainly argues against his seeing it as dizzy gibberish.[13] Moreover, since he not only included "The Door" in *The Second Tree from the Corner* but also in his master collection, *The Poems and Sketches of E. B. White*, published over a dozen years later, his denial of meaning in the story weakens further still. But most telling of all, the ideas in "The Door" mesh with those in other White stories and in a number of his essays. The best example can be found in *The Second Tree from the Corner*'s title story, written a few years earlier than "The Door." In it the autobiographical hero Trexler finds himself facing his own "impossible situation." He has been seeing a psychiatrist in hopes of discovering the cure for his unquenchable longing. But the doctor can't help because his own understanding of human desire turns out to be far less developed than Trexler's. Toward the end of the story, White sums up Trexler's needs (and his own) in a way that would be perfectly comprehensible to the protagonist of "The Door."

> Trexler knew what he wanted, and what, in general, all men wanted; and he was glad, in a way, that it was both inexpressible and unattainable, and that it wasn't a wing [the psychiatrist had defined his need as a new wing for his house in Westport]. He was satisfied to remember that it was deep, formless, enduring, and impossible of fulfillment, and that it made men sick, and that when you sauntered on Third Avenue and looked through the doorways into the dim saloons, you could sometimes pick out from the unregenerate ranks

> the ones who had not forgotten, gazing steadily into the bottoms of glasses on the long chance that they could get another peek at it. Trexler found himself renewed by the remembrance that what he wanted was at once great and microscopic, and that although it borrowed from the nature of large deeds and of youthful love and of old songs and early intimations, it was not any one of these things, and that it had not been isolated or pinned down, and that a man who attempted to define it in the privacy of a doctor's office would fall flat on his face. (102)

Joseph Epstein, attacks the popular notion, broadened again in at least one White obituary, that the author's "inexplicably sunny inclinations" ran "counter to our century's fashion for literary despair." Epstein argues that, in fact, "one has to search very sedulously indeed to find a gloomier writer." He emphasizes the pervasive "melancholy and anxiety" that hung over White's reminiscences of his youth, the dread of nervous breakdown that dogged him through much of his life, his pronounced foreboding of failure, his self-doubts about his intellectual powers, even the way in which his books for children like *Stuart Little*, *Charlotte's Web*, and *The Trumpet and the Swan* reflect his "longings and fears." If Epstein is correct that "sour" idealism led White to find "the cloud in every silver lining," then the author of "The Door" was certainly far better positioned to delineate modern/postmodern angst than one would at first recognize.

Where Epstein seems to be seriously in error, however, is in his attempt to locate the "something" White sought but could not identify in the writer's growing ambition to produce high art as opposed to what he believed to be the smart journalism of his *New Yorker* contributions. For Epstein, this yearning for "significance," dating from the mid-thirties on, was doomed to failure because White suffered from comparative "intellectual indigence."[14] But nothing in "The Door" or the title story in *The Second Tree from the Corner* can be determined to demonstrate such a lamentable lack of mental resources. On the contrary, the story insightfully isolates the twentieth-century human condition, the endless cycle of desire and disillusionment that marks humanity in what most consequential American writers conceive to be the post-religious age. Moreover, nowhere in "The Door" does White so much as hint at art as the "answer." In fact, he argues quite the opposite proposition. At one point in the story he focuses on a mysterious poet who had been killed by his incessant bumping against unyielding doors. Steinhoff has identified the real life model for the poet as White's friend Don Marquis, the creator of *Archy and Mehitabel*, who died exhausted in 1937 after a series of personal tragedies.[15] The poet in "The Door" had "followed all his days" something "he could not name." Finally, he had reached the passive stage after "the preliminary bouts and the convulsions." White attributes to unanswered longing the poet's symptomatic "willingness to let anything be done" to him. In the foreword to *The Second Tree from the Corner*, White says that "a writer, almost by definition, is a person incapable of satisfaction." Of course, by the standards established in "The Door," this would differentiate writers from nonwriters, not in essence, but only in degree and intensity of frustration.

Steinhoff identifies Marquis's poem from a quarter of a century earlier, "The Name," as the source for the doors/walls of desire/disillusionment in White's story. The poem describes a man on a quest who believes he has found the "something he cannot name" in love, then beauty, then God.[16] Steinhoff fails to note, however, White's crucial reworking of the questor's search. Beauty has been replaced by science and materialism, for example. And God, according to the assumptions of "intellectuals," by 1939 long since irrelevant and represented in "The Door" by the Psalms, presents the first passageway that turns out to be a dead end.[17]

But equally telling is the example of the tragic poet himself, whose fall is the most precipitous and most painful of all the seekers' in the story. Through the poet's history, White explicitly rejects art, the refuge of James Joyce, Virginia Woolf, and Wallace Stevens, as an alternative to all-encompassing burnout. And his protagonist's final reach for equilibrium is initiated not in a studio or a garret, but on the street with the people farthest removed from the esoteric workings of "high art." Finally, the evidence persuades that whether or not White absorbed the idea of modern/postmodern man's doomed search for substance from his reading of the twentieth-century American masters, he experienced the very underfulfillment they memorialize in his own special way. "The Door" is a powerful evocation of twentieth-century humanity's serial disenchantment, adrift in an apparently meaningless universe. It also testifies to our penchant for persevering. Moreover, style and structure illustrate ideas in the story. As such, it can function as a transitional text between the modern and postmodern worlds as presented in American fiction.

III

No work of postmodern American literature typifies its time more surely than Don DeLillo's brilliant, serio-comic novel *White Noise*. Its hero, Jack Gladney, head of the Hitler studies program at the College-on-the-Hill, confronts both the idea and the reality of death, thanks to conversations with his wife and colleagues and an "airborne toxic event" that envelopes his town and singles him out for special contamination. Along the way, DeLillo describes a synthetic world much like E. B. White's in "The Door," and he looses a litany of deceiving chemical compounds throughout the narrative (Dacron, Orlon, Lycra Spandex, Krylon, Rust-Oleum, Red Devil, Dristan Ultra). Most foods turn out to be similarly simulated "junk." As if paraphrasing White, Gladney's son Heinrich explains that "nothing is what it seems" (23). But such synthetics have progressed from mentally confusing in "The Door" to life-threatening in *White Noise*. And there are also a number of scattered analogies between rodents and humans in DeLillo's novel, as Gladney's developing medical condition gets likened to those of laboratory rats and mice.

DeLillo also focuses on the desire magnets that have drawn American writers from the "naturalists" forward through the century, the same entities that White identified as his four closing doors. In *White Noise*, for example, Gladney eventually discovers religious faith to be a sham. Early on, DeLillo alerts the reader to this possibility, linking the local churches and an insane asylum in a description of Blacksmith, the town that provides the novel's setting. Meteorology, dispensed through TV weather reports, has replaced theology for Gladney, and the tabloids have become religious texts for the older townspeople. A trip to the cemetery to inspect "the strong simple names" on headstones provides Gladney with a suggestion of vanished "moral rigor" (97). This impression provides a stark contrast to the contemporary scene with its definition of humanity as a mere "tangle of neurons" that bid to render "cowardice, sadism, [and] masochism" morally neutral (200). But Gladney gets conclusive evidence of God's death in the novel's penultimate chapter. He drags his wife's seducer, after shooting and wounding him, to a Catholic emergency room for treatment. There Gladney falls into conversation with Sister Hermann Marie, who stuns him with her straight talk about religious reality. The nun scoffs at his naive assumption that faith survives in the churches. She defines the clergy's role in the world, "to believe things no one else takes seriously," and to comfort non believers with the mistaken assumption that there are still believers (318).

Science stops short of solutions as well. The "miracle" drug Dylar, touted by the charlatan scientist Willie Mink, fails in its supposed ability to erase the fear of death. In fact, scientists are only good at forecasting disasters, including "the eventual heat death of the universe" (10). Medical doctors, like the surgeon who offers "he" a lobotomy in "The Door," are also otherwise helpless in the face of suffering, turning away the Gladneys for untreatable maladies like a child's soulful crying. The foremost fruits of science, the gadgetry of technology, adds to angst by creating "an appetite for immortality," while at the same time threatening "universal extinction" (285).

The "door" of money and conspicuous consumption comes under DeLillo's scrutiny as well. Early on, Gladney reflects on the way "things . . . possessions" teach him to be "wary not of personal failure and defeat but of something more general, something large in scope and content" (6). This intimation of emptiness at the center of what the world offers plays out in a later scene in which Gladney and his family visit a shopping mall. In the midst of the mall's plenty, they are seduced by, among other things, their own images "on mirrored columns, in glassware and chrome," while organ music, conjuring up a cathedral, mixes with "the hum of escalators" (83–84). But Gladney's hopes for his family's fulfillment through his purchases collides with what he knows, namely that commodities cannot compel for the duration. He notes still later, for example, that the discarded detritus of civilization, the "garbage" that makes up the "dark underside of consumer consciousness," may hold clues to our "secret yearnings," and, of course, by implication, to their unrealizability (259). This unbreachable distance between our wants and our world can be observed most instructively in the United States since, as Gladney's chemist friend Winnie Richards points out, "we still lead the world in stimuli" (189).

And even the erotic in *White Noise* requires artificial prompting. In an early bedroom scene, Gladney and his wife Babette note their need to accompany their lovemaking with "trashy magazines" read to each other (29–30). At the same time, the serially married Gladney demonstrates sexual restlessness. His friend Murray Siskind notes the frequent juxtaposition of sex and death in casual conversations with Blacksmith friends, a linkage indicative of their Freudian frustration (217).

On the other hand, Gladney sees family life, and especially his smaller children, as one of the few stays against confusion left in postmodern America. Throughout the novel, he muses on the unspoiled anticipation of his toddler son Wilder, who models "the true universal" by "the way he drops one thing and grabs another" in the context of his young yearning and "freedom from limits," but also in the "inbred desolation" of his crying (50, 77, 209, 289). DeLillo's protagonist makes a habit of checking in on his sleeping children at night, a ritual that leaves him "feeling refreshed and expanded in unnameable ways" (182).

Indeterminate desire dominates Gladney's more generalized thought processes. He ruminates at one point, for example, on the "irony" of humanity, designated to be "the highest form of life on earth and yet ineffably sad" (99). This sadness owes to the restrictions on fulfillment dictated by death, which, once "established," makes it "impossible to lead a satisfying life" (285). Again, Gladney recognizes his own "cosmic . . . yearnings and reachings" at a time when "all the amazement that's left in the world is microscopic" (154, 161). DeLillo also suggests humanity's generic jading through some of the symptoms he links with exposure to the "airborne toxic event." For example, the victims experience frequent episodes of *déjà vu*, a "been there, done that" reflex that suggests satiation.

But all of these discouragements cannot keep DeLillo's characters from indulging their excessive expectation. Gladney himself notes that, despite the odds, humans keep "inventing hope." The novel's final chapter begins with Wilder dodging traffic and crossing a divided highway on his plastic tricycle. The reader may well ask, as if to preface a joke, why does Wilder cross the road? The answer surely must be that he, DeLillo's agent of raw desire, like the tenacious turtle whose road crossing despite the odds stands for the indomitable courage of John Steinbeck's Oakies' in *The Grapes of Wrath*, testifies with his tricycle to the regular rebirth of human desire. DeLillo also renders this proclivity symbolically through the Blacksmith townspeople's magnetized attraction to "postmodern" sunsets, which, thanks to the life-threatening toxic cloud and microorganisms sprayed to disperse it, have become "almost unbearably beautiful" (170). In the novel's closing pages, the citizens congregate on a freeway overpass, and, drawn by a lingering sunset, train their eyes on the west, the direction desire has most often taken in American fiction.

The last paragraph in the novel features Gladney reflecting on the confusion caused by the rearrangement of the shelves in his neighborhood supermarket, the institution defined earlier as a "gateway or pathway" full of "bright psychic data" in the form of replenishing brand-name foods and other consumer goods. The newly scattered items in the store induce "panic" as older customers try "to figure out the pattern." They "turn into the wrong aisle" and "peer along the shelves" in search of order. In their bewilderment they locate the single section that has not been moved, the aisle of generic food, "white packages plainly labeled." Like the ground that invariably meets the foot at the end of "The Door," the generic canned fruits and vegetables, earlier in the novel equated by Murray Siskind to "austerity" and "spiritual consensus," conjure up continuity within confusion, while the "holographic scanners" at the checkout lanes "decode the binary secret of every item, infallibly" (325–26).

Readers of this essay will undoubtedly think of other examples of modern and postmodern works that continue the tradition begun by Crane, Norris, and Dreiser, who chronicle their characters' anguished search for substance and salvation without religious recourse.

Notes

1. The "wonder" quote is from *The Great Gatsby*, 182. The "Gods dead" quote is from *This Side of Paradise*, 282.

2. Lewis, *Pilgrim's Progress*, 9–10.

3. Holman and Harmon, *A Handbook to Literature*, 370.

4. Rueckert, *Kenneth Burke and the Drama of Human Relations*, 138.

5. In one of the few articles about "The Door," William Steinhoff identifies the sources for characters and ideas in the story.

6. Steinhoff, in his *College English* article, " 'The Door,' " contends that "The Man Out in Jersey" must have been inspired by one Samuel W. Rushmore, a Plainfield inventor whose response to what he believed to be an unfair divorce property settlement was to threaten dismantling his house. The case had been receiving considerable publicity in New York at the time White was writing his story.

7. An interesting corollary to White's protagonist's experience can be found in one of Faulkner's novels. At one point Faulkner's Benjy, another character ill-equipped mentally for trying to make sense of his world, enters the Compson family library with his keeper, Luster. Luster turns on the light and the windows go black. Benjy walks to the wall, touches it and thinks: "It was like a door, only it wasn't a door." See *The Sound and the Fury*, 38.

8. One of the puzzles of "The Door" has to do with the "he" character's age. If his loss of faith occurred when he was an adolescent, he would be about thirty-two as the story unfolds, since he has been jumping at ungiving doors, the first of which pretty clearly stands for religion, for twenty years. If the disillusionment occurred when he was in college, he would be in his forties, and, more appropriately, a candidate for a mid-life crisis. An additional possible referent for the "long sweet words with the holy sound" could be maternal ministrations, but this would make "he" very young indeed.

9. For a postmodern reminder (among many) of sexuality's staying power as an illusion of transcendence, see Woody Allen's recent film, *Deconstructing Harry*. In it his cinematic alter ego affirms that "Women are God."

10. Steihoff reveals, in the article cited above, that White had read in *The New York Times*, during February and March of 1939, a series of reports about a model home exhibit at Rockefeller Center. Details in the *Times* articles are appropriated without alteration in White's disordered description of what seems to be a free standing, prototype kitchen where "he's" situation is played out. Steinhoff also conjectures that White may well have read about the newly developed prefrontal lobotomy in a *New York Times* story on 9 March 1939.

11. Sampson, *E. B. White*, 116. Steinhoff argues that the story "ends in health" when "the adventurer escapes from the maze" and emerges "a kind of modern winner" (231–32). But like Sampson, Steinhoff reads the ground/foot lines as just further signs of dizziness.

12. White to Robert L. DeLong Jr., 22 July 1963, in *Letters of E. B. White*, 505. In the letter, White also remembers attending the Rockefeller Center home show in person, not just reading about it, as Steinhoff concludes.

13. White to Astrid P. Coates, *Letters of E. B. White*, 641–42.

14. Epstein, "E. B. White, Dark & Lite," 49.

15. See Steinhoff's article.

16. Ibid.

17. I've noted in my essay that White later denied any intention of question-

ing religion's access to truth. That denial can either be accepted, or, more logically I think, rejected as disingenuous like other of White's remarks about "The Door," or as an example of the not uncommon repentance of an older and more conservative writer confronted with a youthful indiscretion. The last lines of Marquis's poem "The Name" also urge analysis. The speaker in the poem's four stanzas, having failed to locate the something he cannot name elsewhere, seeks the answer in "old chapels." In them he fancies that he has heard "some saint's carven countenance" suggest that all names mean God, perchance." See *Dreams and Dust*, 9–10. Here Marquis is framing in verse, somewhat tentatively to be sure, St. Augustine's argument that the things we desire on earth, the things represented by the doors/walls in White's story, are a foretaste of heaven. Whether White used the conclusion of "The Name" in formulating "The Door" is a nice question. He had obviously read Marquis's poem with considerable concentration. If he did intend to convey the poet's Augustinian gloss, the only evidence would seem to be in those troubling lines about the ground meeting the foot, read as an intimation of order.

Dreiser, Fitzgerald, and the Question of Influence

THOMAS P. RIGGIO

ALTHOUGH THEODORE DREISER (1871–1945) WAS A GENERATION OLDER than F. Scott Fitzgerald (1896–1940), literary historians sometimes place them together in overly determined categories such as The Urban Novel or The Literature of the Twenties. This is owing largely to the serendipitous publication in 1925 of *An American Tragedy* and *The Great Gatsby*. Both books deal with poor midwesterners whose youthful dreams of women, money, and power lead them to ruin. Thematic and narrative affinities have not, however, discouraged critics from building a wall that keeps Dreiser on the side of naturalism and Fitzgerald among the modernists. It's not surprising, then, that the single book-length study dealing with the impact of contemporary writers on Fitzgerald mentions Dreiser only once in passing and concludes that those "who influenced Fitzgerald most significantly were four: Edmund Wilson, H. L. Mencken, Ring Lardner, and Ernest Hemingway."[1]

Naturally, this kind of thinking has stimulated little comparative analysis of the language and imagery of Dreiser and Fitzgerald, who among American writers of their day are the most kindred of spirits. Moreover, what has been said about their relationship does not move beyond source and theme hunting to a consideration of the generational and psychological factors that have been widely accepted as the basis of literary influence.[2] This is perplexing, especially since Fitzgerald frequently spoke about Dreiser, who was the graybeard of American novelists when the younger man began writing.

Questions of literary influence often wait on the evidence of biography. In this case, the biographical record is thin. The writers exchanged no letters, and Fitzgerald's name never appears in Dreiser's surviving correspondence. The only known instance of a meeting between them is in 1923 during a party at Dreiser's New York apartment at St. Luke's Place. Fitzgerald walked in on a lifeless gathering in which Dreiser, a teetotaler at the time, was trying to entertain a group of writers who were looking in vain for liquid refreshment. Fitzgerald arrived drunk, carrying a bottle of champagne under his arm. Evidently he was nervous at the prospect of his first meeting with the author of *Sister Carrie*, *The "Genius"*, and *Twelve Men*, books he greatly admired. Dreiser did not help matters by unceremoniously taking the bottle from him, placing it in his icebox, and moving on to other guests. Llewelyn Powys remembered that Fitzgerald "addressed the elder novelist with maudlin deference. It was as though some young Dick Lovelace had come bursting into Ben Jonson's room."[3] Sherwood Anderson read into Dreiser's manner a deliberate slight, although H. L. Mencken insisted to the contrary that "Fitz came in and was politely treated by Dreiser."[4] All agreed, however, with Ernest Boyd that the tipsy Fitzgerald's unsuccessful attempt to engage Dreiser was "an affecting picture of the Master with the youngest of his disciples."[5]

The only remark attributed to either man at the 1923 party is something Fitzgerald reportedly said in presenting the champagne to his host: "Mr. Dreiser, I get a great kick out of your books."[6] The subsequent history of his statements about Dreiser's work suggests that this was not just drunken flippancy. Even as late as 1937 he listed Dreiser, along with Hemingway and "the early Gertrude Stein" as his "favorite American authors."[7] Moreover, in his familiar role as literary mentor to various women, including his daughter Scottie, Fitzgerald invariably placed Dreiser on his short list of required reading.[8] Among American authors, Dreiser was quite simply Fitzgerald's measuring stick of greatness. In an inscription for Sheila Graham in Frank Norris's *The Octopus*, he wrote "Frank Norris after writing three great books died in 1902 at the age of just thirty. He was our most promising man and might have gone further than Dreiser."[9]

Fitzgerald was not shy in broadcasting his admiration for Dreiser. In a 1924 interview published in the *Smart Set*, B. F. Wilson asked him about his intellectual mentors: "My heroes? Well, I consider H. L. Mencken and Theodore Dreiser the greatest men living in the country today."[10] This supports the reports of Fitzgerald's friends, who noticed what Ernest Boyd describes as his "capacity for hero-worship." Boyd recalls that Fitzgerald "had often discussed the work of Theodore Dreiser, for whom he confessed a respect unusual in his generation."[11] Burton Rascoe was another author who saw that Fitzgerald "had idolized Dreiser as the dean of American novelists."[12]

These reports raise a number of questions. Did Fitzgerald's hero-worship constitute a literary influence, and, if so, what was its nature? Admiration, even hero-worship, does not in itself constitute literary influence. Had Fitzgerald, as Boyd concludes, an "unusual" respect for Dreiser among the writers of his time? Are there, as a result of this esteem, verbal or thematic echoes of Dreiser in his work? Is there evidence of, in Harold Bloom's formulation of the issue of influence, an anxiety in the response of the younger man to his literary forebear, to the degree that he experienced Dreiser as a rival? Finally, is there an intertextual relationship that can shed light on Dreiser as well as on Fitzgerald's writing? Or are we dealing with events and configurations in their shared culture to which both men responded with similar imaginative intensity?

The matter of influence includes, in varying degrees, all of these factors. Although there is no satisfying way to answer such questions, Fitzgerald's own testimony makes it hard to ignore them. For example, in a letter of 3 June 1920 to President John G. Hibben of Princeton, Fitzgerald explained his cynical account of the university in *This Side of Paradise* (1920) with reference to his philosophy of life: "My view of life, President Hibben, is the view of the Theodore Dreisers and Joseph Conrads—that life is too strong and remorseless for the sons of men."[13]

Fitzgerald is here remaking himself in hindsight. It is unlikely that he had read much of Dreiser or Conrad until after writing his first novel, which shows no evidence of their philosophies. To understand his remark, we must factor in Mencken's influence. Fitzgerald later said that he first encountered Mencken when he was reading proofs of *This Side of Paradise*: "I happened across *The Smart Set* one day and thought: 'Here's a man whose name I ought to know. I guess I'll stick it in the proof sheets.' "[14] Fitzgerald surely knew more about Mencken than this statement suggests; he had, in fact, submitted stories to *Smart Set* before he had completed the novel. He dealt with George Jean Nathan, Mencken's co-editor, but it is near impossible for him not to have known about Mencken. Whatever Fitzgerald's knowledge of Mencken, the passage he placed in the proof sheets of *This Side of Paradise* has Amory Blaine "rather surprised by his discovery through a critic named Mencken of several excellent novels: [Norris's] 'Vandover and the Brute,' [Harold Frederic's] 'The Damnation of Theron Ware,' and [Dreiser's] 'Jennie Gerhardt.' "[15] This almost surely was the extent of Fitzgerald's own knowledge of these three authors at the time.

By the time he wrote Hibben, Fitzgerald evidently had read Mencken's *Book of Prefaces*. In that book the critic famously linked Conrad and Dreiser and promoted them as two writers on either side of the Atlantic who shared *his* philosophy, of which Fitzgerald's words to Hibben are an almost verbatim transcription. Mencken's commentary led Fitzgerald to Dreiser's books, and the novelist's letters reveal that immediately after the publication of *This Side of Paradise* he began to read Dreiser closely.

Fitzgerald became openly imitative of the "great man" (and, to a lesser degree, of Frank Norris) in his second novel, *The Beautiful and*

Damned (1922). Few readers of Dreiser could miss the echoes of Hurstwood in Anthony Patch's downward slide from respectability: the slow dwindling of his money, the pride that makes him unable to do work he considers beneath him, and his physical and psychological deterioration—particularly the depression over thoughts of his former glories. There are moments when Fitzgerald openly recreates scenes from *Sister Carrie*. For example, there is the occasion in which Patch, mistaken for a "bum," is tossed out of a restaurant. "The shock stunned him. He lay there for a moment in acute distributed pain. . . . 'You've got to move on, y'bum! Move on.' It was the bulky doorman speaking."[16] At this point, Hurstwood's words, after he had been similarly thrown out onto the street by a backstage doorman, could be spoken by Patch with perfect appropriateness: " 'God damned dog!' he said. 'Damned old cur,' wiping the slush from his worthless coat. 'I—I hired such people as you once.' "[17] In case anyone misses the allusions to Dreiser, Fitzgerald creates a parody of himself in the character of the novelist Richard Caramel, and he has him ostentatiously place his books on the library shelf between the two writers Fitzgerald thought of as the fountainheads of modern American literature: "Wedged in between Mark Twain and Dreiser were eight strange and inappropriate volumes, the works of Richard Caramel."[18]

The desire to be read in the company of Twain and Dreiser was a source of creative energy for Fitzgerald; but it also weighed heavily on him, particularly in the dark hours of self-doubt that he often experienced. The weight became a greater burden after the publication of *An American Tragedy*, when Dreiser became more apparently a source of anxious rivalry for Fitzgerald. After 1925, one notices, Fitzgerald loses few chances to parrot the criticism of Dreiser's wordiness; this was the one area in which Fitzgerald felt secure enough of his talents to claim superiority.

There were few such advantages for Fitzgerald. In early 1926, he wrote to Maxwell Perkins that the plot of his new novel, whose working title was "Our Type" and whose subject was the psychology of a matricidal murderer, "is not unlike Dreiser's in the American Tragedy."[19] This was not meant to be good news for his editor. The shadow of Dreiser's large novel seems to have had a paralyzing effect on Fitzgerald, who never managed to complete this manuscript. Henry Dan Piper notes that Fitzgerald was later nervous as he was planning *Tender Is the Night*, "because he was afraid that Dreiser's *An American Tragedy* might make his novel redundant."[20] Fitzgerald's anxieties suggest that his ambition was to write an "American tragedy" of his own, and, more important, that he sensed between himself and Dreiser a literary kinship so close that the older writer might make his work "redundant."

It is a classic instance of the phenomenon Walter Jackson Bate describes brilliantly in *The Burden of the Past and the English Poet*: the artist's acute awareness of the work of a great predecessor, whom he experiences as both an inspiration and a figure who may have exhausted the possibilities of his art.

Fitzgerald may have felt anxious in part because he had already found in Dreiser sources for his writing. *The Great Gatsby* owes more to Dreiser than the openly imitative *The Beautiful and Damned*. Publicly Fitzgerald told friends that Gatsby was based on a Long Island bootlegger whom he had met.[21] Maxwell Geismar was the first to note that "Vanity, Vanity, Saith the Preacher," a sketch in Dreiser's *Twelve Men* (1919), was the inspiration for *The Great Gatsby*. Dreiser's biographical miniature centers on a man he calls "X" (in reality, Joseph G. Robin, nee Rabinovitch), who begins life penniless as the son of Russian immigrants and acquires great wealth at an early age. He is a colorful but socially insecure man who tries to buy acceptance with lavish displays of wealth. A Trimalcian figure, "X" builds a vast house on Long Island and throws "automobile parties" which attract the new rich and countless hangers-on. Like Gatsby, he has an air of mystery about him and many shady connections, which eventually lead to imprisonment and the loss of wealth. Geismar points out that "the salient details include the obscure birth of the hero, the rejection of his parents, the fierce drive for material success and luxury, including a Long Island estate with a garden of $40,000 roses. It is possible that "Vanity, Vanity" was one of the sources for Fitzgerald's novel—since the younger writer was so impressed with the older one."[22]

Eric Solomon elaborated on Geismar's observation, commenting aptly on the similarities between the narrator in Dreiser's story and Nick Carroway.[23] Ambivalent in their responses, both narrators are repelled and fascinated by the lurid rise and fall of "X" and Gatsby. They are especially intrigued and outraged at the abandonment of their heroes by the followers who clung to them as the masters of bacchanalian revels. Both Nick and Dreiser's narrator believe that Gatsby and "X" are, in Fitzgerald's phrase, "worth the whole damn bunch put together."[24]

One hears in Nick Carroway's descriptions of Gatsby traces of the voice of the narrator in "Vanity, Vanity." The narrative voice in Dreiser's fiction served Fitzgerald, among others, as a vehicle for the writer who is implicitly a critic of society, a storyteller who does not preach social injustice but portrays it as part of the drama of "Life." Dreiser's "X" is introduced, in his role as a Long Island party host, as a social enigma worthy of close scrutiny.

> My host was not visible at first, but I met a score of people whom I knew by reputation. . . . Actresses and society women floated here and there in dreams of afternoon dresses. The automobiles outside were making a perfect uproar. . . . At a glance it was plain to me that he had managed to gather about him the very element it would be most interesting to gather, supposing one desired to be idle, carefree and socially and intellectually gay. . . . I wondered at once at the character of the person who could need, desire or value this [various rooms—music-, dining-, ball-, library and so forth]. A secret bedroom, for instance; a lounging-room! . . . He appeared to have the free, easy, and gracious manner of those who have known much of life and have achieved, in part at least, their desires. He smiled, wished to know if I had met all the guests, hoped that the sideboard had not escaped me, that I had enjoyed the singing. . . . Interestingly enough, and from the first, I was impressed with this man; not because of his wealth (I knew richer men) but because of something about him which suggested dreams, romance, a kind of sense or love of splendor and grandeur which one does not often encounter among the really wealthy. . . . He suggested the huge and Aladdin-like adventures with which so many of the great financiers of the day, the true tigers of Wall Street, were connected.[25]

When "X" is ruined financially, his sycophantic followers abandon him, as they would Gatsby after his death. "I never saw such a running to cover of 'friends' in all my life. Of all those I had seen about his place and in his company . . . all eating his dinners, riding in his cars, drinking his wines, there was scarcely any one now who knew him anything more than 'casually' or 'slightly'—oh, so slightly."[26]

Such passages suggest that Dreiser's importance for Fitzgerald goes beyond the inspiration for plot and character noted in *The Beautiful and Damned* and *The Great Gatsby*. Imitation may be the sincerest mode of flattery, but it represents the least significant form of influence. A more complex level of influence is found in the rhythms and images of *Gatsby*'s prose, which at important moments reveals the ways in which Fitzgerald had imaginatively absorbed Dreiser's language. Fitzgerald's love of the lush, lyrically cadenced phrases of the High Romantics and their Victorian successors attracted him to their presence in Dreiser's writing. The latter's prose is suited to themes that equally obsessed Fitzgerald: the poignancy of the passage of time and of premature death. Despite their many stylistic differences, Fitzgerald and Dreiser have in common a prose whose tonalities are inseparable from their understanding of the world. Like Dreiser, Fitzgerald is a master of pathos, not tragedy, and in 1925 they published two of the most famous American novels in that mode.

Fitzgerald, of course, probably did not sit at his writing desk with Dreiser's books open before him. Still, there are numerous passages in his work that highlight the ways in which he appropriated Dreiser's idiom. Take, for instance, the time after Gatsby's death, when Nick reflects on him and how far he had come from his beginnings as James Gatz:

> his dream must have seemed so close that he could hardly fail to grasp it . . . Gatsby believed in the green light, the orgastic future that year by year recedes before us. It eluded us then, but that's no matter—tomorrow we will run faster, stretch out our arms farther. . . . And one fine morning—
>
> So we beat on, boats against the current, borne back ceaselessly into the past.[27]

If "Vanity, Vanity Saith the Preacher" was one source for the character of Gatsby, a sketch that ends *Twelve Men*—"W. L. S."—suggests the close attention Fitzgerald paid to the cadences and images in Dreiser's writing. "W. L. S." is based on Dreiser's memories of the graphic artist William Louis Sonntag, whose early death becomes the emotional center of the sketch. Dreiser concludes with this passage:

> His dreams were so near fulfillment . . . and then suddenly [his life] had been puffed out before my eyes, as if a hundred bubbles of iridescent hues had been shattered by a breath. We toil so much, we dream so richly, we hasten so fast, and, lo! the green door is opened. We are through it, and its grassy surface has sealed us forever from all which apparently we so much crave—even as, breathlessly, we are still running.[28]

Fitzgerald's "unusual" respect for the older writer can be measured by the extent to which he absorbed the rhythms and language of passages such as this. It is a prose tuned to narrators who, like their creators, find in the sad end of talented dreamers not merely the pathos of unfulfilled aspiration but a symbol of the human condition, which they experience as a race to oblivion. In the passage quoted above, the green light becomes for Gatsby the ironic equivalent of the merciless green door that seals the fate of the richest dreams Dreiser can imagine.

In *Gatsby* Fitzgerald also paid modest tribute to *Sister Carrie*. Robert E. Long has gone further than any critic in claiming that Fitzgerald's novels collectively reflect the "pattern of action in *Sister Carrie*"[29] Long is interested mainly in the influence of the character of Hurstwood on Fitzgerald's failed men—notably Anthony Patch and Richard Diver, both of whom experience "falls" from success and health while other characters provide a counterpoint as they "rise" in the world.

I would add to Long's brief list of references a passage in *Gatsby* that pays quiet homage to the character of Carrie Meeber. At Tom Buchanan's party for his mistress, Myrtle Wilson, Nick learns from her how she met Tom. In her story of the encounter with Tom on the train to New

York, Fitzgerald reimagines Carrie's meeting with Drouet on her trip to visit her sister in Chicago. In both passages seduction becomes inseparable from the attraction of male presence, which is conceived as a function of class—and more particularly the way that class is embodied in clothing.

> "It was on two little seats facing each other that are always the last one left on the train. I was going up to New York to see my sister and spend the night. He had on a dress suit and patent leather shoes, and I couldn't keep my eyes off him, but every time he looked at me, I had to pretend to be looking at the advertisement over his head. When we came to the station he was next to me, and his white shirt-front pressed against my arm, and so I told him I'd have to call a policeman, but he knew I lied. I was so excited that when I got into a taxi with him I didn't hardly know I wasn't getting into a subway train. All I kept thinking about, over and over, was 'You can't live forever; you can't live forever.' "[30]

In this account of Myrtle Wilson's seduction, Fitzgerald provides us with the portrait of a Carrie of the nineteen-twenties, a working-class girl eager to find in the big city an escape, however tawdry, from the poverty of spirit and daily drudgery of her home. Myrtle is shorn of the remnants of Victorian propriety that Carrie Meeber maintains, but she is as responsive to fine suits and patent leather shoes as Dreiser's waif of the 1890s.

Passages such as these raise the question of what elements in the psychological makeup of the two writers led to Fitzgerald's mirroring the work of a stylist so different from himself. Did Fitzgerald, as Harold Bloom argues of all such cases, misread his predecessor, even as he strongly responded to him? Or, to emphasize what Bloom's terms suggest but fail to make clear, did he read Dreiser empathically, finding in him a powerful ally of the imagination, despite the type of Oedipal struggle Bloom posits?

These are, of course, the subjects of a much larger study than this one. I imagine, however, that one must begin with biographical fact. A starting place might be Fitzgerald's youth, which, despite his more genteel beginnings, shares a good deal with Dreiser's working-class upbringing. They were both midwesterners who felt themselves on the social and economic margins of their communities. The shadow of their puritanical parent (for Dreiser his father and for Fitzgerald his mother) can be felt in their best writing, though with considerably more obliqueness in Fitzgerald. I suppose an argument could be made that Dreiser's one year at Indiana University left him with the same mixture of awe-inspired inferiority and prideful disdain as did Fitzgerald's time at Princeton. As writers, they shared an impulse toward the confessional, which probably was rooted in their early Catholicism. In the literary marketplace, they tried to suppress the ethnic and religious sides of their heritage. There are also important similarities in their sexual insecurities, if not in their ways of challenging them. They responded more viscerally and with more ambivalence to the American gospel of wealth than any other writers of their day. They share with only the best writers of any time an enormous sensitivity to human mutability.

This is a short list of biographical factors that might be expanded and explored in the context of intertextual evidence. While I have naturally had to demonstrate the ways in which Fitzgerald incorporated the older writer in his oeuvre, discussion of literary influence, if it is to move beyond notice of mere imitation, should deal as much as possible with the interplay between like sensibilities as with the matter of precedent. Although anxiety over the exhaustion of forms and ideas and over the genius of a predecessor are crucial elements in the dynamics of influence, the affinity between writers that produces such complex reactions deserves attention. For obvious reasons, this element gets lost in practice. In considering, say, Spencer and Keats or Milton and Joyce or Balzac and Dreiser or Shakespeare and the rest of the world, a reader can only speculate on the way the older writer may have responded if the divide between periods could be collapsed.

In the case of Dreiser and Fitzgerald, however, there is more than sufficient overlap to warrant an attempt at expanding the concept of influence to include the idea of reciprocal relationship. We can, that is to say, without risking the charge of idle speculation, pose the question whether a writer can truly be said to influence a significant "other." Or is it necessary that certain psychological and characterological factors of the later writer be present in the work of the predecessor in order for the latter to become an influence? If I may be allowed an excursion into science fiction to restate the question, is it theoretically possible in the case of strong influences that writers *as writers* might be able to exchange chronological periods, regardless of their personal or historical idiosyncrasies? Put another way, is some such similarity of spirit a condition of literary influence?

I confess that I have no answers to these questions, though my experience as a reader leads me to favor the idea that the aesthetic and the psychological are inseparable in cases of artistic influence. In the case of Dreiser and Fitzgerald, we come close to being able to test this proposition. Dreiser outlived Fitzgerald, and therefore he himself had an opportunity to become indebted to the younger writer. At first glance, the evidence seems to point away from any possible reciprocal exchange. To repeat, Dreiser said nothing about Fitzgerald, whom he surely knew about after 1920, if only from their circle of mutual friends. Moreover, by 1925 Fitzgerald was among the hottest new novelists in America. He and Dreiser, in fact, had stories published in a number of the same magazines. Yet there is a strange silence on Dreiser's part, almost as if he consciously (or perhaps subconsciously) refused to recognize Fitzgerald's existence. When asked in the 1930s who were the younger writers he most admired, Dreiser named William Faulkner, Erskine Caldwell, and John Steinbeck, all exact contemporaries of Fitzgerald.[31] When we consider that Dreiser shared with Fitzgerald an imaginative response to American materials unlike that of any of the writers he named, it becomes conceivable that he had indeed read Fitzgerald and perhaps was experiencing some uneasiness of his own over this potential rival. Unless some more concrete information comes to light, though, we will have to be satisfied with educated guesses.

Good educated guesses, however intuitive, have a basis in empirical fact. Although there is no hard evidence that Dreiser ever read Fitzgerald, there are places in Dreiser's writing that strongly suggest that he would have experienced his own shock of recognition had he carefully read the younger novelist. One example, a letter Dreiser wrote to Helen Richardson on 26 May 1924, will stand for numerous instances of this kind. Richardson, a cousin twice removed, was his mistress at the time and later became his second wife. Because of a quarrel, she was living in California and he in New York. The estrangement led to a nine-month separation, during which time Dreiser was working steadily and stressfully on *An American Tragedy*. Dreiser's letters to Richardson attempt to woo her back East; they are equally valuable as a record of his state of mind while in the heat of composition.

Among these letters is the aforementioned one of late May, in which, in the process of flattering his "Babu," Dreiser describes a rare evening away from his writing room. He tells of a party he attended on Long Island Sound at an estate rented by W. C. Fields. The letter is dated less than a year before the publication of *The Great Gatsby*—that is, at the very time when Fitzgerald was most under Dreiser's sway. If the book had already been published, one might very well argue that *Gatsby* had influenced Dreiser's picture of Fields's party. Stated more logically, Dreiser's description of Jazz Age partying among the new rich could serve as a rough gloss on such scenes in Fitzgerald's novel.

118 W. 11th St.[32]

Monday. May 26–1924

Dearest Babu:

Yesterday, because it was clear, I decided to go up to W. C. Fields' place after all. He has just leased a place for the summer in the Sound beyond Larchmont—a $150,000 show property. He has had a very successful year in

Poppy & plainly wants to splurge. No wife but apparently many friends. And he said if I would come as far as Mt. Vernon on the train he would meet me—which he did. In one of two cars that belong to him. And with him were three of the chorus girls of his company and an actor by the name of Lionel Braham, now with The Miracle. In true country-house actor & actress style they were mostly in blues & whites, trim hats, shoes & the like. The conversation consisted of nothing but bright remarks or attempts to make them. Nothing serious. You know the stuff well enough. You used to call it "wise-cracking." there was also of course much ritzing. And being anxious to hold up my end I did my share.

But that place right in the Sound. I wish you might have seen it. It was built by some rich sugar man for some woman he was living with at the time. And afterwards it was sold to F. E. Albee—or E. F. Albee who leases it to Fields this summer. A long sweeping drive in from the main road, a porte cochere at one side, two lamp standards along the road, a great veranda at the back overlooking the sea—and to one side a large [word unintelligible] tennis court. The lawn was perfect & went right down to the water. There are trees, flowers, a pagoda—or lounging room near the water & so on. Inside were four big rooms on the ground floor [word unintelligible] down to the verandah at the back & of course all the luxuries—wines, fruits, cigars & a butler & two men servants to look after you. Out on the lawn were swings & benches with parasols over them & tables before them. And all day after I arrived actors or friends, coming up or going down the road, were coming to and going from this place. They arrived in parties of two, four & six, staying for a little while—some for all day & departed again. That Eddie Jessel that we once saw telephoning his mother from the stage was there nearly all day. He was accompanied by his wife and sister-in-law—the Coleman sisters—whoever they are. Then Holliwell Hobbes (never heard of him before yesterday) arrived with two ritzi girls—actresses—arrived in a car big enough to hold twelve. After them two Jews, a Mr. Lewis & a Mr. Key in a Buick roadster showed up—[word unintelligible] I judged. And after them that Mr. Benchley who did the polite monologue in The Music Box (the financial secy. making his report) and the leading beauty of his show—a miss Saunderson. And after them two Jews connected with the Famous Players Lasky who brought out a new movie by Pola-Negri which was to be shown in the evening on a screen in the library. Finally the veranda, the rooms & the lawn were dotted with people. Four played tennis. Others walked over the ground in pairs. I sat with about 10 around a central outdoor table on which they put cigars, cigarettes, whiskey, candy & magazines.

You would have been amused. Of all the dumb-bells & bone heads give me the average actor and actress. Nothing got the least applause or interest unless it was smutty or smart-aleck. Not a thing. There was a copy of the Theatre Arts Magazine with some really beautiful reproductions of stage sets from the Ancient Mariner, The Emperor Jones & so on. But someone having picked the book up & looked at it casually it went the rounds with such remarks as "do they call that interesting" "Can you beat that stuff" "I can't see a thing in it.'' But the price of cars, who had bought a new one, who owed who what, whether such & such a show was going to close—who was taking a house where—all this got close attention. And, of course, some one asked me if I was related to Dreiser the jeweler.

Then dinner at two. A long automobile ride to a hotel at Greenwich just to promenade & have a few drinks & look at the sea there. Then back for a supper at six-thirty (cold everything). And all the while one actor or another was playing on the piano & another was singing. And two or three more monkeying with the radio try to get Pittsburg—or Chicago. And at least five chorus girls got silly drunk & talked about who was a this or a that & what they would do to so & so if they were in such [word unintelligible] one's place. I sat for the most part & made mental notes.

But to see the Sound & the little yachts out on the water & the sunlight on the grass from the verandah was beautiful. And there was a library of books but no one picked up one.

Then came the moving picture—a fierce, silly thing about Paris & a girl being ruined & then becoming a great star. And someone said to me thats kinda like your book—Sister Carrie—aint it? At about 10 dancing began. And since I dont dance I called on Mr. Fields to get me a car to the depot. And he took me down—without any farewells on my part & I was back here at 1130. But when I looked back on it I liked it—as a spectacle. I've really seen the same thing all my life—some actor or financier or manufacturer getting rich & taking a house for the summer & splurging during his little hour around the candle. But it's still interesting because it emphasizes—for me—how the world goes on doing the same thing over & over & over in precisely the same way. Some of the girls & women there were very pretty & well dressed—but quite without exception in this case brassy & unintelligent. I looked at them & talked with a dozen. Unless you talked sex & flirted they wouldn't talk at all. But automatically I contrasted each & everyone with you—how you thought and how they thought. You wouldn't get very far with that group with any thoughts as to the beauty of the skies or the sea or life. "Oh—yes. it is pretty, isn't it?" You never get "I don't want to see anything beautiful any more" out of them.

Well, Babu—this is what I wanted to write earlier in the day but couldn't. It's 1030 now. I'm tired and about ready to turn in. But I'm going out to mail this first. You're way out west under the pepper trees & I'm here in 11th Street looking up at the lighted clock of the Jefferson Market Police Court. And cats always yowl back here at night. It's only 7PM with you. And when you get this you'll have forgotten what you did Monday evening at 7—Maybe. But if you didn't get a loving long distance thought from me then (a wish I were out there just now & could walk in on her) there's nothing much to telepathy between us.

Good night.

It'll probably be good morning when you read it.

Lovingly

T. D.

Beneath Dreiser's disdain of the theatrical crowd's insouciance and mindless freedom, we can hear him struggling with one of his lifelong demons—a hunger to share in the glitter of this world, which had preyed on his mind from the time he was a boy in Evansville, Indiana. There he watched his brother Paul Dresser freely indulge his large appetite for celebrity and all the fruits forbidden by the god of their father. This side of Dreiser interested Fitzgerald, whose critique of the leisure class contains similar ambivalences. The younger writer had the same feelings about the illusory nature of experience as did his predecessor, but he held on precariously to one illusion that Dreiser could hardly imagine: the sense that the past offered a more heroic moment than was possible in his time. Dreiser's vision was considerably darker. Unlike Fitzgerald, he saw the cars, the parties, the women, the yearning outsiders—the entire social field mined by both men in their fiction—finally as an unsettling reminder that "the world goes on doing the same thing over & over & over in precisely the same way."

Dreiser eventually came to understand, as did Fitzgerald, the generic nature of this scene in American life: "I've really seen the same thing all my life—some actor or financier or manufacturer getting rich & taking a house for the summer & splurging during his little hour around the candle." Out of yearnings for this world as deep as Dreiser's, Fitzgerald was in May of 1924 writing the story of Gatsby, whose demon is that of his author's: the golden girl of his dreams. If Daisy has a close relative in the writing of this period, it is surely Sondra Finchley, an aloof figure in the *Tragedy* who, under different names, appears in Dreiser's memoirs as the distant object of his social and erotic dreams.

Sondra and Daisy, Clyde and Gatsby: close enough fictional relatives to warrant further inquiry into the creative and psychological kinship between Dreiser and Fitzgerald. When I sent Dreiser's letter to a colleague known for his work on both writers, he at first speculated that Fitzgerald might have been at the same party, until a quick check revealed that he was in Europe at the time.[33] Dreiser believed in telepathy, but it is unlikely that either he or Fitzgerald were thinking of each other while he was overlooking Long Island Sound that late spring day. The path of literary influence, nevertheless, is unpredictable and as complex and mysterious as any other personal chemistry. Seen from this distance and with the hindsight provided by the writings of the two men, there may in fact be a sense in which they both were there.

Notes

1. William Goldhurst, *F. Scott Fitzgerald and His Contemporaries*, 11.
2. The most important books dealing with these aspects of literary influence

are: Walter Jackson Bate, *The Burden of the Past and the English Poet*; Harold Bloom, *The Anxiety of Influence: A Theory of Poetry*; Goran Hermeren, *Influence in Art and Literature*; Patrick Colm Hogan, *Joyce, Milton, and the Theory of Influence*.

3. Llewelyn Powys, *The Verdict of Bridlegoose*, 131.

4. See Sherwood Anderson, *Sherwood Anderson's Memoirs*, 336–37; and Sara Mayfield, "Another Fitzgerald Myth Exploded by Mencken."

5. Ernest Boyd, *Portraits: Real and Imaginary*, 222.

6. Qtd. in W. A. Swanberg, *Dreiser*, 272.

7. Matthew J. Bruccoli and Margaret M. Duggan, eds., *Correspondence of F. Scott Fitzgerald*, 484.

8. See, for instance, Fitzgerald's letter of 7 July 1938 to his daughter, Frances Scott Fitzgerald, recommending that she read Dreiser's first novel: "*Sister Carrie*, almost the first piece of American realism, is damn good." See Edmund Wilson, ed., *The Crack-Up*, 298.

9. Bruccoli and Duggan, 342.

10. Fitzgerald, qtd. in B. F. Wilson, "Notes on Personalities."

11. Boyd, 221.

12. Burton Rascoe, *We Were Interrupted*, 301.

13. Bruccoli, ed., *F. Scott Fitzgerald: A Life in Letters*, 40.

14. Bruccoli and Bryer, eds., *F. Scott Fitzgerald in His Own Time: A Miscellany*, 247.

15. Fitzgerald, *The Beautiful and Damned*, 224.

16. Ibid., 438.

17. *Sister Carrie* (Philadelphia: University of Pennsylvania Press, 1981; rpt. 1998), 494.

18. *The Beautiful and Damned*, 422.

19. Qtd. in Robert Sklar, *F. Scott Fitzgerald: The Last Laocoon*, 252.

20. Henry Dan Piper in M. S. Bradbury, ed., *The American Novel and the Nineteen Twenties*, 67.

21. Arthur Mizener, *The Far Side of Paradise*, 186.

22. Maxwell Geismar, *Rebels and Ancestors*, 342.

23. Eric Solomon, "A Source for Fitzgerald's *The Great Gatsby*."

24. *The Great Gatsby*, 154.

25. Dreiser, *Twelve Men*, 1919 (Philadelphia: University of Pennsylvania Press, 1998), 266–68.

26. Ibid., 280.

27. *The Great Gatsby*, 182.

28. *Twelve Men*, 359–60.

29. Robert E. Long, "*Sister Carrie* and the Rhythm of Failure in Fitzgerald."

30. *The Great Gatsby*, 36.

31. Riggio, "Dreiser on Society and Literature: The San Francisco Exposition Interview," 292.

32. The University of Pennsylvania kindly gave permission to publish this letter, housed among the Dreiser papers in the Dreiser Collection at the Van Pelt Library.

33. My colleague is James L. W. West III, the general editor of the Cambridge edition of the works of F. Scott Fitzgerald. My thanks to him for his helpful comments on an earlier version of this essay.

Wright, Dreiser, and Spatial Narrative

YOSHINOBU HAKUTANI

I

AS AFRICAN AMERICANS FOUND THE RURAL SOUTH A LIVING HELL AND dreamed of overcoming racial prejudice and living in northern cities, their writers were intent upon conveying their pains and dreams. The mode of their writing was diametrically opposed to that of nineteenth-century American novelists who often described the mood of pastoral idyl inspired by a longing for simpler agrarian society. This type of fiction was written largely as a reaction to the disharmony and friction that occurred among rugged individualists, strong-willed white men, living in urban society. The new kind of white man was not only able to live in harmony with nature, he would find a bosom friend in the stranger, a dark-skinned man from whom he learned the values of life he had not known. Natty Bumppo in Cooper's leather-stocking novels strikes up friendship with Chingachgook and Hard-Heart, noble savages of the wilderness. Ishmael in *Moby-Dick* is ritualistically wedded to Queequeg, a pagan from the South Seas. Huck Finn discovers a father figure in Jim, a runaway slave.

In twentieth-century American literature, however, a substantial reversal of the antiurban sentiment is found in both European American and African American writings, a new literary tradition often critical of the values expressed in earlier American literature. In *Jennie Gerhardt*, for example, Dreiser described the city as a site of freedom and subjectivity. A realistic modernist like Dreiser, who intimately knew the squalor and corruption city life brought on, used the urban environment as a space in which to dramatize individual liberty and pursuit of happiness. For both men and women, the city was envisioned as a site of confluence between the individual and society, a space which was fluid and wide enough to enable citizens and workers to interact with an industrialized culture.

Much important African American literature which has emerged since the Depression has also been largely urban in character. Although never hesitant to criticize the negative aspects of city life, it has only rarely suggested that pastoral alternatives to the city exist for African Americans. This large and significant body of literature, moreover, contains some surprising celebrations of city life. One way to explain this positive image of the city is to examine the historical experience of African Americans. From the very onset, African Americans were denied imaginative access to a pre-urban homeland in Africa because the institution of slavery did everything possible to stamp out the memory of that world.[1] And the actual experience of slaves in America did not permit them the luxury of romantically imagining the non-urban settings which are so mythically prominent in nineteenth-century American fiction by such writers as Cooper, Melville, and Twain. As Huck Finn and Jim sadly discovered, the territories ahead could be truly liberating only for European Americans. In the era following the literal end of slavery, new strategies for reinslavement were devised in the South where codes of segregation and the practice of sharecropping were to make it impossible for African Americans to establish a positive image of rural life which could serve as a counterbalance to the pull of urban life.

For Richard Wright, Chicago was split between wonder and terror, but it was always preferable to the southern environment he had so categorically rejected. What is remarkable about his impression of Chicago was its dichotomous vision:

> Then there was the fabulous city in which Bigger lived, an indescribable city, huge, roaring, dirty, noisy, raw, stark, brutal; a city of extremes: torrid summers and sub-zero winters, white people and black people, the English language and strange tongues, foreign born and native born, scabby poverty and gaudy luxury, high idealism and hard cynicism! A city so young that, in thinking of its short history, one's mind, as it travels backward in time, is stopped abruptly by the barren stretches of wind-swept prairie! But a city old enough to have caught within the homes of its long, straight streets the symbols and images of man's age-old destiny, of truths as old as the mountains and seas, of dramas as abiding as the soul of man itself![2]

Not only did Chicago in the 1930s and 40s present itself as the center of a powerful industrialized economy, but it was also a striking representation of a modern civilization buttressed by multiculturalism. Small wonder Chicago produced, besides Wright, Margaret Walker, Gwendolyn Brooks, and a host of American writers whose cultural legacies were other than Anglo-Saxon and mostly ethnic, such as Dreiser, James T. Farrell, Nelson Algren, and Saul Bellow.[3]

Farrell was one of the earliest American writers who championed Wright's narrative for an unusual intermixture of realism and lyricism.

He wrote in *Partisan Review* that *Uncle Tom's Children* serves as an exemplary refutation for those who wished to write "such fancy nonsense about fables and allegories." In response to such reviewers as Granville Hicks and Alan Calmer, who wanted Wright to pace more steadily in his narrative and delve more deeply into his material, Farrell argued that Wright effectively uses simple dialogue "as a means of carrying on his narrative, as a medium for poetic and lyrical effects, and as an instrument of characterization."[4] By contrast, as if in return for Wright's unfavorable review of her novel *Their Eyes Were Watching God*, Zora Neale Hurston categorized *Uncle Tom's Children* as a chronicle of hatred with no act of understanding and sympathy. As did some other critics, she opposed Wright's politics, arguing that his stories fail to touch the fundamental truths of African American life.[5]

For Wright, however, what enabled his narrative to convey the truth about African American experience was not an application of literary naturalism but a creation of perspective. Almost a decade earlier than James Baldwin's review of *Native Son*, Wright had posited a theory of African American narrative in "Blueprint for Negro Writing," published in *New Challenge*. This narrative, whether in fiction or in nonfiction, as he argued, must be based on fact and history and cannot be motivated by politics or idealism. African American writing, then, does not assume the role of protest: "even if Negro writers found themselves through some 'ism,' " he asks, "how would that influence their writing? Are they being called upon to 'preach'? To be 'salesmen'? To 'prostitute' their writing? Must they 'sully' themselves? Must they write 'propaganda'?" The inquiry is "a question of awareness, of consciousness; it is, above all, a question of perspective." This perspective, Wright defines, is "that part of a poem, novel, or play which a writer never puts directly upon paper. It is that fixed point in intellectual space where a writer stands to view the struggles, hopes, and sufferings of his people."[6]

Substantiating perspective with "intellectual space," Wright further posits that perspective must not be allied with "world movements" and must be established by the self. Because perspective is "something which he wins through his living," it is "the most difficult of achievement" ("Blueprint" 45–46). This intellectual space comprises, on the one hand, a writer's complex consciousness deeply involved in African American experience and, on the other, a detachment from it. By a detachment Wright means a reflection accomplished in isolation, in a space where neither those afflicted nor those sympathetic to their plight, such as Marxists, are allowed to enter. "The conditions under which I had to work," Wright recalls in *American Hunger*, "were what baffled them [members of the Communist party in Chicago]. Writing had to be done in loneliness."[7]

His attempt to establish perspective and provide it with intellectual space accounts for his lifelong commitment to a narrative by which he is able to convey his own vision of life. His entire work has shown that he was a remarkably resilient thinker and writer. At the outset of his career his writing was deeply influenced by Marxism, but later, as he came to establish his own point of view, he used only the doctrine of Marxist theory on class struggle, which made sense to African American life, but rejected much of the practice, which suppressed freedom and subjectivity.

Although some critics have regarded Wright's work as a product influenced by earlier American and European literary movements, he never considered himself belonging to any of them. In 1941 he told Edwin Seaver: "Dreiser could get his sociology from a Spencer and get his notion of realism from a Zola, but Negro writers can't go to those sources for background . . . In fact, I think in many cases it is good for a Negro writer to get out on his own and get his stuff first hand rather than get it through the regular educational channels" (*Conversations*, 46).

Whatever philosophy Wright had earlier come across, he adamantly adhered to his own theory of narrative. Whether he was interested in Marxism, Zolaesque naturalism, and French existentialism, none of them taught him how to attain his perspective and intellectual space. The Marxist doctrines of class struggle against capitalism proved less relevant to African American life than they did to American life in general. Literary naturalism, based on the concepts of heredity and social environment, would not have applied to African American narrative, for such concepts had less to do with African Americans than they did with European Americans. Racism alone, ever-present in American society, made the social environment of African Americans vastly differ from that of European Americans. By the same token, existentialism, as originally conceived for European society, would not have provided Wright's narrative with the perspective and intellectual space it entailed.

Not only did "Blueprint for Negro Writing," published in 1937, give a clear definition, but Wright also provided a remarkable illustration for his theory. Perspective, he wrote,

> means that a Negro writer must learn to view the life of a Negro living in New York's Harlem or Chicago's South Side with the consciousness that one-sixth of the earth surface belongs to the working class. It means that a Negro writer must create in his readers' minds a relationship between a Negro woman hoeing cotton in the South and the men who loll in swivel chairs in Wall Street and take the fruits of her toil. ("Blueprint," 46)

Focusing on the relationship between African American women workers in the South and European American businessmen in the North, Wright sounded as though he were giving a demonstration of American racial problems. But the perspective he urged the African American writer to achieve does not merely apply to African Americans, it signifies "the hopes and struggles of minority peoples everywhere that the cold facts have begun to tell them something" ("Blueprint," 46).

II

Of his reading in the Chicago period, the recently published *Conversations with Richard Wright* confirms that he paid his utmost attention to such influential American novelists in the twentieth century as Dreiser, Faulkner, and Hemingway.[8] Of the three, Wright was least inspired by Hemingway. In a radio discussion of the New York Federal Writers' Project broadcast in 1938, he said: "I like the work of Hemingway, of course. Who does not? But the two writers whose work I like most today are André Malraux and William Faulkner. I think both of them in their respective fields are saying important things" (*Conversations*, 10). Despite Hemingway's reputation, established by such novels as *The Sun Also Rises*, Wright realized that a Hemingway novel makes a great impression on the reader's mind not for establishing perspective but for creating style. Wright also realized that a Hemingway novel thrives on action, a technique lacking in French novelists like Sartre and Camus.[9] In the 1930s, Wright felt that he belonged to the latest literary generation, which included both Hemingway and Faulkner. He paid a greater tribute to Faulkner because he thought Faulkner's fiction conveys a judicious point of view. In particular, he recognized Faulkner's importance in developing the American novel, in which the "unhappiness" of the American people was realistically described (*Conversations*, 109).

Among all the writers in English, Dreiser had the strongest influence on Wright's mode of understanding American history and culture. "The first great American novelist I came across," Wright said in retrospect shortly before his death, "was Theodore Dreiser. Thanks to him, I discovered a very different world in America" (*Conversations*, 214). As early as 1941, Wright said, "I never could get into Dickens . . . He reeks with sentimentality. Theodore Dreiser . . . is the greatest writer this country has ever produced. His *Jennie Gerhardt* is the greatest novel" (*Conversations*, 38). Toward the end of *Black Boy* he wrote:

> I read Dreiser's *Jennie Gerhardt* and *Sister Carrie* and they revived in me a vivid sense of my mother's suffering; I was overwhelmed. I grew silent, won-

dering about the life around me. It would have been impossible for me to have told anyone what I derived from these novels, for it was nothing less than a sense of life itself. All my life had shaped me for the realism, the naturalism of the modern novel, and I could not read enough of them.[10]

Wright's affinity with Dreiser has conventionally been understood in terms of naturalism, but Wright never considered himself a naturalist.[11] That Wright made no distinction between realism and naturalism in reading Dreiser's novels suggests a predilection for the fiction that mirrors social reality, the writing that not only expresses the sentiments of the socially oppressed but also thrives upon the unalloyed feelings of individuals. This subjectivity on the part of the writer, which Wright deemed the most difficult to achieve, constitutes what he called "perspective" and "intellectual space," the twin elements indispensable to his narrative.

One of the chief reasons why *Jennie Gerhardt* had a strong affinity for Wright is that Dreiser's novel is not a naturalistic novel as is, for example, Stephen Crane's *Maggie: A Girl of the Streets*. As an American realist, Dreiser took pains to deal with young women's search of happiness in the city. Just as the young Wright, finding the rural South a living hell, escaped to Chicago, as so poignantly portrayed in *Black Boy*, Jennie, suffering social ostracism in small Ohio communities, moves to a happier life in Chicago, where she faces less prejudice of class and gender. Unlike Maggie in Crane's novel, to whom the "shutters of the tall buildings were closed like grim lips . . . the lights of the avenues glittered as if from an impossible distance,"[12] Jennie finally finds in Chicago not only privacy and subjectivity but the gay, energetic spirit of life that frees her from oppressive social conventions. Given a slum section of the city and a self-centered family situation, on the contrary, Crane's portrayal of Maggie's life becomes utterly predictable. Growing up in such a family, Maggie has little desire to leave the slum life or to better herself. Although she is described as "blossomed in a mud puddle" and "a most rare and wonderful production of a tenement district, a pretty girl" (141), she is deprived of any sense of autonomy and vision.

In *Jennie Gerhardt* Dreiser achieves what Wright calls "perspective" by gauging the relationship between Jennie and Lester Kane, two individuals placed poles apart in society just as Wright urged his fellow novelists to envision the distance between a black woman cotton picker in the South and a white businessman in Wall Street. Even though Lester is heir to a millionaire business tycoon, he is attracted with great compassion to Jennie, a daughter of poor immigrants, who helps her mother scrub hotel floors in Columbus. Far from a victim of social environment, Lester is described as "a naturally observing mind, Rabelaisian in its strength and tendencies." From Jennie's vantage point, "the multiplicity of evidences of things, the vastness of the panorama of life," of which he is conscious, makes her quest for liberation from class oppression less painful (125). As she moves from Cleveland to Chicago, the multiple and panoramic vision of urban life intensifies. "Yes, Chicago was best," Dreiser declares. "The very largeness and hustle of it" made the concealment of Lester's liaison with Jennie "easy" (173).

Unlike Maggie and her family, who forever remain victims of the big city slum environment, Jennie and her family are endowed with abilities to circumvent the situation and create space for themselves. While Maggie is trapped and her movement is circular at best, Jennie, like the narrator of *Black Boy*, who went from Natchez, Mississippi, to Memphis and then to Chicago, moves from smaller cites to larger ones, from Columbus to Cleveland, and to Chicago. And just like the mature Wright, who later went to New York to broaden his horizon, Jennie is also able to visit the metropolis. Unlike Maggie's brother Jimmie, who cares only about his own life, Jennie's brother Bass, although early on he cares very little for his family, becomes not only concerned about the family's welfare but feels a great sympathy for his sister. In an immigrant family, the oldest son, being young and most acculturated to the American way of life, served as the catalyst for the success of his family.

Most significantly, Wright was inspired by Dreiser's spatial narrative, through which the city in Jennie's ordeal becomes her savior. In Dreiser's narrative, living in a city not only separates her from the restrictive past dominated by class and gender prejudices but gives her the fluid, indeterminate space in which to gain her subjectivity. Furthermore, the spirit of freedom the city inspires in Jennie is also shared with Lester. Whether she succeeds in her search for liberation has a corollary in what happens to his life in Chicago. In *Maggie*, on the contrary, the Bowery life, which is extremely confined, does not allow for the residents' mobility, let alone their travels.

In *Jennie Gerhardt*, the idea and excitement of travel is expressed throughout the novel. As the Gerhardt children walk to the railroad tracks to steal coal, they watch luxurious trains pass by. "Jennie, alone, kept silent," Dreiser remarks, "but the suggestion of travel and comfort was the most appealing to her of all" (28). After his father's death Lester decides to leave the wagon factory owned by his family and departs on a European tour with Jennie, as Wright, while living in exile in Paris, extended his travels to Pagan Spain, West Africa, and Southeast Asia. Jennie, Dreiser writes, "was transported by what she saw and learned":

> It is curious the effect of travel on a thinking mind. At Luxor and Karnak—places Jennie had never dreamed existed—she learned of an older civiliza-

tion, powerful, complex, complete. . . . Now from this point of view—of decayed Greece, fallen Rome, forgotten Egypt, and from the notable differences of the newer civilization, she gained an idea of how pointless are our minor difficulties after all—our minor beliefs. (*JG* 1992: 307)

Although Lester is portrayed initially as an animalistic man, he turns out to be "a product of a combination of elements—religious, commercial, social—modified by the overruling, circumambient atmosphere of liberty in our national life which is productive of almost uncounted freedoms of thought and action" (126). Despite her lack of education and experience, Jennie is also inspired by the same spirit of freedom Lester attains.

In contrast to Crane's deterministic portrayal of Maggie, the fluid, spatial narrative that informs Jennie's liberation had profound influence upon Wright's mode of understanding American history. Dreiser's heroine is a victim of gender prejudice and social, economic oppression. At the outset of his career in Chicago, Wright attempted to acquire his own perspective and intellectual space through the John Reed Club. As he told Edward Aswell, he had a strong affinity for Marxism at that time: "I was a member of the Communist Party for twelve years ONLY because I was a Negro. Indeed the Communist Party had been the only road out of the Black Belt of Chicago for me. Hence Communism had not simply been a fad, a hobby; it had a deeply functional meaning for my life."[13] As Wright also wrote for the *Daily Worker* in 1937, the aim of Marxist African American writers like him was "to render the life of their race in social and realistic terms. For the first time in Negro history, problems such as nationalism in *literary perspective*, the relation of the Negro writers to politics and social movements were formulated and discussed" (emphasis added).[14]

At the very inception of his Chicago period, Wright was indeed intent upon subverting the traditional, hierarchical discourse in American writing, a hegemonic, racist mode of expression. Such a mode of understanding American history was rigid and antithetical to the spirits of freedom and democracy, the twin ideals of American culture. In place of the traditional narrative, Wright wanted to create a spatial model of amelioration. While he lived in Chicago, Marxist writing indeed served his initial purpose: his early writing, and *Uncle Tom's Children* in particular, vividly demonstrated Marxist conceptions of history as the forums in which power relations are understood.

III

"Big Boy Leaves Home," the first story in the 1938 and 1940 editions of *Uncle Tom's Children*, features a young black boy's escape from his violent southern community.[15] Four innocent, happy-go-lucky black boys are discovered naked by a white woman while they are swimming in a pond and later drying their bodies on a white man's premises. When she screams, her male companion without warning begins shooting and kills two of the boys. Big Boy manages to overcome the white man and accidentally kills him. Now the two surviving boys must take flight: Bobo gets captured, but Big Boy reaches home and is told by black church leaders to hide in a kiln until dawn, when a truck will come by to take him to Chicago. While hiding, he poignantly watches Bobo lynched and burned. Witnessing such an event gives Big Boy not only a feeling of isolation, terror, and hatred but a sense of self-awareness and maturity.

Not only is "Big Boy Leaves Home" based upon Wright's personal experience, but the sexual taboo that precipitates this tragedy originates from the fact both black and white people in the South knew so well. The white woman who suddenly appears near the swimming hole, as the story unfolds, is closely guarded and protected by the white world. "In that world," as Blyden Jackson has noted, "at least when 'Big Boy Leaves Home' was written, all Negro males, even young and with their clothes on, were potential rapists. And so this woman screams, and screams again, for someone named Jim, and Jim himself, a white man from her world, comes apace, with a rifle in his hands."[16]

Instead of a comparison between what happens in "Big Boy Leaves Home" and the facts of racism in America, the story has been compared to an ancient myth.[17] In Ovid's *Metamorphoses*, the myth of Actaeon and Diana is told this way:

> Actaeon and his companions are out hunting at midday when Actaeon calls an end to the chase since "Our nets and spears / Dip with the blood of our successful hunting." Nearby, in a grotto pool nestled in a valley, the goddess Diana, herself tired from hunting, disrobed and disarmed, bathes with her maidens. Quite by accident, Actaeon, now alone, comes upon the idyllic scene. Finding no weapon nearby, Diana flings a handful of the pond's water on the hapless hunter, taunting, "Tell people you have seen me, / Diana, naked! Tell them if you can!" He flees from the scene, by stages transformed into a stag, a metamorphosis he does not comprehend (though he marvels at his own speed) until he pauses to drink. Then he "finally sees, reflected, / His features in a quiet pool 'Alas!' / He tries to say, but has no words." Stunned he hears his hounds approach. "The whole pack, with the lust of blood upon them / Come baying . . . Actaeon, once pursuer / Over this very ground, is now pursued . . . He would cry / 'I am Actaeon . . .' / But the words fail." The hounds set upon him "And all together nip and slash and fasten? Till there is no more room for wounds." Meanwhile, his companions arrive, call for him, and rue that he is missing the good show. "And so he died, and so Diana's anger / Was satisfied at last." (Atkinson, 251–52)

The parallels between Wright's story and this classical myth are indeed striking. Both tales begin with idyllic scenes before the plot focuses on an initial encounter between the opposite sexes. Big Boy, the leader of the group, and three friends, who are supposed to be at school, walk through the woods, laughing, beating vines and bushes as if they are hunting anything that interests them. As Big Boy, accompanied by his sidekicks, are pursuing his avocation in a most enjoyable environment, Actaeon, too, with his companions, is hunting in good weather. Before the unexpected appearance of a woman, both Actaeon and Big Boy are at rest, Actaeon tired with hunting and Big Boy warming his body after swimming in the cold pond. Another point of similarity is the hero's fleeing the scene. Before seeing Diana, Actaeon is alone now that his companions have retired from hunting; upon seeing her, he flees the scene. Similarly, Big Boy flees the scene alone since two of his friends are killed and Bobo takes a separate rout and eventually gets captured. Finally, both protagonists sustain serious wounds during their flight. It is, furthermore, significant that the wounding of the hero occurs in two stages. Actaeon suffers what Michael Atkinson calls "the transformative sprinkling with pondwater, which removes his humanity, and the obliterative tearing by the dogs' teeth, which destroys the last form and vestige of life."[18] In Wright's tale, Big Boy first suffers the loss of Buck and Lester, whose blood is sprinkled over him, and secondly he suffers from watching Bobo's body mutilated.

But the points of difference between the tales are equally striking and significant. While in the Roman myth the male protagonist alone encounters a goddess, in Wright's story a group of young boys see an adult woman. However accidental it might be, it is Actaeon who comes upon the scene where Diana is already bathing with her maidens in a secluded pond. The circumstances under which Wright's story begins are reversed: it is the lady who comes upon the scene where Big Boy is already swimming with his friends. The initial setting Wright constructs in "Big Boy Leaves Home" thus poses a serious question whether boys under age should be judged morally wrong when they are seen naked, while swimming, by an adult woman. In the Actaeon myth, given the tradition of privacy behind it, Actaeon is deemed clearly guilty of watching a naked goddess surrounded by her maids. If Big Boy were Actaeon, Big Boy would be arrested as a Peeping Tom in any society. Even if Big Boy were Actaeon, Big Boy's punishment would be only blindness as legend tells that Peeping Tom looked at Lady Godiva riding naked through Coventry and was struck blind. But blindness, the price Peeping Tom paid for his offense, is a far cry from the psychological wounds Big Boy and all other black boys in America indeed suffered: the shooting death of Buck and Lester caused by an army officer on leave and the lynching of Bobo perpetrated by a white mob.

It is also significant that unlike Actaeon, none of the black boys in Wright's story is alone when a member of the opposite sex appears on the scene. The woman in question, moreover, is fully protected by an adult male companion with a shotgun which could legally be used should she be molested and raped by the unarmed black boys. In the myth, however, the goddess is protected neither by those who can overcome a potential seducer nor by any kind of weapon save for her flinging of a few drops of magical pondwater. In terms of crime and punishment, those who are guilty in Wright's story, the lynch mob and the woman who screams, go unpunished, whereas those who are innocent, the four black boys, are physically or psychologically destroyed. In the myth, Actaeon, the only one who is guilty, meets his death while all the innocent, Diana, her maids, and Actaeon's companions all survive the ordeal. If the Actaeon myth and the legend of Peeping Tom tell us anything significant about an ancient system of justice which meted out punishment for humankind, then the system of justice Wright condemns in "Big Boy Leaves Home" is not only unjust but fundamentally corrupt.

While "Big Boy Leaves Home" and the classical myth of Actaeon and Diana are thematically different, Wright's treatment of the sexual theme in this story has a closer resemblance to Dreiser's "Nigger Jeff."[19] It is quite likely that before writing "Big Boy Leaves Home" Wright read "Nigger Jeff." Dreiser's story, in which a white mob lynches a black youth, deals with the same problems of race and miscegenation in America as does Wright's. In "Nigger Jeff," one day a white cub reporter named Elmer Davies is sent out by the city editor to cover the lynching of an alleged black rapist, Jeff Ingalls. Jeff is first captured by a sheriff to await trial, but later taken away by a mob of white men led by the brother and father of a white woman, the supposed rape victim, and finally hanged from a bridge over a stream. After learning the circumstances of the rape, Jeff's behavior, his family's grief, and above all the transcending beauty and serenity of nature against the brutality and criminality of the mob, Davies realizes that his sympathies have shifted.

At the outset of each story, the author stresses the peace and tranquillity of the setting where people, black and white, are meant to enjoy their lives in harmony with nature. In Wright's story, the four innocent, happy black youths, as mentioned earlier, roam about the woods and pasture, laughing, chanting, smelling sweet flowers. "Then a quartet of voices," Wright describes, "blending in harmony, floated high above the tree tops" (*Uncle Tom's Children*, 17). In Dreiser's story, a young impressionable man comes upon the setting on a lovely spring day in the beautiful countryside of Pleasant Valley. As Big Boy and his friends are happy not only with themselves but with the world, Davies, as Dreiser describes, "was dressed in a new spring suit, a new hat and new shoes. In the lapel of his coat was a small bunch of violets . . . he was feeling exceedingly well and good-natured—quite fit, indeed. The world was going unusually well with him. It seemed worth singing about" (*Free*, 76). Under such circumstances no one would expect violence to occur and destroy peace and harmony.

Both stories are told through the protagonist's point of view. In the beginning both Big Boy and Elmer Davies are young and naive, but the violence and injustice they witness make them grow up overnight. In the end, Big Boy, though stunned and speechless, is determined to tell the world what he has learned. As *Black Boy* suggests, Big Boy was modeled after the young Richard Wright himself growing up in the twenties. Dreiser's *A Book about Myself*, one of the finest autobiographies in American literature as *Black Boy* is, also suggests that Elmer Davies was indeed the young Dreiser himself when the future novelist was a newspaper reporter in St. Louis in the early 1890s. As Wright fled the South for Chicago to write his early short stories, Dreiser left the Midwest for New York to write his.

In both stories, the plot, which does not hinge upon a conflict of social forces, thrives on a progression of vision. Each story opens with pastoral idylls, moves through the visions of violence and injustice, and reaches the hero's losing his relative state of innocence. Both writers take much pains to show that the point of view character, the protagonist, rather than society, the antagonist, is capable of vision. The climactic scene in Wright's story, where the victim is hanged and mutilated, is presented with bright firelight. The mob is situated so close to the scene of violence that they cannot see what is transpiring. By hiding in the dark in a kiln, creating space, and establishing perspective, Big Boy can see it far better than can the mob. "Big Boy," Wright says, "shrank when he saw the first flame light the hillside. Would they see im here? Then he remembered you could not see into the dark if you were standing in the light" (48). From his own perspective Dreiser, too, presents the climax for Elmer Davies to see rather than for the mob to see, as Dreiser describes the scene: "The silent company, an articulated, mechanical and therefore terrible thing, moved on. . . . He was breathing heavily and groaning. . . . His eyes were fixed and staring, his face and hands bleeding as if they had been scratched or trampled upon. . . . But Davies could stand it no longer now. He fell back, sick at heart, content to see no more. It seemed a ghastly, murderous thing to do" (103–4). Seeing an asinine murder makes Davies feel as though he became a murderer himself and seems to retard the progression of the story, but the pace of the revelation increases as Dreiser portrays the scene.

In Wright's story, too, Big Boy remains in the kiln through the night after the mob departs and becomes the victim's sole companion. Just as morning comes for a truck to deliver Big Boy to Chicago, dawn breaks for Davies to return to his office. After the crowd depart, Davies thinks of hurrying back to a nearby post office to file a partial report. But he decides against it since he is the only reporter present, just as Big Boy is, and because "he could write a fuller, sadder, more colorful story on the morrow" (105), just as Big Boy could have when he left for Chicago in the morning. This momentary delay in Davies's action gives his revelation a heightened effect.

Moreover, Dreiser's description of dawn in "Nigger Jeff," as that of the opening scene, is tinged with a transcendental vision: "As he still sat there the light of morning broke, a tender lavender and gray in the east. Then came the roseate hues of dawn, all the wondrous coloring of celestial halls, to which the waters of the stream responded." During the lynching, Davies sees the signs of evil on the struggling body, the black mass, and black body hanging limp. The images of the dark are intermingled in his mind with those of the light that suggest hope: "the weak moonlight," "the pale light," "the glimmering water," "the light of morning," "a tender lavender and gray in the east," "the roseate hues of dawn," "[t]he white pebbles [shining] pinkily at the bottom" (*Free*, 105–6). As the story progresses toward the end, signifiers for hope increasingly dominate those for despair.

The same pattern of imagery is also created toward the end of Wright's story. During the night Big Boy has to protect himself from cold wind and rain as well as a persistent dog. Even though morning arrives with the warm sunlight and brightened air, he is still reminded of "a puddle of rainwater" and "the stiff body" of the dead dog lying nearby. "His knees," Wright describes, "were stiff and a thousand needlelike pains shot from the bottom of his feet to the calves of his legs. . . . Through brackish *light* he saw *Will's truck* standing some twenty-five yards away, *the engine running*. . . . On hands and knees he looked around in the *semi-darkness*. . . . Through *two long cracks* fell *thin blades of daylight*. . . . Once he heard *the crow of a rooster*. It made him think of *home*, of *ma* and *pa*" (*Uncle Tom's Children*, 51–52, italics for emphasis). At the final scene the nightmare that has tormented Big Boy throughout the night is now chased out of his mind and destroyed by the blades of the sun: "The truck swerved. He blinked his eyes. The blades of daylight had turned brightly golden. The sun had risen. The track sped over the asphalt miles, sped northward, jolting him, shaking out of his bosom the crumbs of corn bread, making them dance with the splinters and sawdust in the golden blades of sunshine. He turned on his side and slept" (*Uncle Tom's Children,* 53).

In the ending of "Nigger Jeff" as well, Dreiser still makes the hero's consciousness move back and forth between hope and despair as if the images of light and dark were at war. When Davies visits the room when the body is laid and sees the victim's sister sobbing over it, he becomes painfully aware that all "corners of the room were quite dark. Only its middle was brightened by splotches of silvery light." For Davies, another climactic scene of his experience takes place when he dares to lift the sheet covering the body. He can now see exactly where the rope tightened around the neck. The delineation of the light against the dark is, once more, focused on the dead body: "A bar of cool moonlight lay just across the face and breast" (*Free*, 109–10). Such deliberate contrasts between the light and the dark, good and evil, suggest that human beings have failed to see "transcending beauty" and "unity of nature," which are merely illusions to them, and that they have imitated only the cruel and the indifferent which nature appears to signify.

At the end of the story, Davies is overwhelmed not only by the remorse he feels for the victim, as Big Boy does, but also his compassion for the victim's bereft mother he finds in the dark corner of the room:

> Davies began to understand. . . . The night, the tragedy, the grief, he saw it all. But also with the cruel instinct of the budding artist that he already was, he was beginning to meditate on the character of story it would make—the color, the pathos. The knowledge now that it was not always exact justice that was meted out to all and that it was not so much the business of the writer to indict as to interpret was borne in on him with distinctness by the cruel sorrow of the mother, whose blame, if any, was infinitesimal. (*Free*, 110–11)

The importance of such fiction is not the process of the young man's becoming an artist—as Big Boy or the young Richard Wright is surely not trying to become merely an artist. It is the sense of urgency in which the protagonist living in American society is compelled to act as a reformer. In such a narrative, Dreiser and Wright are both able to create their space and perspective. With his final proclamation, "I'll get it all in" (*Free*, 111), Davies's revelation culminates in a feeling of triumph. Although, to Dreiser as well as to Wright, human beings appear necessarily limited by their natural environment and by their racial prejudice, both writers in their respective stories are asserting that human beings are still capable of reforming society.

Indeed, protest fiction, the term critics have assigned "Big Boy Leaves Home," becomes successful literature only if it is endowed with a universal sense of justice as "Big Boy Leaves Home" and "Nigger Jeff" are exemplars. Such a narrative, moreover, must address an actual and pressing social issue, whether it is a lynching a European American writer witnessed in a border state in the 1890s or a problem of race and miscegenation an African American writer encountered in the deep South of the 1920s. As both stories show, great social fiction can be created not so much with the artistry the writer can put into it—much of which is taken for granted in these stories—as with the writer's moral space and perspective the subject matter demands. In "Big Boy Leaves Home," this urgency does not come from the quality of Big Boy's will, nor is it anything to do with the collective will of African Americans. Rather, it comes from the conscience of humanity, the collective will of decent individuals living anywhere. It is a revelation given to Big Boy, as it is given to Elmer Davies. And through the protagonist and with the skill of a gifted writer, it is disseminated to the modern world at large.

IV

Except for the obvious issues of race, Wright and Dreiser shared quite similar experiences before they became novelists. Since their boyhood both had been economically hard pressed; they were always ashamed that they had grown up on the wrong side of the tracks. As boys they witnessed struggling and suffering and felt excluded from society. They grew up hating the fanatic and stifling religion practiced at home. In both lives, the family suffered because of the father's inadequacies as a breadwinner; the son inevitably rebelled against such a father, and the family was somehow put together by the suffering mother. Under these circumstances, their dream of success was merely survival; they tried to hang on to one menial job after another. As a result, both had nurtured a brooding sensibility. At twelve, Wright held "a notion as to what life meant that no education could ever alter, a conviction that the meaning of living came only when one was struggling to wring a meaning out of meaningless suffering" (*Black Boy*, 112), a statement which also echoes in *Dawn*, Dreiser's autobiography of youth.

It would seem that both authors, being literary realists, used authentic court records in writing *An American Tragedy* and *Native Son*. Dreiser drew on the Gillette murder case in upstate New York; Wright on the Leopold and Loeb kidnap-murder as well as the Robert Nixon murder trial and conviction in Chicago. Both titles strongly imply that Clyde and Bigger are the products of American culture and that society, not the individuals involved in the crimes, is to blame. But doesn't such a narrative *always* create tensions in the life of the hero, growing out of an environment over which he has no control and about which he understands very little and, therefore, by which he is *always* victimized. If so, *Native Son* does not exactly fit into this genre. While Dreiser and Wright share the perspective of an disadvantaged individual, the characterization of the individual in his or her respective society considerably differs.

It is true that both novels employ crime as a thematic device. In *Native Son*, the murder of Bessie is the inevitable consequence of Mary Dalton's accidental death; in *An American Tragedy*, Clyde's fleeing the scene of the accident which kills a child leads to his plotting of murder later in the story. Without the presence of crime in the plot neither author would have been able to make significant points about his protagonist. But the focus of the author's idea differs in the two books. Wright's center of interest, unlike Dreiser's, is not crime but its consequences—its psychological effect on his hero. Before committing his crime Bigger is presented as an uneducated, uninformed youth; indeed he is portrayed as a victim of white society who grew up in the worst black ghetto of the nation. We are thus surprised to see him gain identity after the murder. The crime gives him some awareness of himself and of the world of which he has never been capable before. We are surprised to learn that after the murder Bigger is well versed in world affairs. "He liked to hear," Wright tells us, "of how Japan was conquering China; of how Hitler was running the Jews to the ground; of how Mussolini was invading Spain" (*Native Son*, 110). By this time he has learned to think for himself. He is even proud of Japanese, Germans, and Italians, because they "could rule others, for in actions such as these he felt that there was a way to escape from this tight morass of fear and shame that sapped at the base of his life" (109–10).

Despite a death sentence handed down by his white rulers, Bigger now proclaims his own existence. Even Max, who has taken a sympathetic attitude toward the racially oppressed, is bewildered by Bigger's deep urges for freedom and independence. "I didn't want to kill," Bigger tells Max. "But what I killed for, I *am*!" (391–92). Having overcome white oppression, Bigger now stands a heroic exemplar for the members of his race. His brother Buddy, he realized, "was blind . . . went round and round in a groove and did not see things." Bigger sees in Buddy "a certain stillness, an isolation, meaninglessness" (103). And he finds his sister and mother to be equally weak individuals. "Bigger," says Wright, "was paralyzed with shame; he felt violated" (280).

In both *Native Son* and *An American Tragedy* a preacher appears before the trial to console the accused. But in *Native Son* the black preacher is described in derogatory terms. Bigger immediately senses that the Reverend Hammond possesses only a white-washed soul and functions merely as an advocate of white supremacy. Wright offers this explanation: "The preacher's face was black and sad and earnest. . . . He had killed within himself the preacher's haunting picture of life even before he had killed Mary; that had been his first murder. And now the preacher made it walk before his eyes like a ghost in the night, creating within him a sense of exclusion that was as cold as a block of ice." (*Native Son*, 264)

During his act of liberation, too, Bigger is consciously aware of his own undoing and creation. To survive, Bigger is forced to rebel, unlike Clyde, who remains a victim of the tensions between individual will and social determinism. In rebelling, Bigger moves from determinism to freedom. Bigger knows how to escape the confines of his environment and to gain an identity. Even before he acts, he knows exactly how Mary, and Bessie later, has forced him into a vulnerable position. No wonder he convinces himself not only that he has killed to protect himself but also that he has attacked the entire civilization. In *An American Tragedy*, Dreiser molds the tragedy of Clyde Griffiths by generating pity and sympathy for the underprivileged in American society. In *Native Sons*, however, Wright departs from the principles of pity and sympathy which white people have for black citizens. In "How 'Bigger' Was Born," Wright admits that his earlier *Uncle Tom's Children* was "a book which even bankers' daughters could read and weep over and feel good about."[20] In *Native Son*, however, Wright would not allow for such complacency. He warns readers that the book "would be so hard and deep that they would have to face it without the consolation of tears."[21]

The meaning of *Native Son* therefore derives not from crime but from its result. Dreiser's interest in *An American Tragedy*, on the other hand, lies not in the result of crime but in its cause. While Bigger at the end of his violent and bloody life can claim his victory, Clyde at the end of his life remains a failure. *Native Son* thus ends on an optimistic note; *An American Tragedy* as a whole stems from and ends on the dark side of American capitalism. F. O. Matthiessen is right in maintaining that the reason for Dreiser's use of the word *American* in his title "was the overwhelming lure of money-values in our society, more nakedly apparent than in older and more complex social structures."[22] Furthermore, Helen Dreiser seems to confirm Dreiser's central thought in interpreting materialism as the cause of Clyde's tragedy. Commenting on Dreiser's choice of the Chester Gillette murder case for fictionalization, Helen Dreiser writes:

> This problem had been forced on his mind not only by the extreme American enthusiasm for wealth as contrasted with American poverty, but the determination of so many young Americans, boys and girls alike, to obtain wealth

> quickly by marriage. When he realized the nature of the American literature of that period and what was being offered and consumed by publishers and public, he also became aware of the fact that the most interesting American story of the day concerned not only the boy getting the girl, but more emphatically, the poor boy getting the rich girl. Also, he came to know that it was a natural outgrowth of the crude pioneering conditions of American life up to that time, based on the glorification of wealth which started with the early days of slavery and persisted throughout our history.[23]

Dreiser's fascination with this subject resulted in his treatment of Clyde as a victim of the American dream. Bigger, too, a product of the same culture, cherishes a dream of his own. Like anyone else, he reads the newspapers and magazines, goes to the movies, strolls the crowded streets. Bigger is intensely aware of his dreams: "to merge himself with others . . . even though he was black" (*Native Son*, 226). Unlike Dreiser, Wright must have clearly recognized his hero's sense of alienation from the rest of the world. It is an alienation that Wright himself, not Dreiser, often experienced as a boy and as a man. But it never occurs to Bigger that he can pursue such a dream. Indeed, throughout the text Wright amply documents the prevailing social mores, economic facts, and public sentiments to prove that Bigger's actions, attitudes, and feelings have already been determined by his place in American life. It is understandable for James Baldwin to say of *Native Son* that every black person has "his private Bigger Thomas living in the skull."[24] Given such a determined state of mind, Bigger would not be tempted to pursue his dreams. Ironically, the racial oppression and injustice in fact enhance his manhood. To Clyde Griffiths, however, the flame of temptation is brighter and more compelling. He is easily caught, and he thrashes about in a hopeless effort to escape the trap. Under these circumstances, "with his enormous urges and his pathetic equipment,"[25] as Dreiser once characterized the plight of such an individual in America, there is no way out for Clyde but to plot murder.

The central meaning of *An American Tragedy* thus comes from the economic and social forces that overpower Clyde and finally negate his aspirations. Where a Bigger Thomas before liberation must always remain an uninformed, immature youth, a Clyde Griffiths is the one whose mind is already ingrained with that glorious pattern of success; one must climb the social ladder from lower to middle to upper class. Money is necessarily the barometer of that success. At the beginning of the story Dreiser creates social space and perspective by directly showing how the family's mission work in which Clyde is compelled to take part looks contrary to his dreams. Dreiser at once comments that "his parents looked foolish and less than normal—'cheap' was the word. . . .

His life should not be like this. Other boys did not have to do as he did.''[26] A basically sensitive and romantic boy, he cannot help noticing the ''handsome automobiles that sped by, the loitering pedestrians moving off to what interests and comforts he could only surmise; the gay pairs of young people, laughing and jesting and the 'kids' staring, all troubled him with a sense of something different, better, more beautiful than his, or rather their life'' (*AAT*, 10). This scene functions in the story as a great contrast to a similar scene in *Native Son*. Near the beginning Bigger goes to the movies and sees double features. *The Gay Woman*, portraying love and intrigue in upper-class white society, quickly loses his attention, and *Trader Horn*, in which black men and women are dancing in a wild jungle, shows him only life in a remote world. Bigger is thus placed in no-man's-land; he is only vaguely aware that he is excluded from both worlds. Unlike Wright, however, Dreiser places his hero in *An American Tragedy* at the threshold of success and achievement.

The two novelists' divergent attitudes toward the problem of guilt are reflected in the style and structure of their books. *Native Son* is swift in pace and dramatic in tone, and displays considerable subjectivity, involving the reader in experiences of emotional intensity. The thirties were hard times for both white and black people, and it was not possible to take a calm and objective view of the situation. Wright himself was a victim of the hard times and he could speak from his heart. Moreover, Bigger Thomas is a conscious composite portrait of numerous black individuals Wright had known in his life. As indicated in ''How 'Bigger' Was Born,'' all of them defied the Jim Crow order, and all of them suffered for their insurgency.[27] As in the novel, Wright had lived in a cramped and dirty flat. He had visited many such dwellings as an insurance agent.[28] In Chicago, while working at the South Side Boys' Club, he saw other prototypes of Bigger Thomas—fearful, frustrated, and violent youths who struggled for survival in the worst slum conditions.[29]

The twenties, the background of Dreiser's novel, however, had not of course erupted into the kind of social strife witnessed a decade later. Unlike the hostile racial conflicts dramatized in *Native Son*, what is portrayed in *An American Tragedy* is Clyde Griffiths' mind, which is deeply affected by the hopes and failures of the American dream. A later reviewer of *An American Tragedy* accused Dreiser of scanting, ''as all the naturalists do, the element of moral conflict without which no great fiction can be written, for he fobbed the whole wretched business off on that scapegoat of our time, society.''[30] But the depiction of such a conflict was not Dreiser's intention for the novel in the first place. Rather the poignancy of Clyde's tragedy comes from his helpless attraction and attachment to the dream which society had created. Dreiser defines this essential American psyche in an essay:

> Our most outstanding phases, of course, are youth, optimism and illusion. These run through everything we do, affect our judgments and passions, our theories of life. As children we should all have had our fill of these, and yet even at this late date and after the late war, which should have taught us much, it is difficult for any of us to overcome them. Still, no one can refuse to admire the youth and optimism of America, however much they may resent its illusion. There is always something so naive about its method of procedure, so human and tolerant at times; so loutish, stubborn and ignorantly insistent at others, as when carpetbag government was forced on the South after the Civil War and Jefferson Davis detained in prison for years after the war was over.[31]

In contrast to Bigger's violent life, Clyde's mind can only be conveyed by a leisurely pace and undramatic tone. Dreiser's approach is basically psychological, and this allows us to sympathize with the character whose principal weakness is ignorance and naivete. Consequently we become deeply involved with Clyde's fate. Above all, the relative calmness and objectivity in which Clyde's experience is traced stem from a mature vision of the tribulations shared by any of us who have ever dreamed.

The lack of dramatic tone in *An American Tragedy* is also due to change of setting. Dreiser's restless protagonist begins his journey in Kansas City, flees to Chicago, and finally reaches his destination in upstate New York. In contrast, Wright achieves greater dramatic intensity by observing a strict unity of setting. All of the action in *Native Son* takes place in Chicago, a frightening symbol of disparity and oppression in American life. Wright heightens the conflict and sharpens the division between the two worlds earlier in the novel. In the beginning, the Thomases's apartment is described as the most abject place imaginable, while the Dalton mansion suggests the white power structure that ravages black people and destroys their heritage. The conflict is obvious throughout, and the descriptions of the two households present ironic contrasts. Whereas everything at the Thomases' is loud and turbulent, at the Daltons' it is quiet and subdued. But the true nature of the racial oppressor is later revealed: Mr. Dalton, real estate broker and philanthropist, tries to keep African American residents locked in the ghetto and refuses to lower the rents. During the trial, the prosecutor, the press, and the public equally betray the most vocal racial prejudice and hatred. Thus the central action of Book III is for the defense to confront and demolish this wall of injustice before Bigger could be spared his life.

The narrative pattern in *An American Tragedy* is entirely different.

Although the novel is divided into three parts as is *Native Son*, Dreiser's division is based upon change of time, space, and characters. Each part has its own complete narrative, and one part follows another with the same character dominating the central scene. Each unit is joined to the other not only by the principal character but by the turn of events that underlies the theme of the novel. Book I begins with Clyde's dreams of success but ends in an accident that forebodes a disaster. This narrative pattern is repeated in Book II, beginning with a portrayal of the luxurious home of Samuel Griffiths in Lycurgus and ending with the murder. Book III opens with a depiction of Cataraqui County, where Clyde is to be tried and executed. Clyde's defense, resting upon the most sympathetic interpretation of his character as a moral and mental coward, clearly indicates the possibility of hope but nonetheless ends on a note of despair. The death of a child caused by an automobile accident at the end of Book I does not make Clyde legally guilty, but his fleeing the scene of the accident makes him morally culpable. This pattern is also repeated at the end of Book II, where he willfully ignores Roberta's screams for help, an act of transgression for which he is tried and punished. Such a narrative pattern is not given to the death of Mary and Bessie in *Native Son*, since one murder is necessarily caused by the other. Despite the fact that Bessie's death is caused by a premeditated murder, Bigger's crime does not raise the same moral issue as does Clyde's.

In *An American Tragedy* the author's voice is relatively absent. In *Sister Carrie* Dreiser is noted for a lengthy philosophical commentary inserted at every significant turn of event, as well as for a strong tendency to identify with his characters, especially his heroine. But in *An American Tragedy* Dreiser's comments are not only few but short. Despite Clyde's resolution to work hard and steadily once he has reached the luxurious world of the Green-Davidson, Dreiser's comment is devastatingly swift: "The truth was that in this crisis he was as interesting an illustration of the enormous handicaps imposed by ignorance, youth, poverty and fear as one could have found" (*AAT*, 384).

In contrast to *Native Son*, Dreiser in *An American Tragedy* also reduces the author's omniscience by relying upon the method of indirect discourse. When Clyde is helplessly trapped between his loyalty to Roberta and his desire for Sondra, the insoluble dilemma is rendered through his dreams involving a savage black dog, snakes, and reptiles. About the possibility of Roberta's accidental murder, Dreiser depicts how Clyde is trying to dismiss the evil thought but at the same time is being enticed to it. Clyde's actual plot to murder, suggested by the newspaper article, now thrusts itself forward, as the narrator says, "psychogenetically, born of his own turbulent, eager and disappointed seeking.'' This crucial point in Clyde's life is explained in terms of a well-known myth: "there had now suddenly appeared, as the genie at the accidental rubbing of Aladdin's lamp—as the efrit emerging as smoke from the mystic jar in the net of the fisherman'' (*AAT*, 463). The immediate effect of such a passage for the reader is to create compassion for the character whose mind is torn between the two forces with which the character is incapable of coping. Given Clyde's weaknesses, then, the reader is more likely to sympathize with than despise such a soul.

On the contrary, Bigger's manhood—which is as crucial a point in his life as Clyde's dilemma in his—is rendered through direct discourse. It is not the narrator's voice but the character's that expresses his inner life—the newly won freedom. His murder of a white girl makes him bold, ridding him of the fear that has hitherto imprisoned him. In the midst of describing Bigger's intoxication over his personal power and pleasure, Wright shifts the tone of the narrative to let Bigger provide a lofty voice of his own. While preparing a ransom note, Bigger utters: "Now, about the money. How much? Yes; make it ten thousand. *Get ten thousand in 5 and 10 bills and put it in a shoe box*. . . . That's good. . . . He wrote: *Blink your headlights some. When you see a light in a window blink three times throw the box in the snow and drive off. Do what this letter say*'' (*Native Son*, 167). Even more remarkable is Bigger's final statement to Max:

> "What I killed for must've been good!'' Bigger's voice was full of frenzied anguish. "It must have been good! When a man kills, it's for something. . . . I didn't know I was really alive in this world until I felt things hard enough to kill for 'em. . . . It's the truth, Mr. Max. I can say it now, 'cause I'm going to die. I know what I'm saying real good and I know how it sounds. But I'm all right. I feel all right when I look at it that way. . . .'' (*Native Son*, 392)

Bigger's utterance, in fact, startles the condescending lawyer. At this climactic moment Max, awe-stricken, "groped for his hat like a blind man'' (*Native Son*, 392). Interestingly enough, Dreiser's presentation of Clyde in the same predicament is given through indirect discourse:

> He walked along the silent street—only to be compelled to pause and lean against a tree—leafless in the winter—so bare and bleak. Clyde's eyes! That look as he sank limply into that terrible chair, his eyes fixed nervously and, as he thought, appealingly and dazedly upon him and the group surrounding him.
>
> Had he done right? Had his decision before Governor Waltham been truly sound, fair or merciful? Should he have said to him—that perhaps—perhaps—there had been those other influences playing upon him? . . . Was he never to have mental peace again, perhaps? (*AAT*, 811)

In contrast to this portrait of Clyde, who is largely unaware of his guilt and his manhood, the final scene of *Native Son* gives the ending its dramatic impact. Despite his crimes and their judgment by white society, Bigger's final utterance elicits from readers nothing but understanding and respect for the emerging hero.

The sense of ambiguity created by Dreiser's use of portraits, dreams, and ironies in *An American Tragedy* is thus suited to the muddled mind of Clyde Griffiths. Bigger Thomas, however, can hardly be explained in ambivalent terms, for he has opted for the identity of a murderer. Clyde is presented as a victim of the forces over which he has no control, and Dreiser carefully shows that Roberta's murder—the climax of the book—has inevitably resulted from these forces. The principal interest of the novel, centering upon this crime, lies in Clyde's life before the murder and its effect on him. In Book III, Clyde is depicted not merely as a victim of society but more importantly as a victim of his own illusions about life. In the end, then, he still remains an unregenerate character as Dreiser has predicted earlier in the story.

V

Like Clyde, Bigger in *Native Son* is presented in the beginning as an equally naive character, and his life is largely controlled by fear and hatred. He kills Mary Dalton because he fears his own kindness will be misunderstood. He hates in turn what he fears, and his violence is an expression of this hatred. But unlike Clyde, he has learned through his murders how to exercise his will and determination. Each of the three sections of *Native Son* is built on its own climax, and Book III, "Fate," is structured to draw together all the noble achievements of Bigger's life. Significantly enough, each of the changes in Bigger's development is also measured by his own language. The difference in characterization between the two Americans is therefore reflected in the style and structure of the novels. Granted, both novelists deal with similar material, but their treatments of a young man's crime and guilt in American society differ in ideology and in discourse.

In some respect, earlier American writers provided Wright with models for conveying his painful vision. Hawthorne and James, who dealt with the woman's search for freedom and subjectivity, represented by such figures as Hester Prynne and Isabel Archer, focused on an older, more rigid society. But such materials were far removed from what appealed to Wright's endeavor. Twain, who dramatized the relation of European and African Americans in *Huck Finn* and *Pudd'nhead Wilson*, satirized racist society. But his assailing of American life might have sounded quite benign, as Van Wyck Brooks thought that Twain's seriousness about American society was "arrested" by his humor.[32] Despite his high regard for Twain's skills as a humorist, Dreiser, too, was critical of Twain's fictional discourse. As Dreiser noted, Twain's mode of writing diverts its author "almost completely from a serious, realistic, and . . . Dostoevskian, presentation of the anachronisms, the cruelties, as well as the sufferings, of the individual and the world which, at bottom, seem most genuinely to have concerned him."[33]

The closest model that appealed to Wright's understanding of American life was shown by Dreiser, especially by *Jennie Gerhardt* and "Nigger Jeff." It is not surprising that Wright considered Dreiser the greatest writer American culture had produced. It is indeed Chicago that provided the young Richard Wright, as it did Jennie Gerhardt, with ample space in which to move about freely, cherish dreams, and fulfill desires. Having recovered from the first economic depression the nation experienced, Chicago in the 1910s to Dreiser was a throbbing city with space and energy. Wright's Chicago two decades later was similarly a volatile, fluid city, what Wright called "the fabulous city."[34] And, interestingly enough, the nexus of Wright and Dreiser was characterized by mutual admiration. Only recently has it come to light that Dreiser shortly before his death regarded *Black Boy* as a model of writing, "an honest forth right book."[35] In any event, American literary history will record that *Black Boy* is not only one of the greatest autobiographies ever written by an American author but also the greatest achievement of the Chicago Renaissance, a literary movement which would not have flourished without Dreiser's precedence and influence.

Notes

1. Among African American works, perhaps the most successful effort to fictionalize that memory was made by Toni Morrison in *Beloved* (1987).

2. Wright, "How 'Bigger' Was Born," in *Native Son*, xxvi.

3. Dreiser, a son of a poor immigrant, spoke only German in his early childhood. Farrell, who grew up in the Irish-American neighborhoods of Chicago, drew on his early experience in *Studs Lonigan*; both Farrell and Wright were influenced by Dreiser as they influenced each other. Algren, who was also closely associated with Wright, wrote *Never Come Morning*, which Wright said, "deals with Polish life": praising Algren's work, Wright called it "as hard hitting a realistic piece of writing as you will ever read." Bellow, born of Russian immigrant parents in Canada, was raised in Chicago in a multicultural (English, French, and Jewish) household. See Wright, *Conversations with Richard Wright*, eds. Keneth Kinnamon and Michel Fabre, 46. Subsequent references will parenthetically appear in the text as *Conversations*.

4. James T. Farrell, "Lynch Patterns."

5. Zora Neale Hurston, "Stories of Conflict."

6. Wright, "Blueprint for Negro Writing," rpt. in *Richard Wright Reader*, ed. Ellen Wright and Michel Fabre, 45. The essay was originally published in *New Challenge* 2 (Fall 1937): 53–65. Further references to the essay are to *Richard Wright Reader* and are given in the text as "Blueprint."

7. Wright, *American Hunger*, 123.

8. In ranking modern novelists writing in English, as compared with the three Britons, Meredith, Hardy, and the early H. G. Wells, Allen Tate wrote in 1948: "I am convinced that among American novelists who have had large publics since the last war, only Dreiser, Faulkner, and Hemingway are of major importance." See Allen Tate, "Techniques of Fiction," *Visions and Revisions in Modern American Literary Criticism*, ed. Bernard S. Oldsey and Arthur O. Lewis, Jr., 86. Tate's essay first appeared in Tate, *Collected Essays*, 1948.

9. In response to a question of the influence of American novelists on French novelists, Wright said, "Sartre and Camus show that. French writers realized that action was lacking in their novels, at least in the raw, rapid, sure form that characterizes the good American writers (Hemingway, Caldwell, Lewis, and others). We should make clear that this only concerns the focus of some chapters in which the fiction is presented in vivid terms, without apparent style, to lay out a very intense impression. Now, in philosophical and conceptual matters, the influence is null" (*Conversations*, 137).

10. Wright, *Black Boy: A Record of Childhood and Youth*, 274.

11. In a *New York Post* interview in 1938, Wright stated: "I wanted to show exactly what Negro life in the South means today . . . I think the importance of any writing lies in how much felt life is in it." The interviewer stated: "From reading Mencken in Memphis, Richard Wright branched out in Chicago to Henry James and Dostoievsky, to Hemingway, Malraux, Faulkner, Sherwood Anderson and Dreiser, writers of 'the more or less naturalistic school,' although he lays no claims to being, or even wanting to be, a 'naturalistic' writer" (*Conversations*, 4).

12. Stephen Crane, *Great Short Works of Stephen Crane*, 183. Textual references to *Jennie Gerhardt* are to *Jennie Gerhardt*, ed. James L. W. West III (Philadelphia: University of Pennsylvania Press, 1992), and are subsequently given in parentheses.

13. Qtd. in Michel Fabre, *The Unfinished Quest of Richard Wright*, 542.

14. Qtd. in Fabre: 129.

15. Page references to Wright's "Big Boy Leaves Home" are to *Uncle Tom's Children*, 1940.

16. Blyden Jackson, "Richard Wright in a Moment of Truth," 172. Jackson's essay originally appeared in *Southern Literary Journal* 3 (Spring 1971): 3–17.

17. Michael Atkinson, "Richard Wright's 'Big Boy Leaves Home' and a Tale from Ovid: A Metamorphosis Transformed."

18. Ibid., 257.

19. Page references to "Nigger Jeff" are to *Free and Other Stories* and are parenthetically given in the text as *Free*.

20. Wright, "How 'Bigger' Was Born," in *Native Son*, xxvii.

21. Ibid.

22. F. O. Matthiessen, *Dreiser*, 203.

23. Helen Dreiser, *My Life with Dreiser*, 71–72.

24. James Baldwin, "Many Thousands Gone," in *Notes of a Native Son*, 33. The essay first appeared in *Partisan Review* 18 (November–December 1951): 665–80.

25. Qtd. by Matthiessen in *Dreiser*, 189.
26. Dreiser, *An American Tragedy*, 1925 (New York: New American Library, 1964), 12. Page references to this edition are given in the text.
27. Wright, "How 'Bigger' Was Born," in *Native Son*, xii.
28. Wright, "The Man Who Went to Chicago," in *Eight Men*, 210–50.
29. See Keneth Kinnamon, *The Emergence of Richard Wright*, 120.
30. J. Donald Adams, "Speaking of Books."
31. Dreiser, "Some Aspects of Our National Character," in *Hey Rub-A-Dub-Dub*, 24.
32. Although Brooks recognized in Twain a genius and a "tortured conscience," he thought Twain's dedication to humor, "[the] spirit of the artist in him," diluted his philosophy of humankind. See Van Wyck Brooks, "From *The Ordeal of Mark Twain*," in *Adventures of Huckleberry Finn*, eds. Scully Bradley, et al., 295–300.
33. Dreiser, "Mark the Double Twain," 621.
34. Wright, "How 'Bigger' Was Born," in *Native Son*, xxvi.
35. In a letter of 10 July 1945, to Yvette Eastman, one of Dreiser's young mistresses who had a literary ambition, Dreiser wrote:

> Yvette Dear:
> Such a poetic, Lovely letter from you this morning July 10th. You are off on a hill somewhere—up near Brewster, and you fairly sing of the heavens and the earth which considering all you have to do and your unchanging sense of duty always impresses me. I marvel that you dont at least verbally rebel against the conditions that have almost always made you earn your own way. So often I feel that it might be a relief to you if you were to write an honest forth right book like *Black Boy* and in it have your say concerning all the things you have had to endure and so what you think of life. It would be colorful and more dramatic and I feel it would sell, yet not only the data but because of the beauty of your prose. Why not.

See Yvette Eastman, *Dearest Wilding: A Memoir with Love Letters from Theodore Dreiser*, ed. Thomas P. Riggio, 211.

Urban Frontiers, Neighborhoods, and Traps: The City in Dreiser's *Sister Carrie*, Farrell's *Studs Lonigan*, and Wright's *Native Son*

ROBERT BUTLER

THEODORE DREISER, JAMES T. FARRELL, AND RICHARD WRIGHT FORM AN interesting literary triad since they were twentieth-century Chicago novelists who operated within a tradition which may be loosely described as "realistic" and "naturalistic." Moreover, both Farrell and Wright stressed their indebtedness to Dreiser for freeing them from the limitations of conventional fiction, thus enabling them to develop visions and voices which were distinctly modern. Farrell, who greatly admired Dreiser's fiction, knew him personally, and later became his literary confidante and executor, observed in *Reflections at Fifty* that he was awakened as a writer by Dreiser's novels which left an "impression" on him which was both "deep and lasting." Although he was never comfortable with Dreiser's "deterministic vision of man" and also rejected what he felt were his documentary "methods of writing," Farrell was inspired by Dreiser's conception of character and his ability to evoke human experience in a powerful, resonant way. Describing his reading of Dreiser's fiction in his own formative years, Farrell observed:

> More than anything else, I felt wonder and awe: I was strengthened in my feeling that human emotions, feelings, desires, aspirations are valuable and precious. I gained more respect for life, more sympathy for people, more of a sense of human thoughts and feelings in this, our common life.[1]

Wright was likewise strongly affected by Dreiser's example and work. In a 1938 interview he stressed that "I value [Dreiser's work] . . . above, perhaps, any American writer." His praise of Dreiser three years later was even stronger, characterizing him as "the greatest writer this country has ever produced." Furthermore, Wright and Farrell shared a long friendship which went back to the early 1930s and lasted to Wright's premature death in 1960. He considered himself as part of the same "literary generation"[2] as Farrell and was clearly influenced by Farrell's novels, particularly *Studs Lonigan*.

Despite these important biographical connections and literary influences, surprisingly little has been written about the extremely fruitful relationship between these three writers.[3] It is my purpose in this essay to probe some important points of similarity and difference between these three writers as they offer fresh images and interpretations of urban experience in three representative novels, *Sister Carrie*, *Studs Lonigan*, and *Native Son*. Taken together, these masterworks provide a powerful literary record of Chicago from the turn of the century to the end of the Great Depression. And although they clearly reveal important affinities and continuities, emphatically demonstrating the lessons which Farrell and Wright learned from Dreiser and also from each other, they also are distinctively different in style and vision. In the final analysis, these three remarkable novels reveal their authors' unique experiences in the modern American city and their distinctive manner of portraying these experiences in a fresh and compelling vision of urban life.

Dreiser's enormously vital and energetic urban world in *Sister Carrie*, a world which inspires such wonder and terror in its central character, seems at first glance an altogether different literary universe from the unspectacular ethnic neighborhood depicted in *Studs Lonigan* and the frightening ghetto portrayed in *Native Son*. Not only are the social worlds in each novel radically different but the central characters' responses to their respective cities are markedly dissimilar. Because of this, each author employs radically different literary techniques to capture the human experience of these cities. Dreiser relies primarily on naturalistic methods to stress the solidity and dynamism of his large-scale urban environment while Farrell uses a wide range of realistic and impressionistic techniques to bring to life an urban world which is more ordinary and personal. As he revealed in *Reflections at Fifty*:

> I felt closer to Anderson's intimate world than I did to that depicted in Dreiser's massive novels. The neighborhoods of Chicago in which I grew up possessed something of the character of a small town. They were little worlds of their own. Many of the people living in them knew one another. There was a certain amount of gossip of the character that one finds in small towns. One of the largest nationality and religious groups in these neighborhoods was Irish-American and Catholic. I attended a parochial school. Through the school and Sunday Mass the life of these neighborhoods was rendered somewhat more cohesive.[4]

Wright, on the other hand, envisions a city that has deteriorated into a massive ghetto which is anything but an "intimate world" characterized by rituals and institutions making community life more "cohesive." The urban universe of *Native Son* is a painfully alienating environment producing tremendous fear and guilt in its inhabitants. In order to dramatize the terrifying loneliness and estrangement which his central character feels on a daily basis, Wright uses expressionistic and gothic techniques to describe the ghetto as a dark mindscape reflecting the horror of modern urban experience. All three novels can be seen as "seminal" or "paradigmatic" works since they portray the city in powerfully new ways which strongly influence subsequent American literature.

One way to focus sharply on how these novels are both connected and strikingly different in their portrayal of modern urban life is to examine how they use a centrally important motif, the recurrent image of a central character gazing out of windows into urban settings which not only provide epiphanies revealing the nature of urban experience but also clearly reflect the inward lives of these central characters. This motif, which Dreiser perhaps found in his reading of Flaubert's *Madame Bovary*,[5] is used extensively in *Sister Carrie* both as a measure of the social world she must master and also as a reflector of her inward nature and growth. It is used in a similar way in *Studs Lonigan* to reveal Studs's deepest human longings as well as to define the relationship between his personal life and the life of his urban community. *Native Son*, however, brilliantly inverts this motif. When Bigger looks out of windows at the city he is condemned to live in, he perceives neither the dynamic city which triggers Carrie's growth nor does he sense the continuity between the self and neighborhood which often calms and reassures Studs Lonigan. Rather, he perceives himself as doubly trapped, in dilapidated rooms which torment him materially and a fragmented, nightmarish public world which is a grim extension of his ghetto apartment. He feels incarcerated in both worlds which push his mind to the brink of despair and madness.

I

Sister Carrie is enclosed by scenes in which the central character looks out at windows and is stimulated by a vision of the city which fires her imagination by extending to her limitless possibilities for growth which her questing spirit craves. At the beginning of the novel Carrie eagerly looks out of the window of the train as she enters Chicago, beholding the city in "wonder" and "terror" while realizing how "alone" she is in the "great sea of life."[6] She clearly senses the city as a reflector of her deepest longings, for it is "alive with the clatter and clang of life"

(7), a sharp contrast to the stagnant world of the small town in which she was raised. Beholding Chicago in the early evening, which Dreiser describes as "that mystic period . . . when life is changing from one sphere or condition to another" (7), Carrie equates the city with liberating change and excitement, a new world of "theatres" and "parties" (7) which promise her new pleasures and imaginative experience. Although she briefly feels some understandable anxiety at being so abruptly separated from home, such feelings quickly pass and never appear for the remainder of the novel. The "threads" which connect her to the "village" and "home" are "irretrievably broken" (1) at the very beginning of the novel because the modern metropolis touches her at the very core of her being, offering her a protean existence in which she can create an indefinite series of new lives by assuming a variety of roles in an ever-changing city. Looking at Chicago from a train window, she is deeply stirred, thinking "I shall soon be free" (7).

Whenever Carrie's "terror" of the city returns as she directly experiences the harsher features of the urban environment, she is quickly revived by looking out of windows from her position in enclosed space and renewing the positive vision of the city which she imagined in the opening chapter. For example, when she becomes depressed by the "steady round of toil" (10) which characterizes life in Minnie's apartment, she refreshes herself by rocking in a chair by "the open window" and looking at the streets in "silent wonder" (11). While Minnie's world is a trap which will force her to relive her parents' grim working-class existence in Columbia City, Chicago's streets are a sharp break from such a bleak past. As Dreiser notes a few pages later, these streets open up into vast spaces providing new life. They are, in fact, passageways leading to an urban equivalent of the American frontier:

> The City had laid miles and miles of streets and sewers through regions where, perhaps, one solitary house stood out alone—a pioneer of the populous ways to be. There were regions open to the sweeping winds and rain, which were yet lighted throughout the night with long, blinking lines of gas-lamps, fluttering in the wind. Narrow board walks extended out, passing here a house, and there a store, at far intervals, eventually ending on the open prairie. (12)

The city as frontier not only provides Carrie with outward growth in the form of money, new clothes, and a progressively more lavish lifestyle but it also offers psychological and spiritual development as well. Scenes in which she looks out of windows at urban scenes that become increasingly more elegant dramatize both kings of growth. At a point where Carrie has tired of the comfortable but mediocre life she shares with

Drouet, she gazes out of the window of their apartment and is inspired by the tangible and intangible "possibilities" which she sees in Chicago:

> When Drouet was gone, she sat down in her rocking-chair by the window to think about it. As usual, imagination exaggerated the possibilities for her. It was as if he had put fifty cents in her hand and she had exercised the thoughts of a thousand dollars. She saw herself in a score of pathetic situations in which she assumed a tremulous voice and suffering manner. Her mind delighted itself with scenes of luxury and refinement, situations in which she was the cynosure of all eyes, the arbiter of all fates. As she rocked to and fro she felt the tensity of woe in abandonment, the magnificence of wrath after deception, the languour of sorrow after defeat. Thoughts of all the charming women she had seen in plays—every fancy, every illusion which she had concerning the stage—now came back as a returning tide after the ebb. (117–18)

Carrie's quest for outward "luxury" is stressed in this reverie but her inward development is also noted. As she rocks by the window and contemplates the city, she is imaginatively stimulated by imagining herself in a variety of roles which not only draw attention to her, making her "the cynosure of all eyes," but also endow her life with control, making her "the arbiter of all fates." It is precisely at this point in the novel that Carrie has become seriously involved with acting, an activity which transforms her inwardly because it gives her imaginative experience which meets some of her deepest psychological needs. Her acting also develops her will since it provides her with the means of support and mental development she needs to gain some measure of control over her environment. And acting becomes a model for developing a protean self, one capable of assuming a great variety of roles in a dynamic urban world which is always becoming new things. Carrie, who in the novel's first scene finds the theater one of Chicago's most attractive features, eventually comes to see the city itself as an immense theater, a glitteringly protean universe which endows her with the imaginative energy she needs to create a new life.

For the remainder of the novel Carrie continues to experience remarkable physical, emotional, and psychological growth, all of which are reflected in scenes where she looks out of windows and contemplates images of the city which become increasingly more dramatic and rich in meaning. Midway through the novel as she and Hurstwood escape to Montreal on a speeding train, she looks out of the window and conjures up romantic images of two new cities which she feels will transform her life: "Montreal and New York! Even now she was speeding toward those great, strange lands, and could see them if she liked" (200). Some readers have puzzled over this scene, having difficulty finding an adequate motive for Carrie eloping to New York. She clearly feels betrayed by Hurstwood's treachery, has no proof of his divorce, and her earlier infatuation with him has cooled to the point where she clearly realizes that she is not in love with him. But the scene is altogether plausible as Dreiser wrote it and is consistent with other important scenes in the novel because Carrie is not motivated by what she sees inside the train car (a greatly reduced Hurstwood), but is instead motivated by what she imagines as she looks out of the window, a vision of two exotic cities which will provide settings for her continued growth. As was the case in the novel's opening chapter, Carrie equates the modern city with growth which can give her "a newer world" (202) of heightened pleasure, increased status, and personal development. As Hurstwood in this scene looks at the train window and can see only his reflection (a poignant foreshadowing of the narcissism which will contribute to his downfall in New York), Carrie looks "out the window" (204), envisioning a "great city" which can bring her from "bondage to freedom" (209).

Although she receives several setbacks in New York, Carrie's faith in herself and the city are ultimately validated by the radically new life which she achieves in New York. But whenever her confidence ebbs, it is revived when she gazes out of windows and contemplates the city as an emblem of freedom and expanded possibility. At times intimidated by New York's "peculiar indifference" (220), Carrie is refreshed when she looks out of her apartment window at the "great city building up rapidly" (220). After Hurstwood loses his business and becomes "addicted" to the "ease" (267) of hanging around the elegant enclosed space of hotel lobbies, Carrie instinctively separates from him and moves directly into the rough but vital city to secure a job as an actress. As she is being interviewed for a position, she quells her anxiety and self-doubt by viewing "the hard rumble of the city" (279) through the office window. After she leaves Hurstwood and moves into an apartment with Lola, Carrie often takes pleasure in looking "down into busy Broadway" (331) from the vantage point of her penthouse windows.

The considerable human growth which Carrie achieves by the end of the novel is emphasized by the final image of her in the novel sitting in a rocking chair by a window which overlooks a bustling, growing city which can destroy people who lack sufficient imagination and will but rewards her because she has developed these qualities. Her material progress is obviously stressed by the elegance of her apartment. She has finally entered the gates of the walled city which has excluded Hurstwood and is now ready to move steadily upward in American society. And her human growth, which many readers miss, is also sharply signaled in this scene. Intellectually, she has indeed come a long way from the rather shallow "waif" dominated by the various environmental "forces" depicted in the novel's first chapter, for she is reading a novel by Balzac, the same writer who awakened Dreiser's artistic talents and ambitions. Clearly, Ames, who has urged her to drop low comedy roles and pursue more substantial artistic challenges, has "pointed out a farther step" (369) and she is now able to pursue the ideals which he has inspired in her. And Carrie's moral development is also shown when she expresses dissatisfaction to Lola about her outward success and feels genuine compassion for the bums milling below her window as they seek food and shelter. Although Carrie is aware that the city can be a lethal environment, she knows that she has acquired the human traits necessary for success in the city. As she looks at the cold city below her window, she rocks and sings, warmed by the fact that "she saw the city offering more of loveliness than she had ever known" (365).

II

Farrell's *Studs Lonigan* presents a startling different picture of the modern American city but it borrows this technique from Dreiser of using window reveries to make its urban vision clear and coherent. At key points in the trilogy, Farrell defines his city and uses it to reveal his central character's inward nature in scenes which portray Studs looking out of windows at city scenes. Midway through *Young Lonigan*, for example, the narrator tells us that

> Studs awoke to stare sleepily at a June morning that crashed through his bedroom window. The world outside the window was all shine and shimmer. Just looking at it made Studs feel good that he was alive. And it was only the end of June. He still had July and August. And this was one of the days when he would feel swell; one of his days. He drowsed in bed, and glanced out to watch the sun scatter over the yard. He watched a tomcat slink along the fence ledge: he stared at the spot he had newly boarded so that his old man wouldn't yelp about loose boards; he looked about at the patches in the grass that Martin and his gang had torn down playing their cowboy and Indian games. *There was something about the things he watched that seemed to enter Studs as sun entered a field of grass; and as he watched, he felt that the things he saw were part of himself, and he felt as good as if he were warm sunlight; he was all glad to be living, and to be Studs Lonigan.* (Emphasis added)[7]

Farrell's ethnic neighborhood is dramatically different from Dreiser's metropolis in a number of important ways. First of all, it is an extremely familiar world perceived by one who has been inside that world for his entire life rather than a large-scale, dramatic world which is experienced by a newcomer who is fascinated by the city's energy, size, strangeness, and novelty. Studs is completely home in such a place—he feels "swell" when he looks through his bedroom window at a backyard filled with small, familiar objects. It is not a wide-open frontier evoking wonder and terror but a domestic place where the only hint of a frontier are the games of cowboys and Indians which small children play. Secondly, Studs's city is a communal world, a neighborhood populated by his family and friends and other people who share basic beliefs and assumptions about life. This, of course, is a sharp contrast to the city which Carrie gravitates toward, an open space which appeals to her intense individualism by inviting her to develop a unique self which can meet experience on its own terms.

But Farrell the novelist, like Dreiser, uses this window scene to reveal the nature of his character's consciousness and the urban environment which it must interact with. We find out that Studs is not really the cold "tough guy" he appeared to be in the novel's opening scene which describes him glowering into a bathroom mirror as he smokes a forbidden cigarette, but instead is a normal young man with a very "soft" interior nature which delights in the leisure of summer vacation and feels protected and secure in a warm world bathed in sunlight. Moreover, there is a surprisingly poetic quality in Studs which nobody in his social group sees—an imaginative self which regards the things around him as metaphors revealing his true inward nature. In the same way, Carrie's window meditations reveal surprising aspects of her own personality which others are often unaware of—she is not a helpless "waif amid forces" because she is empowered with imagination, intellect, and will, all of which are vividly demonstrated when she transcends the closed space of small rooms by looking out of windows at spacious, growing cities.

Although Studs's urban environment has shrunk to an ethnic neighborhood which is both a place of "spiritual poverty"[8] and a foundation for human growth, it nevertheless reveals his most deeply human qualities when he contemplates it while gazing out various windows. A vivid example of this occurs roughly midway through *Young Lonigan* when Studs returns home after eighth-grade graduation exercises and looks out of his parlor window at a Wabash Street which has been transformed by the dark night and his pensive mood:

> Studs sat by the window. He looked out, watching the night strangeness, listening. The darkness was over everything like a warm bed-cover, and all the little sounds of night seemed to him as if they belonged to some great mystery. He listened to the wind in the tree by the window. The street was queer and didn't seem at all like Wabash Avenue. . . . He thought about the fall, and of the arguments for working that he should have sprung on the old man. He thought of himself on a scaffold, wearing a painter's overalls, chewing to-

> bacco, and talking man-talk, with the other painters; and of pay days and the independence it would bring him. He thought of Studs Lonigan, a free and independent working man. . . . (*YL*, 77–78)

Here Studs clearly resembles the city scene he is contemplating. Both are enveloped in "strangeness" because they are caught in moments of change. Just as the normally familiar Wabash Avenue has an element of "mystery" because it has passed from daylight to darkness, Studs's life is now perplexing to him because he is moving from his stable life as a grammar school student in which his experiences have been structured by others to a new phase where he must make his own decisions about either continuing with his education or dropping out of school and going to work. But he sees the city as offering him viable options—his leaving school will not reduce him to poverty but will make him a "free and independent working man."

Significantly, *Young Lonigan* concludes with Studs again looking out the parlor window at a Wabash Avenue mysteriously darkened by night. But this time Studs's mood has changed, along with the urban scene before him. The tree is now "empty" and Studs is caught in a moment of melancholy, comparing himself to "a sad song" (223). He has made the disastrous decision to drop out of school and work for his father as a house painter, a decision which will greatly empty his future life of new possibilities and growth. In the final two books of the trilogy, which chronicle Studs's decline and downfall, he has all-too-few moments where he is able to envision lucidly the relationship between himself and his urban environment as he gazes out of windows. The tendency toward introspection which brings out his deeply human "soft" nature in *Young Lonigan* is repressed by a social world which demands that he be a "hard" guy given to thoughtless outer action which becomes increasingly more destructive as the trilogy develops. He is typically described therefore in situations which bring out the worst features of his urban environment. In a very real sense, he moves from the role of Carrie in *Young Lonigan*, a youthful aspirant, to the role of Hurstwood in *The Young Manhood of Studs Lonigan* and *Judgment Day*, a pathetic figure crushed by deterministic forces he can neither understand nor control. Accordingly, he is often portrayed in the final two novels as wasting his energy, losing sight of a meaningful future and lapsing into a debilitating melancholy and nostalgia. He is often depicted, therefore, as gazing narcissistically into mirrors, getting drunk in bars, or hanging around on street corners. Like Hurstwood, he becomes addicted to ease, falling into an enervation which saps his energy and gradually destroys his ability to think clearly and act effectively. His death greatly resembles Hurstwood's demise—his health is weakened by bad weather as he desperately searches for work in a city experiencing severe economic distress. Like Hurstwood who finally becomes overwhelmed by "lassitude" (*SC* 1900: 317), Studs succumbs to "weakness and lassitude" wishing "only to sleep, to close his eyes and forget everything."[9]

Danny O'Neill, a character Farrell develops consciously as a foil to Studs, bears close resemblance to Carrie Meeber as he uses imagination, intellect, and will to triumph over the negative forces in the urban environment and use the positive energies of the city to spur his growth. And both figures ultimately transform themselves through a commitment to art. Just as the theaters in New York and Chicago provide Carrie with the role of actress which enable her to tap her imaginative talents, Chicago's schools and libraries liberate Danny O'Neill, making him a writer who can use art both to understand his world and create fruitful directions for himself with that world.

At the end of *The Young Manhood of Studs Lonigan*, Danny is pictured at work in a Chicago gas station where he makes the money necessary to pay his university expenses. Like Carrie, who at the end of her novel is reading a book which stirs her imagination and clarifies her vision, Danny is reading a serious book, Veblen's *The Theory of Business Enterprise*, which induces in him the "elation of intellectual discovery."[10] And like Carrie also, he looks out a window at the city while envisioning a vital future for himself. Although his immediate urban environment confronts him with "dreariness," consisting of a "box-like carburetor factory" (*YM*, 370) and a decaying neighborhood, he can call up in his mind a liberating image of his education providing him with "a newer, cleaner world" (*YM* 372). Just as Carrie uses art as a way of learning how to *act* meaningfully in an environment which threatens to strip her of humanity, Danny discovers that by becoming a writer, he can understand and control his life, gaining "a sense of power" (*YM*, 372) over his experiences. Farrell's city, like Dreiser's city, finally is two radically opposed worlds, a harshly deterministic environment which destroys people like Hurstwood and Studs and a liberating space which offers new lives to people like Carrie and Danny. The city for both writers can be an entrapping room or a window of opportunity.

III

Native Son, although set in roughly the same piece of real estate as *Studs Lonigan* and although deeply influenced by Dreiser's vision of life, presents a vastly different urban world. While Dreiser's and Farrell's characters can either be redeemed or damned by the modern American city, Wright's protagonist sees the city in purely negative terms as a prison, hell, or extended nightmare. Dreiser's metropolis and Farrell's ethnic neighborhood become in *Native Son* a teeming ghetto which contains two equally bleak options, slavery or death.

This is made painfully clear at the opening of the novel where Bigger Thomas looks out a window at the city which he and his family are condemned to inhabit. After killing the rat, he is overcome with revulsion for the life he must live in a one-room tenement apartment and seeks relief in the streets. But as he views these streets through the front door window of his apartment building, he is confronted with more images of entrapment:

> He went down the steps into the vestibule and stood looking out into the street through the plate glass of the front door. Now and then a street car rattled past over steel tracks. He was sick of his life at home. Day in and day out there was nothing but shouts and bickering. But what could he do? Each time he asked himself that question his mind hit a blank wall and he stopped thinking. . . . It maddened him to think that he did not have a wider choice of action. Well, he could not stand here all day like this. What was he to do with himself?[11]

When Carrie Meeber looks out a window at a Chicago Street she envisions a path through a liberating urban frontier. And when Studs Lonigan examines Wabash Street, he is reminded that it is part of a neighborhood of people like himself which form a community. But when Bigger looks out at the nameless street on which his apartment is located, he sees "steel tracks" which remind him of the ghetto which paralyzes his body and traps his mind. Unlike Carrie, whose inward life is stimulated when she observes urban scenes, and Studs whose poetic thoughts are freed when he muses over what he sees in his backyard, Bigger's mind hits a "blank wall" when he observes how the ghetto has laid out his life on tracks leading nowhere. While the city is a catalyst for Carrie's inward development and her achievement of selfhood, Bigger's city is a fiercely deterministic world which will destroy the self by reducing him to a machine or an animal. Unlike Studs who feels at home in his neighborhood and seldom wishes to venture forth from it, Bigger is "sick of his life at home" because the ghetto rooms in which he lives are an extension of cold, hard city which lay outside his windows. He can experience little but "shouts and bickering" in either place. "Maddened" by the fact that he does not have "a wider choice of action" in either his domestic life or his public life, Bigger feels triply alienated, estranged from American society, his community, and himself.

To dramatize the intensity and breadth of Bigger's alienation from an urban world that is fundamentally strange and threatening to him, Wright decided to reject the essentially mimetic styles employed by Farrell and Dreiser in favor of surrealistic techniques.[12] The city in *Native Son* is typically presented as a gothic mindscape reflecting the fear and guilt of Bigger's life which is a direct result of the lack of connection he feels between himself and his social environment. Because his external world offers him so little and because it often threatens to rob him of a significant inward life, Bigger apprehends the city as a process of fragmentation and dislocation, a strange nether world which threatens to destroy him.

For this reason, *Native Son* describes very little of the objectively real urban settings which are rendered so accurately in Dreiser's naturalistic style and Farrell's realistic techniques. The fully reified cities of *Sister Carrie* and *Studs Lonigan* become a Poe-esque landscape of nightmare in Wright's masterpiece. We are never given a precise idea of the year in which *Native Son* takes places, a sharp contrast to the exact dating which Dreiser and Farrell use to make the fictional worlds appear more "real" and to draw important parallels between the lives of their characters and the historical forces at work in their societies.[13] Nor do we see much of the physical details of Bigger's city. Full, clear and coherent descriptions of streets, houses, stores, schools, and other landmarks are never given. The novel's second scene, which describes Bigger leaving his family's apartment and walking down the street, provides a clear example of Wright's highly selective method of depicting city life which is designed more to project the character's psychological response to the city than to give a literal picture of the city. The few details mentioned—a streetcar on tracks, a plate glass window and a political poster which reads "IF YOU BREAK THE LAW, YOU CAN'T WIN!" (16) are clearly designed to suggest what Bigger is thinking and feeling. Shortly after this, when Bigger and Gus meet on the street, the scene is also rendered impressionistically. Observing a high-flying plane and fast-moving automobiles which painfully remind them of the mobility enjoyed by whites but denied to blacks, they realize that black people have been placed in "one corner of the city" that amounts to little more than a "jail" (32). The few details which Wright selects from the external world provide a telling description of the psychological and emotional entrapment which maddens Bigger.

To emphasize further this dislocated quality of Bigger's perceptions, Wright uses Gothic imagery extensively to describe urban reality. This is especially true in Book II where Bigger is overwhelmed by the fears that were triggered in Book I. Going to Bessie's house to draft a ransom note, he perceives the street lamps as "hazy balls of light frozen into motionlessness" (124). After killing Mary, he passes by buildings that appear to him as "skeletons . . . white and silent in the night" (171). In the scene immediately following his brutal murder of Bessie, Bigger wanders the streets caught in a nightmarish world where deserted buildings look like "empty skulls" and where the windows of these buildings "gaped blackly, like . . . eye-sockets" (216).

Because Farrell's characters are seldom pushed to the physical and emotional extremes that convert Bigger Thomas's Chicago into this darkly surrealistic world, their city is presented much more mimetically and lyrically. Lyrical images of the city, almost completely absent from *Native Son*, are used skillfully in *Studs Lonigan*, often being sharply counterpointed with realistic images of city life. Farrell's city, despite its harsh features, can connect with his character's deepest impulses, thereby endowing Studs's inward life with a genuine sense of possibility. Thus the street corners, pool rooms, and bars that threaten to trap Studs Lonigan are consistently contrasted with the parks that allow him to relax, free his mind, and envision a better life for himself. His street fight with Weary Reilley epitomizes his "tough outside part" (*YL*, 160), while his romantic afternoon with Lucy in Washington Park demonstrates that Studs has "a tender inside part" (*YL*, 160) to which his environment can be responsive. Looking out the window of his bedroom at the end of *Young Lonigan*, Studs can see the city and himself in terms of possibilities altogether denied to Bigger—when he sees his neighborhood he feels part of it and regards his neighborhood's image of him as consistent with his own desires to become "Studs Lonigan, a free and independent working man" (*YL*, 78).

When Bigger Thomas looks out of windows, however, the poetic "strangeness" (*YL,* 77) which fertilizes the imagination of Studs Lonigan and the exotic urban images which intrigue Carrie Meeber, become an alienating strangeness which disorients and frightens him as he sees himself as living out an extended nightmare. When he returns home after nearly killing Gus in an irrational poolroom fight, Bigger immediately goes to the window and looks out "dreamily" (43) at the city. But instead of receiving the epiphanies which enlighten and invigorate Studs and Carrie, Bigger is beset with "confused emotions" (44). He has become "disgusted" (44) with the gang which has centered his life in the present and is strickened with anxiety about his future life as the Daltons' chauffeur. His fears are powerfully confirmed when he takes a closer look at the ghetto as nightfall approaches:

> Outside his window he saw the sun dying over the rooftops in the western sky and watched the first shade of dusk fall. Now and then a street car ran past. The rusty radiator hissed at the far end of the room. All day long it had been springlike; but now the dark clouds were slowly swallowing the sun. (44)

From this point on, most of the novel's important scenes will be enacted at night when heavy snows blanket Chicago, creating an eerie world which confuses Bigger and forces him into a variety of self-destructive actions which foreclose his future. As the "sun" illuminating his world dies after being swallowed up by "dark clouds," Bigger's life will also darken until it too is swallowed up by a social environment which forces him into murderous activity.

When Bigger rides with Mary and Jan to Ernie's Chicken Shack, he feels deeply anxious about his proximity to white people in such enclosed space and looks out the car window to seek relief but instead views an urban scene which produces equally intense feelings of entrapment. Just as he sees Jan and Mary as "two vast white looming walls," he views the Chicago skyline as "a vast sweep of tall buildings" (68). On the way back, he drives through Washington Park but envisions a world quite different from the sunny, pastoral world which calms Studs Lonigan and brings out his most deeply human self. The park becomes a grim mindscape reflecting Bigger's deepest fears—as he drunkenly races through the "dark park" (78), he becomes dangerously disoriented: "His sense of the city and park fell away; he was floating in the car . . ." (78). This disorientation is the first step in a sequence of irrational actions culminating in his killing of Mary in a dark room.

At the beginning of Book II when Bigger awakens in his family's one room apartment the morning after he has killed Mary, he immediately looks out the window and sees "snow falling," another hypnotic image which puts Bigger into "a strange spell" which ensnares him in a "deadlock of impulses" (93). He is caught in an eerie world where the borderline between life and death has been blurred and he is "unable to rise to the land of the living" (93). For the remainder of Book II he inhabits such a twilight zone of fear and anxiety which robs him of clear consciousness and the ability to act in humanly productive ways. Again, when he looks out of windows the external scene in the city simply mirrors his confusion rather than providing him with epiphanies which clarify things for characters like Carrie Meeber and Danny O'Neill. After being grilled by Britten for an extended period of time, Bigger looks out of the window of his second-floor room, seeking relief and clarity of mind but is again overcome with images of chaos, a city caught in a physical blizzard which exactly mirrors the psychological storms boiling in him:

> He went to the window and looked out at the swirling snow. He could hear wind rising; it was a blizzard all right. The now moved in no given direction, but filled the world with a vast white storm of flying powder. The sharp currents of wind could be seen in whirls of snow twisting like miniature tornadoes. (182)

Interestingly, Bigger will later jump through this window in his attempt to escape from the police after they have discovered Mary's bones in the furnace but his escape is doomed from the beginning by the hostile urban environment into which he runs. First of all, the snow bank he tumbles into causes him to soil himself by urinating in a "spasm of reflex action" (207). Secondly, the "dark city streets" (207) further confuse him and limit his vision, leading him to "a strange labyrinth" (225) of tangles South Side streets, a "chaos" (225) which Bigger is never able to understand or cope with.

In Book III Bigger has very limited access to windows because he spends all of his time in cramped rooms and his energies are directed toward looking into himself rather than contemplating an external world which he knows he can never return to. His external vision is, for the most part, limited to "staring vacantly at the black steel bars" (336) of his cell or gazing at the walls of the inquest room and courtroom. But when he does get glimpses out of barred windows he is emphatically reminded that the city and the social world it represents fail completely to supply him with meaning for his present or future experiences. His only hope is to recoil from this outward world and undertake a journey into self, hoping to find "some road . . . to a sure and quiet knowledge" (226).

Max tries to rejuvenate Bigger's faith in social and historical experience which transcends self by urging him to look hopefully at images of the city but he fails miserably. In the novel's final scene:

> Max rose and went to a small window; a pale bar of sunshine fell across his white head. And Bigger, looking at him, saw that sunshine for the first time in many days; and as he saw it, the entire cell, with its four close walls, became crushingly real. He glanced down at himself; the shaft of yellow sun cut across his chest with as much weight as a beam forged in lead. With a convulsive gasp, he bent forward and shut his eyes. (386)

Sunlight, which is often used in classic American literature as a symbol of religious awakening and personal conversion,[14] is ironically inverted in this scene as it falls violently with the weight of "lead" over Bigger's chest, inducing a "convulsive gasp" and forcing him to close his eyes. He knows that the sun, which has "died" for him in Book I, will not shine for him much longer. What is "crushingly real" to Bigger is not a hopeful urban prospect outside his windows but the "four closed walls" of his cell.

At the very end of the novel Max once more tries to revive Bigger by looking out his cell window at the city but again fails in his efforts. Coaxing Bigger to look at "the tips of sun-drenched buildings in the Loop"

(389), Max hopes to use this image in a way that might restore Bigger's faith in a vaguely Marxist vision of the future. Explaining that such buildings are part of a civilization centered in "the belief of men" (389) who constructed them, Max tells Bigger that the civilization symbolized by these skyscrapers is dying but will eventually be replaced by a socialist culture centered in people like him. Bigger, of course, finds Max's vision far too abstract and remote from his own human needs. He can not connect Max's "picture" of proletarian brotherhood with "what he had felt all his life" (390) and, as a result, distances himself from Max by laughing and telling him "I reckon I believe in myself. . . . I ain't got nothing else. . . . I got to die . . ." (391). At this point Max is described as "leaning against the window" (391), blocking its view and, in effect, turning it into a wall.

With this gesture, the image of the window, which was so romantically developed in *Sister Carrie* and realistically revised in *Studs Lonigan* is harshly inverted to suggest the essentially bleak urban world which Bigger must encounter. In the final analysis, the city fails to provide *any* human meaning for him, becoming an absurd world which he must recoil from in order to salvage an existentially human identity before he dies. The "faint, wry, bitter smile" (392) on his face as he peers through the bars of his cell door in the novel's final sentence suggest that he is on his way to constructing a marginalized existential identity because he has dispossessed himself of any illusions about the city and the social world it represents and looks instead inside himself for meaning. Unlike Max who is ultimately described as a "blind man" (392), Bigger has a lucid awareness that the only windows which can provide him with hope are the windows of his soul.

Notes

1. James T. Farrell, *Reflections at Fifty*, 132.
2. Keneth Kinnamon and Michel Fabre, eds., *Conversations with Richard Wright*, 15, 38, 32.
3. See Yoshinobu Hakutani's "*Native Son* and *An American Tragedy*: Two Different Interpretations of Crime and Guilt." Hakutani offers a penetrating analysis of important thematic parallels and differences between these two novels. See also Robert Butler's "Farrell's Ethnic Neighborhood and Wright's Urban Ghetto: Two Visions of Chicago's South Side."
4. *Reflections*, 164.
5. Flaubert brilliantly uses this motif in providing epiphanies of Emma Bovary's experience. Emma is often described as feeling suffocated in rooms which symbolize her entrapment in a society which stifles her deepest human longings but she often finds relief when she looks out of the windows of these rooms and imagines a new life for herself. For example, after an argument with Charles,

Emma goes to the window to refresh herself. After the ball at Vaubysard, she leans out of her bedroom window to prolong the illusion of the luxurious life she had experienced at the ball. After Leon goes to Paris, she goes to the window and is refreshed by sunlight as it irradiates her garden.

6. Donald Pizer, ed., *Sister Carrie* (New York: Norton, 1970), 7. All subsequent references to the text are to this Norton Critical Edition and page numbers will be cited parenthetically after the quotation.

7. Farrell, *Young Lonigan* (New York: Avon Books, 1972), 83. All subsequent references to the text are to this edition and page numbers will be cited parenthetically in the text after the quotation.

8. Farrell, *The League of Frightened Philistines*, 86.

9. Farrell, *Judgment Day* (New York: Avon Books, 1973), 404.

10. Farrell, *The Young Manhood of Studs Lonigan* (New York: Avon Books, 1973), 370. All references to the text are to this edition and page numbers will be cited parenthetically after the quotation.

11. Richard Wright, *Native Son* (New York: Harper and Row, 1966), 16. All subsequent references to the text are to this edition and page numbers will be cited parenthetically after the quote.

12. For an excellent discussion of Wright's use of nonrealistic fictional techniques in *Native Son*, see Dan McCall's *The Example of Richard Wright*. McCall argues persuasively that *Native Son* is in the main tradition of gothic fiction established by Poe and Hawthorne since it uses surrealistic techniques to dramatize the "racial nightmare" of American society.

13. For example, Dreiser draws much attention to the fact that *Sister Carrie* opens in 1889, a time when Chicago experienced enormous growth. He also draws our attention to the fact that Hurstwood's business in New York collapses during the financial panic of 1893. Farrell is more elaborate in the dating of the Lonigan trilogy which begins in 1916, a time of apparently great promise for American culture and ends in the late 1920s when America is in the throes of a cultural collapse brought on by the Great Depression. Significantly the turning point of Studs's life in New Year's Eve 1929, a moment when health problems begin which eventually destroy him and when America likewise develops economic, political, and social "health problems" which could lead to its demise.

14. See, for example, Jonathan Edwards's "Personal Narrative" where a beam of sunlight entering his sick room signals his miraculous recovery from a life-threatening illness and becomes a vivid reminder to him of God's grace. Thoreau, likewise, in *Walden* moves from spiritual sickness to spiritual health when a beam of sunlight entering his cabin reinvigorates him by reminding him of the coming spring and the "rebirth" of nature. Natty Bumppo's achievement of a new name and a new life when he slays the Indian in *The Deerslayer* is also symbolized by sunlight suddenly illuminating the scene.

Bibliography

This bibliography contains only those items cited in the text. A year after a work indicates the year in which the work was originally published.

Works by Dreiser

Books

An Amateur Laborer, 1904. Ed. Richard W. Dowell, James L. W. West III, and Neda M. Westlake. Philadelphia: University of Pennsylvania Press, 1983.

An American Tragedy, 1925. New York: New American Library, 1964.

A Book about Myself. New York: Boni and Liveright, 1922.

A Book about Myself (Newspaper Days), 1922. Greenwich: Fawcett, 1965.

The Bulwark. New York: Doubleday, 1946.

Dawn. New York: Horace Liveright, 1931.

Dreiser-Mencken Letters. Ed. Thomas P. Riggio. 2 vols. Philadelphia: University of Pennsylvania Press, 1986.

The Financier. New York: Harper and Brothers, 1912.

Free and Other Stories. New York: Boni and Liveright, 1918.

Fulfilment and Other Tales of Women and Men. Ed. T. D. Nostwich. Santa Rosa: Black Sparrow Press, 1992.

Hey Rub-A-Dub-Dub: A Book of the Mystery and Terror and Wonder of Life. New York: Boni and Liveright, 1920

A History of Myself: Newspaper Days. New York: Horace Liveright, 1931.

A Hoosier Holiday. New York: John Lane, 1916.

Jennie Gerhardt. New York: Harper and Brothers, 1911.

Jennie Gerhardt, 1911. New York: Penguin, 1989.

Jennie Gerhardt. Ed. James L. W. West III. Philadelphia: University of Pennsylvania Press, 1992.

Newspaper Days. Ed. T. D. Nostwich. Philadelphia: University of Pennsylvania Press, 1991.

Notes on Life. Ed. Marguerite Tjader and John J. McAleer. University: University of Alabama Press, 1974.

Selected Magazine Articles of Theodore Dreiser: Life and Art in the American 1890s. Ed. Yoshinobu Hakutani. 2 vols. Rutherford: Fairleigh Dickinson University Press / London & Toronto: Associated University Presses, 1985, 1987.

Sister Carrie. New York: Doubleday, Page & Company, 1900.

Sister Carrie. Rpt. of the 1900 ed. Columbus: Charles E. Merrill, 1969.

Sister Carrie. Ed. Donald Pizer. New York: Norton, 1970.

Sister Carrie. Rpt. of the 1981 ed. New York: Penguin, 1981.

Sister Carrie. Ed. James L. W. West III, John C. Berkey, Alice M. Winters, and Neda M. Westlake. Philadelphia: University of Pennsylvania Press, 1981, rpt. 1998.

Sister Carrie. Ed. Donald Pizer. New York: Norton, 1970, 2nd ed. 1991.

The Stoic. Garden City: Doubleday Company, 1947.

Theodore Dreiser: The American Diaries, 1902–1926. Ed. Thomas P. Riggio, James L. W. West III, and Neda M. Westlake. Philadelphia: University of Pennsylvania Press, 1982.

Theodore Dreiser: A Selection of Uncollected Prose. Ed. Donald Pizer. Detroit: Wayne State University Press, 1977.

Theodore Dreiser's Letters to Louise Campbell. Ed. Louise Campbell. Philadelphia: University of Pennsylvania Press, 1959.

The Titan. New York & London: John Lane, 1914.

A Traveler at Forty. New York: Century, 1913.

Twelve Men, 1919. Philadelphia: University of Pennsylvania Press, 1998.

Unpublished Material

Aglaia, ms. coll. 30, box 351, folder 1, Dreiser Collection, Van Pelt Library, University of Pennsylvania, Philadelphia.

Fall River, 1899, Dreiser Collection, Van Pelt Library, University of Pennsylvania, Philadelphia.

Manuscript notes for *The Financier*, n. d., Dreiser Collection, Van Pelt Library, University of Pennsylvania, Philadelphia.

Theodore Dreiser's Letters to Suzanne Menahan Sekey, 1929–1930, Dreiser Collection, Van Pelt Library, University of Pennsylvania, Philadelphia.

Theodore Dreiser's Letters to Yvette Szekely and Others, ms. coll. 114, Dreiser Collection, Van Pelt Library, University of Pennsylvania, Philadelphia.

This Madness, Aglaia, ms. coll. 30, box 351, folder 2, Dreiser Collection, Van Pelt Library, University of Pennsylvania, Philadelphia.

Short Works

"A Confession of Faith." In *Theodore Dreiser: A Selection of Uncollected Prose*, ed. Donald Pizer.

"The Factory," 1910, no. 5, n. p. Rpt. in *Theodore Dreiser: A Selection of Uncollected Prose*, ed. Donald Pizer, 175–80.

". . . the game as it is played . . ." *New York Times* (15 January 1901). Rpt. in *The Stature of Theodore Dreiser*, eds. Alfred Kazin and Charles Shapiro, 59–60. Bloomington: Indiana University Press, 1955.

"Life Stories of Successful Men—No. 10: Philip D. Armour." *Success* 1 (October 1898): 3–4. Rpt. in *Selected Magazine Articles of Theodore Dreiser*, ed. Yoshinobu Hakutani, 1: 120–29.

"Life Stories of Successful Men—No. 12: Marshall Field." *Success* 2 (December

1898): 7–8. Rpt. in *Selected Magazine Articles of Theodore Dreiser*, ed. Yoshinobu Hakutani, 1: 130–38.

"The Literary Shower." *Ev'ry Month* (1 February 1896): 10–11.

"Mark the Double Twain." *English Journal* 24 (October 1935): 615–27.

"The Mighty Burke." *McClure's* 37 (May 1911): 40–50.

"Muldoon, the Solid Man." Rpt. in *Fulfilment and Other Tales of Women and Men*, ed. T. D. Nostwich. Santa Rosa: Black Sparrow, 1992.

"Neurotic America and the Sex Impulse." In *Hey Rub-A-Dub-Dub*, 1920, London: Constable, 1931.

"Nigger Jeff," 1901. In *Free and Other Stories*, 76–111. New York: Boni and Liveright, 1918.

"Preface." In *Sister Carrie*. New York: Modern Library, 1932.

"Scenes in a Cartridge Factory." *Cosmopolitan* 25 (July 1898): 321–24.

"Some Aspects of Our National Character." In *Hey Rub-A-Dub-Dub*, 24–59. New York: Boni and Liveright, 1920.

"The Strike To-day." *Toledo Blade* (24 March 1894): 1, 6. Rpt. in *Sister Carrie*, ed. Donald Pizer, 417–23.

"Theodore Dreiser's Letter to Yvette Eastman," 10 July 1945. In Yvette Eastman, *Dearest Wilding: A Memoir with Love Letters from Theodore Dreiser*, ed. Thomas P. Riggio, 211. Philadelphia: University of Pennsylvania Press, 1995.

"This Madness: Sidonie." *Cosmopolitan* 86 (June 1929): 83–87, 156–68.

"Three Sketches of the Poor." *New York Call* (23 November 1913): 10.

"The Town of Pullman." *Ainslee's* 3 (March 1899): 189–200.

"The Transmigration of the Sweat Shop." *Puritan* 8 (July 1900): 498–502. Rpt. in *Selected Magazine Articles of Theodore Dreiser*, ed. Yoshinobu Hakutani, 2: 214–21.

"True Art Speaks Plainly." *Booklover's Magazine* 1 (February 1903).

Works by Others

Adams, J. Donald. "Speaking of Books." *New York Times Book Review* (16 February and 6 April 1958).

Aeschylus. *Prometheus Bound*, trans. Henry D. Thoreau. *The Dial* 3. 3 (1843).

———. *Prometheus Bound*, trans. Rex Warner. In *Ten Greek Plays in Contemporary Translations*, ed. E. R. Lind. Boston: Houghton Mifflin, 1957.

Åhnebrink, Lars. *The Beginnings of Naturalism in American Fiction*. Cambridge: Harvard University Press, 1950.

Albertine, Susan. "Triangulating Desire in *Jennie Gerhardt*." In *Dreiser's Jennie Gerhardt*, ed. James L. W. West III, 63–74.

Allen, Woody, Dir. *Deconstructing Harry*. With Woody Allen, Elizabeth Shue, Richard Benjamin, et al. Jean Doumanian Productions, 1997.

Anderson, Sherwood. "An Apology for Crudity." *Dial* (8 November 1917): 437–38. Rpt. in *The Stature of Theodore Dreiser*, eds. Alfred Kazin and Charles Shapiro, 81–83.

———. *Sherwood Anderson's Memoirs*. New York: Harcourt, Brace, 1942.

Anon. Review of *Jennie Gerhardt. Newark Evening News* (16 March 1912). In *Theodore Dreiser: The Critical Reception*, ed. Jack Salzman, 91.

———. "Mr. Dreiser and His Critics." *New York Evening Sun* (18 June 1907). Rpt. in *The Stature of Theodore Dreiser*, eds. Alfred Kazin and Charles Shapiro.

———. Review of *Sister Carrie. Chicago Advance* (27 June 1907). Rpt. in *Theodore Dreiser: The Critical Reception*, ed. Jack Salzman, 42.

———. Review of *Sister Carrie. New York Press* (3 July 1907). Rpt. in *The Stature of Theodore Dreiser*, eds. Alfred Kazin and Charles Shapiro, 68.

Anthony, E. James. "Shame, Guilt, and the Feminine Self in Psychoanalysis." In *Object and Self: A Developmental Approach*, eds. Saul Tuttman, Carol Kaye, and Muriel Zimmerman, 191–234. New York: International Universities Press, 1981.

Atkinson, Michael. "Richard Wright's 'Big Boy Leaves Home' and a Tale from Ovid: A Metamorphosis Transformed." *Studies in Short Fiction* 24 (Summer 1987): 251–61.

Auchincloss, Louis. "Introduction." In *Sister Carrie*, v–xi. Columbus: Charles E. Merrill, 1969.

Auerback, Erich. *Mimesis: The Representation of Reality in Western Literature*. Trans. Willard R. Trask. Princeton: Princeton University Press, 1974.

Bakhtin, Mikhail. *Problems of Dostoevsky's Poetics*. Ed. and trans. Carl Emerson. Minneapolis: University of Minnesota Press, 1984.

Baldiwin, James. "Many Thousands Gone," 1951. In *Notes of a Native Son*, 18–36. New York: Bantam, 1968.

Barker-Benfield, G. J. *Horrors of the Half-Known Life: Male Attitudes toward Women and Sexuality in Nineteenth-Century America*. New York: Harper and Row, 1976.

Barrineau, Nancy Warner. "Housework Is Never Done: Domestic Labor in *Jennie Gerhardt*." In *Dreiser's Jennie Gerhardt*, ed. James L. W. West III, 127–35.

Bassuk, Ellen. "The Rest Cure: Repetition of Resolution of Victorian Women's Conflicts?" In *The Female Body in Western Culture*, ed. Susan Rubin Suleiman, 139–51. Cambridge: Harvard University Press, 1986.

Bate, Walter Jackson. *The Burden of the Past and the English Poet*. Cambridge: Harvard University Press, 1970.

Beard, George. *American Nervousness*. New York: Arno Press, 1881.

Becker, George J., ed. *Documents of Modern Literary Realism*. Princeton: Princeton University Press, 1963.

Beer, Thomas. *The Mauve Decade*. New York: Vintage, 1926.

Berger, John. *Ways of Seeing*. New York: Penguin, 1977.

Bloom, Harold. *The Anxiety of Influence: A Theory of Poetry*. New York: Oxford University Press, 1973.

Bowlby, Rachel. *Just Looking: Consumer Culture in Dreiser, Gissing and Zola*. New York: Methuem, 1985.

Boyd, Ernest. *Portraits: Real and Imaginary*. New York: Doran, 1924.

Boyle, T. Coraghessan. *The Road to Wellville*. New York: Viking, 1993.

Bradbury, M. S., ed. *The American Novel and the Nineteen Twenties*. New York: Crane, Russak, 1971.

Brooks, Peter. *Body Work: Objects of Desire in Modern Narrative*. Cambridge: Harvard University Press, 1993.

Brooks, Van Wyck. "From *The Ordeal of Mark Twain*." In *Adventures of Huckleberry Finn*, eds. Scully Bradley, et al, 295–300. New York: Norton, 1977.

Broucek, Francis J. *Shame and the Self*. New York: Guilford, 1991.

Bruccoli, Matthew J., ed. *F. Scott Fitzgerald: A Life in Letters*. New York: Scribners, 1994.

Bruccoli, Matthew J., and Jackson R. Bryer, eds. *F. Scott Fitzgerald in His Own Time: A Miscellany*. Kent: Kent State University Press, 1971.

Bruccoli, Matthew J. and Margaret M. Duggan. *Correspondence of F. Scott Fitzgerald*. New York: Random House, 1980.

Butler, Elizabeth Beardsley. *Women and the Trades: Pittsburgh, 1907–1908*. New York: Charities Publication Committee, 1909. Rpt. with intro. Maurine Weiner Greenwald. Pittsburgh: University of Pittsburgh Press, 1984.

Butler, Robert. "Farrell's Ethnic Neighborhood and Wright's Urban Ghetto: Two Visions of Chicago's South Side." *MELUS* 18 (Spring 1993): 103–11.

Carnes, Mark. *Secret Ritual and Manhood in Victorian America*. New Haven: Yale University Press, 1989.

Carnes, Mark, and Clyde Griffen, eds. *Meanings for Manhood: Constructions of Masculinity in Victorian America*. Chicago: University of Chicago Press, 1990.

Cather, Willa. *Death Comes for the Archbishop*. New York: Vintage, 1990.

———. *My Ántonia*. New York: Houghton Mifflin, 1918.

———. *O Pioneers!*. New York: Dover, 1913.

Cawelti, John. *Apostles of the Self-Made Man*. Chicago: University of Chicago Press, 1965.

Chase, Richard. *The American Novel and Its Tradition*. New York: Doubleday, 1957.

Coltrane, Robert. "The Crafting of Dreiser's *Twelve Men*." *Papers on Language and Literature* 27 (Spring 1991): 191–206.

Cooper, John Milton. *Walter Hines Page: The Southerner as American*. Chapel Hill: University of North Carolina Press, 1977.

Cooper, Patricia A. *Once a Cigar Maker: Men, Women, and Work Culture in American Cigar Factories, 1900–1919*. Urbana: University of Illinois Press, 1987.

Couvares, Francis G. *The Remaking of Pittsburgh: Class and Culture in an Industrializing City, 1877–1919*. Pittsburgh: University of Pittsburgh Press, 1984.

Crane, Stephen. *Great Short Works of Stephen Crane*. New York: Harper and Row, 1965.

———. *"The Open Boat" and Other Stories*. New York: Dover, 1993.

Cushman, Philip. *The Construction of the Self, Constructing America: A Cultural History of Psychotherapy*. Boston: Addison-Wesley, 1995.

Darwin, Charles. *The Portable Darwin*, eds. Duncan Porter and Peter Graham. New York: Penguin, 1993.

DeLillo, Don. *White Noise*. New York: Penguin, 1984.

Doty, Douglass. Letter to Dreiser, 24 September 1913, Dreiser Collection, Van Pelt Library, University of Pennsylvania, Philadelphia.

Dowell, Richard W. "Introduction." In *An Amateur Laborer*, eds. Richard W. Dowell, James L. W. West III, and Neda M. Westlake.

Dreiser, Helen. *My Life with Dreiser*. Cleveland: World, 1951.

Dudley, Dorothy. *Forgotten Frontiers: Dreiser and the Land of the Free*. New York: Harrison Smith and Robert Haas, 1932.

———. "The 'Suppression' Controversy." In Dudley's *Dreiser and the Land of the Free*. New York: Beechhurst, 1946.

Dunn, Ross E. "Curriculum Critics Err." *The San Diego Union Tribune* (7 December 1994): B–5.

Eakin, Paul John. *Touching the World*, Princeton: Princeton University Press, 1992.

Eastman, Yvette. *Dearest Wilding: A Memoir with Love Letters from Theodore Dreiser*. Ed. Thomas P. Riggio. Philadelphia: University of Pennsylvania Press, 1995.

Eby, Clare Virginia. "Jennie Through the Eyes of Thorstein Veblen." In *Dreiser's Jennie Gerhardt*, ed. James L. W. West III, 91–102.

Epstein, Joseph. "E. B. White, Dark & Lite." *Commentary* 81 (April 1986): 48–56.

Fabre, Michel. *The Unfinished Quest of Richard Wright*, New York: William Morrow, 1973.

Farrell, James T. *Judgment Day*. New York: Avon Books, 1973.

———. *The League of Frightened Philistines*. New York: Vanguard, 1945.

———. "Lynch Patterns." *Partisan Review* 4 (May 1938): 57–58.

———. *Reflections at Fifty*. New York: Vanguard, 1954.

———. *Young Lonigan*. New York: Avon Books, 1972.

———. *The Young Manhood of Studs Lonigan*. New York: Avon Books, 1973.

Faulkner, William. *The Sound and the Fury*, 1929. New York: Norton, 1987.

Feis, Herbert. Letters to Dreiser, 9 February 1921, Dreiser Collection, Van Pelt Library, University of Pennsylvania, Philadelphia.

Filene, Peter. "Men and Manliness." In *Him / Her / Self: Sex Roles in Modern America*. New York: New American Library, 1976.

Filippelli, Ronald L. "Fall River Textile Strikes." In *Labor Conflict in the United States: An Encyclopedia*, ed. Ronald L. Filippelli. New York: Garland, 1990, 175–79.

———. "Homestead Strike." In *Labor Conflict in the United States: An Encyclopedia*, ed. Ronald L. Filippelli, 241–46.

Fisher, Philip. *Hard Facts: Setting and Form in the American Novel*. New York: Oxford University Press, 1985.

Fitzgerald, F. Scott. *Babylon Revisited and Other Stories*. New York: Scribners, 1925.

———. *The Beautiful and Damned*. New York: Scribners, 1922.

———. *The Great Gatsby*, 1925. New York: Scribners, 1953.

———. *This Side of Paradise*, 1915. New York: Scribners, 1925.

Foner, Philip S. *Women and the American Labor Movement from Colonial Times to the Eve of World War I*. New York: Free Press, 1979.

Foster, Alasdair. *Behold the Man: The Male Nude in Photography*. Edingburgh: Stills Gallery, 1988.

Foucault, Michel. "Panopticism." In *Discipline and Punish: The Birth of the Prison*, trans. Alan Sheridan, 195–228. New York: Pantheon, 1977.

Freud, Sigmund. *Civilization and Its Discontents*, 1930. Trans. and ed. James Strachey. New York: Norton, 1961.

———. "The Dissolution of the Oedipus Complex," 1924. In *The Standard Edition of the Complete Psychological Works*, trans. James Strachey. London: Hogarth, 1962–66.

———. "Femininity," 1933 Lecture XXXIII. In *New Introductory Lecture on Psychoanalysis*, trans James Strachey, 112–35. New York: Norton, 1965.

———. "Some Psychical Consequences of the Anatomical Distinction between the Sexes," 1925. In *Standard Edition*, 19: 243–58.

———. *Three Contributions to the Theory of Sex*. In *The Basic Writings of Sigmund Freud*, trans. and ed. A. A. Brill. New York: Putnam, 1986.

Fussell, Paul. *Abroad: British Literary Traveling between the Wars*. New York & Oxford: Oxford University Press, 1980.

Galvin, Kevin. "Dole Hints of Blocking Vote on Foster." *Boston Globe* (17 April 1995): 3.

Geismar, Maxwell. *Rebels and Ancestors: The American Novel 1890–1915*. Boston: Houghton Mifflin / Cambridge: Riverside Press, 1953.

Gerber, Philip L. *Theodore Dreiser*. New York: Twayne, 1964.

Gogol, Miriam. "*The 'Genius'*: Dreiser's Testament to Convention." *CLA Journal* 33 (June 1990): 402–14.

———. "Self Sacrifice and Shame in *Jennie Gerhardt*." In *Dreiser's Jennie Gerhardt*, ed. James L. W. West III, 136–46.

Gogol, Miriam, ed. *Theodore Dreiser: Beyond Naturalism*. New York: New York University Press, 1995.

Goldhurst, William. *F. Scott Fitzgerald and His Contemporaries*. New York: World, 1963.

Grebstein, Sheldon N. "Dreiser's Victorian Vamp." In *Sister Carrie*, ed. Donald Pizer, 541–51.

Green, Harvey. *Fit for America: Health, Fitness, Sport and American Society*. New York: Pantheon, 1986.

Greene, William Chase. *Moira: Fate, Good, and Evil in Greek Thought*. Cambridge: Harvard University Press, 1948.

Greenwald, Maurine Weiner. "Introduction: Women at Work through the Eyes of Elizabeth Beardsley Butler and Lewis Hine." In Butler, *Women and the Trades: Pittsburgh, 1907–1908*, 1984, vii–xlv.

Greg, W. W. "The Rationale of Copy Text." In *Bibliography and Textual Criticism: English and American Literature, 1700 to the Present*, eds. O. M. Brack, Jr. and Warner Barnes, 41–58. Chicago: University of Chicago Press, 1969.

Griffin, Joseph. *The Small Canvas: An Introduction to Dreiser's Short Stories*. Rutherford: Fairleigh Dickinson University Press / London & Toronto: Associated University Presses, 1985.

Hakutani, Yoshinobu. "Dreiser and French Realism." *Texas Studies in Literature and Language* 6 (Summer 1964): 200–12.

———. "*Native Son* and *An American Tragedy*: Two Different Interpretations of Crime and Guilt." *Centennial Review* 23 (Spring 1979): 208–26.

———. "*Sister Carrie* and the Problem of Literary Naturalism." *Twentieth Century Literature* 13 (April 1967): 3–17.

———. *Young Dreiser: A Critical Study*. Rutherford: Fairleigh Dickinson University Press / London & Toronto: Associated University Presses, 1980.

Hancher, Michael. "Three Kinds of Intention." *Modern Language Notes* 87 (1972): 827–51.

Handy, William J. "A Re-examination of Dreiser's *Sister Carrie*." *Texas Studies in Literature and Language* 1 (Autumn 1959): 380–93.

Hapke, Laura. *Tales of the Working Girl: Wage-Earning Women in American Literature, 1890–1925*. New York: Twayne / Macmillan, 1992.

Hermeren, Goran. *Influence in Art and Literature*. Princeton: Princeton University Press, 1975.

Hogan, Patrick Colm. *Joyce, Milton, and the Theory of Influence*. Gainesville: University Press of Florida, 1995.

Holman, Hugh C. and William Harmon. *A Handbook to Literature*, ed. Barbara A. Heinssen. New York: Macmillan, 1992.

Hovey, Richard B., and Ruth S. Ralph. "Dreiser's *The 'Genius'*: Motivation and Structure." *Hartford Studies in Literature* 2 (1970): 169–83.

Howe, Iring. "Afterword." In Theodore Dreiser, *An American Tragedy*, 815–28. New York: New American Library, 1964.

Howells, William Dean. *A Modern Instance*, 1882. Boston: Houghton Mifflin, 1957.

Hurston, Zola Neale. "Stories of Conflict." *Saturday Review of Literature* 17 (2 April 1938): 32.

Hussman, Lawrence E. "Jennie One-Note: Dreiser's Error in Character Development." In *Dreiser's Jennie Gerhardt*, ed. James L. W. West III, 43–50.

Hutchisson, James M. "Death and Dying in *Jennie Gerhardt*." In *Dreiser's Jennie Gerhardt*, ed. James L. W. West III, 208–17.

Irigaray, Luce. *This Sex Which Is Not One*. Trans. Catherine Porter and Carolyn Burke. Ithaca: Cornell University Press, 1985.

Jackson, Blyden. "Richard Wright in a Moment of Truth." In *Modern American Fiction: Form and Function*, ed. Thomas Daniel. Baton Rouge: Louisiana State University Press, 1989.

James, Henry. "The Art of Fiction." In *The Art of Criticism: Henry James on the Theory and the Practice of Fiction*, eds. William Veeder and Susan M. Griffin, 165–83. Chicago: University of Chicago Press, 1986.

Jameson, Fredric. *The Political Unconscious: Narrative as a Socially Symbolic Act*. London: Methuen, 1981.

———. *Postmodernism, or, the Cultural Logic of Late Capitalism*. Durham: Duke University Press, 1991.

Kaplan, Amy. "Romancing the Empire: The Embodiment of American Masculinity in the Popular Historical Novel of the 1890s." *American Literary History* 2.4 (1990): 659–90

———. *The Social Construction of American Realism.* Chicago: University of Chicago Press, 1988.

Karen, Robert. "Shame." *Atlantic Monthly* 269 (February 1992): 40–70.

Kaufman, Gershen. *Shame: The Power of Caring*, 2d ed. Cambridge: Schenkman, 1985.

Kazin, Alfred. "Introduction: Theodore Dreiser and *Sister Carrie* Restored." In *Sister Carrie*, eds. James L. W. West III et al, vii–xviii. New York: Penguin, 1981.

Kazin, Alfred, and Charles Shapiro, eds. *The Stature of Theodore Dreiser.* Bloomington: Indiana Univeristy Press, 1955.

Kinnamon, Keneth. *The Emergence of Richard Wright.* Urbana: University of Illinois Press, 1972.

Kinnamon, Keneth, and Michel Fabre, eds. *Conversations with Richard Wright.* Jackson: University Press of Mississippi, 1993.

Klein, Melanie. "Love, Guilt and Reparation." In Melanie Klein and Joan Riviere, *Love, Hate and Reparation: Two Lectures*, 54–117. London: Hogarth, 1967.

Knapp, Steven, and Walter Benn Michaels. "Against Theory." In *Against Theory: Literary Studies and the New Pragmatism*, ed. W. J. T. Mitchell. Chicago: University of Chicago Press, 1985.

Lacan, Jacques. "The Meaning of the Phallus." In *Feminine Sexuality: Jacques Lacan and the Ecole Freudienne*, eds. Juliet Mitchell and Jacqueline Rose, and trans. Jacqueline Rose. New York: Norton, 1982.

Lapham, Lewis. "Reactionary Chic: How the Nineties Right Recycles the Bombast of the Sixties Left." *Harper's Magazine* (March 1995).

Lehan, Richard. *Theodore Dreiser: His World and His Novels.* Carbondale: Southern Illinois University Press, 1969.

Leverenz, David. "The Last Real Man in America: From Natty Bumppo to Batman." In *Fictions of Masculinity*, ed. Peter F. Murphy, 21–53. New York: New York University Press, 1994.

———. *Manhood and the American Renaissance.* Ithaca: Cornell University Press, 1989.

———. "Manhood, Humiliation and Public Life: Some Stories." *Southwest Review* 71 (August 1986): 442–62.

Lewis, Clive Staples. *Pilgrim's Regress.* Grand Rapids: Erdmans, 1958.

Lewis, Helen B. *Shame and Guilt in Neurosis.* New York: International Universities Press, 1971.

Lingeman, Richard. "The Biographical Significance of *Jennie Gerhardt.*" In *Dreiser's Jennie Gerhardt*, ed. James L. W. West III, 9–16.

———. *Theodore Dreiser: An American Journey, 1908–1945.* vol. 2. New York: Putnam, 1990.

———. *Theodore Dreiser: At the Gates of the City, 1871–1907.* vol. 1. New York: Putnam, 1986.

Lipton, Eunice. "The Laundress in Late Nineteenth-Century French Culture." *Art History* 3 (September 1980): 295–313.

Liveright, Horace. Note to Dreiser, 12 March 1923, Dreiser Collection, Van Pelt Library, University of Pennsylvania, Philadelphia.

London, Bette. "Mary Shelly, *Frankenstein*, and the Spectacle of Masculinity." *PMLA* 108.2 (1993): 235–67.

Long, Robert E. "*Sister Carrie* and the Rhythm of Failure in Fitzgerald." *Fitzgerald Newsletter* no. 28 (Spring 1964): 2.

Lutz, Tom. *American Nervousness, 1903: An Anecdotal History.* Ithaca: Cornell University Press, 1991.

Malkiel, Theresa Serber. *The Diary of a Shirtwaist Striker*, 1910. Rpt. Ithaca: ILR Press, 1990.

Marquis, Don. *Dreams and Dust.* New York: Harper and Brothers, 1950.

Marx, Leo. *The Machine in the Garden: Technology and the Pastoral Ideal in America.* New York: Oxford University Press, 1964.

Matthiessen, F. O. *Theodore Dreiser*. New York: William Sloane, 1951.

Mayfield, Sara. "Another Fitzgerald Myth Exploded by Mencken." *Fitzgerald Newsletter* no.32 (Winter 1966): 207.

McCall, Dan. *The Example of Richard Wright.* New York: Harcourt, Brace, 1969.

McCullough, David. *Mornings on Horseback.* New York: Simon and Schuster, 1981.

McGovern, James. "David Graham Philips and the Virility Impulse of Progressives." *New England Quarterly* 39 (1966): 334–55.

Mencken, H. L. Review of *Jennie Gerhardt*, November 1911, "A Novel of the First Rank." In *Theodore Dreiser: The Critical Reception*, ed. Jack Salzman, 61–64.

Michaels, Walter Benn. "Dreiser's *Financier*: The Man of Business as a Man of Letters." In *American Realism: New Essays*, ed. Eric J. Sundquist. Baltimore & London: Johns Hopkins University Press, 1982.

———. *The Gold Standard and the Logic of Naturalism: American Literature at the Turn of the Century*. Berkeley: University of California Press, 1987.

———. "*Sister Carrie*'s Popular Economy." *Critical Inquiry* 7 (1980): 373–90.

Minter, David. *A Cultural History of the American Novel: Henry James to William Faulkner*. New York: Cambridge University Press, 1994.

Mitchell, Lee Clark. *Determined Fictions: American Literary Naturalism.* New York: Columbia University Press, 1989.

Mitchell, Stephen A. *Hope and Dread in Psychoanalysis.* New York: Basic books, 1992.

Mizener, Arthur. *The Far Side of Paradise.* Boston: Houghton Mifflin, 1951.

Mores, Ellen. *Two Dreisers.* New York: Viking, 1969.

Morrison, Andrew P. *Shame: The Underside of Narcissism.* Hillsdale: Analytic Press, 1989.

Morrison, Toni. *Beloved.* New York: Plume, 1987.

Mukherjee, Arun. *The Gospel of Wealth in the American Novel: The Rhetoric of Dreiser and Some of His Contemporaries.* London: Croom Helm / Totowa: Barnes and Noble, 1987.

———. "*Sister Carrie* at Ninety: An Indian Response." *Dreiser Studies* 21 (Fall 1990): 27–39.

Mulvey, Laura. "Visual Pleasure and Narrative Cinema." *Screen* 16 (Autumn 1975): 6–18.

Mumford, Kevin. " 'Lost Manhood' Found: Male Sexual Impotence and Victorian Culture in the United States." In *American Sexual Politics: Sex, Gender and Race Since the Civil War*, eds. John Fout and Maura Tantillo, 75–99. Chicago: University of Chicago Press, 1993.

Neal, Steve. "Masculinity as Spectacle: Reflections on Men and Mainstream Cinema." *Screen* 24.6 (1983): 2–16.

Norris, Frank. *McTeague*, 1899. New York: Doubleday, 1928.

———. *The Octopus*, 1901. New York: Doubleday, 1956.

Ong, Walter J. *Orality and Literacy: The Technologizing of the Word*. London and New York: Methuen, 1982.

Parrington, Vernon Louis. *The Beginnings of Critical Realism*, vol. 3 of *Main Currents in American Thought*. New York: Harcourt, Brace, 1930.

Person, Ethel S., M. D. *By Force of Fantasy: How We Make Our Lives*. New York: Basic Books, 1995.

Piers, Gerhart, and Milton Singer, eds. *Shame and Guilt: A Psychoanalytic and a Cultural Study*. Springfield: Thomas, 1953.

Pizer, Donald. "Nineteenth-Century American Naturalism: An Essay in Definition." *Bucknell Review* 13 (December 1965): 1–18.

———. *The Novels of Theodore Dreiser: A Critical Study*. Minneapolis: University of Minnesota Press, 1976.

———. "The Problem of Philosophy in the Novel." *Bucknell Review* 18 (March 1970): 53–62.

———. "The Strike." In *Sister Carrie*, ed. Donald Pizer, 416.

Pizer, Donald, ed. *Critical Essays on Theodore Dreiser*. Boston: G. K. Hall, 1981.

Powys, Llewelyn. *The Verdict of Bridlegoose*. New York: Harcourt, Brace, 1926.

Rascoe, Burton. *We Were Interrupted*. New York: Doubleday, 1947.

Reiss, Kathy. *Cheap Amusements: Working Women and Leisure in Turn-of-the-Century New York*. Philadelphia, Temple University Press, 1986.

Richards, Grant. *Author Hunting by an Old Literary Sportsman: Memories of Years Spent Mainly in Publishing, 1887–1925*. New York: Coward-McCann, 1934.

Richardson, Dorothy. *The Long Day: The Story of a New York Working Girl, as Told by Herself*. New York: Century, 1905. Rpt. *The Long Day: The Story of a New York Working Girl*, intro. Cindy Sondik Aron. Charlottesville: University Press of Virginia, 1990.

Riggio, Thomas P. "Dreiser on Society and Literature: The San Francisco Exposition Interview." *American Literary Realism* 11 (Autumn 1978): 284–94.

———. "Europe without Baedeker: The Omitted Hanscha Jower Story—from *A Traveler at Forty*." *Modern Fiction Studies* 23 (Autumn 1977): 423–40.

———. "Introduction." In *Theodore Dreiser: The American Diaries, 1902–1926*, ed. Thomas P. Riggio. Philadelphia: University of Pennsylvania Press, 1982.

Romero, Lora. "Vanishing American: Gender, Empire, and New Historicism." *American Literature* 63 (September 1991): 385–404.

Roosevelt, Theodore. *The Letters of Theodore Roosevelt*, ed. Elting Morrison. Cambridge: Harvard University Press, 1951.

———. *Ranch Life and the Hunting-Trail*, 1888. Rpt. Ann Arbor: University of Michigan Microfilms, 1966.

Rosenberg, Charles E. "Sexuality, Class and Role in 19th-Century America." In *The American Man*, selected by Elizabeth Pleck and Joseph Pleck, 219–54. Englewood Cliffs: Prentice-Hall, 1980.

Ross, Valerie. "Chill History and Rueful Sentiments in *Jennie Gerhardt*." In *Dreiser's Jennie Gerhardt*, ed. James L. W. West III, 27–42.

Rotundo, E. Anthony. *American Manhood: Transformations in Masculinity from the Revolution to the Modern Era*. New York: Basic Books, 1993.

———. "Body and Soul: Changing Ideals of American Middle-Class Manhood, 1770–1920." *Journal of Social History* 16 (1982): 23–38.

Rueckert, William H. *Kenneth Burke and the Drama of Human Relations*, 2d ed. Berkeley: University of California Press, 1982.

Salzman, Jack. "The Editor's Preface." *Modern Fiction Studies* 23 (Autumn 1977): 339–40.

———. "The Publication of *Sister Carrie*: Fact and Fiction." *Library Chronicle* of the University of Pennsylvania 33 (Spring 1967): 119–33.

Salzman, Jack, ed. *Theodore Dreiser: The Critical Reception*. New York: David Lewis, 1972.

Sampson, Edward. *E. B. White*. New York: Twayne, 1974.

Satre, Jean Paul. *Being and Nothingness: An essay on Phenomenological Ontology*, trans. Hazel Barnes. New York: Philosophical Library, 1956.

Schneider, Carl. *Shame, Exposure and Privacy*. Boston: Beacon, 1977.

Scott, Frank H. Letter to Dreiser, 18 November 1911, Dreiser Collection, Van Pelt Library, University of Pennsylvania, Philadelphia.

Scott, Joan Wallach. "Gender: A Useful Category of Analysis." *American Historical Review* 91.5 (1986).

———. *Gender and the Politics of History*. New York: Columbia University Press, 1988.

Sedgwick, Eva Kosofsky. *Between Men: English Literature and Male Homosocial Desire*. New York: Columbia University Press, 1985.

———. "Introduction" and "Gender Asymmetry and Erotic Triangles." Rpt. in *Feminisms: An Anthology of Literary Theory and Criticism*, eds. Robyn Warhol and Diane Price Herndl, 463–86. New Brunswick: Rutgers University Press, 1991.

Seidler, Victor. "Fathering, Authority and Masculinity." In *Male Order: Unwrapping Masculinity*, 272–99. London: Lawrence and Wishart, 1988.

Seltzer, Mark. "The Love-Master." In *Engendering Men: The Question of Male Feminist Criticism*, eds. Joseph Boone and Michael Cadden, 140–58. New York: Routledge, 1990.

Sherman, Stuart P. "The Naturalism of Mr. Dreiser." *Nation* 101 (December 2, 1915): 648–50.

Showalter, Elaine. *Sexual Anarchy: Gender and Culture at the Fin de Siecle*. New York: Viking, 1990.

Sklar, Robert. *F. Scott Fitzgerald: The Last Laocoon*. New York: Oxford University Press, 1967.

Smith-Rosenberg, Carroll. *Disorderly Conduct: Visions of Gender in Victorian America*. New York: Knopf, 1985.

Solomon, Eric. "A Source for Fitzgerald's *The Great Gatsby*." *Modern Language Notes* 73 (March 1958): 186–88.

Spence, Johathan. *To Change China: Western Advisers in China, 1620–1960*. New York: Penguin, 1980.

St. Jean, Shawn. "Social Deconstruction and *An American Tragedy*." *Dreiser Studies* 28 (Spring 1997): 3–24.

Steinbeck, John. *The Long Valley*. New York: Viking, 1956.

Steinhoff, William. " 'The Door': 'The Professor,' 'My Friend the Poet (Deceased),' 'The Washable House,' and 'The Man Out in Jersey.' " *College English* 23 (December 1961): 229–32.

Stepanchev, Stephen. "Dreiser among the Critics." Ph. D. Dissertation, New York University, 1950.

Stewart, Randall. "Dreiser and the Naturalistic Heresy." *Virginia Quarterly Review* 34 (Winter 1958): 100–16.

Susman, Warren I. *Culture as History*. New York: Pantheon Books, 1984.

Swanberg, W. A. *Dreiser*. New York: Scribners, 1965.

Tanselle, G. Thomas. "The Editorial Problem of Final Authorial Intention." *Studies in Bibliography* 29 (1976): 167–211.

Tate, Allen. "Techniques of Fiction," 1948. In *Visions and Revisions in Modern American Literary Criticism*, eds. Bernard S. Oldsey and Arther O. Lewis, Jr., 81–96. New York: E. P. Dutton, 1962.

Tax, Meredith. *The Rising of the Women: Feminist Solidarity and Class Conflict, 1880–1917*. New York: Monthly Review Press, 1980.

Tentler, Leslie Woodcock. *Wage-Earning Women: Industrial Work and Family Life in the United States, 1900–1930*. New York: Oxford University Press, 1979.

Thrane, Gary. "Shame and the Construction of the Self." *The Annual of Psychoanalysis* 7 (1979): 321–41.

Tomkins, Silvan. *Affect / Imagery / Consciousness*. New York: Springer, 1962, 1963.

———. "Shame." In *The Many Faces of Shame*, ed. Nathan Donaldson, 133–61. New York: Guilford Press, 1987.

Trachtenberg, Alan. *The Incorporation of America: Culture and Society in the Gilded Age*. New York: Hill and Wang, 1982.

Trilling, Lionel. "Reality in America." In *The Liberal Imagination: Essays on Literature and Society*. New York: Viking, 1950.

Turner, Frederick Jackson. "The Frontier in American History," 1920. Rpt. in *The Historians' History of the United States*, vol. 1, eds. Andrew S. Berky and James P. Shenton, 462–73. New York: Putnam, 1966.

Twain, Mark. *A Connecticut Yankee in King Arthur's Court*, 1889. New York: Signet, n. d.

Uchida, Yoshitsugu. "A Conflict between Spirituality and Material Civilization in *Sister Carrie*." *Mimesis* 19 (1987): 1–8.

Van Every, Edward. *Muldoon the Solid Man of Sport: His Amazing Story as Related for the First Time by Him to His Friend*. New York: Stokes, 1929.

von Bardeleben, Renate. "Central Europe in Travelogues by Theodore Dreiser: Images of Berlin and Vienna." In *Images of Central Europe in Travelogues and Fiction by North American Writers*, ed. Waldemar Zacharasiewicz, 144–58. Tübingen: Stauffenburg Verlag, 1995.

———. "Dreiser on the European Continent. Part One: Theodore Dreiser, the German Dreisers and Germany." *Dreiser Newsletter* 2 (1971): 4–10

———. "Dreiser's English Virgil." In *Literatur im Kontext—Literature in Context*, eds. Joachim Schwend et al, 345–71. Frankfurt a. M.: Peter Lang, 1992.

———. "Personal, Ethnic, and National Identity: Theodore Dreiser's Difficult Heritage." In *Interdisziplinarität: Deutsche Sprache und Literatur im Spannungsfeld der Kulturen*, eds. Martin Forstner and Klaus von Schilling, 319–40. Frankfurt a. M.: Peter Lang, 1991.

Wanambisi, Monica. "Eight Exemplars of the Twentieth-Century American Novel, 1900–1959." Ph. D. Dissertation, Atlanta University, 1987.

Weiss, Richard. *The American Myth of Success: From Horatio Alger to Norman Vincent Peale*. Urbana: University of Illinois Press, 1988.

West, James L. W. III. "The Composition and Publication of *Jennie Gerhardt*." In *Jennie Gerhadt*, ed. James L. W. West III, 421–56.

———. "Editorial Theory and the Act of Submission." *The Papers of the Bibliographical Society of America* 83 (1983): 169–85.

———. "Fair Copy, Authorial Intention, and 'Versioning.' " *Text: Transactions of Society of Textual Scholarship* 6 (1994): 81–89.

———. "General Assessments." In *Dreiser's Jennie Gerhardt*, ed. James L. W. West III, vii–ix.

———. "Introduction." In Dreiser, *An Amateur Laborer*, eds. Richard W. Dowell et al., xi–lv.

———. *A "Sister Carrie" Portfolio*. Charlottesville: University Press of Virginia, 1985.

———. "The Scholarly Editor as Biographer." *Studies in the Novel* 27 (Fall 1995): 295–303.

West, James L. W. III, ed. *Dreiser's Jennie Gerhardt: New Essays on the Restored Text*. Philadelphia: University of Pennsylvania Press, 1995.

Wheelock, Geo. L. Letter to Dreiser, 12 March 1923, Dreiser Collection, Van Pelt Library, University of Pennsylvania, Philadelphia.

White, E. B. *Letters of E. B. White*, ed. Dorothy Lobrano Guth. New York: Harper and Row, 1976.

———. *The Second Tree from the Corner*. New York: Harper and Brothers, 1954.

Wilson, B. F. "Notes on Personalities." *Smart Set* (April 1924): 33.

Wilson, Christopher P. "Labor and Capital in *Jennie Gerhardt*." In *Dreiser's Jennie Gerhardt*, ed. James L. W. West III, 103–14.

———. "*Sister Carrie* Again." *American Literature* 53 (May 1981): 287–90.

Wilson, Edmund, ed. *The Crack-Up*. New York: New Directions, 1945.

Winkler, Karen J. "Seductions of Biography." *The Chronicle of Higher Education* 27 (October 1993): A6.

Wolfe, Thomas. *Look Homeward Angel*. New York: Scribners, 1929.

———. *The Web and the Rock*. New York: Sun Dial, 1940.

Wright, Richard. *American Hunger*. New York: Harper and Row, 1979.

———. "Big Boy Leaves Home." In *Uncle Tom's Children*, 1940. New York: Harper and Row, 1965.

———. *Black Boy: A Record of Childhood and Youth*, 1945. New York: Harper and Row, 1966.

———. "Blueprint for Negro Writing," 1937. Rpt. in *Richard Wright Reader*, eds. Ellen Wright and Michel Fabre, 36–49. New York: Harper and Row, 1978.

———. *Conversations with Richard Wright*, eds. Keneth Kinnamon and Michel Fabre. Jackson: University Press of Mississippi, 1993.

———. "How 'Bigger'Was Born," 1940. In *Native Son*, vii–xxiv. New York: Harper and Row, 1966.

———. "The Man Who Went to Chicago." In *Eight Men*, 210–50. Cleveland: World, 1961.

———. *Native Son*, 1940. New York: Harper and Row, 1966.

Wurmser, Leon. *The Mask of Shame*. Baltimore & London: Johns Hopkins University Press, 1981.

———. "Shame: The Veiled Companion of Narcissism." In *The Many Faces of Shame*, ed. Donald Nathanson, 64–92. New York: Guilford Press, 1987.

Wyllie, Irvin. *The Self-Made Man in America*. New York: Free Press, 1954.

Zaluda, Scott. "The Secrets of Fraternity: Men and Friendship in *Sister Carrie*." In *Theodore Dreiser: Beyond Naturalism*, ed. Miriam Gogol, 77–94. New York: New York University Press, 1995.

Contributors

STEPHEN C. BRENNAN, Associate Professor of English at Louisiana State University, Shreveport, is the coauthor (with Stephen R. Yarbrough) of *Irving Babbitt* (1987), and currently the coeditor (with Keith Newlin) of *Dreiser Studies.* His articles on Dreiser have appeared in journals such as *Dreiser Studies*, *Studies in the Novel*, *Studies in American Fiction*, and *American Literary Realism*.

ROBERT BUTLER is Professor of English at Canisius College in Buffalo. His publications include *Native Son: The Emergence of a New Black Hero* (1991), *The City in African-American Literature* (coeditor with Yoshinobu Hakutani, 1995), *The Open Journey in Contemporary Black Literature* (1998), and many articles on various topics in *Dreiser Newsletter*, *American Studies*, *Centennial Review*, *Black American Literature Forum*, *African American Review*, *MELUS*, and *CLA Journal*.

KATHY FREDERICKSON has been teaching in the Massachusetts Community College system since 1982, frequently working with military personnel, inmates in Massachusetts Correctional Institutes and in reentry women in Adult Education Programs. In addition to collaborating on classroom projects, her research interests include Dreiser, late-nineteenth and early-twentieth-century American literature, feminist literary criticism, and contemporary American women's fiction and autobiography.

PHILIP GERBER, SUNY Distinguished Professor of English at the State University of New York, Brockport, is the author of many books on various subjects, including *Theodore Dreiser* (1964), *Robert Frost* (1966), *Willa Cather* (1975), *The Plots and Characters in the Fiction of Theodore Dreiser* (1977), *Critical Essays on Robert Frost* (editor, 1982), *Bachelor Bess: the Homesteading Letters of Elizabeth Corey* (editor, 1990), and *Theodore Dreiser Revisited* (1992). He is coediting *The Financier* for the Pennsylvania Dreiser Edition and writing a history of the Trilogy of Desire.

MIRIAM GOGOL, Professor of English at State University of New York Fashion Institute of Technology, is cofounder and past president of the

International Dreiser Society. The editor of *Theodore Dreiser: Beyond Naturalism* (1995), she also has written on Dreiser and other writers.

YOSHINOBU HAKUTANI, Professor of English at Kent State University in Ohio, is General Editor of the Peter Lang series "Modern American Literature." His publications include *Young Dreiser: A Critical Study* (1980); *Critical Essays on Richard Wright* (editor, 1982); *Selected Magazine Articles of Theodore Dreiser: Life and Art in the American 1890s* (editor, 1985–87); *Selected English Writings of Yone Noguchi: An East-West Literary Assimilation* (editor, 1990–92); *The City in African-American Literature* (coeditor with Robert Butler, 1995); *Richard Wright and Racial Discourse* (1996); *Haiku: This Other World* by Richard Wright (coeditor with Robert L. Tener, 1998); Theodore Dreiser, *Art, Music, and Literature, 1897–1902* (editor, 2000).

LAURA HAPKE, Professor of English at Pace University in New York, is the author of *Girls Who Went Wrong: Prostitutes in American Fiction, 1885–1917* (1989); *Tales of the Working Girl: Wage-Earning Women in American Literature, 1890–1925* (1992); *Daughters of the Great Depression: Women, Work, and Fiction in the American 1930s* (1995); and many articles and book chapters on women in American fiction.

LAWRENCE E. HUSSMAN is Professor of English at Wright State University in Ohio. Among his books are *Dreiser and His Fiction: A Twentieth-Century Quest* (1983), *Love That Will Not Let Me Go: My Time with Theodore Dreiser* by Marguerite Tjader (editor, 1998), and *Harbingers of a Century: The Novels of Frank Norris* (1999). He also has written many articles and book chapters on Dreiser and other subjects.

MARSHA S. MOYER is a Teaching Assistant in American history at the University of California, San Diego. Her work on *Sister Carrie* won her a History Graduate Student Writing Prize in 1994 from San Diego State University. Writing a doctoral dissertation on the cultural politics of the Northern California timber industry during the 1980s, she is also interested in examining the cultural and intellectual currents which flow between the public discourses of the environmentalist movement, the New Left, and radical feminist thought.

SHAWN ST. JEAN, Visiting Assistant Professor of English at State University of New York at Fredonia, wrote his doctoral dissertation on Dreiser and Greek mythology at Kent State University. He has published articles on Dreiser and other topics in *Dreiser Studies*, *Studies in the Hu-*

manities, *James Joyce Quarterly*, *The Massachusetts Review*, *Religion and Literature*, *Studies in Bibliography*, and *Studies in Short Fiction*.

KIYOHIKO MURAYAMA, Professor of English at Tokyo Metropolitan University, is the author of *A Study of Theodore Dreiser: America and Tragedy* in Japanese (1987). He published the newest Japanese translation (1997) of the Doubleday edition of *Sister Carrie* with an extensive textual apparatus on both editions. In addition to several books and many articles in Japanese, his work has appeared in *Dreiser Studies* and *CLA Journal*. He is now at work on a book about travel writing in the American 1930s.

THOMAS P. RIGGIO, Professor of English at the University of Connecticut, is General Editor of the University of Pennsylvania Dreiser Edition. Among his editions are *Theodore Dreiser: American Diaries, 1902–1926* (with James L. W. West III and Neda M. Westlake, 1982); *Dreiser-Mencken Letters* (1986); *Dearest Wilding: A Memoir with Love Letters from Theodore Dreiser by Yvette Eastman* (1995); and *Dreiser's Russian Diary* (with James L. W. West III, 1996). Author of many essays on Dreiser and other American writers, he also is writing a Dreiser biography.

RENATE VON BARDELEBEN is University Professor at Institut für Anglistik und Amerikanistik, Johannes Gutenberg-Universität Mainz, in Germany. Among her books are *Das Bild New Yorks im Erzahlwerk von Dreiser und Dos Passos* (1967); *Studien zur amerikanischen Autobiographie: Benjamin Franklin und Mark Twain* (1981); *Missions in Conflict: Essays on U.S.-Mexican Relations and Chicano Culture* (editor, 1986); and *Gender, Self, and Society: Proceedings of the IV International Conference on the Hispanic Cultures of the United States* (editor, 1993).

JAMES L. W. WEST III, Distinguished Professor of English at Pennsylvania State University, is Textual Editor of the University of Pennsylvania Dreiser Edition and General Editor of the Cambridge Edition of the Works of F. Scott Fitzgerald. His editions include *Sister Carrie* (with John C. Berkey, Alice M. Winters, and Neda M. Westlake, 1981), *Theodore Dreiser: American Diaries, 1902–1926* (with Thomas P. Riggio and Neda M. Westlake, 1982), *An Amateur Laborer* (with Richard W. Dowell and Neda M. Westlake, 1983), *Jennie Gerhardt* (1992), *Jennie Gerhardt: New Essays on the Restored Text* (1995), and *Dreiser's Russian Diary* (with Thomas P. Riggio, 1996). He also is the author of *A Sister Carrie Portfolio* (1985) and *William Styron: A Life* (1998).

ANNEMAIRE KONING WHALEY, Assistant Professor of English at East Texas Baptist University, is now completing her doctorate in English at

Louisiana State University in Baton Rouge, where she is doing additional work on textual editing in *Jennie Gerhardt*. She has presented papers at many conferences and published articles in *The Encyclopedia of British Women Writers*, *The Cyclopedia of World Authors*, and *Identities and Issues in Literature*.

Index

Adams, J. Donald: "Speaking of Books," 273
Addams, Jane, 136
Aeschylus, 207; *Agamemnon*, 206; *Oresteia* 207; *Prometheus Bound* 207, 209, 211; *Prometheus the Firebringer*, 207, 211; *Prometheus Unbound*, 207
Åhnebrink, Lars, 23, 36; *The Beginnings of Naturalism in American Fiction*, 36
Albertine, Susan: "Triangulating Desire in *Jennie Gerhardt*," 176
Alger, Horatio, 131, 137
Algren, Nelson, 14, 249, 271; *Never Come Morning*, 271
Allen, Woody, 17, 232; *Deconstructing Harry*, 232
Allerton, S. W., 81
Anderson, Sherwood, 14, 47, 54, 235, 247, 272; "An Apology for Crudity," 54; *Sherwood Anderson's Memoirs*, 247
Anthony, E. James, 124, 136; "Shame, Guilt, and the Feminine Self in Psychoanalysis," 136
Appleby, Joyce: *Telling the Truth about History*, 53
Armour, Philip D., 28, 37, 81
Ashforth, Albert, 193
Aswell, Edward, 255
Atkinson, Michael, 256–57, 272; "Richard Wright's 'Big Boy Leaves Home' and a Tale from Ovid: A Metamorphosis Transformed," 272
Auchincloss, Louis, 14, 30, 37–38; "Introduction to *Sister Carrie*," 37
Auerbach, Erich: *Mimesis*, 76

Bakhtin, Mikhail, 71, 73–74; *Problems of Dostoevsky's Poetics*, 71
Baldwin, James, 250, 265, 272; "Many thousands Gone," 272; *Notes of a Native Son*, 272
Balzac, Honoré de, 34, 68, 76, 242, 280
Barker-Benfield, G. J.: *Horrors of the Half-Known Life: Male Attitudes toward Women and Sexuality in Nineteenth-Century America*, 135
Barrineau, Nancy Warner: "Housework Is Never Done: Domestic Labor in *Jennie Gerhardt*," 176
Barthelme, Donald, 222
Bassuk, Ellen: "The Rest Cure: Repetition or Resolution of Victorian Women's Conflicts?" 137
Bastida, Maria, 183
Bate, Walter Jackson: *The Burden of the Past and the English Poet*, 238, 247
Beard, George M., 128, 136; *American Nervousness*, 136
Becker, George J.: *Documents of Modern Literary Realism*, ed., 37
Beer, Thomas, 42, 54; *The Mauve Decade*, 54
Bellow, Saul, 14, 249, 271
Bentham, Jeremy, 120
Berger, John, 124–25, 136; *Ways of Seeing*, 136
Berkey, John C.: *Sister Carrie* (1981), eds., 63
Bible, the, 203
Blaine, Amory, 236
Bloom, Harold, 195, 236, 241, 247; *The Anxiety of Influence: A Theory of Poetry*, 247
Bouguereau, Adolphe William, 96
Bowlby, Rachel, 66–67, 69; *Just Looking*, 66
Boyd, Ernest, 235, 247; *Portraits: Real and Imaginary*, 247

Boyle, T. Coraghessan: *The Road to Wellville*, 134
Bradbury, M. S.: *The American Novel and the Nineteen Twenties*, ed., 247
Brennan, Stephen C., 16, 138, 193; "This Sex Which Is One: Language and the Masculine Self in *Jennie Gerhardt*," 16, 138
Brill, A. A.: *The Basic Writings of Sigmund Freud*, trans. and ed., 156
Brooks, Gwendolyn, 249
Brooks, Peter, 147, 156; *Body Work: Objects of Desire in Modern Narrative*, 156
Brooks, Van Wyck, 271, 273; *The Ordeal of Mark Twain*, 273
Broucek, Francis J., 119, 122, 126, 134, 136; *Shame and the Self*, 134
Bruccoli, Matthew J.: *Correspondence of F. Scott Fitzgerald*, eds., 247; *F. Scott Fitzgerald: A Life in Letters*, ed., 247; *F. Scott Fitzgerald in His Own Time: A Miscellany*, eds., 247
Bryer, Jackson R.: *F. Scott Fitzgerald in His Own Time: A Miscellany*, eds., 247
Burke, Carolyn: *This Sex Which Is Not One*, trans., 156
Burke, Kenneth, 232
Butler, Elizabeth Beardsley, 107–8, 114; *Women and the Trades: Pittsburgh, 1907–1908*, 107, 114
Butler, Robert, 18, 274, 289; "Farrell's Ethnic Neighborhood and Wright's Urban Ghetto: Two Visions of Chicago's South Side," 289; "Urban Frontiers, Neighborhoods, and Traps: The City in Dreiser's *Sister Carrie*, Farrell's *Studs Lonigan*, and Wright's *Native Son*," 18, 274

Caldwell, Erskine, 243, 272
Calmer, Alan, 250
Campbell, Louise, 193–94
Camus, Albert, 252, 272
Carnegie, Andrew, 78, 106
Carnes, Mark, 122, 133, 135; *Meanings for Manhood: Constructions of Masculinity in Victorian America*, eds., 133; *Secret Ritual and Manhood in Victorian America*, 135
Cather, Willa, 14, 219–21; *Death Comes for the Archbishop*, 221; *My Ántonia*, 220; *O Pioneers!*, 220; "Paul's Case," 220; "Prairie Spring," 220
Cawelti, John, 131, 137; *Apostles of the Self-Made Man*, 137
Chase, Richard, 27, 37; *The American Novel and Its Tradition*, 37
Cheney, Lynn, 53
Chiang Kai-shek, 55
Coates, Astrid P., 232
Coltrane, Robert, 115, 131–33; "The Crafting of Dreiser's *Twelve Men*," 133
Conrad, Joseph, 236
Conroy, Jack, 14
Cooper, James Fenimore, 37, 248–49; *The Deerslayer*, 290
Cooper, John Milton: *Walter Hines Page: The Southerner as American*, 54
Cooper, Patricia A.: *Once a Cigar Maker: Men, Women, and Work Culture in American Cigar Factories, 1900–1919*, 114
Corot, Jean Baptiste Camille, 96
Couvares, Francis, 113
Crane, Stephen, 13, 25, 36, 104, 106, 113, 204, 214–18, 225, 231, 253, 255, 272; *Great Short Works of Stephen Crane*, 272; *Maggie: A Girl of the Streets*, 104, 113, 215–17, 253–54; "The Open Boat," 225; *The Red Badge of Courage*, 25, 36
Cudlipp, Thelma, 95, 138, 155–56, 183
Cushman, Philip: *The Construction of the Self, Constructing America: A Cultural History of Psychotherapy*, 135

Dana, Charles A., 126
Darwin, Charles, 47, 135, 214; "The Expression of the Emotions in Man Animals," 135; *The Portable Darwin*, 135
Davis, Jefferson, 267
DeLillo, Don, 228–31; *White Noise*, 228–30

DeLong, Robert L. Jr., 232
Dickens, Charles, 252
Dickey, James, 14
Dole, Robert, 132, 137
Dostoevsky, Fëdor Mikhailovich, 71, 73–75, 272
Doty, Douglas Z., 179–80, 186
Doubleday, Frank, 23, 36, 49
Doubleday, Nellie, 15, 23, 36, 39–52
Dowell, Richard W., 113, 118, 132–34; "Introduction to *An Amateur Laborer*," 134
Dreiser, Helen Richardson, 192, 243, 264, 272; *My Life with Dreiser*, 272
Dreiser, Sara White (Jug), 37, 58, 156
Dreiser, Theodore
——Books: *An Amateur Laborer*, 104–5, 113, 115, 117, 133–35; *An American Tragedy*, 18, 24, 37–38, 56, 130, 187, 207, 213, 234, 237, 243, 246, 262–70, 273, 289; *A Book about Myself*, 134, 139, 185–86, 259; *The Bulwark*, 219, 225; *Dawn*, 114, 134, 139, 152, 156, 185–86, 192, 262; *Dreiser-Mencken Letters*, 186; *The Financier*, 15, 99, 102–3, 150, 156, 178–79, 182, 186, 191, 205–8, 213, 218; *Free and Other Stories*, 259–61, 272; *The "Genius"*, 17, 46, 117, 196, 218, 235; *Hey Rub-A-Dub-Dub*, 55, 144–45, 150–51, 156, 273; *A Hoosier Holiday*, 16, 145, 154, 156–57; *Jennie Gerhardt*, 14, 16, 63, 97, 102, 104, 107–8, 111–14, 117, 138–39, 144, 147, 150, 155, 161–64, 166–68, 170–72, 174–76, 178, 181, 195, 236, 248, 252–54, 271–72; *Jennie Gerhardt* (1992), 63–64, 155, 161–76, 255, 272; *Newspaper Days*, 77, 105, 114, 185; *Notes on Life*, 149, 156; *Selected Magazine Articles of Theodore Dreiser: Life and Art in the American 1890s*, 13; *Sister Carrie*, 14–16, 18, 23, 25, 27–31, 33–37, 39–40, 42–49, 52–58, 60–63, 65–68, 71–73, 75–78, 104–5, 108, 112–14, 117, 144, 156–57, 162, 181, 213, 217, 235, 237, 240, 247, 252, 268, 274–76, 289–90; *Sister Carrie* (1981), 23, 25–30, 33, 35–37, 54, 57, 60–63, 75, 78, 104, 106, 108–10, 204, 213, 247; *The Stoic*, 101, 207, 210, 219; *Theodore Dreiser: The American Diaries, 1902–1926*, 54, 134; *Theodore Dreiser: A Selection of Uncollected Prose*, 113, 156; *Theodore Dreiser's Letters to Louise Campbell*, 193; *The Titan*, 178, 185–86, 191, 203, 207–9, 218; *A Traveler at Forty*, 16–17, 177–81, 185–86; *The Trilogy of Desire*, 204, 207–8, 210–11; *Twelve Men*, 16, 56, 115, 132–33, 238, 240, 247
——Short works: "Aglaia," 191–92, 195–96; "Barfleur Takes Me in Hand," 181; "A Confession of Faith," 144, 156; "A Counsel to Perfection," 151; "Culhane, the Solid Man," 16, 115; "Elizabeth," 192, 195; "The Factory," 113; "Fall River," 105–6; "Life Stories of Successful Men—No. 10: Philip D. Armour," 37; "Life Stories of Successful Men—No. 12: Marshall Field," 37; "Lilly: A Girl of the Streets," 183; "The Literary Shower," 113; "A London Drawing-Room," 183; "Mark the Double Twain," 273; "The Mighty Burke," 105; "Muldoon, the Solid Man," 115–18, 133; "Neurotic America and the Sex Impulse," 51, 55; "Nigger Jeff," 258, 260–62, 271–72; "Preface to *Sister Carrie*," 54; "Sarah Schanab," 192; "Scared Back to Nature," 115, 128; "Scenes in a Cartridge Factory," 113; "Some Aspects of Our National Character," 273; "This Madness: Sidonie," 191, 195; "Three Sketches of the Poor," 105; "The Town of Pullman," 37; "Transmigration of the Sweatshop," 105; "True Art Speaks Plainly," 54; "Vanity, Vanity, Saith the Preacher," 238, 240; "W. L. S.," 240
Dresser, Paul, 84, 116, 246
Dudley, Dorothy, 44, 49–50, 53–54, 55; *Forgotten Frontiers: Dreiser and the Land of the Free*, 49, 55; "The 'Suppression' Controversy," 54
Duggan, Margaret M.: *Correspondence of F. Scott Fitzgerald*, eds., 247

Dunn, Ross E.: "Curriculum Critics Err," 53

Eakin, Paul John, 184, 186
Eastman, Max Forrester, 17, 187, 190
Eastman, Yvette (Yvette Szekely): *Dearest Wilding: A Memoir*, 17, 187–94, 273
Eby, Clare Virginia: "Jennie Through the Eyes of Thorstein Veblen," 176
Edison, Thomas, 60
Edward VII, King, 99
Edwards, Jonathan: "Personal Narrative," 290
Edwards, Lilly, 183, 186
Ellsworth, Richard, 180
Emerson, Ralph Waldo, 25, 203, 206
Epstein, Joseph, 227, 232; "E. B. White, Dark & Lite," 232

Fabre, Michel, 271–72, 289; *Conversations with Richard Wright*, eds., 289; *Richard Wright Reader*, eds., 272; *The Unfinished Quest of Richard Wright*, 272
Farrell, James T., 13–14, 18, 249–50, 271, 274–75, 280–81, 283–86, 289–90; *Judgment Day*, 282, 290; *The League of Frightened Philistines*, 290; "Lynch Patterns," 271; *Reflections at Fifty*, 274–75, 289; *Studs Lonigan*, 18, 271, 274–76, 280, 283, 285–86, 289–90; *Young Lonigan*, 280–82, 286; *The Young Manhood of Studs Lonigan*, 282–83, 290
Faulkner, William, 14, 54, 232, 243, 252, 272; *The Sound and the Fury*, 232
Feis, Herbert, 185
Field, Marshall, 28, 37, 81–82
Fielding, Henry, 27
Fields, W. C., 243
Filene, Peter: "Men and Manliness," 135
Filippelli, Ronald L.: "Fall River Textile Strikes," 114; "Homestead Strike," 114; *Labor Conflict in the United States: An Encyclopedia*, ed., 114
Fisher, Philip, 130, 137; *Hard Facts: Setting and Form in the American Novel*, 137; "The Life History of Objects: The Naturalist Novel and the City," 137
Fishkin, Shelley Fisher, 194
Fitzgerald, F. Scott, 13–14, 56, 218–20, 234–43, 246–47; "Absolution," 219–20; *The Beautiful and Damned*, 236–39, 247; *The Great Gatsby*, 18, 219, 232, 234, 238–40, 243, 247; *Tender Is the Night*, 237; *This Side of Paradise*, 232, 236
Fitzgerald, Frances Scott (Scottie), 235, 247
Flaubert, Gustave, 26, 276, 289; *Madame Bovary*, 276
Fleming, Berenice, 208
Flynn, Elizabeth Gurley, 107–8, 111
Foner, Philip S., 111, 114; *Women and American Labor Movement from Colonial Times to the Eve of World War I*, 114
Ford, Betty, 43
Ford, Gerald, 43
Foster, Alasdair: *Behold the Man: The Male Nude in Photography*, 136
Foucault, Michel: "Panoticism," 120–21, 135
Frederic, Harold: *The Damnation of Theron Ware*, 236
Frederickson, Kathy: "Working Out to Work Through: Dreiser in Muldoon's Body Shop of Shame," 16, 115
Freud, Sigmund, 124–26, 136, 139, 156; *Civilization and Its Discontents*, 136; "The Dissolution of the Oedipus Complex," 136; "Femininity," 136; "Some Psychical Consequences of the Anatomical Distinction Between the Sexes," 136; *Three Contributions to the Theory of Sex*, 156
Frick, Henry Clay, 106
Fussell, Paul, 184, 186

Galvin, Kevin: "Dole Hints of Blocking Vote on Foster," 137
Gammel, Irene, 194
Geismar, Maxwell, 103, 186, 238, 247; *Rebels and Ancestors*, 103, 186, 247

Gerber, Philip, 15, 79, 213; "Jolly Mrs. Yerkes Is Home from Abroad: Dreiser and the Celebrity Culture," 15, 79; *Theodore Dreiser*, 213
Gillett, Chester, 213
Gillies, Reverend Andrew, 92, 94
Gilman, Charlotte Perkins, 136
Gogol, Miriam, 17, 134, 157, 164, 187, 194; "*The 'Genius'*: Dreiser's Testament to Convention," 134; "Interlocking, Intermeshing Fantasies: Dreiser and *Darest Wilding*," 17, 187; *Theodore Dreiser: Beyond Naturalism*, ed., 157, 194
Goldhurst, William: *F. Scott Fitzgerald and His Contemporaries*, 246
Graham, Sheila, 235
Grant, General Ulysses Simpson, 126
Grebstein, Sheldon, 111
Green, Harvey, 129, 134; *Fit for America: Health, Fitness, Sport and American Society*, 134
Greene, William Chase, 205–7, 210, 213; *Moira: Fate, Good, and Evil in Greek Thought*, 213
Greenwald, Maurine Weiner: "Introduction: Women at Work through the Eyes of Elizabeth Beardsley Butler and Lewis Hine," 114
Griffen, Clyde: *Meanings for Manhood: Constructions of Masculinity in Victorian America*, 133
Griffin, Joseph, 118, 134; *The Small Canvas: An Introduction to Dreiser's Short Stories*, 134
Grigsby, Braxton, 86
Grigsby, Emilie, 15, 86–88, 90–91, 94, 97, 99, 102

Hakutani, Yoshinobu, 23, 37, 134, 248, 289; "Dreiser and French Realism," 37; "*Native Son* and *An American Tragedy*: Two Different Interpretations of Crime and Guilt," 289; "*Sister Carrie* and the Problem of Literary Naturalism," 37; "*Sister Carrie*: Novel and Romance," 15, 23; "Wright, Dreiser, and Spatial Narrative," 18, 248; *Selected Magazine Articles of Theodore Dreiser: Life and Art in the American 1890s*, ed., 13; *Young Dreiser: A Critical Study*, 13, 134
Hals, Frans: "Portrait of a Woman," 96
Hancher, Michael, 185–86
Handy, William J.: "A Re-examination of Dreiser's *Sister Carrie*," 37
Hapke, Laura, 15–16, 104, 114; "Men Strike, Women Sew: Gendered Labor Worlds in Dreiser's Social Protest Art," 15, 104; *Tales of the Working Girl: Wage-Earning Women in American Literature, 1890–1925*, 114
Hardy, Thomas, 32, 37, 138, 214, 272; *Mayor of Casterbridge*, 37
Harmon, William, 232; *A Handbook to Literature*, 232
Hawthorne, Nathaniel, 270, 290
Haywood, Mary Adelaide, 90
Hemingway, Ernest, 14, 56, 234–35, 252, 272; *The Sun Also Rises*, 252
Henry, Arthur, 58, 60–62, 118
Hermeren, Goran: *Influence in Art and Literature*, 247
Herndl, Diane Price: *Feminisms: An Anthology in Literary Theory and Criticism*, ed., 135
Hibben, John G., 236
Hicks, Granville, 250
Hitler, Adolf, 263
Hogan, Patrick Colm: *Joyce, Milton, and the Theory of Influence*, 247
Holbein, Hans, 96
Holman, Hugh C.: *A Handbook to Literature*, 232
Homer: *The Odyssey*, 203
Hovey, Richard B.: "Dreiser's *The 'Genius'*: Motivation and Structure," 134
Howe, Irving, 24, 37; "Afterword to *An American Tragedy*," 37
Howells, William Dean, 32, 38, 75, 77; *A Modern Instance*, 32, 38
Howells, Winifred, 136
Hughitt, Marvin, 81
Hurston, Zora Neale, 250; "Stories of Conflict," 272; *Their Eyes Were Watching God*, 250
Hussman, Lawrence E.: "Expansive

and Unnameable Desire in American Fiction: From 'Naturalism' to Postmodernism," 17, 214
Hutchisson, James M.: "Death and dying in *Jennie Gerhardt*, 176
Huxley, Thomas Henry, 214

Innes, George, 96
Irigaray, Luce, 16, 139–40, 146, 149, 152–53, 156; *This Sex Which Is Not One*, 139, 156

Jackson, Blyden, 256, 272; "Richard Wright in a Moment of Truth," 272
James, Henry, 30, 32, 51–52, 54, 212–13, 270; "The Art of Fiction," 212–13, 272
Jameson, Frederic, 15, 67–68; *The Political Unconscious*, 67–68; *Postmodernism*, 68
Jefferies, Richard, 138, 142, 145–46, 150, 156
Johnson, Robert Underwood, 180
Jonson, Ben, 235
Jower, Hanscha, 183
Joyce, James, 228, 242, 247

Kaplan, Amy, 13, 55, 133, 136; "Romancing the Empire: The Embodiment of American Masculinity in the Popular Historical Novel of the 1890s," 133; *The Social Construction of American Realism*, 13, 55
Karen, Robert, 118, 121, 134; "Shame," 134
Kaufman, Gershen, 118–19, 134; *Shame: The Power of Caring*, 134
Kazin, Alfred, 37, 40, 52, 54–55; "Introduction: Theodore Dreiser and *Sister Carrie* Restored," 37, 54; "Introduction to *The Stature of Theodore Dreiser*," 55; *The Stature of Theodore Dreiser*, eds., 54–55
Keats, John, 242
Kellogg, J. Harvey, 134
Kinnamon, Keneth, 271, 273, 289; *Conversations with Richard Wright*, eds., 271; *The Emergence of Richard Wright*, 273
Klein, Melanie: "Love, Guilt and Reparation," 134
Knight, Clarence A., 90
Kubitz, Estelle, 194

Lacan, Jacques, 135, 148, 152, 156–57; "The Meaning of the Phallus," 135, 156
Laing, R. D., 119
Lamour, Dorothy, 224
Lane, Hugh, 180
Lapham, Lewis: "Reactionary Chic: How the Nineties Right Recycles the Bombast of the Sixties Left," 55
Lardner, Ring, 234
Larsen, Madelyn, 193
Lecky, William Edward Hartpole: *History of European Morals*, 123
Lehan, Richard, 134, 162; *Theodore Dreiser: His World and His Novels*, 134, 176
Leverenz, David, 117, 127, 133, 137; *The Last Real Man*, 127; "The Last Real Man in America from Natty Bumppo to Batman," 133, 137; *Manhood and the American Renaissance*, 133; "Manhood, Humiliation and Public Life: Some Stories," 133
Lewis, Arthur O. Jr.: *Visions and Revisions in Modern American Literary Criticism*, eds., 272
Lewis, C. S., 222, 232; *Pilgrim's Progress*, 232
Lewis, Helen B., 118–19, 122, 134–35; *Shame and Guilt in Neurosis*, 118, 134
Lewis, Sinclair, 14, 54, 272
Libbey, Laura Jean, 104
Liff, Zanvel A., 193
Lingeman, Richard, 114–16, 133–34, 139, 155–56, 162, 180, 185–87, 191, 194–95; "The Biographical Significance of *Jennie Gerhardt*," 176; *Theodore Dreiser: An American Journey, 1908–1945*, 133–34, 155, 186, 194; *Theodore Dreiser: At the Gate of the City, 1871–1907*, 114, 134, 156, 194
Lipton, Eunice, 112
Liveright, Horace, 177, 185, 213
London, Bette, 117, 134; "Mary Shelley, *Frankenstein*, and the Spectacle of Masculinity," 134

Long, Robert E., 240, 247; "*Sister Carrie* and the Rhythm of Failure in Fitzgerald," 247
Louis XV, 96
Lovelace, Dick, 235
Lowry, Malcolm, 56
Luts, Tom, 115, 133, 136; *American Nervousness, 1903: An Anecdotal History*, 133; "Making It Big: Theodore Dreiser, Sex, and Success," 133

Mahler, Gustav, 218
Maier, Norman R. F., 223
Mailer, Norman, 14
Malkiel, Theresa Serber: *Diary of a Shirtwaist Striker*, 111
Malraux, André, 252, 272
Mao Tse-tung, 55
Markham, Kirah, 194
Marquis, Don: *Archy and Mehitabel*, 227; *Dreams and Dust*, 233; "The Name," 228, 233
Marudanayagam, P., 55
Marx, Leo, 128, 136; *The Machine in the Garden: Technology and the Pastoral Ideal in America*, 136
Masters, Edgar Lee, 14
Matthiessen, F. O., 37, 264, 272–73; *Theodore Dreiser*, 37, 272–23
Mayfield, Sara: "Another Fitzgerald Myth Explored by Mencken," 247
McAleer, John J.: *Notes on Life*, eds., 156
McCall, Dan: *The Example of Richard Wright*, 290
McCormick, R. S., 81
McCullough, David: *Mornings on Horseback*, 137
McGovern, James: "David Graham Philips and the Virility Impulse of Progressives," 133
Melville, Herman, 249; *Moby-Dick*, 248
Menahan, Margaret, 189
Mencken, Henry L., 14, 56, 118, 156, 162, 176, 178, 182–83, 186, 234–36, 247, 272; *Books of Prefaces*, 236; "A Novel of the First Rank," 176
Meredith, George, 272
Michaels, Walter Benn, 15, 65–69, 73, 75, 77–78, 205–6, 213; *Against Theory*, 67; *Critical Inquiry*, 66; "Dreiser's *Financier*: The Man of Business as a Man of Letters," 213; *The Gold Standard and the Logic of Naturalism*, 65
Milton, John, 242, 247
Minter, David: *A Cultural History of the American Novel: Henry James to William Faulkner*, 54
Mitchell, Juliet: *Feminine Sexuality: Jacques Lacan and the Ecole Freudienne*, eds., 135, 156
Mitchell, Lee Clark, 204, 206
Mitchell, S. Weir, 136
Mitchell, Stephen A., 190, 195; *Hope and Dread in Psychoanalysis*, 195
Mizener, Arthur: *The Far Side of Paradise*, 247
Mizner, Addison, 92
Mizner, Wilson, 91–95, 97, 102
Moers, Ellen, 13, 40, 54, 103; *Two Dreisers*, 13, 54, 103
Mookerjee, R. N., 55
Morgan, Mary J., 96
Morrison, Andrew P.: *Shame: The Underside of Narcissism*, 134
Morrison, Toni: *Beloved*, 271
Morrison, William, 118
Moyer, Marsha S.: "Dreiser, *Sister Carrie*, and Mrs. Doubleday: Gender and Social Change at the Turn of the Century," 15, 39
Mukherjee, Arun, 51, 55, 77; *The Gospel of Wealth in the American Novel: The Rhetoric of Dreiser and Some of His Contemporaries*, 55, 77; "*Sister Carrie* at Ninety: An Indian Response," 55
Muldoon, William, 16, 115–34, 136–37
Mulvey, Laura: "Visual Pleasure and Narrative Cinema," 136
Mumford, Kevin: " 'Lost Manhood' Found: Male Sexual Impotence and Victorian Culture in the United States," 133
Murayama, Kiyohiko: "But a 'Single Point in a Long Tragedy': *Sister Carrie*'s Equivocal Style," 15, 65
Murphy, Peter F.: *Fictions of Masculinity*, 133
Mussolini, Benito, 263

Nathan, George Jean, 236
Neal, Steve: "Masculinity as Spectacle: Reflections on Men and Mainstream Cinema," 134
Norris, Frank, 13, 26, 32, 36–37, 39–40, 48–49, 113, 204, 214–19, 225, 231, 235–36; *McTeague*, 36, 113, 216–17; *The Octopus*, 32, 37, 217, 225, 235; *The Pit*, 217, 225; *Vandover and the Brute*, 236
Nostwich, T. D., 114, 116, 132–33; *Fulfilment and Other Tales of Women and Men*, ed., 133

Oates, Joyce Carol, 187
Oldsey, Bernard S.: *Visions and Revisions in Modern American Literary Criticism*, eds., 272
Ong, Walter J., 150, 156; *Orality and Literarcy: The Technologizing of the Word*, 156
Ovid, 256, 272; *Metamorphoses*, 256
Owsley, Louis, 90, 95

Page, Walter Hines, 41, 54
Palmer, Potter, 81
Parrington, Vernon Louis, 50, 54; *The Beginnings of Critical Realism*, 54
Peale, Norman Vincent, 137
Peiss, Kathy: *Cheap Amusements*, 109
Perkins, Maxwell, 237
Person, Ethel S., 190, 194–96; *By Force of Fantasy: How We Make Our Lives*, 190, 194
Piers, Gerhart: *Shame and Guilt: A Psychoanalytic and a Cultural Study*, eds., 118, 134
Piper, Henry Dan, 237, 247
Pizer, Donald, 36–37, 55, 106, 113–14, 138, 144, 149, 156, 176, 204, 206, 213, 290; *Critical Essays on Theodore Dreiser*, ed., 55; "Nineteenth-Century American Naturalism: An Essay in Definition," 37; *The Novels of Theodore Dreiser: A Critical Study*, 156, 176; "The Strike," 114
Pleck, Elizabeth: *The American Man*, 136
Pleck, Joseph: *The American Man*, 136
Poe, Edgar Allan, 290
Porter, Catherine: *This Sex Which Is Not One*, trans., 156
Porter, Duncan: *The Portable Darwin*, eds., 135
Powys, Llewelyn, 235, 247; *The Verdict of Bridlegoose*, 247
Pulitzer, Joseph, 84
Pullman, G. M., 28, 37
Pynchon, Thomas, 222

Ralph, Ruth S.: "Dreiser's *The 'Genius'*: Motivation and Structure," 134
Raja, L. Jeganatha, 55
Rascoe, Burton, 235, 247; *We Were Interrupted*, 247
Rehan, Ada, 87
Rembrandt, van Rijn: "Portrait of a Rabbi," 96
Remington, Frederick, 129
Richards, Grant, 177–82, 186; *Author Hunting by an Old Literary Sportsman: Memories of Years Spent Mainly in Publishing, 1887–1925*, 186
Richardson, Dorothy, 112
Riggio, Thomas P., 18, 43, 54, 134, 183, 186, 193–94, 247, 273; "Dreiser: Autobiographical Fragment, 1911," 186; "Dreiser, Fitzgerald, and the Question of Influence," 18, 234; "Dreiser on Society and Literature: The San Francisco Exposition Interview," 247; *Dreiser-Mencken Letters*, 186; "Introduction to *Theodore Dreiser: The American Diaries, 1902–1926*," 134; *Theodore Dreiser: The American Diaries, 1902–1926*, ed., 54
Rodin, Auguste: "Cupid and Psyche," 96
Romero, Lora: "Vanishing American: Gender, Empire, and New Historicism," 136
Roosevelt, Theodore, 129, 132, 137; *The Letters of Theodore Roosevelt*, 137; *Ranch Life and the Hunting-Trail*, 129, 137; *The Strenuous Life*, 129
Root, Elihu, 129
Rosenberg, Charles E.: "Sexuality,

Class and Role in 19th-Century America," 136
Rosenthal, Lillian, 195
Rotundo, E. Anthony, 128, 133, 136; *American Manhood: Transformations in Masculinity from the Revolution to the Modern Era*, 136; "Body and Soul: Changing Ideals of American Middle-Class Manhood, 1770–1920," 133
Rubens, Peter Paul, 96
Rueckert, William H.: *Kenneth Burke and the Drama of Human Relations*, 232
Rushmore, Samuel W., 232

Salzman, Jack, 36, 54, 65, 177, 186; "The Publication of *Sister Carrie*: Fact and Fiction," 36; *Theodore Dreiser: The Critical Reception*, ed., 54, 186
Sampson, Edward, 225, 232; *E. B. White*, 232
Sand, George, 26
Sargent, John Singer, 87
Sartre, Jean Paul, 134, 252, 272; *Being and Nothingness: An Essay on Phenomenological Ontology*, 134
Schneider, Carl, 116, 119, 132–34; *Shame: The Power of Caring*, 132; *Shame, Exposure and Privacy*, 133–34
Schopenhauer, Arthur, 224
Scott, Frank H., 186
Scott, Joan Wallach, 43, 52, 54–55; "Gender: A Useful Category of Analysis," 55; *Gender and the Politics of History*, 54
Scott, Sir Walter, 27, 68
Seaver, Edwin, 251
Sedgwick, Eva Kosofsky: *Between Men: English Literature and Male Homosocial Desire*, 135; "Introduction to *Feminisms: An Anthology of Literary Theory and Criticism*," 135; "Gender Asymmetry and Erotic Triangles," 135
Seidler, Victor: *Education*, 127; "Fathering, Authority and Masculinity," 136
Sekey, Suzanne Menahan (Sue), 17, 188–90, 194, 197–202
Seltzer, Mark, 127–28, 133, 136; "The Love Master," 133, 136
Shakespeare, William, 203, 207, 242; *Macbeth*, 203
Shapiro, Charles, 54–55; *The Stature of Theodore Dreiser*, eds., 54–55
Shawcross, Nancy M., 185, 189, 194
Sheridan, Alan, 135; *Discipline and Punish: The Birth of the Prison*, trans., 120, 135
Sherman, Stuart P., 44, 46–47, 54; "The Naturalism of Mr. Dreiser," 46, 54
Showalter, Elaine: *Sexual Anarchy: Gender and Culture at the Fin de Siecle*, 136
Sinclair, Upton: *The Jungle*, 104
Singer, Milton: *Shame and Guilt: A Psychoanalytic and a Cultural Study*, 118, 134
Singh, Brij Mohan, 55
Siskind, Murray, 231
Sklar, Robert: *F Scott Fitzgerald: The Last Laocoon*, 247
Smith, T. R., 185
Smith, Thomas, 213
Smith-Rosenberg, Carroll: *Disorderly Conduct: Visions of Gender in Victorian America*, 55, 136; "The New Woman as Androgyne: Social Disorder and Gender Crisis, 1870–1936," 136
Solomon, Eric, 238, 247; "A Source for Fitzgerald's *The Great Gatsby*," 247
Sonntag, William Louis, 240
Sophocles, *Oedipus Rex*, 206–7
Spence, Jonathan: *To Change China: Western Advisers in China, 1620–1960*, 55
Spencer, Herbert, 214, 242, 251
St. Jean, Shawn: "Dreiser and American Literary Paganism: A Reading of the Trilogy of Desire," 17, 203; "Social Deconstruction and *An American Tragedy*," 213
Stein, Gertrude, 235
Steinbeck, John, 219, 221, 231, 243; *The Grapes of Wrath*, 231; "The Leader of the People," 222; *The*

Long Valley, 222; *The Pearl*, 222; "The Red Pony," 222
Steinhoff, William, 225, 227–28, 232; " 'The Door,' " 232
Stendhal, Marie Henri Beyle, 76
Stepanchev, Stephen: "Dreiser among the Critics," 44, 54
Stevens, Wallace, 228
Stewart, Randall: "Dreiser and the Naturalistic Heresy," 37
Strachey, James: *Civilization and Its Discontents*, trans., 136
Stuber, Florian, 193
Suleiman, Susan Rubin: *The Female Body in Western Culture*, ed., 137
Sullivan, John L., 131
Susman, Warren I., 44, 53–54; *Culture as History*, 53–54
Swanberg, W. A.: *Dreiser*, 194, 247

Tanselle, G. Thomas, 186
Tate, Allen, 14, 272; *Collected Essays*, 272; "Techniques of Fiction," 272
Tatum, Anna, 192, 194
Tax, Meredith, 111–12, 114; *The Rising of the Women: Feminist Solidarity and Class Conflict, 1880–1917*, 114
Tentler, Leslie Woodcock, 110, 114; *Wage-Earning Women: Industrial Work and Family Life in the United States, 1900–1930*, 114
Thoreau, Henry David, 203, 290; *Walden*, 290
Thrane, Gary, 119, 134–35; "Shame and the Construction of the Self," 134–35
Tjader, Marguerite: Theodore Dreiser, *Notes on Life*, eds., 156
Tomkins, Silvan: *Affect/Imagery/Consciousness*, 136; "Shame," 136
Trachtenberg, Alan, 41, 54; *The Incorporation of America: Culture and Society in the Gilded Age*, 54
Traister, Daniel, 185
Trilling, Lionel, 50–52, 55; "Reality in America," 55
Turner, Frederick Jackson, 44, 116, 133; "The Frontier in American History," 133; *Frontier Thesis*, 44; *The Historians' History of the United States*, 133; "The Significance of the Frontier in American History," 133
Turner, (Joseph Mallord) William, 96
Twain, Mark, 116, 133, 178, 237, 249, 270–72, 273; *A Connecticut Yankee in King Arthur's Court*, 133; *Adventures of Huckleberry Finn*, 270, 273; *Pudd'nhead Wilson*, 270
Tyndall, John, 214

Uchida, Yoshitsugu: "A Conflict between Spirituality and Material Civilization in *Sister Carrie*," 55

Van Dyck, Sir Anthony, 96
Van Every, Edward, 115–17, 129–30, 132–33, 136–37; *Muldoon the Solid Man of Sport: His Amazing Story as Related for the First Time by Him to His Friend*, 133
Veblen, Thorstein, 37, 154, 176, 283; *The Theory of the Leisure Class*, 37; *The Theory of Business Enterprise*, 283
von Bardeleben, Renate, 16, 17, 177, 185–86; "Central Europe in Travelogues by Theodore Dreiser," 186; "Dreiser on the European Continent, Part I," 186; "Dreiser's English Virgil," 185; "From Travel Guide to Autobiography: Recovering the Original of *A Traveler at Forty*," 16, 177; "Personal, Ethnic, and National Identity: Theodore Dreiser's Difficult Heritage," 186

Walker, Margaret, 249
Wanambisi, Monica: "Eight Exemplars of the Twentieth-Century American Novel, 1900–1959," 55
Warhol, Robyn: *Feminisms: An Anthology in Literary Theory and Criticism*, eds., 135
Warner, Rex, 211
Warren, Robert Penn: *Homage to Theodore Dreiser*, 14
Watteau, Jean Antoine, 96
Weiss, Richard: *The American Myth of Success: From Horatio Alger to Norman Vincent Peale*, 137

Wells, H. G., 272
West, James L. W. III, 15, 56, 63–64, 106, 113, 155–56, 161–62, 172, 175–76, 179, 186, 247, 272; "Alcohol and Drinking in *Sister Carrie*," 15, 56; "Composition and Publication of *Jennie Gerhardt*," 176; *Dreiser's Jennie Gerhardt: New Essays on the Restored Text*, ed., 156, 162; "Editorial Theory and the Act of Submission," 179, 186; "Fair Copy, Authorial Intention, and 'Versioning,' " 64; *Jennie Gerhardt* (1992), ed., 63, 155, 161–76, 272; "The Scholarly Editor as Biographer," 64; *Sister Carrie* (1981), eds., 63; *A"Sister Carrie" Portfolio*, 63
Westlake, Neda M., 63, 116; *Sister Carrie* (1981), eds., 63
Whaley, Annemarie Koning, 16–17, 161; "Obscuring the Home: Textual Editing and Dreiser's *Jennie Gerhardt*," 16, 161
Wharton, Edith, 30, 75, 136; *The House of Mirth*, 75
Wheelock, Geo L., 185
White, E. B., 223–29, 232–33; *Charlotte's Web*, 227; "The Door," 223–29, 231–33; *Letters of E. B. White*, 232; "Notes on Our Time," 224; *The Poems and Sketches of E. B. White*, 226; *The Second Tree from the Corner*, 223–24, 226–28; *Stuart Little*, 227; *The Trumpet and the Swan*, 227
Whitman, Walt, 25
Wilson, B. F., 235, 247; "Notes on Personalities," 247
Wilson, Christopher P., 54, 156, 176; "Labor and Capitalism in *Jennie Gerhardt*," 156, 176; "*Sister Carrie* Again," 54
Wilson, Edumund, 234, 247; *The Crack-Up*, ed., 247
Winkler, Karen J., 194; "Seductions of Biography," 194
Winters, Alice M: *Sister Carrie* (1981), eds., 63
Wister, Owen, 129
Wolfe, Thomas, 219, 221; *Look Homeward Angel*, 221; *The Web and the Rock*, 221
Woolf, Virginia, 136, 228
Wordsworth, William: "Preface to *Lyrical Ballads*," 222
Wright, Ellen: *Richard Wright Reader*, eds., 272
Wright, Richard, 13–14, 18, 25, 204, 219, 221, 248–67, 269–76; 283, 285, 289–90; *American Hunger*, 250, 272; "Big Boy Leaves Home," 255–58, 261–62, 272; *Black Boy*, 14, 252, 254, 259, 262, 271–73; "Blueprint for Negro Writing," 250–52, 272; *Conversations with Richard Wright*, 251–52, 271–72, 289; *Eight Men*, 273; "How 'Bigger' Was Born," 264, 266, 271–73; "The Man Who Went to Chicago," 273; *Native Son*, 18, 25, 221, 250, 262–76, 283–86, 289–90; *Uncle Tom's Children*, 250, 255, 258, 260–61, 264
Wurmser, Leon, 118–19, 123, 126, 134–36; *The Mask of Shame*, 119, 123, 134–35; "Shame: The Veiled Companion of Narcissism," 136
Wyllie, Irvin: *The Self-Made Man in America*, 137

Yeats, William Butler, 222
Yerkes, Charles E., 90, 92, 95
Yerkes, Charles Tyson Jr., 15, 79–100, 178, 183, 211, 213
Yerkes, Mary Adelaide (Mollie Moore), 15, 79, 81–102
Yerkes, Susanna, 79, 81

Zaluda, Scott, 156–57; "The Secrets of Fraternity: Men and Friendship in *Sister Carrie*," 156
Zilbergeld, Bernard, 195
Zola, Emile, 24–25, 31, 84, 213–14, 251; *The Experimental Novel*, 213; *Germinal*, 84; *L'Assommoir*, 24–25; *Nana*, 84